Girl Warriors

Girl Warriors

Feminist Revisions of the Hero's Quest in Contemporary Popular Culture

SVENJA HOHENSTEIN

McFarland & Company, Inc., Publishers

Jefferson, North Carolina

ISBN (print) 978-1-4766-7664-7
ISBN (ebook) 978-1-4766-3739-6

LIBRARY OF CONGRESS AND BRITISH LIBRARY
CATALOGUING DATA ARE AVAILABLE

Front cover image: © 2019 Shutterstock

———

Printed in the United States of America

*McFarland & Company, Inc., Publishers
Box 611, Jefferson, North Carolina 28640
www.mcfarlandpub.com*

To Katharina Thalmann,
who helped me slay this dragon

Acknowledgments

I first of all want to thank Michael Butter for being open to supervising a project about a vampire slayer, a girl revolutionary, and a fighting Disney princess, for the time he invested in reading and commenting on my work, and for his thoughtful and constructive feedback. The same applies to my colleagues Annika, Albrecht, Laura, and Sarah, who were always willing to read my chapters and give helpful feedback. I also want to thank Dr. Nicole Falkenhayner and Prof. Ingrid Hotz-Davies for their nuanced criticism and interesting discussions. I am furthermore indebted to the Collaborative Research Center 948, "Heroes, Heroizations, Heroisms," and its integrated research training group for supporting me especially at the beginning of my project. A special thanks goes to the people "behind the scenes": Linda, Janine, Annika, Tom, Aileen, and Hannah, and to the students who attended my seminars on YA Fiction, Girl Power, and Feminism and Popular Culture. I am especially grateful to the fan artists for allowing me to print their images in this book. Thank you also to my friends from Freiburg— Lena, Julia, Christian, Robert, Sabine, Pia, Golnaz, and Steve—for offering shelter, moral support, and coffee whenever I needed it. Most importantly, I want to thank Katharina, my work wife and slapstick sister, without whom this book would not have been written.

Table of Contents

Table of Contents

Introduction

Any culture's or individual's myths of the hero tell us about what attributes are seen as the good, the beautiful, and the true, and thereby teach us culturally valued aspirations.—Pearson xxv

To this day, Joseph Campbell's *The Hero with a Thousand Faces* (1949) remains the most important study on heroic myths.[1] In this study, Campbell compares heroic stories from different time periods and societies around the world and establishes a model of mythological heroism in which the quest or journey—divided into three stages: the separation, initiation, and return—forms the basis of each story (30). Campbell delineates that, in the phase of separation, the hero is called to fulfill his duty and embarks on a quest which, in the beginning, he often does hesitantly and unwillingly. Eventually, he accepts his calling and sets out on a journey during which he has to overcome obstacles and battle evil (36). During the quest, he grows mentally and/or physically, developments which not only allow him to win a "boon" or reward, but also enable him to take on a privileged and dominant position within his community to which he eventually returns (246).

Campbell furthermore maintains that the main function of heroic narratives is to pass on knowledge and traditions and help people to make sense of their lives and their communities (256). Scholars have called attention to the fact that the knowledge and traditions passed on through quest stories cultivate and help to institutionalize binary and hegemonic gender roles as well as patriarchal systems of power (Early and Kennedy 1; Pearson 81). As Mimi Schippers explains, "hegemonic masculinity can include physical strength, the ability to use interpersonal violence in the face of conflict, and authority" (91). Indeed, the similarities between notions of hegemonic masculinity and the traits of the quest hero are striking, as the latter is repeatedly shown to excel in battle, triumph over others, and take on a privileged position in his community. Even though not all of the heroes mentioned by Campbell use physical strength or violence to achieve their aims, the ability to fight

1

or win battles is a crucial feature of many of them. Consequently, the figure of the warrior emerges as one important subcategory of mythical heroes, a character whose representation casts physical strength, independence, and authority as heroic and valuable.[2]

Whereas the portrayal of male warriors validates and stabilizes patriarchal power through the celebration of hegemonic masculinity, the representation of women and girls in quest stories does so by enforcing notions of hegemonic femininity as weak, passive, and vulnerable (cf. Schippers 91). In typical quest stories, women are either cast as helpless and passive damsels in distress in need of rescue, or as beautiful princesses who serve as a reward for the brave deeds of the hero (Pearson 2). Notably, the binary gender allocations embodied by the archetypes of the hero and the damsel are crucial in this context, because the characteristics of hegemonic masculinity

> guarantee men's legitimate dominance over women *only when they are symbolically paired with a complementary and inferior quality attached to femininity*. Thus, the significance of masculinity and femininity in gender hegemony is that they establish symbolic meanings for the relationship between women and men that provide the legitimating rationale for social relations ensuring the ascendancy and dominance of men [Schippers 91; emphasis added].

That quest stories perpetuate hegemonic gender relations can also be observed in other scenarios in which women are attributed the role of the evil witch. As she has to be killed in order for the hero to proceed on his journey, this role or archetype speaks strongly of the fear of powerful or subversive, that is, non-hegemonic femininity (Pearson 2). Similarly, the few accounts of female warriors such as the Amazons or Joan of Arc were frequently marginalized and viewed as exceptions or momentary transgressions from the norm, which highlights that they were perceived as a threat to the hegemonic order, too (Early 17).

What is more, in Western cultures more specifically, for a long time, the role of the hero has also been reserved for privileged white men, "a socially, politically, and economically powerful subgroup of the human race." By contrast, "racial minorities, the poor, and women [were] seen as secondary characters, important only as obstacles, aids, or rewards" for the hero (Pearson and Pope 4). Based on these observations, the quest is also often considered an elitist myth, made up by privileged men who designed the heroic ideal in their own image and in order to maintain and affirm their own superiority and power.

It is important to note, however, that even though the model of the quest hero has proven to be a very influential, popular, and resilient one, who or what is considered to be heroic is subject to change. In fact, there is no such thing as a set of basic features that are essentially heroic. On the contrary, as the introductory quote states, heroic figures "tell us about what attributes are seen as the good, the beautiful, and the true" by a given society (Pearson xxv). In other words, they communicate which traits and behaviors are regarded as valuable or extraordinary by a specific society at a particular historical moment. Heroic characters and narratives, as well as the concepts of heroism and gender perpetuated through them, are constructed and "discursively produced through historical, cultural, and social contexts" (Keller 3). Indeed, "the hero exists in the eye of the beholder [only]. Every hero must be a hero *to* someone" (Strate 21). This means that people achieve heroic status because their audiences or worshippers declare specific qualities to be extraordinary; communities do not merely witness a person becoming a hero or recognize a person's timeless heroic qualities, but they rather enable his or her heroization. The dominance of the mythical quest hero or warrior is then not so much a sign that hegemonic masculinity is essentially heroic, but it rather testifies to the prevalence of patriarchal ideas and structures which continue to permeate and influence Western societies, cultures, and narratives.

Accordingly, retellings of quest stories can reflect upon and offer insights into changing gender norms and concepts of heroism. In this book, I look at rewritings of quest stories in which teenage girls set out on heroic journeys in order to trace how narrative patterns as well as conceptualizations of gender and heroism influence and inform each other. To be more precise, I analyze Buffy Summers from the TV series *Buffy the Vampire Slayer* (1997–2003), Katniss Everdeen, the female protagonist of the *Hunger Games* trilogy (2008–2010), and the Disney princess Merida of DunBroch, who stars in the animated movie *Brave* (2012). I have chosen these popular culture characters because they are not merely sidekicks, but the protagonists of their respective stories, who set out on quests of their own at the end of which they successfully bring down patriarchal power systems. What is more, all of them are teenage girls who are experienced in dealing with weapons, so that in these narratives, male warriors are exchanged with female ones, a feature which has the potential to fundamentally challenge the hegemonic gender roles and notions of heroism usually perpetuated by quest stories.

While writers and producers play an important role in the creation of heroic figures, audiences, fans, and worshippers also take part in the construction of heroes. This is why my study also includes a reception analysis of what John Fiske has called secondary and tertiary texts (118–19), that is, paratexts or promotional material and works created by fans such as fan art and fan fiction. Since heroism and normative girlhood are both subject to societal and cultural negotiations, looking at these additional texts helps to shed light on how both categories are conceptualized outside of the fictional universes. In addition, an analysis of the fan texts also offers new perspectives on how heroic characters and the social norms and values they represent can be questioned and changed. While the male quest hero can be regarded as the product of a top-down process during which those who were already in power preserved and legitimized their rule by creating heroes in their own likeness, the Internet has facilitated a bottom-up approach in which groups that were previously marginalized are given the opportunity to create innovative heroic figures that more adequately represent the lives, values, and norms of people who are not privileged, white, heterosexual men.

It is my claim that the representations of Buffy, Katniss, and Merida across primary, secondary, and tertiary texts establish concepts of heroism and girlhood inspired by feminist values and ideas. Taken together, the manifold and diverse portrayals of the girl warriors work against the archetypes of the male hero and the damsel in distress, or rather the hegemonic gender allocations they usually maintain. The representations of the teenage heroines challenge the myth that heroes must be white, masculine, heterosexual, and privileged patriarchs and they also rework notions of ideal girlhood to include girls of color or queer girls, for instance. The texts furthermore emphasize that girls can and should use the tools of feminism to fight for equality. Both the primary texts and works by fans also reflect that feminist thought and theory are not only increasingly regarded as—to hark back once more to the introductory quote—potentially good, beautiful, and true, but that they, along with the girl warriors, have moved closer to the mainstream.

By studying representations of teenage girls, I first of all aim to counter a biased and at times dismissive approach to this specific group visible in the more general fields of both youth studies and feminism. Indeed, it is striking that, on the one hand, "female adolescence is typically a highly controlled and managed process, with considerable social pressure being applied to ensure that girls safely transition into normative womanhood" (Dean and Laidler). Yet, on the other hand, for decades, scholars largely focused on the study of boys and boyhood, casting girlhood "as a preparation for womanhood rather than an identity in its own right" (Currie, Kelly, and Pomerantz 5). In this context, Dawn Currie, Deirdre Kelly, and Shauna Pomerantz point out that "while this neglect reflected the way that girls, in general, were not legitimate occupants of the kinds of public spaces accessible to especially male researchers, it also signals a more general cultural devaluation of girls and young women" (17). Notably, said devaluation can also be observed within feminist scholarship. Here, girls are perceived as "'the other' of feminism's womanhood" and feminists "consciously [distance] themselves from association with this category," which is thought to connote immaturity, dependence, and childishness (4, 5).[3] Due to this othering, their marginalization within feminist discourse and analysis, and a shortage of in-depth critical engagement with girl culture and girls themselves, there exists a persistent belief that girls and young women are not interested in feminism, do not identify as feminists themselves, and tend to conform to patriarchal norms and demands instead of resisting them (Driscoll, *Girls* 11; Keller 2, 3).

Since I am concerned with representations of teenage girls in popular culture specifically, I also engage in the academic debate about the so-called Girl Power movement, a popular culture phenomenon that first emerged in the mid–1990s. Icons of Girl Power were public figures such as the Spice Girls, and its defining feature was a reappraisal of femininity as a tool for female empowerment and independence (Genz and Brabon 76). Followers of the movement—the so-called "Girlies"—believed that they could use their femininity and sexuality, which had long been regarded as a tool of patriarchal control, in order to achieve their private and professional goals and liberate themselves from cultural norms and requirements regarding the role, look, and behavior of girls and women (77). In addition to the Spice Girls, Girl Power brought forth a variety of innovative female characters whose representations broke with traditional gender norms and conventions (cf. Brown; Byers; Hopkins). Among them was the figure of the girl warrior. Shows such as *Buffy the Vampire Slayer* (henceforth abbreviated *BtVS*) or *Dark Angel* (2000–2002), which both featured teenage girls that were skilled fighters or "hot chicks with superpowers," populated the TV stations of that time ("End of Days").

Girl Power at large became a mainstream cultural phenomenon already in the 1990s and "continues to be ubiquitous in mainstream media addressed to teen girls" to this day (Zaslow 159). By contrast, the girl warriors themselves initially remained in marginal or subcultural positions. To name just one example, even though it is a fan favorite today, *BtVS* never received extremely high ratings nor did it win any prestigious prizes or accolades. By contrast, highly successful franchises such as *The Hunger Games* or Disney princess movies attest that, in the 2010s, girl warriors have moved closer to the mainstream. After all, the *Hunger Games* broke records both with regard to sales of the novels and movie tickets and *Brave* won an Oscar for "Best Animated Feature Film."

Ever since their emergence more than twenty years ago, girl warriors have been subject of heated debates concerning the question whether or not they can be regarded as empowering or even feminist role models. This debate was rendered rather complicated not least because it coincided with a debate over the status of the feminist movement and its aims and values in general. On the one hand, the post–1990s are branded as the era of "post-feminism" (Levine 170). Post-feminism is an ambiguous period and has been defined and interpreted in numerous ways (Genz and Brabon 1). Basically, post-feminism "is said to effect a de-collectivization of the feminist movement as it translates feminist social goals and political ideas into matters of individual choice or lifestyle" (36–37). Post-feminism is seen as a period in which women are told that gender equality has been achieved and political activism has become unnecessary, making issues such as contraception, beauty standards, or career opportunities matters of private concern and individual choice (36). Post-feminism interpreted in this manner is seen as a countermovement against feminist political activism and feminist social critique. Many critics believe that the result of post-feminism is a silencing and marginalization of women's concerns and problems and thus ultimately disempowering (51).

On the other hand, during the early 1990s, there also emerged a feminist movement called third wave feminism, which stands in stark opposition to post-feminist thought and theory. Third wavers are politically active and "see their work founded on second wave principles, yet distinguished by a number of political and cultural differences" (156). Like second wave feminism, third wave feminism aims at fighting and overcoming patriarchal power structures through consciousness raising, political involvement, and group activism. It distinguishes itself from the second wave because it appropriates feminist thinking to the late 20th and early 21st century by opening up feminism to oppressed and marginalized groups, situating itself in the realm of popular culture, and challenging the essentialist aspects of second wave feminism and its perception of womanhood (158–59). This is visible, for instance, with regard to the manner in which the third wave defines sisterhood, as it is no longer meant to include only women, but generally "refers to unification, strength in numbers, and shared interest" of a group of people independent of their sex, age, race, or ethnicity (Payne-Mulliken and Renagar 68). Third wave feminism's most important concern is to address and acknowledge the ambiguities and contradictions of essentialist concepts such as gender, class, and race. It wants to raise awareness for and deconstruct the pattern of binary opposites that have informed Western thinking and supported male superiority for centuries (Genz and Brabon 156). Third wavers call for a perception of all people as having ambivalent and changing identities and thus also advocate for a contradictory notion of womanhood that is influenced by both feminine and masculine features (Levine 177).

Third wavers and the critics of Girl Power as a post-feminist movement, then, claim girl warriors for themselves and see them as either empowering or dis-empowering female role models, respectively. However, the latter assessment is far more prevalent. Indeed, girl warriors have been read as advocates of a post-feminist agenda time and again, and the majority of scholars dealing with these characters maintain that, even though, as active, skilled, and violent characters, they break with gender conventions to some extent, their adherence to more stereotypical femininity, especially with regard to their outer appearance, which is frequently described as sexy and/or fetishized, ultimately re-embeds them into patriarchal discourses (cf. Brown; Hopkins). Critics maintain, for instance, that Girl Power's celebration of femininity must be seen as a trap through which girls are constituted as sexual objects and subjected to invisible and self-imposed patriarchal rules and norms. From this point of view, embracing and emphasizing one's femininity as girl warriors, for instance, frequently do, is not a potentially liberating and empowering act, but one that results in limitations and patriarchal oppression, since "the Girlie look is similar to, if not synonymous with, patriarchal ideals of feminine beauty" (Genz and Brabon 79).

Moreover, critics point out that "girls who diverge from the norm by virtue of their race, class, sexuality, body type, and ability are largely invisible within popularized discourses of girl power" (Currie, Kelly, and Pomerantz 48). After all, the majority of female heroes are white, conventionally beautiful, heterosexual, and middle-class, traits that have cast doubt on their progressiveness (Brown 143; Hains 103–04). Critics point out that even though these characters open up the realm of heroism to some extent, the exclusion of "girls who are large, differently abled, queer, and/or poor" still results in the fact that heroism is defined within highly constrained bounds (Projansky 1). As a result, Girl Power discourse and girl warriors are criticized not only for marginalizing girls that do not adhere to the norms of idealized femininity, but they are also accused of "papering over the enduring and perhaps deepening inequalities generated by class and race stratifications" (Harris 35).

It has also been claimed time and again that through its focus on outer appearance and lifestyle, in Girl Power discourse, power is often solely cast as the power to buy commodities. As Rebecca Hains laments, "this unfortunate rendering of power as consumer power is one of several ways in which girl power's dominance is problematic" (93). What is more, since it is a popular culture phenomenon, many regard Girl Power and narratives about girl heroes as commercialized and commodified and thus as lacking in actual political or feminist content (Hains 99; McRobbie 538; Riordan 282). Critics state that "girl power has a home in neo-liberalism, which places emphasis on self-improvement, self-correction, and individual empowerment over social change or state support" (Zaslow 158–59). In her monograph *Future Girl: Young Women in the Twenty-First Century*, youth sociologist Anita Harris even claims that young women who adhere to the Girl Power ideal, that is Harris' eponymous future girls, have been established in Western cultures as the demographic that is particularly suited to "embrace and manage the political, economic, and social conditions of contemporary societies" and their neo-liberal ideologies (2).

Indeed, many accuse the movement along with the female characters it brings forth of being anti-feminist not only because of the non-political themes it addresses. They also hold its popularity responsible for the fact that actual feminist thought and theory are kept out of the mainstream media and therefore out of public awareness (Early and Kennedy 4; Hains 92). In this context, the independent and powerful girl warriors are criticized for luring girls into the belief that the times of a powerful patriarchy are over, that feminism is outdated, and that they as young girls have reached equality and can now do and be anything they want (Brown 142). Even Jeffrey Brown, who advocates for a more nuanced engagement with female action heroes in general, argues that when it comes to girl heroes specifically, there exists a danger "that young women may buy into the fantasy that they, like fictional action heroines, really do live in a world where women have achieved equality and can do anything" (155).

In more recent debates, however, scholars have started to read not just girl warriors, but female heroes in general in a more nuanced fashion. Brown, Sarah Hagelin, or Elizabeth Hills, for instance, have taken on a more neutral position, underlining that the female warrior or action heroine should rather be seen as a complicated, complex, and ambivalent phenomenon that cannot easily be categorized into good vs. bad, empowering vs. disempowering, or progressive vs. conservative. Unlike their male counterparts, who are invariably masculine, female warriors combine and fuse feminine and masculine gender traits; they are not either or, but both at the same time. Therefore, their portrayals offer more than a simple inversion of gender and instead highlight that this issue is more complex than many other mainstream cultural texts want their consumers to believe. This echoes third wave feminism's conception of identity as "multifaceted and layered" and mirrors "its emphasis on paradox, conflict, multiplicity, and messiness" (Dicker and Piepmeier 10, 16).

Hills in particular also insists that femininity in itself should not be automatically regarded as a disqualifier for heroism (43). This evaluation harks back to the assessment of female warriors within third wave feminism, where Girl Power and its vindication of femininity are celebrated rather than denounced. Indeed, third wavers such as Jennifer Baumgardner and Amy Richards postulate that women and girls should not have to become more masculine in order to be taken seriously or to be able to compete with men in different aspects of their everyday lives (*Manifesta* 137). Consequently, third wavers read female heroes in general and girl warriors specifically as potentially empowering and subversive role models who teach their (female) audiences that they can be both stereotypically feminine *and* strong and independent (Levine; Payne-Mulliken and Renagar).

What is more, Brown, Hills, and Hagelin also offer a more general critique of previous feminist academic work on female warriors at large, which, as they put it, frequently falls back into a binary approach that simplifies these fictional characters as well as the gender discourses and other cultural and societal issues addressed and negotiated through their narratives. Hagelin in particular makes aware of the paradox within much of feminist scholarship when she states that, while many accuse female warriors of reiterating patriarchal discourses and gender hierarchies, feminist analyses actually frequently do the same. This is because the aspects of the heroines that connote traditional femininity are repeatedly read as disempowering and/or objectifying, so that "the very things that scholars criticize [...] are also the things patriarchal culture has used to denigrate women" (10). In her criticism, Hagelin concludes that "we as scholars often fall into a similar trap—to crave female characters who are stripped of the vestiges of 'femininity' that signal the way our subjectivities have been formed by patriarchy" (12).

In marked contrast to many of their predecessors studying the phenomenon, more recent works on Girl Power also maintain that "popularity and quality are not incompatible and that a text or act might have a popular *and* authentically feminist message" (Zaslow 159). According to this view, the presence of girl warriors, feminist themes and ideas, as well as narratives of female empowerment and strength within popular culture should be seen as a positive development instead of being dismissed simply because it is commercial and/or popular (6). While scholars such as Catherine Driscoll and Emilie Zaslow posit that it is important to "take seriously the tension between agency and complicity that is, and will indefinitely be, at the core of girls' media, particularly in girl power media culture," they also argue that resistance and empowerment always takes place within existing power structures and that a certain amount of complicity, that is, engagement with said structures, can therefore never be completely avoided (Driscoll, *Girls* 280–81; Zaslow 32). In other words, working within and calling upon the structures of commercial popular media discourses is a necessary part of the feminist struggle that takes place within this field. They also encourage others to conduct more research on female adolescence, as the manifold representations and concepts of girls and young women serve as "crucial markers of cultural specificity and social change" (Driscoll, *Girls* 7).

Taken together, many of the more recent studies attempt to refute the aforementioned stereotypes concerning (teenage) girls and girl culture more generally. Currie, Kelly, and Pomerantz, for instance, question the notion of young women as helpless victims of both the media and commodities they consume and instead insist that many female teenagers critically engage with the representations they encounter in the media (29). What is more, just like Jessalynn Keller in *Girls' Feminist Blogging* (2016), Zaslow in *Feminism, Inc.* (2006), or Mary Celeste Kearney in *Girls Make Media* (2006), they also call for an increase in academic work that more directly engages with girls and young women themselves instead of simply analyzing the manner in which they are represented in the media.

This book heeds these requests and will join, engage in, and expand upon the various debates about Girl Power, feminism, female heroes, new heroic archetypes, and the regressive or progressive potential of these characters. I focus on girl warriors in particular to challenge some of the negative assumptions that have been made regarding such heroines as disempowering role models, on the one hand, and the conceptualization of their audiences as non-political consumers and potential victims of the media, on the other one. In doing so, I refute the widespread assumption made by many feminist scholars that behaving according to the scripts of stereotypical femininity is invariably disempowering. Just like the scholars who have joined the debate more recently, I understand portrayals of female heroism in general, and girl warriors specifically, as highly complex and complicated phenomena. Indeed, while I do offer a reading that casts Buffy, Katniss, and Merida as feminist figures, their very complexity, as I show in the second half of this book, leaves room for alternative, that is, both progressive and reactionary readings. Finally, this book also attempts to close the gap that exists in the study of teenage girls to some extent and refute the stereotype that (teenage) girls are not interested in feminism. To this end, I include analyses of media created by teenage girls and young women themselves to show that the texts and images they generate engage in a variety of feminist discourses that subvert patriarchal gender roles and power structures.

In this context, it is important to briefly explain how I define feminism. Indeed, the division of the feminist movement into multiple subcategories makes it hard, if not impossible, to talk about feminism today as one unified movement. For the purpose of this book, I draw together some of the most prominent features found across a variety of feminist groups. I define feminism along the lines of the third wave as a political movement that retains theories and strategies from its second wave predecessor at the same time that it strives to be more inclusive and diverse. It endeavors to subvert patriarchal power structures and gender hierarchies through the revaluation and equalization of traditional femininity as well as a reconceptualization of gender as non-binary. It also works with an intersectional approach that acknowledges and celebrates diversity and insists on the inclusion of previously marginalized groups such as people of color or the LGBTQ community. Moreover, contemporary feminisms rely on both popular culture and the Internet as spaces in which feminist ideas can be spread and debated, and activism can be fostered (Munro 23).

Because it brings together academic discourses, questions, and debates from different fields such as girl studies, gender studies, feminisms, digital media, reception analysis, film and television studies, and fan studies, this study relies on a variety of methods, theories, and approaches to analyze how notions of heroism and gender are conceptualized in *BtVS*, the *Hunger Games*, and *Brave*, as well as the secondary and tertiary texts that surround these narratives. Whereas discourse analysis and close reading will be used throughout this work to analyze both form and content of the different texts, the lens will continuously shift between a focus on gender and heroism, respectively, in order to observe how the two categories influence and inform each other.

With regard to the analysis of gender specifically, Judith Butler's theory of gender performativity is an indispensable tool to grasp why girl warriors are characters that have the ability to de-naturalize and de-stabilize gender categories. Butler suggests that "gender is a performance that produces the illusion of an inner sex or essence or psychic gender chore; it produces [...] the illusion of an inner depth" ("Imitation" 267). As Butler emphasizes, even though gender roles are artificially constructed and maintained, many people regard both feminine and masculine behavior and appearance as determined by biological factors and therefore as natural (*Gender Trouble* 10). She suggests that the artificial nature of gender can be exposed through acts that make aware of the performances needed to preserve the categories, such as parody or drag (186). Female warriors can produce a similar effect as their blurring of gendered traits and behaviors also has the potential to shatter binary and naturalized gender norms.

Since many of the texts analyzed in this book are visual or audio-visual, I also draw from feminist film analysis, as it offers concepts and methods that are helpful in analyzing how and to which effect the bodies of the heroines are represented. Here, Laura Mulvey's concept of the male gaze established in "Visual Pleasure and Narrative Cinema" will serve as one central source. In this article, the author posits that the bodies of women and girls are invariably staged in movies to cater to a male heterosexual gaze. This means that they are cast as passive objects whose main function it is to afford pleasure to the male onlooker. This concept has been highly influential, but it has also been repeatedly reworked and adapted, so that I will rely on both the theory itself and on revisions and updates that question Mulvey's model of male power and female objectification. Those are, for instance, the analyses of cinematic female action heroines by Jeffrey Brown or Sarah Hagelin.

My research is also indebted to the field of cultural studies, most importantly because its conceptualization of popular culture as a site of struggle over meaning makes it possible to see girl warriors not simply as commodified goods and representatives of conservative values imposed from above by the culture industries, but as characters whose portrayal has the potential to resist or negotiate hegemonic concepts of both girlhood and heroism (cf. Storey 8–9). What is more, cultural studies is not only interested in the texts produced by the culture industries themselves, but it also insists on the importance of consumption for the process of meaning making (63–65). Here, the field of fan studies comes into play as well, especially because it regards audiences not as passive consumers, but as active interpreters who have the potential to "demonstrate resistance and agency" (Lopez 432).[4] Fan scholars insist that works produced by fans, such as fan art or fan fiction, should be regarded as texts in their own right and studied as such (Hellekson and Busse; Jenkins, *Textual* 46; Pugh). A close reading of the different media produced by fans can thus offer important insight regarding the impact heroic characters such as Buffy, Merida, and Katniss have on their audiences, how they are interpreted, and how their stories, characters, or outer appearance are adapted and changed as a form of criticism of the original texts.

This book is divided into two parts. In Part I: Representations of Girl Warriors in Primary Texts, Chapters 1 through 3, I look at narrative conventions more closely in order to trace how retellings of mythical quest stories can influence the concepts of both gender and heroism represented in such narratives. So far, there exist only a few studies that analyze stories in which women set out on heroic quests, let alone any that engage with teenage girls in particular. Already in their 1981 monograph *The Female Hero in American and British Literature*, Caroline Pearson and Catherine Pope point out that the female hero as an archetypal figure has been neglected by both literary and cultural studies (viii), yet this situation remains largely unchanged. After all, in 2014, in her introduction to the anthology *A Quest of Her Own: Essays on the Female Hero in Modern Fantasy*, editor Lori Campbell still laments that "very little substantive work has been done on the female hero" (5). In fact, she merely mentions one other academic study, namely Jennifer Stuller's *Ink-Stained Amazons and Cinematic Warriors: Superwomen in Modern Mythology* (2010) that engages with the female hero and heroic archetypes specifically. In all of these works, the authors describe a model of female heroism and quest stories that are informed by and simultaneously rework either the complete model or individual aspects of the male quest hero in order for the respective stories to account for experiences and challenges encountered by women and girls specifically.

All of these works are helpful for my analysis, yet there are also a number of issues which set my research and approach apart from these texts. Pearson and Pope most thoroughly use Campbell's model of the mythical quest hero to analyze fictional female characters, yet their focus on 19th- and 20th-century realist fiction stands in stark contrast to my analysis of contemporary popular culture heroines. Likewise, *A Quest of Her Own* focuses on modern fantasy literature exclusively. Still, the authors of this anthology identify some tropes and characteristics of female heroes in this genre which can be connected to my own findings, thus establishing a more comprehensive notion of female heroes in contemporary popular culture. Finally, just like this study, Stuller's work on female heroes covers a variety of genres such as movies, TV shows, and comics. She also dedicates a section to a description of how writers, artists, directors, or actors create, engage with, and influence portrayals of heroic characters.

The only authors who at least mention feminist features of heroic quest stories more specifically are Pearson and Pope. They argue, for instance, that while "on the archetypal level the journey to self-discovery is the same for both the male and female hero" (viii), the latter faces different obstacles than her male counterpart and is occasionally even hindered from completing her quest due to her sex and gender (16, 18). The authors rely, however, on a notion of feminism that casts stereotypical femininity as inferior to masculinity because they identify a female character as heroic if she rejects the norms of traditional femininity and "elects instead to develop within herself the heroic qualities society has seen as male" (177). While it acknowledges that gender is non-binary, this model still enforces a gender hierarchy in which traditional masculinity is cast as heroic and traditional femininity as an obstacle that needs to be overcome (cf. 18, 49–50, 68). Even though they also point out that, at the end of her quest, the female hero occasionally starts to validate her femininity as well, Pearson and Pope's analysis still insists that it is her masculine traits that turn a woman into a heroic character (177–78).

A different notion of femininity within the realm of female heroism can be found in the more contemporary works analyzed in the studies conducted by Campbell and Stuller. They posit that in fantasy novels, TV shows, movies, and comics, traditional femininity is often not staged as incompatible with heroism, but frequently presented as a heroic quality in its own right, as it is crucial for the heroine's success (L. Campbell 284; Stuller 88, 92). In this context, they identify aspects such as romantic love, friendship, and community as central parts of narratives that feature female heroes (L. Campbell 284; Stuller 87–88). Stuller also demonstrates that the majority of female heroes does not strive to attain power over others, but to nurture and work within a community (88). However, even though Stuller and Campbell mention that changing gender norms can be held accountable for the appropriation of heroic stories and features, they do not account for feminist influences or representations of feminist discourses in any detail.

In this context in particular, my research closes two gaps: first of all, the analysis of more contemporary teenage heroines such as Buffy, Katniss, and Merida, and, secondly, the identification of elements in rewritings of quest stories that are decidedly feminist. Buffy Summers is probably one of the best-studied female characters of popular culture but no study has yet drawn together the various different elements in order to set up a more comprehensive model of female heroism, which is exactly what I attempt to do. What is more, there exists only one in-depth analysis of Merida's role as a heroine, namely Zoe Jaques' "'The Huntress Who Delights in Arrows.'" Notably, her article is also one of a few in which Katniss is analyzed with regard to notions of heroism. Even though in the wake of the success of *The Hunger Games*, a number of essay collections were published, many of these "are journalistic rather than academic in nature," touching on "a large number of issues [without developing] them in detail" (Lethbridge 102). In fact, Katniss' role as a heroine has so far only been explicitly studied by Jaques and by Stefanie Lethbridge, who both compare the heroine of the *Hunger Games* franchise to (mythical) archetypes such as the anti-hero or the victim and other heroic forebears such as the goddesses Diana or Artemis.

By contrast, I compare the girl warriors to male quest heroes to show that they undermine a variety of archetypes and tropes, not only regarding myths, but also concerning the specific genres from which they stem, namely horror, YA fiction, and Disney princess movies. In doing so, I establish a model of female heroism I call the feminist quest heroine. The feminist quest heroine follows the well-established pattern of the classic heroic journey quite closely, yet her narrative changes and subverts central aspects of both the quest and of typical characteristics of the male hero. In fact, the narratives deviate from the model of the quest hero in exactly those moments that usually maintain and celebrate traditional masculinity and male superiority and instead replace them with feminist elements. In these narratives, the quest is turned from a story that supports a patriarchal world view into one that celebrates a feminist one, which shows that quest narratives can be rewritten to incorporate feminist thought and theory. In delineating the model of the feminist quest heroine, I take up and affirm some of the features of female heroism established by previous scholars, such as the importance of community or the revaluation of femininity, but also highlight that said features hark back to and promote feminist ideas and concepts. I furthermore point out some additional qualities that are staged as heroic, most importantly the fight against patriarchal oppression, thus contributing to and expanding on the model of female heroism.

The first chapter on *BtVS* establishes the model of the feminist quest heroine. I analyze four central modifications of the traditional quest narrative to demonstrate that the series creates a model of heroism that incorporates and celebrates feminist thought and theory. Those are the hybrid gender of the heroine, the portrayal of her body, her engagement in relationships, and different forms of power negotiated in the show. While I use episodes from all seven seasons to set up the model, the musical episode "Once More, with Feeling" serves as a focal point in this chapter, as its songs and dance numbers engage with and prominently highlight the four modifications.

In Chapter 2, the focus lies on Katniss Everdeen, one of the most prominent girl warriors of recent years. The popularity of this character attests that girl warriors have moved from the subcultural spheres that Buffy occupied towards a position closer to the mainstream. It is my aim to show that the model of the feminist quest heroine has been adapted in the *Hunger Games* trilogy to not only account for changes in Western cultures and politics, but to highlight that thoughts and behaviors reminiscent of feminist theory can serve as suitable tools to address contemporary challenges such as the power and influence of the media or political oppression and exploitation. I set out by analyzing gender role portrayals as well as systemic forms of oppression in the fictional world of Panem. I then show that the trilogy draws attention to strategies through which the representation of teenage girls in the media can take on new meanings and subvert established systems of power. Finally, the chapter also traces Katniss' personal development and her coming into political consciousness in order to highlight instances in which feminist discourse informs the type of activism and heroism created in the novels.

The final girl warrior I analyze is Disney's Princess Merida, the character who has so far received the least academic attention of the three heroines. In this chapter, I read Merida against the background of her Disney princess predecessors and suggest that she is, indeed, the first feminist Disney princess. This is because in *Brave*, the princess or damsel-in-distress archetype is revised to include elements of the feminist quest heroine. In contrast to the first two chapters, my focus lies not so much on the question how the feminist quest heroine subverts notions of masculine superiority and male power, but in this case, I analyze how the model can be used to subvert the archetype of the damsel in distress, too. I identify tropes of princess stories that usually reinforce notions of traditional femininity, most importantly the celebration of romantic love and the enmity between women, and demonstrate that *Brave* subverts these tropes and infuses the princess story with a feminist message. The inclusion of elements of the feminist quest heroine and a feminist message into a Disney princess movie clearly underlines that feminist ideas, albeit in alleviated form, have arrived in the mainstream.

Even though I explicitly focus on the damsel in distress only in Chapter 3, this archetype will also occasionally come up in the first two chapters in order to show that the feminist quest heroine subverts both the archetype of the warrior and the damsel. Whereas the heroines' whiteness, conventional beauty, and heterosexuality are features that have previously been used to criticize girl heroes, I want to explicitly engage with these traits not in order to dismiss the feminist potential of these characters based on these issues, but, on the contrary, to delineate that it is exactly these features that are essential for the establishment of a feminist message. In fact, only by having them adhere to the tropes of idealized femininity to some extent can the texts challenge the archetype of the damsel, who has traditionally not only been conceptualized as young, white, beautiful, heterosexual, and privileged, but also as passive, vulnerable, and dependent on male help and guidance. In fact, this archetype has historically addressed and conceptualized white privileged femininity in particular. As Sarah Hagelin observes, there remains a "stubborn [...] association of whiteness with vulnerability" because "twenti-eth-century American culture has taught women, particularly privileged, white women, to understand themselves as especially vulnerable" (15). As I will show in each chapter, the girl heroines undermine the archetype of the damsel by breaking the connection between race, gender, youth, and vulner-ability. Notably, they do not shed the markers of the damsel archetype to do so, but features of stereotypical femininity are negotiated and revalued as part of the heroic and not as a contrast to it. This is a central element to establish the feminist message, as patriarchal gender hierarchies are chal-lenged and subverted.

In addition to the male quest hero and the damsel, Buffy, Katniss, and Merida challenge a third heroic trope, namely that of the so-called "strong female character." The term has surfaced in the popular press specifically to criticize the fact that often, "being a badass isn't a safeguard from being one-dimensional, inessential to the story, or primarily on-screen decor" (Will-more). The "strong female character" serves as an umbrella term for different modes of representations of female heroism. It usually refers to masculinized, one-dimensional female fighting machines whose main function it often is to appeal to a male heterosexual gaze, which is why they are also frequently referred to as the "Fighting Fuck Toy" (Heldman). In any case, the strong female character is reactionary, as it articulates a type of heroism that rein-forces traditional notions of both gender and heroism.[5] Buffy, Katniss, and Merida stand in stark contrast to the strong female character, as they are nei-ther one-dimensional, nor hypersexualized or inessential to the story.

In Part II: Representations of Girl Warriors in Secondary and Tertiary Texts, Chapters 4 through 6, I show that the feminist issues represented by the girl heroines are used or addressed in fundamentally different ways in the secondary and tertiary texts. To be more precise, said texts either recast the girl warriors according to more traditional and established archetypes or they embrace, emphasize, and at times expand upon the feminist ideas com-municated in their stories. The promotional material tends to hark back to more conventional gender role portrayals and archetypal tropes, and thus ultimately contains and diminishes the feminist potential laid out in the pri-mary texts. The works of fan art and fan fiction, by contrast, have a tendency to highlight the feminist subtext, to bring it to the fore, and, at times, to take it further. They do so by expanding on female heroes to include characters that are queer or girls of color, for instance, and thus also address and incor-porate the criticism regarding the whiteness, conventional beauty, and het-erosexuality of popular culture's girl warriors.

In Chapter 4, I analyze a variety of paratexts whose aim it is to promote and sell the heroines and their stories to a mainstream audience. Looking at these texts makes it possible to draw conclusions on the notions of heroism and girlhood in a broader cultural and societal context (cf. Gray 24). This is because as entities used to sell commodities, paratexts aim at representing primary texts in a manner that makes them appealing and interesting to a broad clientele. In other words, paratexts mirror the themes or ideas of a specific text deemed important or valuable enough to be used as a marketing tool. In the case of the girl warriors, the paratexts marginalize or erase the feminist subtext of the primary texts and instead represent the young women in a manner that harks back to more stereotypical notions of both femininity and heroism. Even though their representation develops in some aspects, Buffy, Katniss, and Merida are repeatedly portrayed in ways that either adhere to the model of the masculinized male warrior hero or in a manner that sexualizes and objectifies them.

The final two chapters deal with fan fiction and fan art, respectively. Even though there also exists a plethora of texts that work into different or even opposite directions, I concentrate on texts in which the feminist features of the primary texts are highlighted. In their numerous works, fans praise the innovative notions of female heroism represented in *BtVS*, the *Hunger Games*, and *Brave*, and repeatedly hark back to and celebrate elements of the feminist quest heroine. In addition, they also create pieces of art that diversify conceptualizations of heroism and girlhood even more. To be more precise, the pieces of fan fiction analyzed in Chapter 5 negotiate questions of heroism, gender, and (queer) sexualities. I analyze a specific subgenre of fan fiction, namely femslash, that is, texts in which two female characters engage in a romantic and/or sexual relationship. These works follow a queer agenda that challenges the dominance of heteronormativity found in the majority of representations of heroic characters in mainstream popular culture by creating heroines that work against these ideals. The authors of femslash thus insist that queer girls can be heroines, too, or that being queer should not be seen as incompatible with heroism.

Finally, through an analysis of fan art in Chapter 6, I show that fans participate in a variety of intersectional feminist online discourses that comment on the representation of women, girls, and heroic characters in contemporary popular culture. They first of all posit that female heroes such as Buffy, Katniss, and Merida can serve as feminist role models precisely because, as girl warriors, they undermine a number of stereotypical portrayals of female characters usually found in the mainstream media. Again, features of the feminist quest heroine show up time and again as traits of these heroines that are deemed particularly innovative or empowering. Secondly, fans also criticize the fact that girl warriors, and heroic figures in general, are usually portrayed as white/Caucasian. In their fan art, they use a strategy called "racebending," a term that refers to either changing the outer appearance of a white character to portray them as a person of color, or the replacing of a white character with one of color. By representing women and girls of color in heroic roles previously occupied by white characters, these fans expand on the concept of idealized girlhood and maintain that people of color should be represented as heroes, too.

While the fan texts hence celebrate and support the feminist demands for diversity, equality, and inclusion through their production of heroines who adhere to and represent these very principles, through their containment of the feminist subtext, the paratexts indirectly show that feminist ideas are not yet mainstream enough to be used in the promotion and selling of these heroines to a general U.S. audience. Still, the diversification of features and characters that are deemed potentially heroic speaks strongly of the impact of feminist thought and theory on the creators of heroic figures, both professional and non-professional ones.

I

Representations of Girl Warriors in Primary Texts

◆ ◆ 1 ◆ ◆

Establishing the Feminist Quest Heroine in *Buffy the Vampire Slayer*

> BUFFY: And what are we, if not women up for a challenge?
> WILLOW: Exactly, did we not put the grrr in girl?
> —"Living Conditions"

This short conversation between Buffy Summers and her best friend Willow Rosenberg neatly sums up the premise of *BtVS*. Buffy is, indeed, a woman, or rather teenage girl up for a challenge since she is the Slayer, the one girl in the world chosen by destiny and armed with supernatural strength to "stand against the vampires, the demons and the forces of darkness" ("Welcome"). The series, which ran over seven seasons from 1997 to 2003, featured weekly villains in the form of monsters, demons, and vampires, as well as different "Big Bads": major antagonists who posed a threat throughout the course of a whole season. However, no matter how evil and powerful they were, Buffy still ultimately always defeated the monsters and saved the world. In order to do so, she received the help of a so-called Watcher, Rupert Giles, who trained her and conducted research on the different supernatural villains Buffy fought. In addition, she was also supported by her group of friends, the so-called "Scoobies," and her vampire boyfriends Angel and Spike.

While the exchange between Buffy and Willow hence sums up the show itself, it also alludes to the cultural and historical context in which the series was created. To be more precise, when Willow talks about putting "the grrr in girl," she refers to the Riot Grrrls, a subcultural movement that was established in the early 1990s by young women who belonged to all-female punk bands. Their aim was to create a space in which girls could speak out against the sexism they encountered within the field of punk rock itself as well as in their everyday lives more generally (Zaslow 29). Bands such as Bikini Kill coined the term Girl Power, or Grrrl Power, and their activism was informed by both second wave feminism and punk: Riot Grrls were anti-capitalist and created their own music and zines, for instance; they also encouraged their members not to consume mainstream commodities and regularly met to talk about the problems and challenges they faced as young women, an activity that closely resembles the consciousness raising format central to second wave feminism (cf. Hains 97).What is more, their style of clothing adhered to a "girlie aesthetic" that connoted stereotypical femininity, yet they openly staged outrage about the sexism they experienced (Currie, Kelly, and Pomerantz 7), a rage that is made explicit through the onomatopoetic growl written into the word "grrrl."

The Riot Grrrl movement is frequently regarded as the "authentic predecessor to a commercial girl power media culture," yet critics usually name additional developments that led to the emergence of Girl Power as a mainstream discourse (Zaslow 29). The second development that can be connected to the establishment of Girl Power is the countermovement against the traditionalism and conservatism concerning the role of women in American society in the 1980s and early 1990s. As described by Susan Faludi in her book *Backlash: The Undeclared War Against American Women* (1991), during this time, American culture showed a heightened interest in war, fighting, and celebrating the figure of the tough and violent male warrior, while at the same time erasing images of women from the public sphere or portraying them as passive and/or mute (78, 125–26). As a reaction to this regressive discourse, there emerged a trend in U.S. popular culture to depict women and girls as "strong, independent, professionally successful and assertive characters" who challenged "traditional gender norms" (Allrath, Gymnich, and Surkamp 29).

Finally, the emergence of the Girl Power discourse also coincided with what Zaslow describes as "the apex of the popularization of feminist psychological studies of girls" (13). The idea of what scholars have since termed the "Ophelia" or "'at-risk' discourse" was developed in the highly successful parenting guide *Reviving Ophelia: Saving the Selves of Adolescent Girls* (1994) and academic studies such as *Making Connections: The Relational Worlds of Adolescent Girls at Emma Willard School* (1990), or *Schoolgirls: Young Women, Self-Esteem, and the Confidence Gap* (1994). The authors of these books reported that girls suffered from a severe loss of self-esteem once they reached adolescence. Due to societal pressures regarding their outer appearance and behavior, which were only strengthened by the media, girls were said to learn to silence their voices and hate their bodies, which resulted in failure at school, self-mutilation, and eating disorders (cf. Day, Green-Barteet, and Montz 5). Even though the Ophelia discourse was frequently criticized for pathologizing teenage girls, its conceptualization of female adolescence as fragile, vulnerable, and even dangerous for those who went through it still gained a lot of attention at the time (Harris 140–42; Zaslow 17).

Against this background, Buffy can be regarded as a heroine who was created, among other things, as a reaction to an increased interest in girls and girlhood in the 1990s and the discourses about the Ophelia complex and Girl Power. Indeed, the show engages with, and at times challenges, many of the major discourses surrounding the Girl Power movement. First of all, Buffy embodies the apparent dichotomy of being stereotypically feminine on the one hand—she is interested in girlie things such as fashion, makeup, boys, and spending time with her friends—and being an empowered girl on the other hand, as she is the Slayer. Notions of stereotypical masculinity and femininity become mixed and blurred in this mini-skirt-wearing warrior, who is chosen by destiny to protect the world from monsters, demons, and the occasional apocalypse. By portraying its female protagonist in this specific manner, the show counters the stereotype that a blonde, Californian, teenage girl cannot be strong, resilient, and responsible for saving the world. Consequently, Buffy's creator Joss Whedon not only designed a female warrior who fights against monsters and demons, but Buffy slays gender norms and expectations as successfully and thoroughly as the vampires she turns into dust.

In addition to gender conventions, *BtVS* also challenges genre conventions. As Whedon himself stated, the show was initially conceived as a subversion of the genre of horror and the stereotypical manner in which many horror movies portray female characters. The series first of all works against the trope of the "pretty [...] blond girl in the alley [...] who keeps getting killed. [...] She was fun, she had sex, she was vivacious. But then she would get punished for it" (Whedon qtd. in Vint 6). The TV show clearly undermines this trope, as it portrays Buffy as a hyper-feminine, fun, and sexually active girl who kills monsters instead of being killed by them. Secondly, by insisting that girls do not have to take over masculine character traits in order to survive, the show subverts an additional trope frequently encountered in the horror genre, namely that of the so-called "Final Girl." As established by Carol Clover in *Men, Women and Chainsaws* (1992), in a typical horror movie, the final girl is the only character to survive the killer's attacks. In contrast to the female victim, however, the final girl is rather masculinized and does neither have sex nor any other kind of fun (39, 40). Both tropes are hence problematic with regard to their portrayal of gender because they suggest that masculinity is needed in order to survive, an idea which *BtVS* certainly defies.

As a consequence, Buffy not only serves as a prime example of the new type of female protagonist that emerged after the backlash of the 1980s, but she can also be seen as a response to the worries about teenage girls as potential victims brought forth by the Ophelia discourse. This is because in the fictional universe, the fights against monsters, demons, and vampires serve as symbols of the real-life struggles teenagers in general and adolescent girls in particular face on a regular basis (cf. Chandler 3; Magee 885; Wilcox 3, 12). Even though the TV show demonstrates time and again that, indeed, high school, adolescence, and even young adulthood can be hell, it refuses to cast its female protagonist or her friends as victims, and instead lets them successfully slay the real and metaphorical demons which haunt them. Noticeably, it is exactly this mixing and blurring of the real and the fantastic in *BtVS* which allows the show to first create an alternative reality in which experiments and changes can take place. With regard to the TV series, the experiments with gender conventions are one of the most interesting transformations since "the blurred boundaries that are possible in speculative texts open up space necessary to examine arguments and gendered ideologies which govern what is, and what is not, possible in the 'real' world" (Buttsworth 185). The combination of a patriarchal world and an innovative female character such as Buffy calls attention to, challenges, and even shows ways of how to defy both patriarchal power systems and gender norms.

What is more, the usage of elements of myth and fantasy not only makes it possible for the show to subvert contemporary notions of gender, but contemporary notions of heroism and heroic myths, too. At a first glance, Buffy resembles and echoes the mythological male hero in a number of features. She is smart, physically strong and brave, knows how to use weapons, and can take care of herself. What is more, just like her male counterparts, Buffy has been chosen by destiny to become the Slayer and does not embrace her extraordinary status and her new role from the beginning of her calling. During the course of her adventures, however, she starts to acknowledge the opportunities and possibilities her heroic status affords her and she eventually accepts and embraces her role as the Slayer (Bowman). After all, Buffy even sacrifices herself twice in order to save the world ("Gift"; Prophecy"). Finally, the Slayer also has to go through the problematic phase of the return: Buffy is reluctant to accept her life on earth after she has been resurrected and pulled out of heaven by her friends ("After Life"). Due to her blissful experience in heaven, she has trouble accepting the reality with which she is confronted after her return to the real world, and just like the heroes described in Campbell's monomyth, Buffy receives help to come to terms with ordinary life, namely from the vampire Spike (cf. Bowman).

Based on these observations, I argue that *BtVS* establishes a model of heroism which casts both traditional femininity and feminist theory and activism as potentially heroic. As I will demonstrate, this model, which I call the feminist quest heroine, lets its female protagonist closely follow the typical narratives of quest stories in which men occupy the roles of heroes only to then deviate from the model in exactly those moments that usually affirm the hero's masculinity in order to replace it with stereotypical femininity. As a consequence, the patriarchal and heteronormative agenda inherent in traditional heroic tales is replaced with a feminist one. Buffy can be regarded as a feminist heroine because her character not only fights against the patriarchal forces in her world by using methods resembling feminist activism, but she also undermines well-established connotations with regard to both traditional femininity and masculinity, calls into question the very existence of a binary model of gender, and reconceptualizes femininity and girlhood as empowered and potentially subversive states of being. *BtVS* does so by turning the quest from a story about male power and dominance into an account of female empowerment and agency.[1] This is achieved through four major modifications of the quest narrative on which I will focus in the following pages.

First, of all, it is very simply the heroine's hybrid gender itself that breaks the association between heroism and masculinity. While for centuries, heroism in general and warriorhood in particular were strongly connected to masculine traits such as bravery and strength, in *BtVS*, they become connected to femininity as well. Due to the fact that heroism is not only connected to masculine character traits, but masculine and muscular bodies, Buffy's petite frame serves as an additional subversion to the model of traditional male heroism. Therefore, the portrayal of Buffy's body will be the focus of attention in the second part of my analysis. After that, I turn to the platonic relationships in which the Slayer engages. Since traditional heroes usually work alone and without support (J. Campbell, *Hero* 246), the inclusion of a network of friends is another feature that challenges conservative models of male heroism. What is more, it also introduces the feminist concept of sisterhood. Last but not least, I analyze the way in which Buffy brings down the patriarchal forces of her world and establishes a new system of power. Notably, this new power system is non-hierarchical and inclusive and thus echoes systems of power propagated by feminist movements.

I have chosen the musical episode "Once More, with Feeling" as a focus to delineate how these four modifications of the quest narrative function. While I also refer to numerous other episodes, I use "Once More, with Feeling" as an anchor to which I return time and again in order to trace the kind of heroism established in the show. In this episode, a demon whose presence makes people burst out into song is summoned to Buffy's hometown Sunnydale. Through these acts of singing and dancing, people express their feelings and emotions, which, if they are particularly strong, frequently lead to spontaneous self-combustion. Since Buffy has recently been resurrected by her friends, who believe that they saved her from hell, while only Spike knows that, in fact, they pulled her out of heaven, a lot of feelings and truths are revealed throughout "Once More, with Feeling." This particular episode is especially suited for an analysis of the kind of heroism established in *BtVS*, as it dedicates one or several songs to each of the main themes I want to address.

"But you're just a girl": The Subversion of Heroism and Gender Norms

Considering that the protagonist of *BtVS* is a teenage girl, gender can be regarded as "the biggest transgression of warrior iconography" represented in the series (Buttsworth 185). That is why I interpret it as the basis of and the source for all other digressions from the image of the mythological male warrior. As already mentioned, for centuries, the role of the warrior has been largely assumed by men and hailed as the epitome of masculinity (Pearson 2). The entrance of a petite, blonde Californian teenage girl into the realm of warriorhood disrupts this pattern and invites audiences to reflect on concepts of warriorhood and heroism, as well as hegemonic masculinity and femininity.

In "Once More, with Feeling," Buffy's exceptional role as a female warrior is given particular prominence because the very first song of the episode— "Going through the Motions"—depicts the Slayer on patrol, effortlessly fighting and killing numerous vampires and demons. The mere fact that she can simultaneously sing a song about her personal feelings and engage in combat with supernatural beings not only highlights the campy style of the series at large, but also clearly shows off the Slayer's power and skills. In addition, the musical fighting scene demonstrates that her character blurs binary gender notions. After all, Buffy talks about her feelings, an activity typically connected to hegemonic femininity, at the same time that she slays vampires, an activity that usually connotes hegemonic masculinity. The manner in which *BtVS* undermines traditional gender roles in the realm of heroism in particular is furthermore underscored because its female protagonist does not rescue a damsel in distress, but a tall, muscular, and handsome man, from the hands of a demon. Hence, the very first song of the episode represents Buffy, and the manner in which the series challenges traditional concepts of gender and heroism, in a nutshell: in this heroic tale, a young beautiful woman effortlessly fights vampires and demons and rescues helpless men from peril and distress, all without breaking a sweat.

The adding of feminine attributes to a model of heroism that has been exclusively connected to masculinity influences the image of the traditional warrior hero and changes the pattern of what can be seen as heroic. Through the depiction of Buffy as a skilled warrior the show not only counters stereotypes of gender roles in general, but of teenage girls in particular. On the one hand, Buffy is portrayed in accordance with the image of the typical teenage girl, as she is occasionally moody, unmotivated, emotional, irrational, or unpleasant (Sainato 141). On the other hand, even though Buffy has these flaws and weaknesses, she is still the heroine of the series. In fact, it is exactly her imperfections that render her a heroine, because her very ability to deal with or to overcome personal flaws is a skill that is presented as part of Buffy's heroism. This is another aspect that is emphasized in the very first song featured in "Once More, with Feeling." As mentioned above, Buffy was pulled out of heaven by her friends and consequently suffers from depression, singing that she is just "going through the motions / losing all [her] drive." At the same time, however, and in spite of her psychological issues, Buffy has no problems to fight and kill vampires and demons. In fact, that she is able to do so by "going through the motions," that is, by not putting a lot of effort into it, makes her powers appear even more impressive.

BtVS furthermore works against a dis-empowering portrayal of everything girly by showing that many of Buffy's rather feminine traits allow her to be a better Slayer. The departure from the traditional model of warrioring shows that women and girls can not only be strong when they take on masculine attributes, but that they can be even more successful if they embrace femininity at the same time. On numerous occasions, the show maintains that "the social conventions of mainstream femininity, which have so often been used to argue that women cannot be warriors, are often precisely what makes Buffy such an effective soldier" (Buttsworth 185). This advantage is demonstrated, for instance, already in the very first episode of the series, when Buffy is able to identify a vampire due to his unfashionable outfit, as according to her, "only someone living underground for ten years would think *that* was still the look" ("Welcome"). In this scene, Buffy plays out a quality typically connected to femininity—namely her knowledge of fashion—in order to spot a vampire in a room full of people and can consequently save her friend Willow from said vampire. *BtVS* thus works against the devaluation of feminine attributes, such as an interest in clothes and trendiness, as predominantly shallow and unimportant.

In fact, Buffy is able to take on a superior position not in spite of her feminine features and her status as a teenage girl, but because of them. Indeed, "with Buffy, the heroic becomes not just reconciled with the feminine, but ruled by it" (Byers 171). This is because the Slayer's supernatural strength puts her in an equal position with regard to the creatures she has to fight, but it is her femininity that lifts her to a superior one. On *BtVS*, femininity is not a limiting quality, but it is of irreplaceable value for the Slayer and her fight against evil. This feminization of the warrior hero echoes the ideals of the Girl Power movement as it shows that "you don't have to make something masculine in order to make it valued by society" (Baumgardner and Richards,

"Feminism" 63). The series elevates teenage girls' knowledge and lifestyle to a potentially heroic status, opening up the realm of who can be a hero and what can be regarded as heroic to include issues that have not been connected to the concept before.

In addition, the show counters one of the common points of criticism regarding Girl Power media, namely that girlhood is depicted in an idealized fashion as powerful and unproblematic (cf. Brown). By contrast, *BtVS* addresses a number of issues, problems, and threats that "normal" teenage girls face on a regular basis such as problems with parents, peer pressure, cliques, violent boyfriends, or popularity contests among girls, which cannot all be analyzed in detail here. What all of these examples have in common, however, is that in each case, the series demonstrates that girls should actively resist and defend themselves against discrimination, victimization, and the gender norms that might constrain them. The show hence engages in the Ophelia discourse in so far as it shows that while teenage girls are confronted with limiting gender norms on a regular basis, they can also fight their victimization and overcome the challenges of adolescence.

Buffy, for instance, is regularly confronted with the norms of hegemonic femininity as she was, for instance, expelled from her former school due to her aggressive behavior, and at Sunnydale High, her principal also has issues with her unruly personality ("Welcome"). Instead of having Buffy conform to societal demands, the series emphasizes that her unruly emotions are important for her as they render her a better fighter. The show stresses that emotions such as anger and fury, which usually connote hegemonic masculinity, can actually be productive and empowering. It does so, for instance, during a conversation between the two Slayers Buffy and Kendra when Buffy explains: "My emotions give me power. They're total assets! You feel it, right? How the anger gives you fire? A Slayer needs that" ("What's My Line (Part 1)"). This statement demonstrates that the show conceptualizes Buffy's emotions not as limiting or distracting. On the contrary, she is able to use them to her own advantage, as they render her a better fighter. In contrast to Kendra, who likes to keep "an even mind" and relies on her technique only, Buffy uses her technique, her instincts, *and* her emotions to win a fight, thus underlining the positive aspects of her fury ("What's My Line (Part 1)"). *BtVS* consequently reworks notions of hegemonic femininity and girlhood by demonstrating that even though societal norms might tell them that they should be temperate, friendly, and kind, girls can and should voice their "outrage at the world's injustices" (Dicker and Piepmeier 22).

In "Once More, with Feeling," too, the importance of Buffy's defiant emotions is staged, as there is a whole song dedicated to them, namely "Walk through the Fire." The song deals with the fact that, due to her expulsion from heaven, Buffy has lost the passion a Slayer needs to fight evil. In the song, this is expressed through the metaphor of fire, which Buffy has lost. At the same time that she comments on this loss in her song, Buffy also asserts: "I want the fire back!" This demonstrates that she knows of the value of her emotions in general, and her fury and anger in particular. By insisting that the Slayer needs these emotions in order to successfully fight evil, the show reflects another common feminist belief, namely that girls have to embrace their anger about their oppression if they want to become powerful enough to change their societies and the injustices that cause their outrage in the first place (Helford 18).

In this context, it is not only violent emotions, but also actual physical violence that plays a central role in the TV show. Here, *BtVS* goes a step further in countering gender stereotypes and norms of appropriate feminine behavior, as Buffy is not only allowed to show her destructive emotions, but also to let them out in a violent fashion when she slays vampires and demons. Keeping in mind that stereotypical femininity is often connected to both passivity and peacefulness, depicting Buffy in this fashion "challenges assumptions about violence that are organized around sexual difference, offering a space to reconceptualise the relationship between gender, power and aggression" (Parks 119). In this context, Lisa Parks argues that even though the show has often been criticized and even censored for its "spectacular displays of physical aggression," *BtVS* uses said displays to make aware of certain issues and problems connected to violence rather than to promulgate or celebrate violence itself (118–19).[2] One of these issues is the idea that self-defensive behavior can be regarded as a feminist practice (124).

Through her use of physical violence, Buffy not only shows that girls can be as powerful and strong as men, but she also demonstrates that they do not need a man to protect them as she can successfully defend herself and the members of her community, both female and male ones. As mentioned before, this is indicated in "Once More, with Feeling," as it is a handsome young man whom she rescues from the hands of evil. In addition, the show also demonstrates that girls can, in fact, resist and overcome victimization, as Buffy's acts of violence disrupt "the gender ideology that makes men's violence against women seem inevitable" (McCaughey ix). All in all, physical violence can be seen as part and parcel of the shows feminist agenda as it deconstructs binary concepts of gender and portrays ways in which women and girls can fight the oppressive patriarchal forces in their societies. The show hence also counters the notion that the Girl Power discourse is a nonpolitical one. After all, the vampires and monsters Buffy slays stand in as representatives of abusers, rapists, and patriarchal dominance in general (Chandler 1).

The final issue regarding teenage girls' lives that is a central topic of the TV show is romantic love and sex. In *BtVS*, romantic love plays an important role. Indeed, Buffy falls in love and has relationships with men several times throughout the course of the series. By portraying her in this manner, the TV show counters yet another feature of male heroism and that is "the tendency of the lonely hero to evade romantic commitment" (Wilcox 9). Indeed, in classic quest stories, the romantic interest never accompanies the hero on his journey, but she "has to remain in wait for him either at the start or the end of the road" (Auden 49). In a slight variation of this pattern, which Rhonda Wilcox refers to as the "Little Joe Phenomenon," the romantic partner might be present during the quest for a short time, but eventually dies and thus supports the portrayal of the hero as a man who "must be left fatally free of romantic entanglements" (9–10). By having Buffy engage in romantic relationships, the series includes yet another element that has previously been incompatible with heroism.

At the same time, it is important to note that, even though being in love is shown to be compatible with being a hero, it is not staged as a heroic quality in its own right. In other words, even though love and romance do play a part in Buffy's life, her romantic entanglements neither define her nor do they render her a heroine. The show thus subverts another ideal central to the concept of hegemonic femininity, and that is the importance of romantic love. Buffy always remains at the center of the story and she usually puts her obligations before her desire for romance (Hopkins 115). This is demonstrated most clearly in the final episode of season two when Buffy kills Angel, the, until then, love of her life, in order to fulfill her duty to save the world ("Becoming (Part 2)").

Furthermore, the show emphasizes that its heroine is not willing to gain self-worth and define herself only by being in a relationship. Buffy is self-confident enough to completely abstain from a relationship if the man of interest does not fulfill her expectations and understands that she has to get self-confidence from herself and not from others, which is demonstrated, for instance, when she tells Xander: "I don't need a guy right now. I need me. I need to get comfortable being alone with Buffy" ("I Was Made"). The show's highlighting of the idea that Buffy does not define herself through her romantic relationships, but that she is comfortable being single, echoes the feminist belief that women should not depend on male approval or define their self-worth based on their attractiveness to men (cf. Vint 10). Ultimately, *BtVS* thus shows that girls and women should be confident because of what they themselves can achieve and they should learn to accept and like who they are instead of subordinating themselves to male judgment.

In spite of the innovative and empowering portrayal of romantic love on the show, the central position that this topic takes up has given a number of critics cause to comment on the apparent heteronormativity represented in *BtVS* and to criticize the romantic entanglements as stereotypical depictions of love and sexuality that reduce the radical potential of the series with regard to its depiction of gender roles (cf. Magoulick 737–41). What these critics overlook is that Buffy was created to subvert and rework the damsel in distress archetype as well as the gendered tropes of the horror genre. Therefore, I suggest that it is, in fact, imperative for the show to feature heterosexual relationships because only through this can these stereotypes be fully revoked. This is because romance is one of the corner stones on which the portrayal of traditional gender roles and the conservation of heteronormativity in many traditional narratives rest. After all, every damsel is rescued by a male love interest, every girl who has sex in horror movies is eventually killed off, and every girl who does not survives. Consequently, these stories reiterate images of female helplessness and victimhood and male strength and courage time and again and also establish a very conservative stance regarding female sexuality. Thus, to simply leave out romantic plots in general, or replace heterosexual with homosexual romance would rob the show of the opportunity to rewrite and innovate these narrative tropes.

Indeed, the show successfully challenges heteronormativity because even though Buffy is heterosexual, her behavior and her relationships with men are a far cry from being heteronormative. This is because her status as a female warrior opens up opportunities to rework and re-envision heterosexual relationships and the roles women and men take up in them. During the course of the show, Buffy falls in love with different men whose characters represent different degrees of traditional femininity and masculinity, respectively.[3] The major love interests on the show are the two vampires Angel and Spike, who often act as the sidekicks and enablers of Buffy's heroism and strength (McCracken 121). In "Once More, with Feeling," for instance, Spike sings, "I better help her out," stressing his role as helper rather than leader and thus taking on a role typically connected to femininity. What is more, while Buffy rejects the role of the female victim when she tells Angel, "Oh, you know me. Not much with the damseling" ("Chosen"), her vampire lovers are regularly rescued and protected by her, a narrative device that undermines traditional gender roles even more ("Graduation Day [Part 1]"; "Showtime"; "What's My Line [Part 2]").

However, it is not simply a gender reversal that is depicted in *BtVS*, but rather a blurring of gender roles that takes place. This is because Buffy, Angel, and Spike all act in ways that can be described as both stereotypically masculine and feminine at the same time. In "Once More, with Feeling," gender roles are, for instance, made a topic in Spike's song "Rest in Peace." In this song, Spike serenades Buffy and opens up about his feelings for her when he sings that he "died so many years ago / but [she] can make him feel / like it isn't so." He also tells Buffy that being with him "touches him more than [he] can say," describing his heart as "a traitor" that "would break his chest" "if

[it] could [still] beat." While admittedly, Spike is, in part, so open about his emotions because of the musical curse that afflicts Sunnydale's inhabitants, his use of poetic language also refers back to his occupation as a writer of love poems before he became a vampire and can thus be regarded as a general characteristic of him ("Fool"; cf. also Spicer). As a poet, Spike was derided by his peers for being too emotional and sentimental, or, in other words, not masculine enough, and his feminine attributes also shine through in this song when he bares his emotions to Buffy, who, in a manner reminiscent of stereotypical masculinity, seems embarrassed and annoyed by his confession.

The gender roles which the different parties take on in this relationship are furthermore reworked when Spike kneels down in front of the Slayer, telling her that he is her "willing slave." While there is certainly a sexual innuendo in this line, it also mirrors the power dynamics between the two: Spike knows of Buffy's strength and he willingly submits himself to her power, taking on a role in this relationship usually connected to stereotypical femininity. Nevertheless, even though Spike takes on a submissive position and is rescued by Buffy on numerous occasions, he is also still a vampire with supernatural strength and repeatedly acts in heroic and brave manners himself. Indeed, in the musical episode, after Buffy has saved her little sister Dawn, it is Spike who saves Buffy when he stops her dancing, which would have let to spontaneous combustion and death. In this episode, Spike acts both in a manner connected to stereotypical femininity when he sings the love song, and in a manner connected to stereotypical masculinity when he saves Buffy. His character and his behavior in this particular episode consequently mirror and contribute to the complex gender role portrayal characteristic of *BtVS* at large. What is more, his hybridized gender position is also celebrated at the end of the episode when he and Buffy share their first kiss.

As a consequence of this specific portrayal of romantic relationships, gender scripts are negotiated and accommodated since the show manages to create characters with gender identities that elude clear binary categorizations. As Arwen Spicer observes,

> *Buffy* repeatedly depicts a hybridization of conventional gender roles within individual personalities in ways that evade categorization. The traditional tropes of gender persist, but they become so dissociated from their traditional correlations to physical sex that they often interrogate more than support the gender roles they typically define [5].

Ultimately, this hybridization also leads to an innovative portrayal of heterosexual relationships. Instead of reaffirming hegemonic gender roles and male dominance and female obedience, *BtVS* draws a picture of romance in which the male and female partner are equally important as they rescue and support each other. What is more, through its portrayal of men as helpers and supporters of Buffy's heroism, *BtVS* depicts a more complex kind of man, namely one who "embraces his masculinity when he must, and subjectifies himself to [a powerful woman] the rest of the time, because he knows her power trumps his" (Camron 17). The show thus offers role models not only for women and girls, but for boys and young men, too.

At the same time that it celebrates this particular type of male character, *BtVS* explicitly criticizes hegemonic masculinity through its portrayal of Angel, who starts out as an effeminate character but is turned into his evil alter ego Angelus after he has had sex with Buffy, loses his soul, and becomes a stalking, abusive, and even murderous character ("Innocence"). When his soul is taken from him, Angel is turned into a representative of normative masculinity, and this kind of masculinity is shown to be problematic and threatening for Buffy as well as her family and friends (McCracken 128). Through its portrayal of Angel as a kind of domestic abuser, the show clearly alludes to problems caused by hegemonic masculinity in the real world. After all, Angel's desire to torture and kill Buffy reflects the societal problem that today, "a woman is more likely to be killed at the hands of a man she loves than by anyone else" (Dicker and Piepmeier 6).

Even though it thus represents sexual relationships not in an idealized fashion, but as being prone to conflict, *BtVS* ultimately maintains that young women should have a fulfilling and self-determined sex life and depicts female sexuality in a positive and empowering manner. This is because it is not only Buffy herself, but also the other female characters who engage in sexual relationships so that on this show, "girls are both narrative and sexual 'tops,' who are allowed to follow their sexual desires. Buffy, Willow, Cordelia, Faith, and Anya are the program's active romantic pursuers, and they savor the control they have over their sexual and social interactions with their love objects" (McCracken 126). The portrayal of sexually active girls and young women underlines the show's status as an innovator when it comes to the representation of female characters in popular culture. This is because popular culture texts very often mirror the fact that "[f]or centuries, Western society has been suspicious of female sexuality; [and] even in contemporary American culture, women are often criticized for being sexually active" (Chandler 38). In contrast to this, the female characters on *BtVS* are neither punished nor criticized for being sexually active and they do not lose their status as heroic characters, either.

The show thus also echoes third wave feminism and its "rebellion against the false impression that since women don't want to be sexually exploited, they don't want to be sexual," and furthermore works against the stereotype that feminists are men-haters (Baumgardner and Richards, *Manifesta* 137). The third wave refuses to regard sex as merely a symbol of patriarchal power and a tool for female oppression. Even though the movement admits that sex and heterosexual relationships both contain the potential to exploit women and girls, this does not mean that they necessarily have to do so (137). As an effect, this progressive notion of sexuality destroys the binary portrayal of female passivity and submission and men's action and authority in sexual matters, and shows that girls can be both, sexy and sexual active on the one hand, and strong and self-determined on the other (Vint 8). *BtVS* rather calls for a reworking and adjustment of gender roles in heterosexual relationships and delineates the opportunities that an equal relationship can offer. It also expands on the concept of heroism to include female characters who are sexually active, thus breaking with a taboo and turning sexual activity into something that is no longer incompatible with heroism or with being a female role model.

"I may be dead, but I'm still pretty": Reworking Gendered Bodies

Considering that "the hero is embodied, essentially, in the body of *male youth*," Buffy's female and feminine body poses yet another challenge to the established norms of heroism and gender categories respectively (Byers 172; emphasis added). While the traditional male warrior's body has been described as massive and visibly strong, Buffy adheres exactly to the standard of ideal femininity as she is small, petite, and light (Brown 33; Buttsworth 190). These bodily features are clearly highlighted in "Once More, with Feeling," where she sports fashionable outfits and sings in a high soprano voice. During the song "Something to Sing About," for instance, she is clad in a red tank top and matching lipstick and dances seductively, swaying her hips and tossing her long blonde hair. Notably, however, the dance choreography is interspersed with fighting scenes in which Buffy takes on and beats three male opponents. Through the portrayal of a hyper-feminine body that simultaneously displays strength and fighting skills, *BtVS* once again points to the artificiality and constructedness of binary gender categories and well-established stereotypes of female weakness and male strength.

In order to achieve this, it is important for Buffy to look stereotypically feminine or rather hyper-feminine on the one hand and perform in a manner typically attributed to masculinity on the other hand. This is because very often, female warriors are re-embedded into a binary gender discourse and simply read as masculine, or as male warriors in drag. Indeed, a number of critics have argued that there is a danger for female warriors to "become reinscribed within the patriarchal order as a hero who is acceptable because she is really a masculine figure in a woman's body" (Spicer 4). This is problematic as the reading of female warriors as male characters makes it impossible to challenge traditional gender roles, because "if a female character seen as kicking ass must be read as masculine, then women are systematically denied as a gender capable of behaving in any way other than passive" (Brown 33). Therefore, it is crucial that Buffy's body is portrayed according to the conventions, or even exaggerated versions, of femininity since the very discrepancy between her appearance and her behavior makes it harder to regard and dismiss the heroine as a masculine character. In other words, through the portrayal of Buffy's outer appearance as hyper-feminine, "the audience's gender beliefs are more directly destabilized because the image of a petite, pretty woman in a dress kicking ass denies the narrative logic that allows viewers to deride the heroine as a butch or as a woman trying to be a man" (33). Hence, the series creates an image of female strength and power that cannot be easily denied or refuted.

Nevertheless, time and again, Buffy's outer appearance and her adherence to a feminine beauty ideal have been the reason for criticism concerning the heroines' seeming compliance with oppressive patriarchal standards of feminine beauty. For instance, Buffy has often been criticized for wearing sexy and fashionable clothes and for being pretty and skinny (M. Johnson 1; Wilcox and Lavery xviii). Numerous critics have argued that the show cannot be regarded as a feminist text since its protagonist, as well as most of her co-actresses, confirm and thus support patriarchal standards of feminine beauty and act as negative and limiting role models for young women and girls (Pender, "I'm Buffy" 43). What is overlooked in these cases is that even though the heroine's appearance may comply with standards of feminine beauty and fragility, her performance and behavior do not. Although Buffy is sexy, her "sex appeal plays little to no part in her success as a slayer" (Levine 180). Instead, she is "physically and mentally active in saving the world" and her body thus symbolizes "a kind of resilience, strength and confidence" that can be regarded as both innovative and empowering (Karras).

Nevertheless, the show still addresses Buffy's outer appearance and how her petite stature influences the way her opponents see her. In the beginning of the series, for example, the Slayer has an advantage due to her size and beauty. This is because demons and vampires regularly underestimate her and are more ready to attack Buffy due to her apparent fragility and helplessness. Hence, Buffy has the element of surprise on her side which makes it easier for her to kill her attackers. Through the portrayal of these specific scenes, the show not only demonstrates that girls are often regarded as easy prey, but it simultaneously shatters these stereotypes by having Buffy defeat the attackers. In contrast to this, later on in the series, it is shown that Buffy has overcome the status of potential victim as she has established a reputation for herself so that often, vampires and demons flee without even putting up a fight when they find out that Buffy is the Slayer. The idea that supernatural creatures are so afraid of the petite and pretty girl that they do not even dare attack her makes Buffy's strength appear even more remarkable.

Consequently, Buffy's body is not simply used as decoration or adornment, but it fulfills a function as an effective and reliable weapon (Brown 25). As the Slayer, she is endowed with supernatural power and strength in order to "stand against [...] the forces of darkness" (opening narration). Hence, she is not only stronger than other girls, but more forceful than humans in general; even her military-trained boyfriend Riley stands no chance against her in a fight, although he takes drugs to enhance his physical prowess ("New Man"; "Out of My Mind"). Besides that, Buffy has no problems beating supernatural creatures in a fight, either. She is not merely as powerful as a man, but her physical strength generally exceeds that of most living creatures (Karras). Therefore, at a first glance, Buffy's bodily strength and her fighting skills echo the model of the classic male warrior. Her manner of fighting, however, does not simply copy the male model, but it is an extraordinary style in which masculine "hand-to-hand" combat and feminine "acrobatic agility and grace" are combined to achieve success (Early 19). Buffy's fighting style does therefore not only reflect her hybrid gender identity, but it also demonstrates that a combination of feminine and masculine attributes can create a unique and successful way to slay the vampires and monsters with which she is confronted on a daily basis.

At the same time, *BtVS* also shows that women and girls can be strong even if they are not huge and muscular or have supernatural strength. This is because the show underlines time and again that it is also her training that renders the Slayer a competent fighter. "Once More, with Feeling," for instance, highlights this by dedicating a whole song to a training montage in which Giles has Buffy engage in different athletic activities and practice various fighting techniques and styles: he throws blades at her, lets her kick a wooden plank, work out on a pommel horse, and hit a punching bag. While she herself is instructed by her watcher Giles or spars with Angel, Riley, or Spike, Buffy also trains and encourages others to fight demons and vampires. This holds true not only for the Scoobies, but is especially emphasized in the final season of the show when Buffy trains a group of potentials, all of whom are teenage girls that—as their title suggests—have the potential to be called as the next Slayer, but do not have any superpowers yet. In spite of their lack of supernatural abilities, Buffy successfully teaches the girls how to defend themselves and to fight back. She hence not only empowers those girls, but she indirectly also encourages young women in general to overcome their anxieties and trust in their own strength.

In addition to highlighting female power and strength, the unconventional portrayal of Buffy's body also works against the common trend in culture to objectify and eroticize the female body (McCracken 120). *BtVS*, for instance, turns the roles of male and female bodies around because it "repositions the female heroine as active, productive, and impenetrable in relation to a male body that is passive, non-procreative, and highly penetrable" (123). Indeed, even though Buffy is injured and wounded repeatedly, a lot of pain and suffering is diverted onto Spike and Angel respectively, and both vampires are "beaten, stabbed, burned, staked, and shot with arrows" on many occasions throughout the series (117). Thus, Buffy's vampire boyfriends Spike and Angel, take on "to an excessive degree, two roles most associated with women, the spectacularized, eroticized body and the traumatized body" (120). Although the bodies of the women on the show are also on display, since they often wear fashionable and skimpy clothes, they are never as strongly fetishized and shown in long detail by the camera as are most of the men and especially Buffy's boyfriends (120). Consequently, *BtVS* turns around genre and gender conventions by showing and eroticizing the male bodies on screen and putting women in the powerful position of onlookers (Karras). Time and again, Angel and Spike take off their shirts in order to serve as "eye-candy" for both the young women in the fictional world and the audience in front of the TV screen (McCracken 117).

However, whereas in her role as the Slayer, Buffy is not limited by her stereotypically feminine body, in her everyday life, she still often has to adhere to standards of femininity or is at least confronted with them. This holds not only true with regard to her violent behavior and attitude described above, but she also has to conform to said standards with regard to her body and especially her clothes. It has been noted before that Buffy has widely been criticized because she dresses in trendy and skimpy clothes. Notably, the problem of dressing appropriately is also dealt with in the series itself. In one episode, for example, Buffy tries to find the right outfit for her first night out in Sunnydale. This particular scene works as a kind of meta-comment which points out that women and young girls are heavily judged and assessed according to their looks: Buffy is standing in front of her mirror at home, alternatively holding two different outfits—a sexy leather dress and a long dress with a floral pattern—in front of her. While holding up the first dress she says, "Hi! I'm an enormous slut!" and "Hi! Would you like a copy of the Watchtower?" while she is trying out the other one ("Welcome"). Here, it is apparent that Buffy herself is aware that the clothes she wears carry a certain message and that she will be judged and treated according to her outfit. Once again, fashion—an issue typically connected to traditional femininity—is thus portrayed as something that can be potentially empowering because Buffy can actively use her outer appearance and her outfit to influence how others will see her. Nevertheless, the alternatives with which Buffy is confronted—being seen as promiscuous or as a member of Jehovah's Witnesses—not only mirror the stereotypical depiction of women as virgin or whore, but further reflect that in the patriarchal society in which she lives, there is only a limited range of roles for her to take on.

All in all, critics who interpret Buffy's hyper-feminine body in a disempowering manner step into the trap of seeing femininity in general as a disempowering and victimizing tool of the patriarchy. As they condemn femininity per se, many critics overlook that Buffy not only actively uses her body as a weapon and understands the controlling and constraining potential of norms of appearance, but that in addition, she is able to manipulate these standards in order to reach her own goals. She thus breaks the connection between femininity and powerlessness and demonstrates that heroes can come in shapes and sizes other than the tall and muscular male warrior.

"A Slayer with family and friends": The Power of Connections

Another way in which *BtVS* challenges traditional portrayals of male heroism is through Buffy's numerous relationships; romantic, platonic, as well as familial ones. In fact, Giles, Willow, Xander, and the other changing members of Buffy's circle of support become so important for the Slayer's mission that they even receive their own title, namely the "Slayerettes" or "Scoobies." While the traditional hero is predominantly presented as a man who must endure his quest alone, the fact that Buffy

> isn't afraid to ask for help, and constructs around her a group of peers [...] that provide it, is quite unusual in [...] heroic genres. Victimization is far more often solitary, as is the hero who struggles against it. That Buffy stays connected to her peers through change, conflict and loss is a central, and quite feminist, preoccupation of the narrative [Coulombe 214].

Through its focus on interpersonal relationships, the show criticizes the classic representation of a lonely, independent, and masculine hero who strives for power and dominance by adding yet another feminine and feminist feature to the image of the female warrior and that is connectedness. Said connectedness can be regarded as feminine, because the desire for relationships and the tendency to define oneself through one's bonds to other people can, according to American psychologist Carol Gilligan, be observed more often in women than in men (32–33).[4]

The importance of friendships for the success of Buffy's heroic journey is clearly expressed in "Once More, with Feeling" through the various songs the cast sings. The Slayer herself, for example, directly refers to the importance of togetherness in the song entitled "If We're Together" when she sings: "What can't we face if we're together? / What's in this place that we can't whether? / Apocalypse.... We've all been there. / The same old trips! Why should we care?" By using rhetorical questions and the personal pronoun "we" time and again, Buffy underlines the importance of the group for the fight against evil and assures the Scoobies that if they stick together, nothing and no one will be able to defeat them. Furthermore, the scene that features this song takes place in the Magic Shop, where all of the Scoobies sit around a table, conducting research together, and suggesting theories about the potential cause for the singing and dancing. Even though all of the theories they suggest quickly turn out to be unsustainable, the fact that each member helps in conducting research and in proposing solutions calls attention to the level of equality in this group.

At the same time, the episode also contains a theme frequently encountered in the context of interpersonal relationships on *BtVS*, namely the potential conflicts that these bonds bring with them. After all, "Once More, with Feeling" is deeply concerned with people singing about emotions, feelings, and inner conflicts which they have so far kept tightly under wraps. Both the songs "Walk through the Fire" and "Where Do We Go from Here" deal with the problems the Scoobies face and the sense of isolation many of them experience. This is, for instance, expressed when they sing that they "walk alone in fear" or when Buffy muses that "one by one they turned from [her]." Similar to the sexual relationships mentioned above, platonic relationships on *BtVS* are not shown to be easy to uphold, either. Still, the different members of Buffy's circle of friends do not leave the group, but rather work through their conflicts and problems. Again, this is indicated in the musical episode when the Scoobies sing: "We'll see it through / that's what we're always here to do / so we will walk through the fire." Indeed, these lines have a double meaning. On the one hand, they refer to the fact that the group goes to support Buffy in her fight against evil, and, on the other one, also insinuate that the Scoobies work on and overcome their own interpersonal conflicts and problems time and again.

Indeed, it is not only this particular episode that stresses the importance of mutual support and connectedness, but this happens very early on in the series. After all, the group of friends is created already in the second episode when the rule that "the Slayer must work in secret" is broken when Willow and Xander learn about Buffy's secret identity ("What's My Line (Part 2)"). The series repeatedly emphasizes that the Chosen One appreciates and fights for her relationships since Buffy is convinced "that her friends provide as much security as they pose risks" (Fuchs 101). While, admittedly, her attachments to others render Buffy more vulnerable and attackable—numerous enemies try to get to Buffy and defeat her by threatening her friends and family ("Once More"; "Passion"; "Weight of the World"; "Yoko Factor")—the Slayer still fosters these relationships because she understands the value of them. Spike, for instance, comments on Buffy's advantage over former Slayers due to her numerous interpersonal connections when he tells her: "Every Slayer has a death wish. Even you. *The only reason you've lasted as long as you have is you've got ties to the world*: your mum, your brat kid sister, the Scoobies.... They all tie you here" ("Fool"; emphasis added). Using the metaphor of ties, Spike suggests that Buffy is a better fighter because of her numerous relationships which make her persevere in situations in which other Slayers would long have given up. However, the Scoobies and her family not only support Buffy in her fight against evil in this indirect manner, but they are also present both on the battlefield and in the library where they help to conduct research on the different demons and monsters.

Thus, through the positive and empowering depiction of joint action, another idea of feminist theory, which has been "an integral part of the feminist movement since its beginning," is represented, namely sisterhood (Payne-Mulliken and Renagar 58). "Sisterhood refers to unification, strength in numbers, and shared interest" (68), and it is exactly these features that accurately describe the Scoobies. Said form of joint action and group effort can furthermore be regarded as typical of third wave feminism, since this particular movement "strives to include more diverse voices, including those of men and those of non-white heritage. Consequently, sisterhood for the third wave truly means the unification of all and the oppression of none" (58). This attitude is featured in the show since the bond of sisterhood includes both male and female characters as well as werewolves, demons and vampires, who, according to Fuchs, can be regarded as representatives of racial diversity (105–6). By portraying the group as being made up of a variety of people, the text expands the definition of sisterhood and shows that regardless of one's personal background and identity, working together empowers and strengthens each individual (Payne-Mulliken and Renagar 67).

Notably, it is not only Buffy who profits from the empowering potential of sisterhood, but the other Scoobies do so, too. Consequently, the positive effects of joint action, connectedness, and the inclusion of different and diverse characters are highlighted even more. Because of its insistence on diversity, there is also another innovation that results from the crucial roles that the heroine's friends take on in *BtVS*: the realm of heroism is opened up to include a larger variety of characteristics (Sainato 142). While the traditional quest story can be interpreted as "an elitist myth, which at its base embodies the notion that some people take their heroic journeys while others simply serve and sacrifice," *BtVS* is more inclusive (Pearson 2). This is because the heroine's friends and allies are not merely depicted as sidekicks whose only task it is to enable Buffy's heroism, but many of them take on central and indispensable roles themselves, embarking on their own heroic journeys alongside the female protagonist, and ultimately become heroines and heroes in their own right (Kord and Krimmer 144; Sainato 142).

In this context, it is crucial to note that like Buffy, who is an unlikely heroine due to her gender and age, many of the secondary characters do not appear to have heroic potential either, at least not with regard to the standards of classic heroism (cf. Sainato 142). Xander and Willow, for instance, are regarded as "losers" by their more popular peers at school and are therefore marked as outsiders of mainstream society ("When She Was"). In contrast to this, they are central characters and literal insiders in the world of demons and monsters, and both of them become heroes by overcoming their own challenges and saving the world on their own behalf ("Chosen"; "Grave").

Xander, for example, is an unlikely hero because he is not depicted as the average teenage boy but is feminized since he "lacks [...] traditional masculinity" (Camron 6). In "Once More, with Feeling," for instance, Anya describes Xander in adherence to the archetype of the damsel in distress when she sings: "When things get rough he / Just hides behind his Buffy." Xander is furthermore feminized when the episode reveals that the person who summoned the demon also has to marry it. Since it is Xander who did so, he asks the demon whether he has to become his "queen." The choice of the word "queen," as well as the fact that it is Xander, and not Anya, Tara, or Willow, one of the numerous female members of the gang, who is threatened with having to become the demon's bride casts Xander in a role strongly connected to notions of traditional femininity. This feminization is only further emphasized by the fact that until Xander admits to having summoned the demon, the role of the potential bride is occupied by 15-year-old Dawn.

As this example demonstrates, Xander's actions and his role on the show cannot be categorized according to the standards of male heroism and its glorification of masculinity. Instead, Xander's individual and unique kind of heroism is predominantly established through his decency, loyalty, and love for his friends (Kord and Krimmer 149). The idea that unwavering love and loyalty can be heroic qualities is most explicitly staged in the finale of season six when Xander saves the world from an apocalypse simply by expressing his love for his best friend Willow ("Grave"). What is more, unlike the majority of the other members of the Scooby Gang, Xander does not have any supernatural abilities, so that he generally occupies an inferior position in comparison to both his friends and the enemies the Scoobies fight on a daily basis. Still, time and again, Xander is willing to risk his life in order to help his friends and thus demonstrates not only his bravery but, first and foremost, his unwavering loyalty (Camron 15).

Willow, too, is an unlikely heroine for several reasons. First of all, she starts out as an intelligent and friendly, yet extremely shy and insecure girl (L. Schultz 195). Her intelligence is called attention to in "Once More, with Feeling" when Tara describes her as "the brainy type." During the course of the series, however, she also develops into a powerful witch and can contribute to Buffy's mission through her magical skills as well as her intelligence and research abilities (Hopkins 117; Sainato 142). In fact, her powers become so potent that the demon in the musical episode even states that he can "smell [her] power" ("Once More"). In spite of her supernatural powers, however, Willow still defies notions of traditional heroism. This is not just because she is a girl and a geek, but the innovative depiction of heroism and the diversity of role models that the series promulgates are further expressed when Willow has her coming out in season four and engages in a lesbian relationship with Tara, a young woman she meets in college ("New Moon"). This is worth mentioning because homosexuality in itself is a topic that, at the time the show first aired, was hardly ever dealt with on TV, and Willow and Tara are, in fact, the first lesbian couple portrayed on prime time TV at large (Driver 57–58).

It is thus noteworthy that *BtVS* in general, and "Once More, with Feeling" in particular, openly deal with and even celebrate their love. The episode dedicates a whole song entitled "Under Your Spell" to their relationship, which Tara describes in very romantic terms, comparing Willow to the sun and stating that she makes her believe in true love. Even more importantly, the song ends in Willow's and Tara's bedroom, where the latter lies on the bed and sings: "The moon to the tide / I can feel you inside. / I'm under your spell / surging like the sea / holding you so helplessly. / I break with every swell / lost in ecstasy / spread beneath my willow tree / you make me complete." While the lyrics already deal with female sexual desire, the action in the scene underscores the topic even more, since Willow, after leaning over Tara, moves downward and out of the frame, which insinuates that she engages in oral sex with her girlfriend. This scene not only reflects that female sexuality and desire is a prominent topic on *BtVS* in general, but it is even more remarkable as it depicts a lesbian couple. Through the portrayal of Willow as a smart, sexually active, and homosexual character on the one hand, and an indispensable part of the Scoobies, on the other one, a person that would usually not even be represented in the media is given a central and powerful role in *BtVS*. As a consequence, the series represents homosexuality in a positive manner and "promotes diversity" more generally, as it casts a smart, geeky, gay girl not only as a role model but as a heroine in her own right (Sainato 142).

Buffy's connectedness to other people and the fact that she relies on them to support her can be criticized as limiting her heroism because she is not portrayed as being completely independent and autonomous. However, this depiction of female heroism is one that is more approachable for young women and in no way denies Buffy's strength and agency. With regard to the issues of relationships and bonds, her situation mirrors "the struggle that many young women face to be strong, independent, articulate, ambitious, and powerful. And this is done without erasing women's desire for connection" (Byers 172). *BtVS* shows that girls should not be afraid to demonstrate and make use of their power, strength, and skills. At the same time, it also maintains that being interdependent and nurtured by others does not automatically render them weak or oppressed. On the contrary, Buffy's connectedness is empowering because her investment in her numerous relationships make her a more successful Slayer. Consequently, once again, a concept connected to traditional femininity that has been deemed inferior to its masculine counterpart and thus incompatible with notions of heroism is elevated to an equal or even superior status.

"Every girl who could have the power, will have the power": Power and Selfhood

Just like the traditional male hero, Buffy embarks on a heroic quest, experiences adventures, fights battles, and eventually "[discovers] the treasure of [her] true [self]" (Pearson 1). In this respect, the female warrior follows and adheres to the pattern of male heroism because her quest, just as in the case of her male counterparts, can be regarded as a journey towards maturation and individuation (Brannon 1). At the same time, her journey is infused or rather inspired by feminist thought and theory, because Buffy's quest adheres to the model of consciousness-raising, a central issue in feminist thinking. "The consciousness-raising format provides a model of the transformations involved in coming to feminist consciousness: becoming aware of inequalities, identifying our own part in them, and then taking steps to change them" (Dicker and Piepmeier 14). Both the things which she learns during her journey and the outcome of the her heroic struggle, or in Campbell's terms, the 'boon' which she bestows upon her world, are hence fundamentally different from that of the traditional male warrior. While male warriors strive for personal power, superiority, and dominance over others and re-establish a patriarchal order once they return from their heroic journeys (Pearson 2–3), the heroine of *BtVS* does not fight to become ruler of her world. On the contrary, her expansion of the mind lets her realize that she can share her power and destroy the patriarchal system by which she and others are oppressed, and thus empowers and frees herself *and* others. Hence, concepts of power propagated by third wave feminism are not only included into the plot of the show, but also inspire the notion of heroism established in *BtVS*. This is because the system of power that Buffy establishes—the gift she bestows—resembles the heterarchical and mutually supportive concept of empowerment propagated by the idea of sisterhood to a large degree.

The show first of all challenges patriarchal power and hierarchies on a micro-level through its portrayal of one of the most central relationships, namely that between Buffy and her Watcher, Rupert Giles. On the one hand, this particular bond exactly reproduces the model of the male quest hero described by Campbell (*Hero* 69). Just as the generic masculine hero, Buffy receives the assistance of a guide, that is, her Watcher, once she sets out on her heroic quest. However, while the roles of guide and charge that Giles and Buffy take on are very similar to those featured in the classical quest story, the relationship that develops between the two is rather unique and innovative as it challenges ideas of male authority and female submissiveness and thus also undermines the idealization and naturalization of male authority established in the typical quest story (cf. Owen). While at a first glance, the differences in both gender and age between Buffy and her Watcher bring to mind patriarchal fatherhood and male authority, their relationship in fact redefines these very concepts as it is "characterized by mutual respect and affection, not by differences in power or competence" (Kord and Krimmer 146).

This is clearly demonstrated in "Once More, with Feeling" with the help of the song Giles sings during the training montage mentioned before. In this song entitled "Standing," he describes traditional fatherhood in a manner that reflects the show's overall stance on patriarchal structures, namely as something that restricts girls,' or in this case Buffy's, development and independence. On the one hand, Giles underlines that he clearly believes in his charge's heroic potential when he sings: "Your path's unbeaten / and it's all uphill / and you can meet it." On the other hand, he continues with "but you never will. / And I'm the reason / that you're standing still." This self-evaluation demonstrates that the Watcher understands that his attempts to protect Buffy from following her own path, from facing the challenges of being a Slayer and an adult woman hinder her from evolving and growing up.

What is more, he insists that it is his adherence to traditional fatherhood that results in Buffy's stagnation, as he sings: "Wish I could play the father / and take you by the hand / Wish I could stay / But now I understand / I'm standing in your way." In these lines, he maintains that leading the Slayer instead of letting her lead, which he describes as playing the father and taking her by the hand, has dire consequences because it allows Buffy to remain passive and immature. This is furthermore pointed out when Giles observes that, because of his fatherly behavior, Buffy "just [lies] there / when [she] should be standing tall." Even though the relationship between Buffy and her Watcher is admittedly more equal than traditional patriarchal relationships, this scene still highlights that an adherence to the more traditional notions of being a father and a daughter restricts the latter in her personal development. Since Giles actually leaves Buffy for a certain amount of time, the series also communicates the idea that the heroine needs to be free from fatherly supervision, no matter how well intended, in order to fully grow into her role. In contrast to the model of the traditional patriarch, Giles does not try to keep Buffy under his influence and power, but helps her to become an independent and self-determined woman (cf. LaRossa 25). *BtVS* hence turns the figure of the guide from a supporter of masculine power into an enabler of female heroism and empowerment.

However, *BtVS* not only challenges patriarchal power, but it furthermore establishes an alternative system. Unlike traditional warrior heroes, Buffy "is not interested in simply inverting the paradigm (in which one side must dominate and control the other) but in finding a new way to cooperatively work for a common cause" (Brannon 6). The concept of sisterhood is put into opposition to patriarchal power because the show draws a clear distinction between patriarchal and hierarchical power on the one hand, and shared, non-hierarchical systems of power on the other. On *BtVS*,

> [the] first power [...] is the power to overcome obstacles, to coerce others to do one's bidding, or to destroy a power bent on evil. In all of these cases, the power is a straightforwardly patriarchal one. It is characterized by a top-down command structure, by one leader being in charge while the others follow, with a highly individualized system of personal power [...]. The second type is fundamentally different, and it poses both a critique and a threat to the previous easy, dominant view. This is shared power, and its goal is the empowerment of all [Durand 45].

While critics agree that the show is highly concerned with different concepts of power and emphasizes the positive effects of shared power (cf. Brannon; Durand), it is crucial to remember that this issue is not an isolated topic but is, in fact, deeply connected to the female protagonist's heroic journey and her personal development. After all, Buffy's interest in power structures and the recognition of the oppressive forces of patriarchal systems, as well as the liberating possibilities of shared power, are triggered by her personal development and maturation. Only by learning about herself, her aims and values, and her place in the world can Buffy arrive at an evaluation of the power structures in which she herself is so deeply embedded and start to question the validity and dominance of said system. In this context, the heroine's quest plays an important role so that Buffy's personal development will be analyzed in detail here in order to trace not only her journey towards achieving agency and selfhood, but also to paint a picture of how these achievements enable her to change the mechanisms of power at play in her world.

In the beginning of the series, Buffy is largely defined and controlled by others so that her role as the Slayer can be interpreted as a fixed identity category as described by Judith Butler. This is because being the Slayer comes with certain rules of conduct that work as "normalizing categories of oppressive structures" ("Imitation" 255). While Buffy bends the old rules and traditions regarding her duty as the Slayer to a certain extent—by letting her friends in on her secret identity, for example—she usually behaves according to the rules set up by the Watchers' Council, the institution that controls the Slayer. She thus defends a system of values and norms that is not her own, but that of the institution of which she is a part. This is portrayed, for instance, in the final battle against the Master in season one. In this episode, Buffy is informed about a prophecy which predicts that she "will face the Master and she will die" ("Prophecy"). Even though Buffy is shocked by this prediction, she does not question the validity of the prophecy nor her part in it. After trying to quit and run away, Buffy reclaims her role as the Slayer and sets out to fight the Master, dies at his hands, and thus fulfills her fate as well as the demands of the identity category she has been assigned.[5] The fact that she can only act according to her own values and aims when she rejects to fulfill the task she is given as the Slayer, or has to act according to the rules set up by others and sacrifice herself when she does ultimately reclaim this role, shows that in the beginning of the series, Buffy's own personality, her needs and values, are often not part of her Slayer identity.

Over the course of time, however, Buffy increasingly claims the role she is given for herself, infuses it with her own values and aims, and thus achieves a larger amount of agency. Noticeably, only then is she able to defeat the ruling forces which oppress not only her, but also her friends and allies. Buffy increasingly understands that in addition to the obvious villains, namely evil demons and vampires, seemingly good and righteous institutions such as the Watchers' Council are dangerous and potentially harmful, too. Indeed, the Council threatens and harms Buffy and her friends on numerous occasions, for instance when they test her Slayer skills without telling her ("Helpless"), or refuse to save her non-human friends because they regard them as evil and less worthy than humans ("Graduation Day (Part 1)"). The show hence ultimately also criticizes hierarchical and institutionalized systems of power represented by the Council.

In this context, an important insight that triggers Buffy's development is her realization that under the Council's threats, rules, tests, and adherence to tradition lies the attempt to control her and to use the Slayer's power for their own purposes (Brannon 4). In other words, Buffy understands that the role of the Slayer has been utilized as an oppressive identity category in order to control her and her power. This idea is played out in season five when a delegation of the Council visits Sunnydale in order to determine whether Buffy is worthy of the information that they have about Glory, the main antagonist of that season ("Checkpoint"). Here, the series points out how important the acquisition and cultivation of power is for the Watchers' Council, because even though they are "faced with the destruction of the world that they are powerless to stop, they cling to the little power they have remaining," and try to subject Buffy and the Scoobies to their authority and rule (Durand 50). As Quentin Travers, the head of the group, explains, the delegates will conduct "an exhaustive examination of [Buffy's] procedures and abilities" ("Checkpoint") and only help her if she passes the test, or, in other words, "the only way they plan to provide any information is through Buffy's submission to their power" (Durand 51).

The Council tries to maintain its power not only by trying to control and constrain the Slayer, but they attempt to define and trivialize Buffy herself as well as her status within the organization. Travers describes Buffy with the help of a disempowering metaphor that speaks strongly of the autocratic and impersonal worldview of the Council: "I think your Watcher hasn't reminded you lately of the resolute status of the players in our little game. The Council fights evil. The Slayer is the instrument by which we fight. The Council remains; the Slayers change" ("Checkpoint"). By using the metaphor of an "instrument" or tool to describe and define both Buffy and the role she is given, Travers tries to convince her of her passive and insignificant status in the "little game" between good and evil. Through this description, the Council wants to intimidate Buffy and embed her firmly in the hierarchy of power of which the delegates are the heads.

Due to her personal development, however, Buffy can resist this disempowering definition and disconnects herself from the power structures of the organization. She demonstrates that she "will no longer accept uncritically authoritarian patriarchal rule as symbolized by the Watchers' Council" (Early 22). In doing so, the heroine "resists being trapped into a fixed identity; she may not be able to escape being the Slayer, but when she realizes that she cannot break away from her responsibilities, she seeks to redefine the meaning and office of the Slayer itself" (L. Schultz 198). No longer does Buffy let others decide what she has to do and how she has to fight evil in order to properly fill her role as the Chosen One. Buffy understands that behind its self-confident attitude, the Council hides that it is merely craving for more power in order to maintain its superiority over the Slayer. This is indicated when Buffy tells the Scoobies: "Everyone [is] just lining up to tell me how unimportant I am. And I've finally figured out why. Power. I have it. They don't. This bothers them" ("Checkpoint"). In rejecting their authority and claiming her own power, she clearly expresses her independence from institutionalized patriarchal power.

Buffy's fight against the patriarchy culminates in the final season of the show when the Slayer can establish a new system of power which is characterized by an elimination of hierarchies. In this season, Buffy is confronted with two enemies who symbolize patriarchal power. The first is a "pitch-perfect stereotype of the misogynist, Southern, Christian fundamentalist"

(Levine 184) and the second is a group called the "Shadow Men," a trio of African Shamans who created the first Slayer millennia ago. During her visit with the Shadow Men, Buffy finds out more about the origins and creation of said Slayer and she also learns more about the role and heritage of her Slayer destiny ("Get It"). The Shadow Men reveal that they created the first Slayer by exposing her to and uniting her with the energy of a demon, an action which has clear parallels to rape or sexual abuse and thus underlines the misogynist, ruthless, and oppressive qualities of the first group of Watchers (Payne-Mulliken and Renagar 65). Thus, the Shadow Men work as a metaphor for patriarchal power because they subdued and violated a girl in order to achieve their own aims when they created the first Slayer (66). They hence function as an additional example of an inconsiderate and impersonal institution, because they are not interested in Buffy herself or her needs, but instead try to embed Buffy in their own hierarchy of power in order to manipulate and control her (66).

Even though she finds herself in a desperate situation, Buffy refuses to play according to the rules of patriarchal power. Instead, she starts to question and eventually reconceptualizes the system of power at its most basic level (Durand 55). She does so by going against the rule that only one girl can be the Slayer when she asks Willow to cast a spell that will empower each potential all over the world. In a speech in which she tells the Scoobies and the potentials about her plan, Buffy indicates that she rejects patriarchal traditions, power, and knowledge when she proclaims:

> So here's the part where you make a choice. [...] What if you could have that power now? In every generation *one* Slayer is born because a bunch of men who died thousands of years ago made up that rule. They were powerful men. This woman [Willow] is more powerful than all of them combined. So I say we change the rule. I say *my* power should be *our* power. [...] From now on, *every* girl in the world who might be a Slayer *will* be a Slayer. Every girl who *could* have the power *will* have the power. *Can* stand up, *will* stand up. Slayers: every one of us. Make your choice! Are you ready to be strong? ["Chosen"].

In this speech, Buffy explains that the rules and traditions of the Slayer only exist because it has always been common knowledge and belief that only *one* girl could have the status of the Slayer at a time, and only *one* girl could be that powerful. In contrast to this, throughout her heroic journey, Buffy has learned that it is shared power and connectedness that truly offer strength because "shared power is increased, not diluted" (Brannon 13). By sharing her power with girls from all over the world, Buffy not only defies and ultimately destroys patriarchal power, but she promulgates a concept of power in which people fight together to create a better world for everyone (Durand 55).

Through the image of shared power, the series addresses additional issues of third wave feminism. For instance, "in transferring power from a privileged, white, Californian teenager to a heterogeneous group of women from different national, racial, and socio-economic backgrounds, the show's final season addresses [...] the issue of cultural diversity that has been at the forefront of third wave feminist theorizing" (Pender, "Kicking Ass" 8). Thus, the series supports and highlights the need for feminist activism and female empowerment to be diverse and inclusive, and it provides viewers with an alternative to well-established and naturalized patriarchal systems of power (Levine 171, 185). Buffy, the newly-called Slayers, and the Scoobies fight together and can therefore defeat an army of vampires. Consequently, they once again serve as inspiring role models whose portrayal establishes innovative conceptions of heroism, because in this approach to shared power, sisterhood, and activism, "people, particularly young girls and women, can find strength, knowledge and power" (Payne-Mulliken and Renagar 71).

The positive image of shared action and power is further underlined as Buffy not only empowers others and helps them to overcome their fears, weaknesses, and insecurities—as presented in the final episode of the show when girls all over the world feel their strength and start to fight for themselves ("Chosen")—but she herself can also finally come to terms with her own issues. Throughout the show, Buffy has struggled with her extraordinary status as the Chosen One, which made her feel isolated and displaced (Fuchs 98, 100). By changing the destiny of the Slayer, the heroine overcomes the major challenge of her quest, namely "an isolation enforced by a patriarchal structure that feared the power which it bestowed" (Brannon 1). Finally, Buffy has gained agency because she has become a more self-determined subject who is free to choose who she wants to be and what she wants to do. She can resume fighting evil if she wants to, but since she is "not the one and only chosen anymore," she can also lead the life of an ordinary young woman ("Chosen"). With regard to her heroic journey and Campbell's model of the heroic quest, Buffy has reached the "freedom to live" stage (Hero 37). The heroine is no longer primarily concerned with the fight against evil and her survival, but she is free to lead a life of her own choice.

Conclusion

As this chapter has demonstrated, on the one hand, BtVS is firmly embedded in and responds to the gender discourses at work in the late 1990s, as it engages in Girl Power discourse by starring as protagonist a hyperfeminine girl warrior who subverts gender norms and stereotypes of girls as victims. On the other hand, the show also engages in more timeless issues, namely the conceptualization of heroism. However, this conceptualization, too, is heavily influenced by then contemporary political, cultural, and societal discourses as it establishes a model of heroism that is reflective of Girl Power and third wave feminist thought and theory. The feminist quest heroine as portrayed by Buffy undermines notions of male heroism, power, and superiority and infuses the concept of heroism with new meaning. On the one hand, Buffy's adherence to the model of the masculine quest hero establishes her status as a warrior and heroine in her own right. On the other one, however, the deviation from the model in exactly those moments or with regard to qualities which usually emphasize and celebrate traditional masculinity—and the weaving in of a feminist agenda that portrays traditional femininity and girlhood in a supportive and empowering manner—breaks the connection between heroism and hegemonic masculinity. Thus, the show not only maintains that women and girls can be heroes, too, but, moreover, the model of the feminist quest heroine insists that they can be heroic without having to copy a masculinist and patriarchal standard, or, in other words, that "a woman does not have to act like a man to be a hero" (Bowman).

At the same time that it is progressive when it comes to portrayals of gender and heroism, the series has been criticized for its representation of race. First of all, *BtVS* has only white actresses and actors in its main cast, an issue that seems to be opposed to third wave feminism's interest in race and ethnicity (cf. Ono; Fuchs). What is more, the few people of color who can be seen on the show predominantly take on the roles of villains or sidekicks. Kent Ono, for instance, observes that the black Slayer Kendra is marginalized, stereotyped, and quickly killed off after she joins the Scoobies in the second season of the show. Moreover, he points out that the episode "Inka Mummy Girl" portrays a South American girl as a villainous exotic femme fatale (173–77).

Nevertheless, even though the criticism concerning racial exclusivity is certainly a valid one, critics have also argued that the series depicts racial and bodily diversity through different means. Cynthia Fuchs, for example, points out that each of Buffy's Slayer predecessors is shown to have been of non-white origin, a feature which not only makes visible, but also de-naturalizes Buffy's own whiteness (102). She furthermore claims that the series depicts racial diversity through the portrayal of demons, monsters, and vampires (105–06). Others have also pointed out that, in the last episode of the show, when Willow's spell activates potentials all over the world, the series follows a more inclusive agenda by showing that girls with different ethnic and racial backgrounds are called to be Slayers (Pender, "Kicking Ass" 8). Finally, I suggest that it is important for Buffy to be white and middle-class because, in the context of the Ophelia discourse, it was this group of girls specifically which was reported to suffer most from a loss of self-esteem when they reached adolescence (Zaslow 21). As a girl who is white and middle-class herself, Buffy can thus act as an empowering role model for these young women in particular.

In spite of the fact that it has since developed into a cult TV series, *BtVS* was a rather marginal phenomenon when it first aired. This shows that, in the late 1990s and early 2000s, its campy attitude, subversive portrayal of gender, sex, and sexuality, reconceptualization of heroism, and feminist message did not hold mainstream appeal yet. At the same time, the fact that the show became a "touchstone for popular culture" (Magee 888), made its "way into a larger social consciousness" (Stuller 12), and still exudes a cultural influence today, attests to the fact that the themes and issues addressed in *BtVS* speak to and inspire a large number of people, both fans of the series and creators of popular culture. Indeed, Buffy became an icon "that enabled the presence of even more female heroes in popular entertainment media" (12), two of which will be analyzed in the next chapters.

◆ ◆ 2 ◆ ◆

Adapting the Feminist Quest Heroine

The Hunger Games' *Katniss Everdeen*

> The very moment when the idea came to me for *The Hunger Games* [...] happened one night when I was very tired and I was lying in bed channel surfing. I happened upon a reality program, recorded live, that pitted young people against each other for money. As I sleepily watched, the lines of reality started to blur for me and the idea for the book emerged.—Collins qtd. in Blasingame 727

Dystopian or post-disaster fiction has become one of the most successful genres among young (and not so young) adult readers in recent years (Braith-waite 6). As numerous critics have explained, dystopian settings and stories are especially suited to address the interests and concerns of teenage readers, as the major themes of these novels, such as the search for identity, belief in a better future, or struggle with authorities are topics with which many young people can identify (7). The poster girl of this genre is Katniss Everdeen, the protagonist of the extremely successful *Hunger Games* trilogy, which has been turned into a franchise spanning movie adaptations, computer games, toys, as well as make-up and fashion lines.[1]

The *Hunger Games* trilogy tackles all of the issues frequently found in YA dystopian fiction. It features a teenage protagonist who struggles against an oppressive political regime. This specific one uses propagandistic media, modern slavery, and—as the title suggests—hunger in order to maintain its power. Even though the story is set in the distant future, "the novels address specific political and economic forces that afflict not only [the fictional state of] Panem but also our contemporary society" (Clemente 21). The connections and continuities between this speculative world and contemporary U.S. society and culture are remarked on early on in the novel, as it is said that Panem "rose out of the ashes of a place that was once called North America"

(Collins, *Hunger Games* 18).[2] The political system is described as totalitarian and hierarchically structured with "a shining Capitol ringed by thirteen districts" (18). While "the brutal dictatorship of the Capitol over the [...] districts and the forms of social control and colonial oppression are always at the forefront of the story," the novels also pay attention to "popular culture from the present, such as reality TV, and professional sports championships" (Blasingame 726).

This blurring of politics and popular culture, which is already alluded to in the introductory quote by the novels' author Suzanne Collins, is most strongly mirrored in the fact that the female protagonist lives in a world where adults sacrifice children and teenagers for the sake of both entertainment and oppression. At the beginning of the trilogy, Katniss is chosen in a lottery to take part in a reality TV show entitled "The Hunger Games," which is broadcast across the nation. In this show, the so-called "tributes," a boy and a girl from each district aged between twelve and eighteen, are thrust into an arena to kill each other on live TV until only one of them—the victor—remains. These games take place every year to commemorate an uprising that took place several decades ago. They are officially treated as "a festivity, a sporting event" (Collins, *HG* 19), but Katniss explains that, in fact, they are designed to punish, humiliate, and torture the citizens of the districts and to firmly keep them in their powerless position (18–19). Katniss, however, defies the power of the Capitol at the end of the Games when she threatens to commit suicide. This feat helps her and Peeta Mellark, the male tribute from her district, to win the Hunger Games, but it also eventually, over the course of the second and third installments, sets into motion a political rebellion in which Katniss herself takes on a central role. In the end, the power of the Capitol is overthrown and a new, democratic political system is established.

While the story and setting of the trilogy are hence rather typical of the genre of YA dystopian fiction, Katniss is an unusual protagonist for this particular kind of scenario simply because she is a teenage girl. On the one hand, female protagonists have always been represented in YA fiction ever since the emergence of the genre in the U.S. during the first half of the twentieth century. On the other hand, however, novels featuring female protagonists were aimed at girls specifically and predominantly occupied with topics such as domesticity, dating, and romance, whereas it was boys' stories that included action and adventures (Cart 8). This distinction, in which the plots and themes are strictly separated according to the intended reader's gender, has, in fact, not changed throughout the history of YA fiction, which is emphasized by literary scholar Michael Cart when he observes that "then, as now, it was firmly believed there were girl books and boy books and never the twain would meet" (8).

Whereas gender distinctions remained fairly stable, some other YA genre conventions did undergo a number of changes and alterations. The preoccupation of the novels, for instance, moved away from innocent and trivial topics that were dominant in the first half of the 20th century (14–17) to realistic and often dark depictions of teenagers' concerns and struggles in the 1960s and 1970s (29, 30). After the genre went almost extinct in the early 1990s (53), the second half of the decade brought forth a renaissance, a new golden age of YA fiction (57). Highly successful series such as Joanne K. Rowling's *Harry Potter* (1997–2007) and Stephenie Meyer's *Twilight* (2005–2008) revived the genre by introducing fantastic and supernatural elements, so that in the first decade of the 21st century, novels intended for a teenaged readership were populated by wizards, werewolves, and vampires (Day, Green-Barteet, and Montz 6–7).

Harry Potter and *Twilight* not only represent the emerging trend of speculative worlds in YA fiction of which dystopian fiction is one subcategory, but they also exemplify the pertinacity of traditional gender roles in this genre. *Harry Potter* has a male protagonist whose story follows the model of the mythical quest hero, as he enters a magical world, experiences adventures and trials, and ultimately kills his evil antagonist Lord Voldemort. Even though the series features a strong-willed, clever, and brave female sidekick in Hermione Granger, her actions and skills are often merely used to enable and further Harry's heroic journey. *Twilight*, on the other hand, does feature a female protagonist: Bella Swan. Her story, however, revolves around her romantic relationship with the vampire Edward Cullen and the question whether the couple can be together. Moreover, Bella reinforces the archetype of the damsel in distress, as she has to be rescued by male characters time and again.

By contrast, the *Hunger Games* trilogy can be regarded as an innovative work of YA fiction because it combines the typical features of the genre as represented in *Twilight* and *Harry Potter* to original ends: it features a teenage girl as the heroine of an action-driven story. Notably, this is done in a fashion that establishes Katniss as a feminist quest heroine. This is because, on the one hand, just like traditional male heroes, Katniss goes through the main phases of Campbell's model of the quest. When she is reaped for the Games and separated from her family, Katniss does not actively decide to set out on her heroic journey, but she is chosen by destiny and rises to the occasion (cf. Campbell, *Hero* 30, 36). During the phase of initiation, she undergoes trials and adventures, and, in the end, her rebellious actions make it possible to bestow a gift upon her society, namely a new political system.

On the other hand, however, Katniss defies gender norms in exactly those moments of her quest that would usually maintain and celebrate connections between heroism and masculinity and validate hegemonic gender relations. This is because, just like Buffy, she is a teenaged girl warrior whose gender identity and outer appearance challenge the connection between heroism and masculinity. As I will show during the course of this chapter, in contrast to male heroes who are predominantly masculine, Katniss' gender identity can be described as hybrid. More importantly, she uses both her masculine and feminine traits to succeed in her quest. As a consequence, just as in *BtVS*, stereotypical femininity is revalued and represented as potentially heroic.

What is more, Katniss can also be described as a feminist quest heroine because she does not fight alone, but is supported by friends and allies, so that her quest narrative, too, advocates for the feminist concept of sisterhood. Most importantly, however, Katniss' story adheres to the model of the feminist quest heroine because she does not fight to become the ruler of her world but destroys and flattens patriarchal hierarchies of power. In fact, her quest, too, follows the consciousness-raising format established by second wave feminism. As a consequence, Katniss heroic journey is cast as a development towards feminist or political consciousness and activism. The novels hence stray from YA conventions where female protagonists are frequently shown to develop and mature because of the romantic relationships in which they engage (Platt 73). This deviation is yet another aspect through which the novels infuse their narrative with a feminist message, as they advocate for feminist forms of activism and heterarchical systems of power. Once again, the trilogy establishes notions of heroism and girlhood similar to those found in *BtVS*, as both narratives insist that their female protagonists' development into politically conscious, critical, and subversive young women is what renders these characters heroines and role models.

At the same time that it reiterates many of the ideas and themes found in *BtVS*, the *Hunger Games* trilogy also infuses the concept of female heroism with new meaning, adapting it to fit a 21st-century background and (young adult) readership. It is interesting to note that, just like Buffy, Katniss emerged after a feminist backlash. As described by scholars such as Susan Faludi in *The Terror Dream* (2007) and Michael Kimmel in *Manhood in America* (2017), the attacks on 9/11 led to a resurgence and reappraisal of traditional masculinity and archetypes such as the warrior. Indeed, the similarities between the late 1980s and early 2000s are striking, because

> just as the 1980s saw a backlash against the feminism of the 1970s, the feminism of the 1990s took a back seat to patriotism and family values in the wake of the attacks of September 11, 2001. Liberal values in general and feminist and pacifist sensibilities in particular were seen as unpatriotic in light of these attacks, and American women were asked to be thankful that they were not living in Afghanistan and thus should not complain about the inequalities that remain in American society. Suddenly, feminism was out of season [DiPaolo 178].

By featuring a feminist quest heroine, the *Hunger Games* trilogy works against the backlash and the idealization of male warriorhood and infuses popular culture with feminist thought and theory.

Besides that, it is also deeply concerned with the theme of war, that is, who fights it, how and why, and what are the tragic and traumatic consequences of warfare (cf. Dominus). The novels thus critically engage with events such as 9/11 and the ensuing wars in the Middle East. In addition, through their portrayal of an extreme version of reality TV and the hype surrounding it, they also respond to changes in Western media landscapes such as the success of reality TV in the first decade of the 21st century. The release of the first novel moreover coincided with the financial crisis in the fall of 2008 and articulated many of the discourses that began to spread in the aftermath of the collapse of the stock market, especially the widening gap between the rich and the poor. Even though the financial crisis can thus not be regarded as an inspiration for the story, by featuring a heroine that fights for the economically oppressed, the *Hunger Games* puts questions of class and class conflicts at the core of its narrative and reflects contemporary concerns and political and social developments which emerged at the same time that the novels did.

Since Katniss is a YA heroine as well as a political rebel who struggles with issues and injustice also to be found in contemporary Western cultures and U.S. culture more specifically, my argument is two-fold. First of all, the *Hunger Games* trilogy establishes an innovative model of both gender and heroism in the context of contemporary YA dystopian fiction, infusing the genre with a feminist message. In addition, by having a teenage girl take on the role of political rebel and soldier whose aim it is to bring down an oppressive patriarchal system, the trilogy reconceptualizes the notion of what it means to be a hero and a teenage girl in the 21st century, adding a feminist flavor to both. Through its usage of a feminist quest heroine, the trilogy suggests that approaches reminiscent of feminist thought and activism are effective means to tackle the challenges Katniss, and by extension contemporary U.S. or Western societies, face. The novels hence dramatize ways in which economic exploitation, the de-politicization through the media, or political oppression can be overcome through political activism inspired by feminist thought and theory.

As it is Katniss' personal development, her coming into political consciousness, and the ensuing fight against oppression that take center stage in the novels, this chapter closely traces said development in order to show that the *Hunger Games* trilogy employs a variety of feminist concepts and ideas. I also regularly bring up the model of the feminist quest heroine to identify moments in which the novels undermine heroic conventions established in typical quest narratives. In the first part, I start out by discussing how gender is conceptualized in the trilogy and show that it breaks with the binaries usually found in heroic stories. I also demonstrate that, at this stage of the narrative, Katniss is characterized as a non-political person who does not see any reason in trying to fight the political system. Through an analysis of the heroine's various performances for the cameras in the second subchapter, I illustrate that, in the trilogy, representations of the teenage girl are used in a manner that subverts the de-politicizing or oppressive functions of the media in Panem. I furthermore trace Katniss' growing comprehension of both the power of the media and the political system. In the last part, I focus on Katniss' role in the rebellion as the Mockingjay and a rebel soldier. In this context, the growing group of friends, allies, and rebels Katniss gathers around her will be analyzed as well in order to explain why they can be described with the feminist term of "sisterhood" and why their fight can be said to be inspired by notions of feminist activism.

"There's nothing you can do": Gender and Oppression in Panem

Although she is not as hyper-feminine as Buffy, as a girl warrior, Katniss challenges binary and hierarchical concepts of femininity and masculinity, too. From the very first scene onwards, when the only hint that the narrator might be a girl is the "long dark braid" which Katniss tucks into her hood, *The Hunger Games* mixes and blurs gender categories and thus echoes the feminist conceptualization of gender as hybrid and fluid rather than binary and stable (4). Indeed, Katniss' behavior and character traits constantly oscillate between hegemonic femininity and masculinity, not only in the beginning of the first novel, but throughout the trilogy as a whole. On the one hand, Katniss is rather masculinized as she is sturdy, emotionally and physically tough, and straight-forward. Her decision to volunteer as a tribute and protect her sister Prim, her fighting skills, as well as her physical and emotional resilience can be regarded as attributes commonly connected to hegemonic masculinity, too (J. Miller 147). On the other hand, the caring relationships between her and her sister Prim and, later on, Rue (Collins, *HG* 202), Wiress (*CF* 324), and Finnick (*MJ* 175), also signify Katniss' feminine side, her compassionate, caring, and kind character.[3]

That this girl warrior is an accomplished archer blurs gender boundaries even further. Even though Katniss describes in detail how she learned to use her bow and arrow and how long it took her to feel comfortable and safe in the woods surrounding her district (*HG* 51), she also maintains that she has an innate talent for shooting, as she states that "[i]t's more than experience. It's a natural gift [...] the way [she] can shoot at an animal in almost complete darkness and still take it down with one arrow" (*CF* 6). By portraying Katniss as a girl with an innate talent for archery, the novels undermine the notion that women and girls are naturally and inherently non-violent. In other words, they deconstruct the connection between sex and gender. Katniss' talent hence exemplifies feminist claims that gender traits are an outcome of socialization and that women and girls are not friendly and peaceful because they are female, but because they are raised and educated to behave in this specific manner. In addition to being socialized into behaving in more masculine manners, Katniss also has a *natural inclination* for shooting and archery, a fact that destabilizes naturalized connections between girlhood and actions and behaviors connected to stereotypical femininity.[4]

The novels furthermore dramatize notions of gender held by feminist theory because time and again, they present gender roles as performative. For instance, Katniss explains that she took on the roles of both mother and father for her younger sister Prim after her father had died in a mining accident and her mother suffered from depression (*HG* 27). This means that she acts as provider and nurturer at the same time, both of which are highly gendered roles commonly connected to stereotypical masculinity and femininity, respectively. When Katniss states, "I had lost not only a father, but a mother as well. At eleven years old, with Prim just seven, I *took over* as head of the family," the novel explicitly presents this role as performative (*HG* 27; emphasis added). This is because the verb "take over" insinuates that these gendered roles can be learned.

That Katniss takes over, or is forced to take over traits and behaviors connected to stereotypical masculinity also draws attention to the fact that Panem's society is a patriarchal one. After all, it is made clear that the gendered traits that connote masculinity are much more valuable for Katniss herself and for the people living in District 12 at large. In fact, Katniss needs to behave in a masculinized manner to survive and to be able to support her mother and sister who are both stereotypically feminine (cf. Myers 136). The importance or value of traditional masculinity is, for instance, also alluded to by Katniss when she states that Gale could easily find a wife especially because he can work in the mines, hunt, and thus provide for a family (Collins, *HG* 10). Regarding this portrayal of gender, Zoe Jaques claims that the trilogy reinforces traditional gender hierarchies to some extent because it "repeatedly offsets and opposes male and female capabilities, with the latter seeming ineffectual, fragile, or self-absorbed" (152). I contend, however, that it rather indicates that Panem in general and District 12 in particular are patriarchal societies in which traditional femininity is frequently regarded as a weakness rather than an asset.

The novels further underline this notion through the portrayal of heterosexual romantic relationships, or rather the love triangle, because Katniss' inability to choose between her two love interests Peeta and Gale mirrors the heroine's inability to embrace the more stereotypically feminine aspects of her identity. Indeed, in this story, the love triangle is given new meaning as it symbolizes the heroine's struggle for identity, which in turn calls attention to the patriarchal gender hierarchies at work in Panem.[5] To be more precise, Gale symbolizes Katniss's masculine side as his character is constructed according to the models of the romantic hero and hegemonic masculinity (J. Miller 155).[6] Peeta, on the other hand, symbolizes the feminine aspects of Katniss' personality. Her fellow tribute is commonly described as a feminized character as he is open, kind, eloquent, and trusting, and although he is physically strong and brave, he tries to abstain from violence against others (Collins, *HG* 25–32, 48, 89, 130; *CF* 54, 124). That Katniss is afraid to start a relationship with Peeta and embrace her feminine side insinuates that, in the patriarchal society in which she lives, character traits connected to stereotypical femininity are seen as a source of weakness and vulnerability.

Through its particular portrayal of romantic love, the trilogy also reworks narrative conventions of YA fiction, where "the coming-of-age narrative is found in the transformation of characters from girlhood to womanhood through romance" (Platt 73). By contrast, in the *Hunger Games*, this transformation is triggered through political activism. The trilogy challenges the centrality of romantic love prominent in many YA texts, especially those directed at a female readership such as the *Twilight* series, because even though romantic love does play a role in the story, it is a comparably minor one, with issues such as politics and rebellion taking on more central positions. Indeed, it is Katniss' struggle to survive and to fight alongside the rebels to bring down the oppressive political system that takes center stage time and again. Romantic love is marginalized, for example, when Katniss states that she "can't think about kissing when [she has] got a rebellion to incite" (*CF* 125–26) and when she observes that she could "survive just fine without either" Peeta or Gale (*MJ* 330). These examples stress that the plot is not driven by the female protagonist's search for true love, but rather by her aim to support the rebels, her thirst for revenge, and her desire to kill President Snow, all of which are mentioned on countless occasions throughout the second and third parts of the trilogy (cf. *CF* 117–19, 122–24, 127, 141, 164, 166, 167, 329; *MJ* 30–31, 168–69, 183, 191, 195, 229, 234, 332).

It is also important to notice that, in this quest story, oppression is shown to be systemic. After all, the first few pages of *The Hunger Games* already indicate that, in Panem, the government systematically establishes and maintains class differences in order to stop the oppressed from uniting or rebelling. Katniss articulates this when she explains that unequal rations of food are used to separate the population within the district itself because they are "a way to plant hatred between the starving workers of the Seam and those who generally count on supper and […] ensure that we will never trust one another" (14). The same method is used for the districts at large, as here, too, artificially created differences in wealth are used to cause jealousy and hatred between the districts; feelings that are supposed to stop Panem's citizens from uniting against their oppressors (19).

This portrayal of oppression due to class and gender and how the two categories interact works against one of the more common points of criticism regarding girl warriors and Girl Power characters in general, namely that their stories do not acknowledge issues such as systemic, intersectional, or patriarchal oppression (Currie, Kelly, and Pomerantz 49). Katniss is not a girl who lives "in a world where women […] can do anything" but her life is heavily influenced and constrained by a patriarchal system of oppression that puts her at a disadvantage because of her gender and class position (Brown 155). While the novels maintain that gender is performed, the particular gender performances of hunting and trading, which Katniss learns to carry out because she has no other choice, speak strongly of the fact that Panem is a patriarchal society that systematically oppresses its citizens not only based on their class affiliation, but because of their gender, too.

At the same time that it presents these systemic and intersectional oppressions, *The Hunger Games* characterizes Katniss as a non-political person. Whereas, on the one hand, she is aware that the people in the districts are exploited, on the other one, protesting or resisting are not yet options for her. The hunting scene with Gale, for instance, emphasizes her non-political stance when Katniss gets irritated about his plans to leave District 12, an act which she regards as "preposterous" and absurd, and therefore pointless to even talk about (9). Said passage also highlights that Katniss is so concerned with day-to-day problems, such as finding food, that she is not able to think about anything else, especially not about how to change her personal situation, let alone that of a whole society. Even though she is suspicious of the official historical account of the rebellion, she does not "spend much time thinking about it. Whatever the truth is, [she does not] see how it will help [her] get food on the table" (42). This illustrates that, on the one hand, Katniss' role as family provider keeps her from *doing* anything defiant, and, on the other one, also stops her from *thinking* subversive thoughts or questioning the Capitol's power.

What is more, it is not merely her thoughts and behavior, but also Katniss' identity which is influenced through her role as family provider. This is because Katniss' self-realization and individuation are not possible as she is completely occupied with keeping herself and her loved ones alive (Braithwaite 7). *The Hunger Games* thus emphasizes the Capitol's power to control and restrict its citizens both mentally and physically with the help of poverty and hunger. Katniss herself remarks on this during the Hunger Games when she wonders what her future would look like if she won. Since most of her life "has been consumed with the acquisition of food," Katniss is "not really sure who [she is], what [her] identity is" (Collins, *HG* 310). Selfhood, individuation, or her personal development have always been marginal issues in her life. This is another feature that Katniss and Buffy share, as just like Buffy's role as a Slayer controlled by the Watchers' Council, Katniss' occupation as family provider, too, can be regarded as an identity category that hinders her from developing her own identity, let alone a political consciousness or agenda (cf. J. Butler, "Imitation" 255).

By portraying Katniss in the manner just described, the trilogy expands on the notion of heroism to include someone who is not only a girl, but, at least initially, poor, underprivileged, and politically powerless. The novels thus rework the traditional quest narrative to include and give a voice to someone with an inferior class and gender position instead of focusing on "a socially, politically, and economically powerful subgroup of the human race," namely upper-class white men (Pearson and Pope 4). This quest story thus casts the fight against systemic patriarchal oppression and marginalization as potentially heroic.

"I could do so much": Medialized Strategies of Resistance

While she is characterized as a non-political person in the beginning of the trilogy, Katniss' relationship to politics changes once she is reaped for the Games and becomes part of the propaganda system and the power struggles in Panem. Indeed, she increasingly gains political consciousness and develops the will to resist and even rebel against the Capitol's power. In this context, the *Hunger Games* trilogy establishes a contemporary model of the feminist quest heroine that shows how media representations that usually render girls and women powerless and objectified can be used to establish and support a political agenda. This is because during the course of the story, Katniss succeeds more and more in infusing her media representations with political meaning, thus turning the spectacle of the Games into events brimming with political meaning and defiant potential. This is made possible because both bodily features as well as interests that are connected to stereotypical femininity, such as fashion and styling, are portrayed in an innovative manner, namely as potential tools of empowerment and rebellion. Consequently, it is an empowering and feminist subtext that is established here, as interests that are usually considered trivial or unimportant are given new meaning and value. At the same time, the novels also criticize the manner in which girls and women are represented and used in both the media landscapes of Panem and contemporary Western cultures. This is because they show that when she enters the Hunger Games, is presented on TV, and groomed to become a celebrity, Katniss initially takes on stereotypically feminine gender performances that bring to mind notions of female passivity, sexualization, and objectification.

Before I turn to her representation in the media specifically, I briefly want to illustrate that the portrayal of Katniss' body more generally defies heroic conventions, as it challenges the norm that the bodies of heroes must adhere to ideals of hegemonic masculinity, that they must be tall, muscular, and visibly strong. In fact, time and again, the novels emphasize that their female protagonist rather conforms to the physical standards of ideal femininity because Katniss is described as small and thin (Collins, *HG* 181; *MJ* 234). As I will further elaborate in Chapter 6, it is problematic that Katniss, along with many other popular female (teenage) protagonists, adheres to Western beauty standards to a large degree. Nevertheless, her representation as a lethal warrior still specifically targets and undermines the damsel in distress archetype typically connected to this type of female character, because her portrayal as a girl warrior challenges persistent connections between female youth, beauty, and helplessness. This is achieved because instead of portraying her bodily features as a disadvantage, the novels maintain that Katniss is a better warrior because of her feminine physique. Since she is not as tall and heavy as the career tributes, for example, she can run very fast and escape her persecutors by climbing trees (*HG* 149, 181). Moreover, Katniss' body is also very resilient, which is yet another aspect that bears a striking resemblance to the portrayal of the female hero's body in *BtVS*. Katniss is vulnerable and she gets hurt several times throughout the trilogy. However, she never gets as badly injured as Gale and Peeta, for instance (*HG* 188, 340; *CF* 112–13). Consequently, stereotypical patterns of representation and resulting connotations of female and male bodies as weak or strong, respectively, are distorted and reworked in this quest story.

The Hunger Games calls upon stereotypical representations of gender in the media more specifically when, in preparation for the Games, Katniss is made to move from a more masculine gender position, which she occupied at home in District 12, to one where she behaves in ways that are more stereotypically feminine (J. Miller 146). This adherence to traditional gender roles is described as a common tactic among those reaped for the Games. Even though in these instances, the performed gender and the sex of the respective tribute are in accordance with binary gender notions, they still dramatize the idea that gender is not a naturally given fact. The male tributes, for instance, present themselves as a "monstrous boy" and a "ruthless killing machine," or as a "giant," "built like an ox" (Collins, *HG* 125, 126). By contrast, the female tributes are "sexy," "provocative," or "sly" (125). Katniss, too, is told to become more feminine, to be cheery, friendly, and charming all the time, instead of behaving like her usual hostile self (115–18). The clear division between female and male tributes is commented on by Katniss, who laments that if she were a male tribute, she "could get away with sullen and hostile and it would be just fine" (126).

That Katniss initially does not want to abide by the norms of stereotypical femininity, even though this will help her to get sponsors, draws attention to the fundamental difference between male and female tributes when it comes to the question of power. While the first are allowed to be active, and it is their self-fashioning as powerful agents that renders them fan favorites, the female tributes need to behave in a passive manner and present themselves as objects of adoration. This need to be likeable makes them more dependent on the whims and opinions of the Capitol citizens, which means that they ultimately occupy less powerful positions than the male tributes. The importance for the teenage girls to be passive recipients rather than active doers is also pointed out when Peeta confesses his love for Katniss during a public interview. By making her "look desirable," he makes Katniss appear more feminine, as his desire creates an image of her as an object, a position that adheres to notions of stereotypical femininity (135). While Katniss is initially outraged by this treatment, Haymitch explains that she should be thankful that Peeta has established this image of her, because it will help her win sponsors. However, it highlights that Katniss is dependent on others to create this favorable image of her. It is indeed striking that in spite of the fact that Katniss is an accomplished archer and thus an actual contender in a game in which children need to kill others to win, she is not allowed to present these abilities that connote traditional masculinity on TV, but is instead forced to become more feminine and thus more passive.

All of these examples highlight that Panem's media industries perpetuate traditional and binary notions of gender, ascribing girls more passive roles and allowing boys to be active and aggressive. By drawing parallels between the Hunger Games and contemporary reality TV shows and celebrity culture, the novels indirectly comment on U.S. mainstream media and the Western entertainment industry at large by insinuating that they, too, preserve traditional and hegemonic gender roles and represent girls and young women according to the scripts of stereotypical femininity.

Indeed, in addition to her personality, Katniss is also rendered more feminine and more passive and dependent with regard to her outer appearance. In preparation for the Games, for instance, the tribute is handed over to a prep team that administers the following treatments in order to remove the most obvious digressions from the beauty ideal in the Capitol. These include scrubbing down [her] body with a gritty foam that has removed not only dirt but at least three layers of skin, turning [her] nails into uniform shapes, and primarily, ridding [her] body of hair. [Her] legs, arms, torso, underarms, and parts of [her] eyebrows have been stripped of the stuff, leaving [her] like a plugged bird, ready for roasting [61].

These bodily corrections are an exaggerated version of beauty treatments that women and girls undergo both in the U.S. and many other parts of the world today (J. Miller 153). Thus, in this scene, the novel stages the connections between femininity, beauty ideals, and the objectification and sexualization of girls and women, both in Panem and contemporary Western societies. This is achieved because during her make-over, Katniss is turned into a person that adheres to the beauty standards of the Capitol at the same time that she is also turned into an object to be looked at, to give pleasure to others. Katniss herself does initially not receive any pleasure from her changed appearance, but, on the contrary, the peelings, manicure, and hair removal make her feel vulnerable and exposed. Hence, the novel also makes aware of and denounces beauty standards that turn women and girls into passive objects that can be looked at, criticized, and consumed by others.

More important than this mere critique of beauty ideals and the objectification of female bodies, however, is that the novels project the idea that beauty norms, and the perpetuation of them through the media, can have political consequences. To be more precise, *The Hunger Games* warns against the loss of political engagement and awareness due to diversions such as rigid norms of beauty. This is achieved through the portrayal of the citizens of the Capitol as docile bodies, that is bodies "that may be subjected, used, transformed, and improved" (Foucault 136). According to Michel Foucault, discipline "dissociates power from the body, on the one hand, it turns it into an 'aptitude,' a 'capacity,' which it seeks to increase; on the other hand, it reverses the course of energy, the power that might result from it, and turns it into a relation of strict subjection" (138). In the *Hunger Games* trilogy, discipline exists in the form of beauty norms which indirectly strengthen the power of Panem's rulers because, first of all, they influence and control the citizens, and secondly, the people's attention is diverted and turned away from concerns of political, economic, or social nature (Van Dyke 256).[7] This idea is referred to in the novels through the mentioning of *Panem et Circenses*. Just like the people in ancient Rome, the citizens of the Capitol have "given up their political responsibilities and [...] power" "in return for full bellies and entertainment" (Collins, *MJ* 223).

While in contemporary Western societies, beauty norms are still highly gendered and women spend more time and money on their bodies than men do, in Panem, matters are more complicated. On the one hand, the need to adhere to certain standards of beauty applies to both men and women. Katniss' prep team is one case to exemplify this claim, because all of them have altered their bodies regardless of their gender: Venia has "gold tattoos above her eyebrows," Flavius wears "purple lipstick," and Octavia's "entire body has been dyed a pale shade of pea green" (*HG* 61–62). Critic Jessica Miller praises the parallels concerning standards of beauty and conceives of them as a positive development that reflects a level of equality between men and women (153). In contrast to this positive interpretation, I see the relative equality of beauty standards rather as an equality of oppression that renders both men and women "docile bodies" in Foucault's sense.

However, Katniss' negative attitude towards the fact that she is represented in the media and turned into a public figure changes when she realizes that she can subvert the Capitol's power by using the media to convey her own (political) messages (J. Miller 158; Van Dyke 264). Instead of becoming a docile body herself by embodying the common concept of the tribute as a symbol of oppression, exploitation, and entertainment, Katniss understands that she has the ability "to show the Capitol they don't own [her]. That [she is] more than just a piece in their Games," more than just a docile body to represent and affirm the power of the Capitol (Collins, *HG* 236). She does so for the very first time after Rue's death when she decorates the body of her fellow tribute with flowers. In this scene, Katniss arranges Rue's body as a sign of protest, or, as she herself describes it, in order "to shame them, to make them accountable," knowing that the Gamemakers will "have to show" the dead girl's body to audiences across Panem (236–37).

By decorating Rue's body and mourning her, Katniss accuses the Capitol of doing something wrong and points out that the Games are not the festivities, entertainment, and sources of honor they are commonly made out to be in the dominant discourse, but an exploitative and inhuman demonstration of the Capitol's power. This scene illustrates that in the trilogy, the feminist quest heroine has been adapted to engage with more contemporary issues. Indeed, her actions comment on contemporary media landscapes and suggest means on how to defy and subvert media that depoliticize their audiences and dehumanize the people they represent. Katniss' actions and thoughts indicate that she knows how the media representation of the Hunger Games works as she consciously stages Rue's body and hence her act of defiance for the cameras. Katniss communicates her rebellious agenda by using the very same media channel that the Gamemakers employ but turns the purpose of the TV broadcast on its head when she uses it to criticize the Games. This also stresses that Katniss understands that she can influence and manipulate the images and the messages they contain.

What is more, this scene also highlights the connections between becoming angry and coming into political consciousness, because Katniss' hate and fury make her realize that it is not the tributes who are the evil ones, but that the Capitol is the source and the driving force of both the Hunger Games and the people's oppression in general. This is articulated when she states that

> *it's the Capitol I hate* for doing this to all of us. Gale's voice is in my head. His ravings against the Capitol no longer pointless, no longer to be ignored. Rue's death has *forced me to confront my own fury* against the cruelty, the injustice they inflict upon us. [...] There's no way to take revenge on the Capitol. Is there? [236; emphasis added].

Due to the emotions triggered by Rue's death, Katniss realizes whom she hates and why, and she begins to think about challenging the Capitol. In other words, in this moment, she "consciously starts to reject her position as victim [and] starts to become an agent" (Lethbridge 96). The strong emotions she feels wake her from the passivity concerning the Capitol and make her think about actions to take revenge on the people who rule Panem. Notably, Katniss does not keep these emotions to herself, but she openly displays them when she performs the three finger salute as a sign of her hate and resistance/antagonism. The effect of these actions is immediate, as the people of District 11 send Katniss some bread as a demonstration of their thankfulness and their support. The novels hence clearly point out that contemporary media landscapes can be used for political representations and even mobilization. After all, her display of anger is broadcast across the nation and inspires others to embrace their own outrage and become active in the fight against oppression.

Besides that, Katniss also uses her outer appearance and her style, ergo entities that connote traditional femininity, to take part in and ultimately influence the political discourses at work in Panem. Hence, new meaning is given to fashion, style, and beauty, as they are infused with political and subversive content. This portrayal supports the feminist claim that performing femininity does not automatically and invariably lead to objectification that renders women and girls powerless, but can be potentially empowering. In this context, it is her stylist Cinna who takes on a central role in teaching Katniss how to perform a more feminine role on the one hand, and, on the other one, how to empower herself by influencing her representation in the media. In the opening ceremony for the first Games, for instance, Katniss is dressed in an outfit that burns with synthetic fire, the empowering potential of which is clearly articulated by the tribute herself when she states: "Cinna has given me a great advantage. No one will forget me. Not my look, not my name. Katniss. The girl who was on fire" (Collins, *HG* 70). As this statement underlines, playing the role of the "girl on fire" empowers Katniss on two different levels. First of all, it creates a star persona that the people in the Capitol can remember and potentially sponsor. As a consequence, the probability that Katniss will win the Games is heightened, which tips the odds in her favor to some extent, as it gives her hope and allows her to enter the arena with more confidence.

In addition, Cinna also enables Katniss to understand and handle the dangerous political power struggles in which she becomes entangled (Van Dyke 263). For instance, after she has won the Games, her stylist presents her as a young and naïve girl and not as the courageous and powerful victor that she is. Katniss observes:

> I look, very simply, like a girl. [...] Innocent. Harmless. Yes, it is shocking that Cinna has pulled this off when you remember I've just won the Games. This is a very calculated look. Nothing Cinna designs is arbitrary. [...] [I]t's a reminder that the Games are not quite finished. And beneath his benign reply, I sense a warning [Collins, *HG* 355].

In this scene, Katniss adheres to the standards of hegemonic femininity because her make-up and her outfit, which is padded in certain places to give her curves, emphasize her girlishness and thus, by implication, her alleged naïveté and innocence. At the same time, this particular look projects the subversive potential of outer appearance because her outfit, which seemingly renders her passive and harmless, actually makes it possible to conceal the subversive and rebellious potential of her act of defiance in the arena and therefore enables her to protect herself and Peeta.

Indeed, the scene also points out that Katniss undergoes a learning process when it comes to political issues. While she does "not [immediately] understand Cinna's design" when he clads her into the girlish outfit, she soon realizes that it is supposed to carry a certain message to President Snow, namely that she is only an "innocent" girl (366, 360). Once Katniss understands the role she is supposed to play, she supports the intended meaning of her outfit by behaving like a teenage girl in love, flinging herself into Peeta's arms, kissing him, and snuggling up to him (361). Ultimately, Katniss learns to take on femininity as a conscious act or a performance and the heroine increasingly understands how she can influence and change the connotations to femininity that would usually render her powerless and docile (J. Miller 156).

In this context, a development is furthermore traceable with regard to the purpose and effect of Katniss' clothes, as they become increasingly laden with rebellious and political messages. These changes are brought about when Katniss realizes that without a complete change of the system, the oppression from the Capitol will never stop. Even though she survives the Hunger Games and returns to District 12 as a victor, Katniss soon comes to understand that this new role is yet another identity category supposed to firmly embed her in the political power structures and stop her from becoming politically active. In other words, it is yet another "ploy to distract [her] and keep [her] from doing anything else inflammatory in the districts" (Collins, *CF* 150). Ironically, the very fact that President Snow tries to submit her to a new identity category, to distract her and contain her defiant potential, makes Katniss recognize that she can actually play an essential part in the rebellion. When she muses that since she "set it in motion, [she] could do so much" more to support the rebellion, the novels demonstrate that Katniss becomes aware of her own rebellious potential and that she also realizes that playing a vital part in the rebellion will ultimately enable her to protect the people close to her as well as the people of Panem and its future generations (123).

Her development into a politically active and resistant rebel is signified not only through the representation of her thoughts, but, notably, also through her clothes. Indeed, in contrast to the first Games, when Katniss' different dresses are rather employed for personal reasons, namely to win sponsors or even to protect her and Peeta by deflecting from her political potential and power, in *Catching Fire*, they are used for exactly the opposite purpose, namely to openly stage and emphasize her status as a defiant subject and symbol for the rebels. The wedding gown that turns into a mockingjay costume during the interview for the Quarter Quell, the jubilee version of the Hunger Games that forces Katniss and Peeta to take part in the Hunger Games once more, serves as an example to illustrate this claim. President Snow forces Katniss to wear her wedding dress for the interview because by "turning her bridal gown into a shroud," he wants to humiliate her and show that she, as an offender of his power, is not allowed a happy future (248). Just like a bride who is given to her husband whom she has to obey, Katniss is supposed to symbolize a bride that is given into the hands and powers of the Capitol.

However, when the wedding gown burns away on stage to reveal a mockingjay costume, this degrading image is destroyed both literally and figuratively. By becoming the Mockingjay and turning into the rallying point for the rebels, Katniss symbolizes and hence also claims political power. Indeed, the political implications of her wardrobe are summarized by Katniss herself when she asserts that "what will be seen as a flashy costume change in the Capitol is resonating in an entirely different way throughout the districts" (253). Even though the citizens of the Capitol merely regard her costume change as entertainment, Katniss understands that, once again, Cinna has been able to convey a political agenda to the rest of Panem through the use of Katniss and her costumes. By burning away the wedding dress that symbolizes Katniss' submissiveness to the power of the Capitol and turning her into the Mockingjay instead, Cinna stages her secession from the power of President Snow and also teaches Katniss the possibility of political resistance through style.

During the rebellion that plays out in *Mockingjay*, the media in general, and television in particular, take on an even more crucial status than they did in the first two installments. Time and again, through the repeated description of the television spots, their production, content, and airing, the novel indicates that the "war in Panem is, in many ways, fought on and through TV" (Day 174). The Capitol, for instance, broadcasts footage of Peeta to convince the rebels to stop fighting and to warn Katniss more specifically against continuing on her revolutionary path. Just like the Capitol, District 13 uses television for propagandistic reasons, too. They hence challenge and disturb one of the central sources of power that the Capitol possesses. While each part of the trilogy has emphasized that the Capitol depends on "its ability to manipulate media and control the flow of information," the rebels succeed in destroying this monopoly of power when they hack the broadcasting system and feed their own material into the lines of communication (Latham and Hollister 35).

In this context, it is not only the rebel propaganda in general, but Katniss specifically who plays and indispensable role in destroying the monopoly of power over the media and hence the power over the kind of information and (political) discourses spread across Panem. This is because Katniss is shown in the majority of rebel propaganda, so that, once again, media representations of a teenage girl are staged as effective tools to spread political contents and mobilize others. To be more precise, the so-called "propos," short propaganda videos that are broadcast in the districts and the Capitol, focus on Katniss exclusively and portray her as the defiant and fearless "rallying point" of the rebellion (Collins, *MJ* 44, 10). More importantly, it is stressed that this staging of the rebellious female hero is highly successful. After all, Katniss is told after the airing of the first propos that "the rebels, who were barely maintaining a foothold in several districts, have rallied. They have actually taken 3 and 11 […] and have made inroads in several other districts as well" (119).

By staging Katniss as a subversive and empowering media personality, the novels challenge the notion that popular media representations of girls tend to be non-political or disempowering. Indeed, in the novels, the exact opposite is the case, as it is the heroine's media presence that allows her to effectively communicate political and resistant messages and to mobilize others to join the rebellion against the Capitol. Notably, she frequently does so by using fashion and style, which usually do not connote ideas such as political subversion or rebellion. The novels hence demonstrate a notion prevalent in third wave feminism, namely that popular culture and the performance of femininity are means through which feminist and political messages can be spread and even amplified.

A *"journey [that] has not been undertaken alone":* *Sisterhood and Agency*

In the *Hunger Games* trilogy, the adapted model of the feminist quest heroine also reflects upon contemporary manifestations of power as well as political and social issues. Just like *BtVS*, the *Hunger Games* trilogy is deeply concerned with the issue of power, but in contrast to Buffy's heroic journey, Katniss' quest takes place on a public and decidedly political level. The message that the *Hunger Games* send is that it is heroic to be politically active and defiant of political power and oppressive regimes. It thus clearly echoes the feminist claim that "political engagement and activism are crucial components of a feminist consciousness in the twenty-first century" (Dicker and Piepmeier 8). In this context, the concept of sisterhood is celebrated, as it becomes more and more central throughout *Catching Fire* and *Mockingjay*. Time and again, the novels underline that unification and mutual support are important for successful (political) empowerment, thus echoing the third wave's belief that "feminism is not simply about women's issues but is a broad-based political movement that seeks freedom for all those who are oppressed" (8). Katniss embodies exactly these feminist ideals: by becoming politically active, she and her fellow rebels help to bring down the patriarchal forces in order to bring freedom to all the people of Panem, ergo "all those who are oppressed."

The Quarter Quell interview scene analyzed above is not only helpful in examining how Katniss can use fashion to communicate a political agenda, but it also accentuates the potential power of uniting for a common cause. On the one hand, the individual interviews with each contender already undermine the rules of the Games and defy the Capitol, as the victors-turned-tributes "come out fighting" and call for a cancellation of the Games (Collins, *CF* 250–51). On the other hand, Katniss asserts that the demonstration of solidarity among the victors has an even greater impact when she notes: "[…] all twenty-four of us stand in one unbroken line in what must be *the first public show of unity* among the districts since the Dark Days. […] We victors staged our own uprising" (258, 259; emphasis added). This portrayal of unity, which is initiated by Katniss when she reaches out to hold hands with her fellow tribute Chaff, perfectly exemplifies the third wave's conception of sisterhood, as this form of joint action and empowerment "strives to include more diverse voices, including those of men and those of non-white heritage" (Payne-Mulliken and Renagar 58). In fact, the rebellious group of victors is very diverse as its members are of different ages and genders, different races and ethnicities, different classes, and even different abilities, as some of them, such as Chaff, who has lost an arm, or Peeta, who has a prosthetic leg, have been permanently injured by the Games.

The composition of the group first of all reflects that "sisterhood [...] means the unification of all and the oppression of none" (58). Secondly, the scene also establishes that the group achieves more power by working together. Even though some of the victors only join the demonstration of unity hesitantly and break the alliance once they enter the Games, many of them, such as Johanna, Finnick, Wiress, Beete, or the Morphlings truly form an alliance to save Katniss and support the rebellion. Moreover, the television screens turn to black as soon as the people in charge realize what is going on, an action that furthermore draws attention to the power of this demonstration of solidarity. Indeed, the demonstration of unity and loyalty must be seen as a radical political act in Panem because in this dystopian society, "trust and friendship are enemies of the state" (Day 173). By contrast, the collective struggle of the victors can be described as radical as it symbolizes "the reinvention of solidarity" in a society that is built on antagonism and separation (Fisher 33). Throughout the first two installments of the trilogy, readers learn that the districts are isolated and there is no communication, let alone unification, among the districts. What is more, not only do the people in the districts hardly know anything about each other, but, through the spectacle of the Hunger Games, for instance, they are even encouraged to see each other as enemies (Culver 97). The isolation and enmity between the districts is created through a conscious effort by the Capitol to keep the oppressed from joining together and challenge the political power system. Therefore, the victors' decision to publicly unite and hold hands goes directly against the Capitol's agenda, as it demonstrates unity among the victors in particular, and, by extension also works as a symbol of unification and the potential to defy the Capitol in all of Panem.

The scene in which the victors stage their uprising is a turning point for both, the people of Panem and Katniss herself. The magnitude of the political statement that is delivered through this demonstration of unity is reflected in Katniss' feelings, as she feels "empowered" by what happened on stage (Collins, CF 258). This shows that she recognizes the advantages that connectedness and group effort can bring to her agenda to defy the Capitol, which is an important step towards overthrowing President Snow. Katniss' feeling of strength and empowerment through a connection to others stands in stark contrast to how she conducted herself at the beginning of the trilogy when, apart from Gale, Katniss had no good friends at all (HG 6, 112).

Indeed, Katniss slowly realizes that she is not completely self-sufficient and gradually "ceases to resent the way that the bonds [...] restrain her freedom of action, and [...] comes to value instead what they offer her in return: a connection to other people" (Culver 100). Over the course of the novels, the female protagonist finds herself in numerous situations in which she has to depend on others: Haymitch develops a winning strategy for her; Rue becomes an ally; District 11 sends Katniss bread during the Games; Cinna designs her empowering outfits; and Katniss' own district lies to the authorities about Gale's true identity (*HG* 58, 238; *CF* 252, 12). The list could be continued, but should suffice to illustrate that there are a large number of instances in which the heroine receives help, protection, and encouragement from others. The girl warrior values these bonds because they are based on mutual support and responsibility. In this mutuality and interdependency, Katniss experiences a new kind of relationship, one in which she is not invariably confronted with additional responsibilities and constraints, but can rely on others to help and relieve her from certain burdens. Through the portrayal of her friendships and the numerous advantages that result from them, the novels revalue yet another attribute usually connected to femininity, and that is the desire for connection. Indeed, they emphasize that the cultivation of friendships and alliances gives Katniss an advantage over her antagonists.

The trilogy not only stages sisterhood as advocated by third wave feminism by making a point about how political change can be brought about and oppression overcome through group efforts that include people from a variety of backgrounds, but in a similar fashion to *BtVS* and characters such as Xander and Willow, diversity in the *Hunger Games* also entails the personality traits and skills characters possess. Thus, the trilogy is innovative with respect to the question of who is fighting the oppressive regime, but also of how they are fighting it. In addition to Katniss, who, due to her young age, low class position, and gender subverts standards of traditional heroism, many of the secondary characters do the same. Peeta, for instance, is a feminized character and thus an unlikely hero. Although he is physically strong and brave, he lacks aggressiveness or an inclination for violence. Rather, his actions are motivated by his loyalty and caring attitude. His character thus broadens the realm of heroic possibility for male characters to include actions that are motivated by intelligence, knowledge, and care.[8]

Heroic conventions are also challenged in the case of Rue, the 12-year-old tribute from District 11. In a conversation between her and Rue, Katniss directly comments on the importance of skills that do not necessarily fit the model of traditional heroism, but are nevertheless valuable, when she tells her fellow tribute: "We're strong, too [...]. Just in a different way" (Collins, *HG* 206). Here, Katniss points out that the two girls have additional skills, such as the knowledge of how to find food, that give them an advantage over the career tributes, who are dependent on their physical strength alone. She thus underlines that there are a number of skills other than physical strength and the ability to fight that can help them to survive and defeat their enemies and oppressors. In addition, since Rue is described in the novels as a black girl, the portrayal of her character also points to the goal of third wave feminism to include and advocate for people of color (cf. *CF* 126, 54–58). All in all, due to the fact that the individual efforts of characters such as Katniss, Peeta, Rue, and many of the other rebels are shown to be important for bringing down the political regime, the realm of heroism is opened up in the *Hunger Games* trilogy to include a larger variety of characteristics and skills.

At the same time that the trilogy emphasizes that a successful rebellion is only possible through joint actions and unification—it is the combination of Katniss' fierceness, Peeta's eloquence, Prim's care, Cinna's artistic designs, the victors' effort to protect the heroine, and the action of many more people and their individual skills that eventually overthrows President Snow's regime—it does in no way deny Katniss' central status as the protagonist and heroine of the story. On the contrary, the relationships to other people help Katniss to develop into a political rebel as her "most momentous […] decisions stem from her powerful attachments to others" (Myers 142). By emphasizing that Katniss' protective and compassionate actions undermine the power of the Capitol and trigger her political activism, the novels portray yet another feature connected to stereotypical femininity in a positive manner. This is the case, for example, when she sings for Rue while she is dying or holds out the berries so she and Peeta can both win the Games. In fact, in a society in which compassion, help, and loyalty are seen as defiant acts, Katniss' "defender-of-the-helpless act," as Johanna Mason calls it, can only be regarded as radical and subversive (Collins, *MJ* 221).

In spite of the central role as both the catalyst and a driving force of the rebellion, Katniss has also frequently been criticized for merely being reactive and not possessing any true agency and self-determination. Amanda Firestone, for instance, argues that

> [a]gency is the ability to make decisions and effectively enact those decisions to achieve specific results, whereas activity simply denotes physical action that doesn't necessarily require intense thought. Although Katniss has lethal skills with a bow and arrow, using them in survival situations doesn't necessarily assert her agency [215].

While critics such as Firestone ascribe Katniss a lack of agency and see her as an object that is used by the power players in Panem, I suggest that it is rather Katniss' *struggle* against the power players and for agency, her attempts to set up and follow her own (political) agenda, and her efforts to understand the ways in which she is used by Coin and Snow that best describe her position within the trilogy. Katniss is neither completely influenced and determined by others, nor is she able to always act on her own behalf and follow her own aims. Even though she is frequently turned into an object, for instance when she is reaped as a tribute or chosen to become the Mockingjay, Katniss also finds ways to resist the expectations that come along with these roles and to infuse them with her own meaning and agenda. Consequently, the *Hunger Games* trilogy establishes a discourse about female agency that "continues to resonate with girls today" (Fritz 29). This is because agency is shown to be something for which Katniss needs to fight continuously, something that she achieves only for it to be taken away again. Katniss's struggle for agency thus realistically mirrors the same struggle many readers themselves, especially adolescent and/or female ones, face on a daily basis.

For example, in contrast to Firestone's claim that Katniss does not have the ability to make her own decisions and effectively enact those to achieve specific results, her becoming the Mockingjay is clearly depicted as a deliberate choice that enables Katniss to reach specific results, namely to stop the oppression of the people in Panem. When Prim asks her whether she decided to become the Mockingjay because she wants to or because she feels forced to do so, Katniss answers: "No, I want to. I have to, if it will help the rebels defeat Snow" (Collins, *MJ* 34). As described above, it has been Katniss' wish to support the rebels ever since she returned from the Victory Tour. Hence, at the same time that the role of the Mockingjay is created by others and supposed to support their agenda, Katniss' taking on of the role is still a deliberate act that helps and empowers her as well, as it allows her to further her own agenda along with that of the rebel leaders. Thus, instead of indicating that she relents to outside pressures, the usage of the verb "have to" in this particular context rather signifies her desire to support the rebels in order to reach her own goals. Moreover, that she acts in order to achieve specific results is also underlined when she comes up with a list of conditions that will protect herself as well as her friends and family (38).

Katniss' constant struggle for agency not only manifests itself in her inner conflict whether to, but also how to embody the role of the Mockingjay. Even though Katniss makes a conscious choice and briefly empowers herself when she agrees to become the Mockingjay under certain conditions, her power and agency are directly reined in again by President Coin when she publicly announces that Katniss will be put to trial and probably executed if she does not obey her orders (58). Here, the novel draws a parallel between District 13 and the Capitol when Katniss observes that, in addition to the Gamemakers, President Snow, and the rebels, Coin is "another power player who has decided to use [her] as a piece in her games, although things never seem to go according to plan" (59). In this short observation, Katniss aptly describes how others try to use her to become more powerful, but she also alludes to her own role within this game of power: the reason why things never seem to go according to plan is because Katniss never simply takes on the roles and behaviors she is supposed to, but instead disrupts the plans and subverts and, at times, even destroys the power relations in which she is embedded.

In fact, during her stay in District 13, Katniss' values and aims are contrasted with those of District 13 in general and its president Alma Coin in particular time and again. Although she presents herself as the savior of Panem, Katniss gradually comprehends that even though Coin may fight against the oppressive powers of the Capitol, "she uses the same playbook as President Snow" to do so (Averill 175). Indeed, Coin is aptly named, as the president of District 13 "may be female to Snow's male, [yet] they're two sides of the same coin" (J. Miller 154). By giving the role of the power-craving patriarch to a woman and a man respectively, the *Hunger Games* trilogy shows that female power is not necessarily preferable to male power. Instead, the novels maintain that it does not matter who is in power, but emphasize that the system of patriarchal and hierarchical power in general is problematic.[9] After all, the kind of oppressive and autocratic power she wants to execute is directly criticized when President Coin is assassinated by Katniss (Collins, *MJ* 372). Notably, it is the insight into the discrepancy between her own aims and values and those of Coin that ultimately results in Katniss' dissociation from the leader of District 13 and, more importantly, the system of power for which she stands.

The idea that even in District 13, Katniss continues to be used as a piece in the power games for Panem is highlighted when she comes to realize that the seemingly empowering role of the Mockingjay rather constrains and exploits her. In fact, both the role as Mockingjay and the manner in which she is treated resemble her treatment as a tribute to an uncanny extent. As she observes:

> What they want for me is to truly take on the role they designed for me. The symbol of the revolution. The Mockingjay. [...] They have a whole team of people to make me over, dress me, write my speeches, orchestrate my appearances—as if *that* doesn't sound horribly familiar—and all I have to do is play my part [10].

As a tribute, Katniss is exploited to signify the power of the Capitol and as the Mockingjay, she is exploited to signify the power of the rebels. Just as she was during the Hunger Games, in District 13, Katniss is initially turned into a symbol, a commodity, an object for consumption, and a tool that serves the aims of other people, in this case Alma Coin and the rebel leaders.

It is furthermore made clear that this particular treatment is very similar to that of the tributes in the Games in an additional regard, and that is the adherence to stereotypical scripts of femininity. Indeed, when it comes to the Mockingjay's outer appearance, the rebel leaders abide by gender norms and conventions of more typical media representations, as the female protagonist is given a complete make-over to make her look more mature and, notably, more sexy (70). Katniss indicates that the character into which she is turned looks completely unfamiliar to her when she speaks about herself in the third person and affirms: "I do not know who that person [on screen] is" (70–71).

What is more, she emphasizes that, as a public figure whose appearance is used to achieve a specific effect, she has to live up to a certain ideal when she observes that when it comes to looks "a televised rebel has her own standards to live up to" (60). Although Katniss has taken on the role voluntarily, the Mockingjay turns out to be an oppressive identity category similar to the ones by which she has been influenced before. Becoming the Mockingjay initially means becoming a piece of propaganda, a weapon wielded by others.

At the same time, the novel stresses the need for Katniss to resist these manipulations and furthermore suggests that she can only successfully inspire the rebels and act as a heroine for them if she infuses the role of the Mockingjay with her own characteristics and values. This is insinuated when she fails spectacularly at aptly fulfilling the role she is given during the first shoot for the propos as she can neither identify with the words she is supposed to say nor with the look that she sports (70–72). During a meeting after the shoot, Haymitch draws attention to the fact that the moments in which Katniss "genuinely moved" people are all "unscripted," which means that Katniss acted in a more authentic and spontaneous manner and not according to a given identity category (74, 75).

Notably, however, these moments were also ones in which the heroine acted in a more feminine manner. This indicates that Katniss' femininity is an important part of her character in general, and her unique kind of heroism in particular. Indeed, this scene highlights the complexity of both gender portrayals and conceptualizations of femininity and heroism at work in the trilogy. While the feminine identity category imposed from above renders Katniss passive, inauthentic, and thus rids her of heroic potential, her own character traits that connote femininity are shown to be part and parcel of her heroism. Indeed, *Mockingjay* stresses that it is not only her defiance and fighting skills, but her more stereotypically feminine features that render her a heroine for the people of Panem. In this context, her girlhood in particular is cast in a heroic light when one of the rebels tells Haymitch that they should "wash her face" to take off the heavy make-up. When the same rebel states that "she's still a girl and you made her look thirty-five," the novel indicates that neither Katniss' youth nor her gender are seen as contradictions to her status as a heroine, but rather as an essential part of it (77).

That her femininity is an indispensable part of her heroism is also illustrated in the scene in which Katniss visits a military hospital in District 8 and personally interacts with the wounded people around her. This scene casts notions connected to traditional femininity as heroic on two levels. First of all, it is once again an activity usually connected to stereotypical femininity, namely taking care of the wounded, that is staged in the propaganda spots as inspiring and heroic. Secondly, this scene also demonstrates that Katniss regards herself not as an unattached leader or rallying point but as a part of the rebels. This is articulated when she asserts that she "belong[s] to them" (90). When she gives her first defiant speech as the Mockingjay after the hospital has been bombed by the Capitol, the novel combines these two aspects. On the one hand, it dramatizes the idea that Katniss is most strongly motivated by the urge to protect and help others rather than by her need to prove her own strength or power, as it is the death of the wounded that propels her into action. On the other hand, when she directly addresses President Snow and warns him, "If we burn, you burn with us" (100), the novel also calls attention to her sense of community. After all, the use of the pronoun "we" clearly underlines that Katniss sees herself as part of the rebel army rather than an isolated leader.

This scene also calls attention to the importance of sisterhood, of mutual support, and group effort. This is because Katniss only becomes aware of her own powerful position within the rebellion when she visits the fellow rebels and sees that what "has so often felt like a solitary journey, has not been undertaken alone. I have had thousands upon thousands of people from the districts at my side" (90). When she sees the large number of people who all look up to her and fight for the same cause, Katniss not only feels a sort of belonging and support, but she also understands that she is more important and therefore more powerful than both Coin and Snow want her to believe. This is highlighted when she observes:

> A new sensation begins to germinate inside me [...]. Power. I have a kind of power I never knew I possessed. Snow knew it, as soon as I held out those berries. [...] And Coin knows now. So much so that she must publicly remind her people that I am not in control [90].

The realization that others try to control her due to her central status within the rebellion closely resembles Buffy's observation about the same issue: "Power. I have it. They don't. This bothers them" ("Checkpoint"). However, in contrast to Buffy, who stops working for and with the Watchers' Council, Katniss does not completely sever the ties to the forces that try to control her. Still, the recognition of her own powerful position and the witnessing of the rebel's loyalty and support allow her to reassess her own role within the rebellion and also encourage her to keep fighting and to keep on playing the role of the Mockingjay.

In addition, the scene also serves as one example to show that Katniss is able to make the role of the Mockingjay her own on different occasions and frequently frees herself from the oppressive forces of the different power players, if only for short amounts of time. Hence, it is not merely at the very end of the rebellion when Katniss assassinates Coin that she "finds a Mockingjay identity that's authentic, one with which she truly can identify," as Jill Olthouse claims (53). Indeed, when Katniss states that she is "held aloft in a cloud of heat that generates not from [her] surroundings, but from [her] own being" (Collins, *MJ* 100), the novel indicates that in this instance, her role as the Mockingjay and her own wish to defy the Capitol become one, enabling her to give a speech that dramatizes her own defiant potential and serves as a motivation for the rebels as well.

Last but not least, Katniss' powerful position and her ability to garner support from others are also illustrated when she becomes the leader of the star squad, the troupe of soldiers that accompany her during the siege of the Capitol. Even though Katniss never performs as leader of the rebellion as a whole—she encourages the rebels and gives them hope, but never makes any strategic decisions on a grander scale—the narrative alludes to her ability to lead a group of people through the portrayal of the star squad and their mission to reach Snow's mansion. In this context, the story presents a specific way of leading others, since Katniss does not lead by force, but the others follow her because they want to and because they believe in her ability to kill Snow and end his authoritarian regime (324–25). The scene in which Katniss and her team go underground in order to find President Snow and kill him can, first of all, be regarded as a moment of agency, as Katniss takes the deliberate decision not to return to the camp in order to follow her personal agenda established in *Catching Fire* and pursued ever since, namely to kill Snow. In addition, it also speaks strongly of Katniss' essential role within the rebellion as a whole and her leadership potential in particular. This is because the star squad serves as a symbol of the rebel army in particular and the people of Panem at large as it consists of victors, people from the Capitol, soldiers from District 13, as well as people from the other districts. Their willingness to support Katniss, to follow her, to accept her authority, and to die for her underline Katniss' influential status and peoples' readiness to accept her as a leader and trust in her goals.

Nevertheless, that Katniss does not go on her underground mission to kill President Snow alone, but is accompanied by fellow soldiers, many of whom are her friends, also means that she is never completely autonomous and free in her choices. Even though she can be regarded as the leader insofar as it is her goal that they are trying to reach, Katniss is still also dependent on the help of the squad, especially on their knowledge of the Capitol (299), their allies (318), and their fighting skills (309–12). Her connection to other people and the fact that she cares for their well-being hence once again deconstructs the idealization of masculine heroism. By becoming autonomous and superior rulers, traditional male heroes ultimately represent and reaffirm models of patriarchal power (Pearson and Pope 3). As critic Tarina Quraishi states: "With independence comes the temptation of apathy." In contrast to this, Katniss neither becomes fully independent nor detached from and disinterested in the people around her, but she establishes friendships and support systems, shares the power she gains, empowers others, and consequently flattens or destroys the hierarchies of patriarchal power by which she and others are oppressed. Ultimately, Katniss' engagement in various friendships, alliances, and relationships undermines the image of the lonely and independent warrior and opens up the realm of heroism to include people who love and care for others.

Ultimately, Katniss' triumph over patriarchal power structures also highlights her status as a feminist quest heroine. With regard to her role as the hero of her story, Katniss has reached the "freedom to live stage" described in Campbell's heroic model and is finally able to lead a life in which she herself can more freely determine how she wants to live (cf. Campbell, *Hero* 37). However, her particular way of life sets itself apart from that of male heroes, who usually take on powerful and superior positions. By contrast, Katniss turns away from politics, goes back to her home district, marries Peeta, and has children. Whereas many read this return to a more stereotypically feminine role in a negative light and hence reiterate the derogatory discourse surrounding traditional femininity more generally (Berlatsky; Firestone; Lethbridge 99; Quraishi), her return to District 12 and a life far removed from the political power players can also be seen as an affirmation of Katniss' heroic status and her feminist achievements: since it has been her aim to overthrow Snow's oppressive regime and to make sure that children will no longer be threatened by the Hunger Games, her becoming a mother and living in a changed District 12 emphasizes that she has achieved exactly what she set out to do in the beginning of the trilogy and thus confirms her heroic accomplishments.

Conclusion

Katniss can be regarded as a feminist quest heroine because she, too, challenges the conventions found in traditional quest stories, that is the gender and class affiliation of the hero, his muscular male body, and his lonely quest that leads to personal empowerment and reinstates hierarchical and patriarchal power structures. However, through its portrayal of Katniss Everdeen as a media-savvy driver of political change who constantly struggles for power and agency, the *Hunger Games* trilogy adapts the model of the feminist quest heroine for her journey to reflect and comment on contemporary social, cultural, and political challenges and demands.

Moreover, by depicting a female character in an action-driven plot, the *Hunger Games* trilogy has radically altered the world of YA (dystopian) fiction, because to the same extent that its female protagonist undermines and revolutionizes the politics at work in her society, the trilogy has changed the politics of the genre, too. After all, in the wake of the success of the novels, numerous YA dystopian novels, trilogies, and series, all of which featured a female protagonist, such as *Divergent* (2011–2013), *Matched* (2010–2012), *The Selection* (2012), *Birthmarked* (2010–2012), *Delirium* (2011–2013), or *The Girl of Fire and Thorns* (2011–2013) were published. Ultimately, the popularity of the trilogy, its feminist heroine, and the *Hunger Games* franchise as a whole attest that alternative quest stories, girl warriors, and third wave feminist theory have moved from the subcultural spaces that *BtVS* occupied to spaces closer to mainstream popular culture, where they are celebrated by cultural critics, journalists, and audiences alike (cf. Berlatsky; Lewit).

However, whereas the *Hunger Games* trilogy establishes innovative gender discourses with regard to Katniss herself and many other secondary characters, it also creates a homophobic and transphobic discourse through its portrayal of queer characters. This is because the novels draw the Capitol citizens according to queer stock characters and connect them, along with their alternative lifestyle, to inhuman decadence, stupidity, and evilness. The novels thus echo and strengthen a number of prejudices about the LGBTQ community. The derogatory portrayal of said community is not only rather conservative in general, but it also stands in direct opposition to contemporary feminist movements and the third wave in particular, which strives to be intersectional and to include, represent, and support all those who are oppressed by patriarchal systems, including people who identify as gay or trans.

The homophobic discourse is, for instance, established through the portrayal of the Capitol and its inhabitants in accordance to the aesthetics of "camp," which is "a style […] that favors 'exaggeration,' 'artifice,' and 'extremity'" (Bergman 4–5). According to Susan Sontag, camp is both "disengaged, depoliticized—or at least apolitical" and "a certain mode of aestheticism" that is not primarily concerned with beauty, but with a "degree of artifice, of stylization" (277). Based on these definitions, the style prevalent in the Capitol can indeed be described as camp. Not only are the citizens of the Capitol not interested in politics, but, as Katniss describes, their clothes, hairstyle, makeup, and even the buildings in the Capitol "seem artificial, the pinks too deep, the greens too bright, the yellows painful to the eyes" (Collins, *HG* 59). In addition, the bodily modifications that the people in the Capitol undergo are also exaggerated, artificial, and extreme, as they dye and tattoo their skin and use plastic surgery to modify their bodies even further (63). Katniss describes them as "oddly dressed people with bizarre hair and painted faces" who are "total idiots" (63) and a "rotten lot [that] is despicable" (64). Since camp is closely "affiliated with homosexual culture" (Bergman 5), the trilogy creates a homophobic subtext, because it harshly criticizes the campy style of the Capitol and directly connects it to human degeneration, heartlessness, and indifference to others (cf. *HG* 60, 65; *CF* 204–5).

The portrayal of the artificial bodily modifications as part of the camp aesthetic of the Capitol can be read as transphobic, as well. Even though the novels never explicitly mention procedures such as gender-affirming surgeries, the bodily modifications that the people in the Capitol undergo can still be regarded as trans practices or "transmogrification—that is, strange or grotesque transformation: transformation that is characterized by distortion, exaggeration, and extravagance" (Sullivan 553). The fashions and extravagancies of the Capitol, especially with regard to bodily modifications, largely resemble those practices. Indeed, Nikki Sullivan maintains that

> procedures as diverse as mastectomies, penectomies, hormone treatments, tattooing, breast enhancement, implants, corsetry, rhinoplasty, scarification, branding, and so on [...] all function, in varying ways and to varying degrees, to explicitly transform bodily being—they are all [...] "trans" practices [552)].

As trans practices, the bodily modifications that the people in the Capitol undergo can also be regarded as anti-essentialist "because [they] actively [defy] the idea that bodies need to or should operate in accordance with how they 'naturally' operate" (Jakubowski). The changing of the color of the skin or implants described in the trilogy work in this fashion since they do away with allegedly natural boundaries or rules of outer appearance. Finally, the trilogy also more explicitly alludes to gender transitions and transgressions because it describes the male citizens of the Capitol as effeminate characters (Collins, *HG* 61, 62, 124, 366).

While literary critic Jennifer Mitchell claims that these bodily modifications "[reveal] the Capitol's fluid approach to gender" and "decry traditional gendered traits," she ignores that said approach to gender is commented on in a derogatory manner time and again (135, 136). Katniss describes their result in a fashion reminiscent of stereotypical transphobic notions of gender affirming procedures, namely as bodily modifications that go beyond what is perceived of as natural. The people of the Capitol are not only described as ugly, because, according to Katniss, they are "so dyed, stenciled, and surgically altered [that] they're grotesque." These types of surgeries are condemned even more because they render the Capitol citizens non-human, which Katniss points out, for instance, when she describes her prep-team as "a trio of oddly colored birds" or "pets" (Collins, *HG* 63, 62; *CF* 247).[10] By changing the color of their bodies or using implants, the people in the Capitol attempt to overcome traditional conceptions of human outer appearance altogether. These performances and manipulations can thus be seen as practices that make aware of the instability and artificiality of gender roles and essentialist notions of what human bodies should look like. However, since they are so harshly judged, these anti-essentialist notions are condemned and portrayed as unnatural and "freakish" (*HG* 125).

The most obvious denunciation of queerness and homosexuality can, however, be found in the depiction of sex and sexuality in the trilogy. First of all, homosexuality is outright neglected in the novels because there is not one character, let alone a heroic one, who is openly gay. In addition, the novels establish homophobic undertones through the connection between homosexuality and the Capitol and heterosexuality and the districts, respectively. In the districts, heterosexuality is compulsory, as throughout the whole trilogy, the only romantic relationships mentioned between people from the districts are heterosexual ones. In contrast to this, homosexuality is only referenced, or rather alluded to, in the context of the Capitol, namely when Finnick confesses that he was sold as a sex-slave to both men and women (*MJ* 170). By describing it as something that exists in the Capitol only, the story casts homosexuality in a negative light. This notion is strengthened even more as the only time it is hinted at, it is described in the context of prostitution. Therefore, homosexuality is, on the one hand, connected to the flamboyant and narcissistic lifestyle of the Capitol citizens and, on the other one, to the Capitol and the oppressive regime of President Snow.

Finally, through the conceptualization of the Capitol as a queer space, the novels perpetuate another stereotype about gay characters, namely the idea that homosexuals are unproductive. The idea that homosexuality is unnatural as it does not lead to reproduction has long been used to argue against gay marriage (Rohy 101–02) and it is metaphorically inscribed into the *Hunger Games* trilogy, too, as in the queer spaces of the Capitol, nothing is made but only consumed, whereas food and commodities are produced in the straight spaces of the districts. The narrative hence portrays the Capitol as queer, silly, decadent, and inferior, and the more rural spaces of the districts as authentic, natural, masculine, and superior, especially when it comes to questions of morality. Ultimately, through their establishment of homophobic and transphobic discourses, the *Hunger Games* trilogy suggests that an urban lifestyle along with increased freedoms in sexuality, body images, and gender roles will eventually lead to horrors such as the Hunger Games and it is therefore highly problematic in its portrayal of queerness as silly, inhumane, and potentially dangerous. What is more, while the novels expand on the notions of heroism when it comes to gender, class, or race, their outright rejection to include LGBTQ characters into their realm of heroism severely limits the innovative approach to heroism established in the trilogy. Yet, this neglect also opens up an opportunity for alternative readings that counter the reactionary portrayals of sexuality in the novels, which is a topic that will be explored in detail in Chapter 5.

$$\blacklozenge \ \blacklozenge \ 3 \ \blacklozenge \ \blacklozenge$$

Mainstreaming the Feminist Quest Heroine
Brave *and the Warrior Princess*

[H]ere in America, we are in the midst of a royal moment. To call
princesses a "trend" among girls is like calling *Harry Potter* a book.
—Orenstein, "What's Wrong"

Fairy tales have been part of Western cultures for centuries and one of
the best known characters depicted in these tales is that of the princess. While
the princess has been an iconic figure for a long time, the introductory quote
from Peggy Orenstein claims that in recent years, the prevalence and popularity of princesses have reached new heights. Fairy tale princesses have not
only become a part of mainstream popular culture in general but of girls'
lives and girls' popular culture in particular (Rothschild 4). In addition to a
new wave of Disney princess movies that were released between 2009 and
2016, there has been an increasing number of live-action fairy tale adaptations
featuring princesses as leading ladies, for example *Mirror Mirror* (2012), *Snow
White and the Huntsman* (2012), *Into the Woods* (2014), *Cinderella* (2015),
and *Beauty and the Beast* (2017). Other icons of girl culture such as Barbie
have jumped on the bandwagon as well: movies entitled *Barbie as Rapunzel*
(2002), *Barbie: Princess Charm School* (2011), or *Barbie: The Pearl Princess*
(2014) are just a selection of almost 30 movies that portray Barbie as a
princess. In addition to the movies, there also exists an overwhelming number
and range of merchandise products that cater to the princess hype. Young
girls can engage with their objects of affection by reading books, seeing musi-
cals, listening to CDs, visiting theme parks, playing games online, sleeping
in princess bed linen, or dressing up as their favorite princess—and these are
just a few of the items and activities that are available. Even grown-up princess
devotees can take part in the fandom by wearing princess lingerie or by get-

ting married in princess-inspired wedding gowns (cf. Ng; Rothschild 7). In light of this, it is indeed an understatement to merely call princesses a trend as they have clearly evolved into a staple of mainstream girl culture.

Not least due to their popularity, princesses and the fairy tales that feature them have come under increased scrutiny because they serve as a vital tool for education and socialization. Since they frequently deal with archetypal characters and follow a formulaic plot structure in which a brave man battles evil and rescues a beautiful woman, fairy tales can be regarded as a subcategory of Campbell's monomyth; one that is aimed at children specifically (cf. Zipes, *Fairy Tale* 2, 3). Even though they were not originally intended for them, over time, fairy tales have been "institutionalized as an aesthetic and social means through which questions and issues of civilité, proper behavior and demeanor in all kinds of situations" could be easily and effectively taught to children (11).[1] In this context, it is important to note that just like myths in general, fairy tales, too, often reinforce traditional gender hierarchies and teach patriarchal values to their young audiences (9). Many critics hence regard fairy tale princesses as potentially problematic and even harmful archetypes and role models for young girls because they often perpetuate traditional notions of idealized and extreme femininity that include passivity, obedience, the search for romance, domesticity, and an adherence to Western beauty ideals (Clapp-Itnyre 7; DiPaolo 169; Rothschild 1–2, 9, 13). What is more, critics warn that having role models that are passive, innocent, and praised for their beauty instead of their actions might harm the self-esteem of young girls and severely limit their aspirations and goals (Baker-Sperry and Grauerholz 724; Fisher and Silber 121).[2]

Again, however, it is important to keep in mind that, just like heroes, princesses are not representatives of natural and unchangeable human characteristics, but their stories and traits rather serve as indicators of societal, political, or cultural norms and values regarding gender roles in general and femininity in particular (Rothschild 2–3; Stover 8). This is why an "examination of princess stories can shed light on American culture as a whole in addition to girl culture" (Rothschild 13). On the one hand, the continuous portrayal of hegemonic femininity through damsel-in-distress characters testifies to the prevalence of patriarchal and binary notions of gender in Western cultures at large, and U.S. culture in particular. On the other hand, to the same amount that the connection between masculinity and heroism is constructed and maintained through myth, the connection between femininity and victimhood is constructed, too. In other words, there is neither anything inherently heroic in traditional masculinity nor is there anything inherently non-heroic in femininity. Thus, even though the archetypes in fairy tales frequently perpetuate traditional gender roles and heroic concepts, they are potentially subject to change.

Indeed, there recently emerged a type of princess that challenges the notions of ideal femininity symbolized by the archetype and that is the so-called "Warrior Princess." These princesses are brave, mentally and physically strong, skilled fighters, able to protect themselves and others, and definitely not in need of rescue by a handsome Prince Charming. Representatives of this kind of princess are, for instance, the Snow Whites in the movies *Snow White and the Huntsman* and *Mirror Mirror*. Warrior Princesses can also be found on TV, for example in the series *Once Upon a Time* (2011-present), which stages many of the well-known fairy tale princesses as independent and self-sufficient young women. The Snow White in this series, for instance, is not confined to doing the dwarfs' chores. Instead, she lives on her own in the forest, fights against the Evil Queen, and meets her Prince Charming when she attempts to rob him—a feat which she easily accomplishes not least because the prince is surprised that he is being robbed by a girl ("Snow Falls").

Another princess to defy tradition is Merida of DunBroch, the female protagonist of the animated Disney movie *Brave*. Not only is Merida skilled in archery and horseback riding, but she also hates to dress up in ball gowns, and, most importantly, refuses to get married. In fact, Merida takes her destiny into her own hands and defies the ancient patriarchal tradition of arranged marriage by participating in the contest for her hand in marriage herself, easily beating all of her male suitors and winning self-ownership. However, this defiance of traditions causes a fight between Merida and her mother Queen Elinor. In an attempt to magically change her mother's stance on her refusal to get married, the princess accidentally, with the help of a witch, turns Elinor into a bear. When the princess finds out that her mother has to be returned to human form within three days, she sets out on a quest to find a way to reverse the spell and save her mother.

Brave is a particularly remarkable princess movie not only because of its female protagonist, but also because this Oscar-winning film was produced by Disney and Pixar, two film studios which had previously not been known for their innovatory portrayal of female characters. Indeed, Pixar, a computer animation film studio that became a subsidiary of the Walt Disney Company in May 2006, had actually never even created a movie with a female lead before *Brave* (Corliss 68). *Time* magazine's Joel Stein adequately sums up the relationship between the film studio and its female characters when he claims that "Pixar has a girl problem. All of its unfathomably successful movies [...] have male leads. Very male leads: cowboys, astronauts, robots, cars, Ed Asner." With regard to the depiction of women and girls, Pixar thus fits right into the Disney Corporation which, throughout its long history, "has never been synonymous with feminism" either (DiPaolo 169). On the contrary, the corporation has rather been widely and repeatedly criticized for its conservative stance on gender roles and its dated representation of women and girls (cf. Bruce 2; England, Descartes, and Collier-Meek 556; Towbin et al. 24). Disney is said to reproduce and inculcate a world view in which binary gender roles are the norm: men have power and agency, women who are submissive and obedient are rewarded with marriage, and disobedient and powerful women are punished for their attempts to defy the patriarchal *status quo* (Bruce 2).[3]

Because of its tendency to perpetuate conservative gender roles, the Disney Corporation specifically, as well as the princess characters it produces, are mentioned time and again in the context of media representations that are potentially harmful for young female audiences (Do Rozario 34; Hines and Ayres 4; Whelan 26–27). This is because the company is both one of the biggest producers of entertainment for children and of princess characters. Starting with *Snow White and the Seven Dwarfs* in 1937, the corporation has since produced twelve highly popular princess movies which are usually divided into three different groups or waves. The first wave comprises *Snow White* (1937), *Cinderella* (1951), and *Sleeping Beauty* (1959). Ariel from *The Little Mermaid* (1989), Belle from *Beauty and the Beast* (1991), and the eponymous characters of the movies *Pocahontas* (1995) and *Mulan* (1998) make up the group that belongs to the second wave of Disney princesses. The third wave features movies created after the turn of the century and includes Tiana from *The Princess and the Frog* (2009), Rapunzel, who stars in the movie *Tangled* (2010), *Brave*'s Merida, Anna and Elsa from *Frozen* (2013), and *Moana* (2016).

In addition to the films in which they appear, many of these princess characters are marketed through a campaign that was launched in 2000 and brings together the so-called "Official Disney Princesses" into one franchise that, today, offers more than 25,000 merchandise products (Whelan 25). The latest member to join the official line-up in 2013 was Merida, a princess who sets herself apart from her royal predecessors by virtue of both her behavior and outer appearance. As described above, Merida differs from traditional (Disney) princesses in fundamental ways and can, as I argue, even be regarded as the first feminist Disney princess. This is achieved because *Brave* merges the archetype of the hero and the damsel by featuring a princess character as the protagonist of a quest story. More importantly, Merida adheres to the model of the feminist quest heroine because, just like Katniss and Buffy, she is a girl warrior who sets out on a heroic journey during which she matures and develops in a manner that allows her to overthrow the patriarchal system at work in her society. She also does so by forging connections to other people, or her mother, to be more precise. By mixing and blurring the role of princess and hero within the character of Merida, *Brave* ultimately defies traditional notions of princesshood and heroism and challenges the persistent idea that the two roles are diametrically opposed.

Whereas in the previous chapters, I focused more intensely on the manner in which the model of the feminist quest heroine undermines the archetype and idealization of the male warrior, in this chapter, I concentrate on the way in which the model can be used to revise the archetype of the damsel in distress. At a first glance, Buffy, Katniss, and Merida are quite different because the first two feminize the masculine warrior and the latter masculinizes the hyper-feminine princess or damsel in distress. The result of both types of reworkings, however, is the same, as they establish a complex female hero who uses both stereotypically feminine and masculine skills to succeed in her quest. Through its depiction of Merida as a warrior princess, *Brave* does not only revalue stereotypical femininity and girlhood, but revises and expands upon notions of ideal femininity and girlhood by rendering both more complex and inclusive.

I show that the inclusion of the feminist quest heroine into a princess story is achieved through two major modifications to the classical Disney princess movie. This is, first of all, the portrayal of a mother-daughter relationship and the inclusion of a complete nuclear family, which makes it possible for *Brave* to openly criticize the gender roles and conventions often found in Disney princess movies. Moreover, the film also alludes to notions of sisterhood because the relationship with her mother enables the princess to forge an empowering connection to another person. Secondly, the replacement of the theme of romantic love with a heroic journey infuses the narrative with a feminist message, as this makes it possible for the film to address issues such as the princess' development, agency, and the defiance of patriarchal power. I analyze the two modifications separately, comparing *Brave* and its female protagonist to its predecessors of the first and second waves of Disney princess movies. In each part, I concentrate on both form and content to demonstrate that *Brave* engages with and reworks a number of Disney's tropes and traditions that usually reinforce a patriarchal world view. In this context, I further show that the princesses of the second wave cannot be seen as feminist role models, even though numerous attempts have been made in the past to interpret them as more evolved when it comes to issues of female agency and independence.

"You changed!" "Oh darling, we both have": Revising Royal Families

Even though heroes and damsels are often conceptualized as direct opposites, there is one thing that they do have in common, namely that both remain alone until the first rescues the latter at the end of his heroic journey and the two can live together happily ever after. The effect of this loneliness, however, it fundamentally different: while the solitude of the hero during his quest establishes his masculinity, strength, and independence, that of the damsel strengthens a patriarchal system that separates women and girls from each other and instead insists that the only relevant relationship they should have are those with their (future) husbands (Pearson and Pope 180). In other words, the traditional princess story

> divides girls from one another, from themselves, and from adult women. [Watching] fairy tale after fairy tale, [girls] come to see that they must relinquish ties to other women so that all their energies can be harnessed in preparation for the fiercely competitive race towards men's approval [Fisher and Silber 129–30].

By depicting women as antagonists or rivals, such stories also take on a decidedly anti-feminist stance, as they conceal the possibility of female friendship and solidarity, as well as that of sisterhood and the common fight against patriarchal systems. Indeed, princess stories rather support such systems, as they stage marriage as the ultimate happy ending of a woman's life.

Since the model of the feminist quest heroine demonstrates that connections to other people are essential, and, more importantly, that said connections can be instrumental in the fight against patriarchal oppression, it can be used to revise not only the archetype of the male hero, but that of the damsel, too. Using the model fills the princess story with female role models and celebrates female solidarity as well as concepts of love other than romantic ones. These are changes that turn princess stories from anti-feminist texts into narratives with a feminist message. This is achieved in *Brave* through the staging of the complicated yet loving relationship between Merida and her mother. That it is the relationship between two female characters, and not the search for romantic love, which takes center stage in this princess movie is one central element that sets *Brave* apart from its predecessors. To be more precise, in the film, the tropes of the princess and the (evil) queen are rewritten to challenge both genre conventions and the patriarchal subtext perpetuated through more traditional representations of princesses and evil queens. Indeed, *Brave* does not only feature a princess and a queen, but a complete nuclear family, which offers additional opportunities to rework the notions of the lonely princess waiting for Prince Charming to rescue her.

Before turning to *Brave*, I briefly delineate the manner in which previous princess movies have portrayed female characters and how tropes were used to enforce misogynist discourses and traditional notions of femininity. It has been noted by many that strong, empowering, and equal relationships between two women are quasi non-existent in the Disney universe. On the contrary, women are shown as adversaries who have to outrival each other in order to gain male approval in general or the love of a handsome Prince Charming in particular (Fisher and Silber 121; Rothschild 66). What is more, whereas witches or stepmothers take on the roles of villains in princess movies, biological mothers are largely absent. In fact, while the role of mothers in Disney movies at large has been an object of debate and analysis for a long time, as she is generally "more stereotypically (and ideologically) drawn than any other character" (Haas 197), it is striking that in princess movies specifically, mothers are not drawn at all, as they simply do not exist. In many cases, mothers have even been removed in the process of adaptation when they existed in the original fairy tale (196). By eliminating mothers from its scripts, Disney first of all marginalizes female characters on a quantitative level.[4] Secondly, erasing mothers from the storyline devalues motherhood, as well as mother's identities and their work (196) and eradicates any chance for the princesses to find in her mother a "model of maternal agency" or to "find contentment in the company of [a] compassionate [mother]" (Fisher and Silber 126, 130).

Indeed, in the movies of the first wave, adult women are cast as the exact opposite of compassionate nurturers, taking on the roles of antagonists, evil stepmothers, and witches instead. More importantly, the movies communicate the idea that it is their non-adherence to traditional gender roles which renders these women villains instead of role models. All of the female antagonists in the princess movies of the first wave defy standards of traditional femininity on numerous levels (cf. Ayres 42): They are not passive but active; the aim of their actions is to empower themselves or to harm others, not to support or nurture others; and, most importantly, they use their sexuality and beauty to gain even more power, not to become the obedient wife of a handsome prince.

These women's powerful status is furthermore emphasized through the manner in which they are drawn. The movements and posture of the female villains Maleficent, Lady Tremaine, and the Evil Queen serve to underscore their confidence, as they "dominate the screen with every move; their gestures are grand, their voices commanding." Indeed, their bodies connote power and authority as they are designed as "tall, powerful-looking, sexual [and] mature womanly hourglasses" (Rothschild 81). Moreover, the female villains are presented as women who use their good looks and sexuality not in order to please others, but to get what they want: they are "sexual subjects, not sexual objects" (Bell 116). All of the first wave movies stress the connection between female sexuality and power and, at the same time, insist that female maturity and sexuality, if they are connected to agency, must be regarded as threatening and deserving of punishment or even death (Bell 117; Rothschild 60).

When it comes to the depiction of additional female characters, the princess movies of the second wave take the marginalization and eradication of women even a step further. Except for Ursula in *The Little Mermaid*, the villains in these newer films are men, either single ones as Gaston in *Beauty and the Beast*, or whole groups of them as in *Mulan* and *Pocahontas*. Even though this could be regarded as a positive development because women are not merely divided into good and evil anymore, it limits the range of roles women can take on even more. In fact, idealized femininity is still present in the form of princesses, but representatives of female maturity, sexuality, and power are completely banned from these films. What is more, hardly any other female characters have been added to the scripts, while men—as fathers, princes, and antagonists—are featured in large numbers and given central and influential roles. The result of this is that "[men] are so dominant that women, beyond the titular princesses, are hard to find in these films" (Rothschild 147). Thus, the movies of the second wave obliterate female characters and role models in the same manner as those of the first wave—an observation which ultimately affirms the claim that these films are only feminist on the surface.

Brave must be regarded as radical in this context because this Disney princess movie not only features a biological mother, but a mature and powerful female character that is ultimately depicted in a positive light and as a potential role model for her daughter. Indeed, in *Brave*, the act of mothering is neither "erased [nor] naturalized [or] devalued" (Haas 196). In fact, the question of how to properly raise a child, or rather a princess, is an important topic in the film and a source of debate and conflict. Even though Elinor initially appears to be "powerfully evil" and adheres to the archetype of the evil queen to some extent (196), *Brave* reworks this trope, thus countering the vilification of powerful women so often found in previous Disney princess movies.

Elinor adheres to the trope of the evil queen especially in the beginning of the movie, when she acts as Merida's antagonist and the fights between mother and daughter take center stage. Whereas Elinor wants her daughter to behave according to the scripts of traditional femininity and tries to teach her how to be a proper princess, Merida continuously rejects her mother's ideas and refuses to behave according to her rules. Nevertheless, instead of casting the older woman as a villain trying to harm a perfectly innocent princess, the movie insinuates that both, mother and daughter, are responsible for the conflict. This is highlighted, for instance, in a scene after Merida has won her own hand in marriage and the fight between mother and daughter escalates. Here, both behave in a problematic manner, because Merida destroys a precious tapestry on which Elinor has worked, slicing through the family portrait embroidered on it, and severing off Elinor from the rest of the family. At the same time, Elinor destroys one of Merida's most important belongings, too, when she throws her bow into a fireplace.

While both mother and daughter hence behave in offensive and hurtful manners, *Brave* insists that they are not evil or mean, but that their conflict rather arises out of a lack of communication skills. This idea is dramatized in a scene in which, instead of talking directly to each other, Elinor talks to her husband and Merida to her horse Angus. However, since the scene repeatedly cuts from Merida to Elinor and back, their monologues are presented as a dialogue between the two. During this dialogue, both explain the reasons for their anger and their motivations for behaving the way they do. Elinor underlines that she regards the education her daughter receives as something positive and the sheltered life she leads as a privilege, as it is "everything [she and her husband] never had." Merida rather sees it as the exact opposite, lamenting that she wants her "freedom" (*Brave*). More importantly, the movie also draws attention to the fact that, in spite of their numerous fights, the two do love each other. This is articulated when Merida explains that she is "not doing anything of this to hurt [Elinor]" and her mother wishes that her daughter "could just try to see [that what she does, she does] out of love" (*Brave*). The movie thus alludes to the trope of the evil queen or stepmother to some extent, only to then revise the notion of female wickedness by demonstrating that Elinor is not motivated by hate, jealousy, or evilness, but by love for her daughter and concern for her future. It hence also puts a focus on the actual work of mothering, dealing with the hopes and conflicts Elinor encounters.

While the movie admittedly stages the relationship between Merida and her mother as a complicated one, it is neither rooted in the queen's jealousy of the princess' youth and beauty nor depicted as a struggle for male approval, as was the case in the majority of *Brave*'s predecessors. Instead, it is a realistic account of the struggles and conflicts between a teenage daughter and her mother. Elinor is not the epitome of female wickedness just as Merida is not an embodiment of the perfect princess, but both possess virtues and flaws. Through the portrayal of the female characters in this way, *Brave* erases the duality between evil queen and angelic princess that has existed in princess movies for decades and replaces it with a model of a female relationship in which the two parties eventually support and positively influence each other.

In this context, *Brave* not only enters new territory as it puts the relationship between a princess and her mother at the center of attention, but it is even more innovative—at least in the context of Disney princess movies—as it is the first to feature a nuclear family that consists of parents and siblings. In fact, the voicing and undermining of gender expectations and norms are in large part made possible through the inclusion of a nuclear family that consists of both female and male members. By featuring a daughter, a mother, a father, and three brothers, the film can address a number of issues which challenge the audience's view of traditional tropes and patterns usually found in Disney princess movies. In addition to providing comic relief, for instance,

Merida's three little brothers are instrumental for the movie to criticize gender differences in socialization and education. When the three princes Hamish, Hubert, and Harris are introduced by Merida as "wee devils," who "can get away with murder" while she "can never get away with anything," the film highlights the different roles that the princes and the princess have to take on. The boys are allowed to run around the castle unsupervised and play tricks on others. By contrast, Merida is taught by her mother to recite poetry, play musical instruments, and behave like a proper princess. The movie makes aware of and, by having Merida complain about this issue, also criticizes the differences in socialization and upbringing that reinstate and maintain binary gender roles.

In addition, *Brave* also criticizes traditional ideals of femininity perpetuated through the (Disney) princess. On the one hand, Queen Elinor tries to raise a girl that neatly resembles the image of the Disney princess. On the other one, Merida herself complains about the role that is imposed upon her and thus makes aware of the restrictive nature of idealized femininity in general and traditional princesshood in particular. When she observes, "I'm the princess. I'm the example. I've got duties, responsibilities, expectations. My whole life is planned out!," the movie emphasizes how limiting gender norms, and those of stereotypical femininity specifically, can potentially be. In a similar manner to *BtVS* and the *Hunger Games*, *Brave* advocates for non-binary gender conceptions. It does so by making aware of the frustrations Merida experiences when she is forced to take on a hyper-feminine position on one side of the gender scale and insinuates that the princess has a more hybrid and complicated gender identity: she enjoys activities such as archery and horseback riding, but she is also nurturing, which is indicated through her relationship with her little brothers or her horse, for instance.

Nevertheless, even though it asserts that Merida regards the role she is supposed to take on as limiting, *Brave* does not, as some have argued, devalue stereotypical femininity *per se* (cf. Jaques 151), but rather shows that the Scottish kingdom in which she lives is a patriarchal society. After all, gender roles are not only divided into binary opposites, but they are also given different value. Merida is, first of all, confronted with numerous rules and norms in her daily lessons, as, according to Queen Elinor, "a princess does not chortle, doesn't stuff her gob, rises early, is compassionate, patient, cautious, clean, and, above all, a princess strives for … well … *perfection!*" (*Brave*). That the princess rejects these rules of appropriate feminine behavior and appearance and sees them as a burden which restricts her freedom demonstrates that she lives in a world which works according to a patriarchal gender hierarchy that equates stereotypical femininity with limits and boredom and stereotypical masculinity with excitement, adventure, and freedom. What is more, when Merida goes out to ride her horse and shoot her bow and arrow, the movie underlines that the princess prefers to behave according to the scripts of stereotypical masculinity. This calls attention to the fact that she has internalized the norms of patriarchy and values stereotypical masculinity more than stereotypical femininity.

A similar tendency can be observed in Queen Elinor, as she tries to hold up the patriarchal system of power at work in her society by adhering to tradition and marrying her daughter off to another future clan chief. In addition, Elinor is caught in conservative ideas and ideals about the proper role and behavior of women—or princesses, to be more precise—and she also consciously perpetuates binary gender roles by trying to instill the rules of appropriate femininity in her daughter. In this context, *Brave* also draws attention to the power of fairy tales and legends to naturalize and uphold specific systems of power. After all, Elinor tries to convince Merida to submit to tradition and thus patriarchal power by using the legend of an "ancient kingdom" that fell into "chaos and ruin" simply because the old rules and traditions set up by previous rulers were not obeyed. While Merida mocks the tale when she tells her mother that it is "a nice story," Elinor warns her and insists that "it's not just a story. […] Legends are lessons and they ring with truth" (*Brave*). This conversation first of all emphasizes how devoted Queen Elinor is to tradition and how embedded she is in the patriarchal system, which in turn stops her from questioning or changing the rules of her society. Secondly, Merida's sarcastic remark can also be read as a meta-comment that points out that legends should not be taken too seriously and that norms, traditions, and the narratives that perpetuate them can be changed, which is exactly what *Brave* attempts to do.

Through its portrayal of Queen Elinor as an upholder of tradition, *Brave* points out that women, too, take part in the maintenance of oppressive power structures. It also indirectly criticizes this, as it is this behavior in particular that leads to conflict with her daughter. At the same time, her role as queen and authoritative figure is also depicted in a more positive light. Indeed, as a queen, she is shown to be authoritative, experienced, competent, and knowledgeable of political protocol. This is demonstrated, for instance, in a scene that depicts the opening ceremony of the highland games. Even though King Fergus initially rises to speak, he quickly starts stammering and is lost for words, so that Elinor has to come to his aid and finish his speech for him. What is more, she is also the one who reminds the clansmen of the rules of the game and articulates her knowledge about the legal and historical roots of the competition when she explains that "in accordance with our laws, by the rights of our heritage, only the first born of each of the great leaders may be presented as champion" (*Brave*). Here, the movie paints a positive picture of female maturity, power, and authority, as it stresses that Elinor is in charge and that she is the one who "holds the kingdom together" (Robertson 12). It hence challenges the trope of the evil queen and the notion that powerful women are dangerous and must be punished, replacing it with a woman whose rule is not only tolerated but justified.

The visual portrayal of Queen Elinor also contributes to the more positive depiction of female power. Even though she is considerably taller than Merida, a feature which symbolizes the difference in age between the two characters, in comparison to Kind Fergus, who is extremely tall and broad, Elinor still appears rather petite and slender. Notably, this difference in size is in no way reflected in the amount of competence and respect the king and queen possess. As delineated above, Fergus is repeatedly shown to be inept when it comes to his official duties as king and it is his wife who takes over his duties and is in charge of the proceedings. Moreover, Fergus uses his bodily strength and fighting skills to gain respect or rule whereas Elinor uses her character and her skills to do the same. She commands, for instance, a room full of unruly clansmen without once raising her voice. Hence, the movie asserts that women do not have to be physically strong in order to be respected; it is Elinor's natural authority and queenly demeanor that make the clansmen listen to her. The movie therefore breaks the connection between female power, evilness, and danger, infusing it instead with positive notions of competence, knowledge, and much needed leadership.

Through this particular portrayal of King Fergus and Queen Elinor, gender roles are further complicated and fairy tale tropes are reworked. At a first glance, Fergus appears to be a stereotypical king: he has power, is physically strong, and brave. Since he is a king, husband, and father, his status also brings to mind the role of the patriarch. In those regards, he adheres to the norms of traditional masculinity in crucial ways. Yet, his behavior also frequently deviates from the norms of traditional masculinity. First of all, and in marked contrast to his wife, he encourages Merida to be adventurous and independent. Indeed, it is Fergus who gives Merida her first bow and arrow, assuring her that "learning to fight is essential," no matter whether one is a prince or a princess (*Brave*). Whereas Jaques argues that this gift is problematic as it supports a patriarchal system and "initiates [the princess] into a male order" (162), I suggest that it rather depicts a non-traditional and empowering father-daughter relationship. After all, instead of protecting and sheltering his daughter, Fergus encourages her to break with gender traditions. Moreover, he also does not behave like the typical patriarch because he usually leaves it to his wife to be strict and authoritarian with their children and rather tries to avoid conflict, which is shown when he refuses to take part in an argument between Merida and her mother.

In addition, the movie also challenges the idealization of male heroes. On the one hand, Kind Fergus serves as an example of traditional warriorhood as he himself is the protagonist of legends filled with battles, beasts, and danger, one of which is even told at the beginning of the movie. On the other hand, this first impression is quickly challenged in order to reveal that, in fact, King Fergus—the allegedly brave hero of many legends—is also rather childish and irresponsible in many ways. *Brave* establishes this idea first of all when it portrays his wife as more competent and authoritarian than he is. Secondly, he and the other clansmen who visit during the highland games also behave more like children than adults or accomplished rulers. They get into fights, call each other names, present their bare behinds in an attempt to offend one another, and need to be regularly called to order by Queen Elinor, who takes on the role of a surrogate mother for these adult men. Here, the movie challenges the notion of male heroism to a large extent as, instead of putting these warrior heroes on a pedestal and presenting them according to heroic conventions, they are rather depicted as chaotic, childish, irresponsible, and in need of female guidance.

All in all, *Brave* complicates and questions binary gender roles and norms with regard to each family member except for the little brothers, who are still used as a foil to put emphasis on the difference in upbringing. It hence calls on the feminist notion that gender roles are learned and non-binary. With regard to Elinor, it is quite ironic that while she wants to turn her daughter into a paragon of ideal femininity, she herself behaves in manners that defy traditional gender roles. Even though Elinor herself has accomplished the stereotypical feminine skills she teaches her daughter, she also possesses traits and shows behaviors that rather connote stereotypical masculinity, especially in her role as ruler and queen. By portraying the nuclear family in this manner, the movie replaces archetypes with more complex characters. It depicts a patriarch who supports his daughter's breaking of gender conventions, a queen and mother who is not evil but competent and concerned about her child's well-being, and a princess who is neither perfect nor hyper-feminine.

"I'll be shooting for my own hand": Replacing Romantic Love

The lack of a love story is the second crucial transgression from the Disney norm that sets *Brave* apart from the other princess movies and allows the film to infuse the narrative with a feminist message. While "the theme of romance is the only recurring theme in every single Disney princess film from all generations," *Brave* is the first to break this pattern as it does not eventually pair its princess off with a male love interest (Stephens 102). The movie consequently undermines the function of the traditional romance story which has been used to reinforce traditional gender notions and patriarchal ideas and ultimately marginalized the princess character. Instead of dreaming about her Prince Charming, Merida embarks on a heroic journey that changes her destiny and patriarchal tradition. Thus, Merida emerges as a feminist quest heroine whose story and character question the norms of hegemonic femininity and its connotations with passivity, helplessness, and physical and moral perfection.

Indeed, it is the love story in particular, and the manner in which it has been portrayed in princess movies, that call attention to the status of the Disney Corporation as a preserver of traditional gender roles and patriarchal ideals. Whereas romance did already play an essential role in the original fairy tales, it was even more heavily emphasized by Disney when they adapted the literary tales for the screen (Rothschild 61). Even though adaptation theory has long established the notion that an adaptation does not have to be true to the original text in order to be good (cf. Bluestone 5–6; Leitch 3), it is still important to point out that in the case of its princess movies, Disney changed the source material in very specific ways, namely in a manner that renders the princesses even more stereotypically feminine and consequently more conservative than their literary predecessors. Through the focus on romance and heterosexual love, romantic ideas and ideals such as finding one's true love and true love's kiss have become essential elements of fairy tale adaptations in general, and princess stories in particular (Rothschild 63, 65). The pervasiveness of these traditional concepts underlines Disney's powerful status as a creator of cultural tropes. At the same time, however, the elimination of this conservative element in *Brave* also demonstrates that norms of hegemonic femininity are changing as even Disney creates a princess story that does not include a romantic story line.

The trope of finding true love has been widely criticized by (feminist) scholars, especially because it is seen as one of the main pillars on which Disney's depictions of traditional gender roles rests. This claim holds especially true for the generation of the princesses of the first wave—Snow White, Aurora, and Cinderella—whose only ambition in life is to find a suitable husband or rather, as Brenda Ayres puts it, to be found by him: "Finding *him* is not an option; she is to *be* found, passive voice" (40). Indeed, "passive" is the keyword when it comes to the description of the Disney princesses of the first wave, since it highlights their status as emblems of traditional femininity. In all of the films, a lack of activity, development, and change are recurring elements both with regard to their behavior as well as their personalities (Towbin et al. 30; Zipes, *Happily* 93–94). No matter what happens to them, the princesses remain friendly, obedient, and innocent, waiting for their prince to rescue them.

Notably, it is not only their behavior and character traits that adhere to an idealized notion of femininity, but their bodies, too, are drawn in an idealized fashion. The most important factor that contributes to this effect is their beauty: Snow White, Aurora, and Cinderella are paragons of female beauty as their bodies are designed according to "male fantasies of female biological perfection. [...] Disney's heroines all feature tiny waists, large breasts, curvy hips, and sensuous hair" (Bean 55). What is more, they all wear beautiful gowns that accentuate the "hyper-idealized, highly sexualized female form beneath" the fabric (55). All of the first wave princesses are white, a portrayal which connects whiteness to both beauty and goodness and suggests that being white is a prerequisite for becoming a princess (Bell 110; Lester 294–95; Rothschild 72). In addition, the princesses also move with grace and elegance, as the animated characters were all modeled after real-life professional ballet dancers.[5] In short, the bodies of the princesses are designed in a way that emulates and creates a certain standard of female attractiveness that is highly idealized and reflects conservative gender ideals where a woman's main purpose is to cater to the male gaze and look attractive for men (Rothschild 73).

There is, however, one exception in which the princesses are allowed or even expected to behave actively, and that is when it comes to the domestic sphere. Snow White, Aurora, and Cinderella can all be considered prime examples of the "Angel-in-the-House stereotype," that is, a woman who is obedient to her husband and takes care of both her family and the household without objection or complaint (Manley 81–82; cf. also Ayres 39). Adding to this portrayal of the princesses as eligible wives and mothers is the interaction with their animal friends. Not only does this plot device help to characterize the princesses as charming and special (Rothschild 56), but it also shows that they are motherly and nurturing.[6] Hence, the films perpetuate reactionary gender roles and, at the same time, further the central status of romantic love as they hint at the idea that the young women will be able to fulfill their designated roles as future wives and mothers.

While the princesses are consistently depicted according to the scripts of hegemonic femininity, namely as damsels in distress, the princes are portrayed as the heroes who ride to the rescue and save the day. Their traits and behaviors thus reinforce notions of hegemonic masculinity. What is more, some critics go so far as to argue that even though the princesses are the titular characters of the movies, it is rather the stories of the princes and other male characters that are central to these films (Ayres 40; Rothschild 61, 65).[7] This claim is, for instance, backed up by the observation that the princes are present both at the end and in the beginnings of the films, so that "the brief glimpse Disney offers into the lives of their princesses begins and ends with the princesses' romantic involvement with men" (Whelan 28). Indeed, men act as initiators and drivers of the story and are also responsible for the happy ending.

The idea that it is not the lives of the princesses that play a central role in the movies but the lives and legacies of the princes is further supported by the specific kind of happy ending featured in every princess movie, namely a wedding. Each young woman marries a future king, and the movies communicate the idea, albeit to different degrees, that the princesses are needed as future wives and, most importantly, mothers—they are needed to produce heirs, ensure the legacy of the king, and keep the patriarchal system intact. The importance of conceiving heirs is another example of how the plot is set into motion because of male desires and needs (Rothschild 65). All in all, both the princesses' characters and their stories are marginalized to a large extent since they are embedded in a patriarchal discourse concerned with male privilege and power. In the end, Snow White, Aurora, and Cinderella are merely means to ensure that the patriarchal power system can prevail.

However, it is not only the princes' lives that frame the stories, but the topic of romance is also present from beginning to end. In the movies of the first wave, audiences are primed in a variety of ways to expect a love story and a happy ending. These specific expectations are, first of all, raised by the status of the movies as adaptations of well-known and beloved fairy tales (cf. Fisher and Silber 126). The relationship between the movies and their literary predecessors is strongly emphasized, since "[each] of [the] early princess films opens with a real-world, live-action scene of a storybook with ornate, gothic covers. The books then flip open, revealing the texts that set the scene for the story to come" (Rothschild 54). In two cases, namely *Cinderella* and *Sleeping Beauty*, there is also an omniscient voice-over narrator who recites the beginning of the respective stories. By employing these real-world scenarios, the movies forge a connection to the original texts (Whelan 22), and in doing so, also establish the major themes and values, namely romantic love and heteronormative gender roles.[8]

Harking back to the literary tradition and arousing specific expectations also has an impact on the role of the princesses within the movies. By portraying a written text in a book and having an omniscient narrator, the movies give narrative agency to an authority outside of the fictional world because it is not the princesses who tell the story, but hetero-diegetic narrators. Consequently, as demonstrated with the help of the books, everything is literally already fixed in writing and thus unchangeable. As a result, the tales told in the films are not the princesses' stories but stories *about* the princesses. The movies underline that the young women have no narrative agency and no influence on the outcome of the narratives.

When it comes to the representation of hegemonic gender roles and heteronormative relationships, many of the observations made in the context of the Disney princess movies of the first wave also hold true for those of the second wave. Just as with their predecessors, in each movie, the young women and their stories are marginalized in favor of men (cf. Rothschild 143). What is more, this "framing of women's lives" by men, as Jack Zipes calls it (*Fairy Tale* 89), is even more obvious than in the movies of the first wave. Many of the first wave films start with the introduction of the conflict by showing the dire and/or dangerous situations in which the princesses find themselves and only then present the prince as love interest and heroic rescuer from said situations. By contrast, each and every princess movie of the second wave presents the male protagonist in the very first scene of the movie. The only exception is *Mulan*, which nevertheless still starts with the introduction of the male antagonist and not the female protagonist. Hence, in these films, the framing does not only take part on a symbolic level, as was the case with the first wave, but the princes literally frame the action as they are the only characters present at the beginning and the end of each movie.

The introduction of the male love interest at the very beginning of the movie is key to establishing the theme of romance. This has, of course, already been the case in the movies of the first wave. Yet, for the second wave, it becomes even more crucial to assure the audience that they can indeed expect a romantic movie because there are specific changes regarding the princesses that make it necessary to establish this topic right at the beginning of each film. Since these princess movies have all been produced in the aftermath of second wave feminism, the female characters have been adapted to changes in gender role expectations to some extent (Rothschild 135–36; Stover 5). Generally speaking, they have been revised in a way that makes them appear more active and independent. Therefore, the introduction of the male love interests at the beginning of the movies assures the audience that they can expect a love story in spite of the updated characteristics of the princesses.

In spite of the critique the second wave princesses face, the fact remains that in these movies, the concept of the Disney princess has been updated to meet contemporary demands regarding gender roles and femininity (Rothschild 135). Ariel and her fellow second wave princesses are more active and self-confident than Snow White, Cinderella, and Aurora. Whereas the princesses of the first wave merely dreamed of Prince Charming to find and rescue them, the princesses of the second wave still dream, but they do not primarily dream about love, at least in the beginning of the films, but about adventures, knowledge, and change (Clapp-Itnyre 10; Ross 56; Rothschild 74).

What is more, the movies of the second wave also start to offer a more inclusive notion of female beauty. In this context, a development can be observed within the movies of the second wave itself. While Ariel and Belle are both of Caucasian descent and sport bodies that are highly idealized and resemble those of pin-up girls or burlesque dancers (Bell 110, 114), the second wave eventually comes to encompass more diverse princesses: Mulan and

Pocahontas are of Chinese and Native American descent, respectively, thus widening the range of those who can become a princess. In addition, both young women are portrayed as athletic, active, and strong, so that their bodies and their movements do no longer resemble those of dancers but of sportswomen, symbolizing independence, activity, and strength (Do Rozario 46–47).[9]

Nevertheless, in the end, all of the second wave princesses still represent idealized and fetishized forms of feminine beauty. In spite of the fact that each is supposed to represent a different type of woman, they all share the same characteristics: they have long and lustrous hair, their faces are youthful with big eyes and small mouths, they are slender, and have a tiny waistline. In other words, the range has expanded to a little extent, but each princess is still "a paragon of her own type of beauty" (Rothschild 136). Furthermore, the purpose of the princesses' good looks remains the same as they mainly use it to secure male approval and find a suitable husband. In this regard, the second wave princesses do not differ from the princesses of the first wave at all; being adored by a handsome Prince Charming is still the ultimate goal of all Disney princesses.

What is more, just like their first wave predecessors, many of the female protagonists are accomplished when it comes to domestic matters. Even though domesticity has increasingly lost its function as an indicator of ideal femininity and does not play one of the most central roles anymore, it is still used to characterize the princesses as friendly, caring, and self-sacrificing characters (England, Descartes, and Collier-Meek 563). This is also highlighted through their connection to animals. In fact, most second wave princesses do not have only one, but rather a whole set of animal friends with distinct names and characteristics. While these help to establish the princesses as caring and friendly, they ultimately take away from the centrality of the female characters and thus support the marginalization of the princesses' stories. It is also noteworthy that all of the animal sidekicks, and most of the enchanted servants in the case of *Beauty and the Beast*, are male characters, so that, once again, female characters and their stories are marginalized whereas male characters and their adventures are put front and center.

Finally, the most important parallel is, of course, that just as the princesses of the first wave, all of the second wave princesses fall in love with a handsome, brave, and strong young man:

> The princess always won the love of the prince by the end of the Disney Princess films, and this portrayal of romance provides a strongly gendered message. The child viewer is provided with consistent exposure to the social script that one falls in love either very quickly, at first sight (*Snow White, Sleeping Beauty*), against all odds (*Beauty and the Beast, Mulan,* [...]), or both (*Cinderella, The Little Mermaid,* [...] *Pocahontas*) [England, Descartes, and Collier-Meek 565].

Both in the first and second wave movies, many of the princesses fall in love at first sight *and* against all odds. In this excerpt, Dawn England, Lara Descartes, and Melissa Collier-Meek also point out that the message behind portraying love in this stereotypical way can be harmful for a young audience if they watch these love stories time and again. Nevertheless, it is also visible that some kind of development has taken place, since two of the second wave princesses—Belle and Mulan—get to know their male love interest a little better before they actually fall in love with them. In other words, love at first sight is no longer the only option to depict how people fall in love with each other. Hence, the newer "princess movies show a more balanced portrayal of relationship formation" (565). Still, the central position that the topic of relationship formation occupies in these movies indicates how little has changed in the conceptualization of the princesses in particular and female characters in general within the realm of Disney princess movies.

As mentioned above, Merida is the first Disney princess whose story does not include a male love interest at all. In fact, the central conflict is established because Merida refuses to get married to one of the suitors her parents have chosen for her. This is not to say that it is only the lack of her involvement in a romantic relationship that renders Merida a feminist princess. *Brave* is not a movie that condemns romantic love *per se*, but rather portrays it in a more nuanced fashion. It includes, for instance, a positive example of a happy marriage in the form of Merida's parents King Fergus and Queen Elinor. Moreover, there are a number of scenes that underline that the princess does not oppose marriage in general. When she states that she is "not ready" for marriage, and asks the clan chiefs to allow their children to "find love in [their] own time" and "decide for themselves who they will love," she rather points out that she feels too young and wants to marry out of love and not because of political necessity. Being only 16 years old, and thus falling into the same age category as the rest of the princesses who are between 14 (Snow White) and 19 years of age (Cinderella), Merida offers a more realistic depiction of how a teenage girl might feel about getting married, especially to someone she does not know or love.

In this regard, *Brave* uses romance in a similar manner as the texts analyzed in the previous chapters, namely to challenge gender and genre conventions. While *Buffy the Vampire Slayer* includes romantic relationships to work against the notion perpetuated in horror movies that girls have to be punished for being sexually active, and the *Hunger Games* repurposes the YA love triangle to reflect upon Katniss' struggle for identity and the patriarchal society of Panem, *Brave* erases the romantic story arch in order to work against the genre specific norm set up in traditional fairy tales, namely that every princess needs a prince to live happily ever after. By having a princess end up happily without a Prince Charming by her side, the movie underscores the feminist idea that women and girls can be happy on their own and should not define themselves or their worth based on romantic relationships (cf. Vint 10). What is more, whereas in traditional princess movies, romantic love and weddings are used to symbolically reinstate patriarchal families and power systems, *Brave* refuses to support, idealize, or perpetuate such systems. Instead, it focuses on the princess, her quest, and the manner in which she changes tradition and subverts patriarchal power.

Merida's central status is clearly emphasized on a formal level through a variety of features and changes in narrative conventions. For instance, in contrast to many of its predecessors, *Brave* does not rely on techniques of narration that make use of hetero-diegetic voice-over. Instead, the voice of the princess herself can be heard loud and clear throughout the movie, both on the level of the story as well as on the level of narration, because she herself tells the story. This gives Merida a higher amount of agency in comparison to her predecessors, as she is the one who narrates, and ultimately shapes, her story and her life. In fact, *Brave* is not only different in the context of Disney princess movies, as it is the first installment that makes use of voice-over narration to enable the princess to tell her story in her own voice and with her own words, but it is also subversive on a more general level: as Lynda Haas observes, "an opening voice-over by a woman is unusual in mainstream cinema" and hence, *Brave* takes on an exceptional position both in the realm of Disney movies as well as with regard to mainstream cinema at large (198).

Interestingly, Merida's narration also renders the concept of agency the focal point of the movie, a feature that further asserts the feminist flavor of *Brave*. In the film, voice-over is used to a large extent to talk about fate and destiny and whether and how people can influence their lives. Being able to influence your own life and change your destiny is, according to Merida herself, not an easy task, as she states that "there are those who say fate is something beyond our command, that destiny is not our own. But I know better. Our fate lives within us. You only have to be brave enough to see it" (*Brave*). In her statement, the female protagonist emphasizes that being in command of your life and taking charge of it is a feat not everyone will accomplish, but she also refers to the title of the movie itself. What is made clear through Merida's comment is that, on the one hand, the title "Brave" refers to mental and physical strength in dangerous situations, features that Merida certainly possesses. On the other hand, her comment also points out that becoming independent and responsible, to be in command of your own life—in short, to achieve autonomy and agency, two concepts central to feminist thought and theory—also calls for a brave person.

Another formal element that is taken up and revised in *Brave* is the framing of the narrative and the introductory scene. Whereas, previously, Disney princess movies used the introductory scene to set up the dire situation in which the female protagonist is caught and/or to introduce the male love interest and the theme of romance, *Brave* uses this scene to introduce Merida and her family. The audience witnesses one of Merida's earlier birthdays, when she is out in the forest with her parents, plays hide and seek with her mother, and, most importantly, receives her first bow and arrow as a gift from her father, who also immediately starts to teach her how to shoot. By depicting a little princess who is fond of archery, the movie calls attention to its status as a subversive and revisionist tale and stages gender and genre transgressions as one of its main themes. In addition, it also foreshadows the conflict between Merida and her mother, as Elinor questions the appropriateness of the gift when she tells her husband that Merida "is a lady" (*Brave*). Moreover, *Brave* undermines genre conventions not only in its very first scene, but in its last scene, too. Instead of presenting a wedding as the ultimate happy ending, the movie has the suitors sail away and instead stages the restored relationship between princess and queen as the happy ending to this fairy tale.

Other formal features set *Brave* even further apart from its predecessors. It is, for instance, generally "darker and geared towards more mature audiences" than the average Disney princess film (Imondi). Indeed, the world of Princess Merida is not one that is filled with songs, animal friends, and fairy godmothers. On the contrary, as with the love story, *Brave* leaves out many of these stereotypical features of Disney princess films, hence defying both genre conventions and corresponding gender roles once again. For instance, *Brave* is the only Disney princess movie that cannot be described as a musical. In fact, there is not one song that is sung directly by the characters themselves. The film also changes or rather adapts the representation of the animal friend without completely erasing this feature. On the one hand, Merida's horse Angus plays a key role in the depiction of the princess as an adventurous and independent teenage girl. The Clydesdale—a race that is known for its size and strength—mirrors Merida's strength and energy and, at the same time, riding it affords her a wider range of freedom and mobility. On the other hand, however, he is not as significant as many of his predecessors, so that he does not take away from Merida's central role in the movie. In fact, he is used as a device to expand on the characterization of the princess and underline her hybrid gender identity, as her interactions with her horse demonstrate that she is both, brave and adventurous, ergo stereotypically masculine, and caring and nurturing, ergo stereotypically feminine.

Finally, *Brave* also charts new territory in the context of animated bodies. Merida sports a feminine body that challenges established conventions of Disney princess movies both with regard to her face and body type. Whereas *BtVS* and the *Hunger Games* feature female heroes with stereotypically feminine frames in order to subvert the notion that true heroes must be visibly strong, *Brave* features a princess who is not as hyper-feminine as her prede-cessors to show that such characters do not have to be slender, beautiful, and passive. The film consequently expands on the notion of who can be a princess as it opens up the realm of normative femininity to include a larger variety of body types, facial features, or hair styles and colors. When it comes to her face, for example, Merida stands in stark contrast to the rest of the Disney princesses because her eyes are not as huge, her mouth is not as tiny, and her features are not as "conventionally pretty" as those of the typical princess (Stephens 103). In other words, she is not idealized but looks "like a real girl, complete with the 'imperfections' that all people have" (A. Smith).

This observation also holds true for Merida's body. Once again, her por-trayal can be described as more realistic than that of other Disney princesses, as the proportions of her body are not overdrawn or hyper-sexualized (cf. A. Smith). However, even though the princess' body is neither hyper-feminine nor curvaceous, it is still clearly feminine. This is established through her size, long hair, and because she wears dresses, for instance. At the same time, Merida is also shown to be a warrior, as she is skilled with her bow and arrow and does not shy away from fighting physically, either. "The resulting char-acter is," as Bridget Whelan states, "not a 'hero in drag' but a new heroine […], a new kind of princess" (29). In a similar manner to Buffy and Katniss, Merida adheres to the model of the feminist quest heroine as she combines bodily features that connote femininity with physical abilities traditionally connected to masculinity and hence challenges binary notions of gender. The film imbues the image of the princess with new empowered meaning and consequently insists that princesses in particular and girls in general can be warriors, too.

In this context, the usage of costume also fulfills a subversive function. While Kelly Bean observes that in stereotypical princess movies, the elaborate and colorful gowns that each princess wears merely serve to "expose […] a hyper-idealized, highly sexualized form beneath" (55), Merida's clothes serve a very different purpose. Her outfit is not designed in a manner that presents her mainly as an object through emphasizing her feminine body and thus catering to the male gaze. Rather, her dress enables the princess to act as a subject, as it affords her a larger amount of mobility and freedom. Hers is not an elaborate, low-cut, and tight-fitting gown, but a simple dress held in a dark blue and sewn in a way that leaves room at her shoulders and elbows, allowing Merida to move around freely, to ride her horse, and to shoot her bow and arrow.

What is more, *Brave* draws a clear contrast between its protagonist's everyday clothes and general princess attire when Merida has to put on a more stereotypical—and more restrictive—gown before she meets her male suitors. This particular dress looks like a proper princess ball gown with silk fabric, golden elements, and a tight-fitting cut. Yet, it is immediately stressed that Merida feels restrained and uncomfortable, as she tells her mother that her dress is "too tight," and that she can neither breathe nor move (*Brave*). The restraining features of proper princess attire are further pronounced by the fact that Merida can only move around very slowly and gingerly. This conscious depiction of the confining features of princess attire certainly causes a comic effect. In addition, it also makes audiences aware that the dress serves as a symbol for the restrictiveness of idealized princesshood and of female beauty ideals in general, as the princess clearly struggles with the clothes that are supposed to show her off as a beautiful princess and future bride.

In addition to her face, body, and clothes, there is yet another important element regarding the innovative portrayal of Merida's looks and that is her hair. Indeed, when it comes to her outer appearance, Merida's hair has received special attention on two levels. First of all, the animators had to invent a new program to successfully portray the princess's curly red hair in a realistic and lifelike manner (cf. Lorditch). In this regard, Merida actually resembles many of her Disney predecessors, as "the princess has [...] always been rendered in the cinematic trends occurring at her original release" (Do Rozario 36). Interestingly, in addition to using this new technology to enhance the experience of the viewer, Disney also employs it to make a point about the character of the female protagonist, namely to highlight that she is a defiant and unruly character.

In this context, *Brave* can be regarded as subversive or even radical because it has its female protagonist work against and (literally) destroy gender restrictions time and again. Not only does she repeatedly pull out a lock of her curly hair that is supposed to be hidden underneath a white headdress, but, when she partakes in the archery contest, she takes off said headdress and lets her hair flow freely in the wind. This act contributes to her portrayal as a strong and independent girl to a large extent, as the princess's ginger curls mirror her fiery, wild, and untamed personality (Robertson 12, 16). In addition, Merida also destroys her princess gown when she rips it in order to be able to shoot her bow and arrow during said contest. This act of defiance works on two levels: First of all, Merida rebels against rules of gendered behavior in her society, namely that only men are allowed to compete for a woman's hand in marriage when she decides to enter the competition herself. Secondly, she also deconstructs associations between gendered behavior and gendered looks when she destroys her dress. In a similar manner to Buffy and Katniss, Merida openly stages her anger about the restrictions and limits which the norms of femininity, symbolized by her dress, put upon her. She does so both verbally, when she exclaims "curse this dress!" as well as physically by ripping the garment, shooting her arrows, and confronting her mother with an angry facial expression.

This fury and her resulting behavior have rather dire consequences, as they lead to a fight with her mother. Here, the movie once again draws attention to the fact that Merida lives in a patriarchal society in which the defiance of gender expectations is met with repercussions. After all, as a reaction to Merida's behavior and a form of punishment, Queen Elinor even burns her bow, the symbol of her gender transgressions. At the same time, however, *Brave* makes it clear that Merida's anger is justified as the shooting scene celebrates her behavior along with her archery skills, even filming the final shot in slow motion. While it hence makes aware that girls behaving in a defiant fashion might be punished, the movie still subverts the patriarchal discourse at work on the level of the narrative and asserts that girls should defend themselves against societal structures, gender norms, or traditions that confine them. This is yet another element that contributes to the feminist message established in *Brave*, as gender transgressions and the defiance of patriarchal power are celebrated and justified in this scene.

All in all, eliminating the romantic story arch, revising the princess' outer appearance along with a variety of other formal codes and plot conventions, and allowing Merida to narrate her own story enables the movie to focus on the princess herself and to stage her as a complex and self-determined character. *Brave* thus features an active and strong princess with a more realistic body and hence not only renders princesshood more inclusive and diverse, but also establishes a role model that encourages girls to have aims in life other than finding romantic love.

"I've decided to [...] break tradition": Merida's Heroic Journey

Just as every other feminist quest heroine, Merida first has to overcome obstacles, understand her own role and status within the system of power, and find allies in order to successfully bring down a patriarchal system. In this context, the manner in which the movie merges and consequently subverts and complicates conventions of fairy tales, myths, heroes, and princesses becomes apparent once again. As Campbell posits in *The Hero with a Thousand Faces*,

> [t]ypically, the hero of the fairy tale achieves a domestic, microcosmic triumph, and the hero of myth a world-historical, macrocosmic triumph. Whereas the former—the youngest or despised child who becomes the master of extraordinary powers—prevails over his personal oppressors, the latter brings back from his adventure the means for the regeneration of his society as a whole [38].

First of all, the use of the personal pronoun "he" alludes once again to the fact that in both fairy tale and myth, heroes are usually male. Having a female character, let alone a princess, take on this role hence undermines heroic conventions on its most basic level. Secondly, *Brave* also changes the type of triumph: while Merida does achieve a "domestic, microcosmic triumph" and "prevails over [her] personal oppressors" when she solves the problems with her mother, the fact that she changes the traditions of marriage at large can also be described as "a world-historical, macrocosmic triumph." This is especially noteworthy because by changing the rules of arranged marriage, Merida successfully subverts the patriarchal system at work in her society. This is a feat that no other Disney princess has accomplished before.

What is more, Merida is neither the youngest nor a despised child. As mentioned above, even though the princess fights with her mother, the latter still loves her daughter and only wants what is best for her. Nevertheless, in the beginning of the film, Merida is certainly not pleasant, obedient, or patient, but rather stubborn, defiant, and short-tempered. The princess rolls her eyes and groans during her lessons, she yells at Elinor during their fights, and deliberately ignores her mother's instruction not to "lose another arrow" when she takes part in the shooting contest (*Brave*). Whereas this behavior has been called out by Jaques to be an "egocentric" act of "infantilism" (161, 162), I suggest that it is an important means to challenge the conventions of both princesshood and girlhood perpetuated in Disney movies specifically and fairy tales at large. To be more precise, *Brave* subverts the idea that princesses "are not allowed any defects" (Stone 45), that they should, as Queen Elinor herself states, strive "for perfection" (*Brave*).

Merida's more unpleasant character traits are another fundamental aspect through which *Brave* establishes a new type of princess that challenges the very ideals of femininity usually perpetuated by such characters. After all, *Brave* justifies Merida's emotions and her behavior in the face of forced marriage at age sixteen and the other limits that behaving according to the scripts of traditional princesshood bring with them. The film thus counters the stereotype that teenage girls are silly, overly emotional, and dramatic and, in a similar manner to *BtVS* and the *Hunger Games*, establishes a feminist subtext by allowing its female protagonist to clearly voice her outrage about the patriarchal oppression she faces.

In marked contrast to Buffy and Katniss, however, Merida is not chosen by destiny, but she herself brings about the obstacles, or rather the problem that sends her on her heroic journey, when she turns her mother into a bear. Even though, admittedly, the princess does not know that this is exactly what will happen, she still tells the witch very clearly and emphatically that she wants "a spell to change [her] mum" because "that will change [her] fate" (*Brave*). By depicting Merida in this fashion, the movie succeeds in challenging another trope often found in Disney princess movies, which is the idea that princesses are innocent, victims of their circumstances, and therefore in need of rescue. Merida is neither innocent nor a victim of her circumstances, but fully responsible for causing problems in the first place. Still, she is not punished for her insistence to change her fate, but emerges as the heroine of the story because she successfully overcomes the obstacles and saves her mother. Thus, additional aspects are added to the concept of heroic princess-hood and girlhood established in *Brave*, namely the ability to take on and deal with problems and challenges instead of waiting for a Prince Charming to solve them.

Because of its focus on Merida and her mother, the film is also able to introduce the concept of sisterhood, an issue central to feminist thinking and feminist quest stories. It therefore once again echoes feminist discourses also established in *BtVS* and the *Hunger Games*, albeit on a much smaller scale, as this group exists of two women only. In a similar manner to Katniss, Buffy, and their respective allies, Merida and Elinor learn that in order to empower themselves, they have to work together, learn from each other, and support one another. Jack Zipes has noted that in traditional fairy tale movies, "there is no character development because the characters are stereotypes, arranged according to a credo of domestication of the imagination" (*Fairy Tale* 94). What is more, parallel to the lack of change in character, there is no change in the power system either (*Breaking the Magic Spell* 112). *Brave* undermines both of these assumptions by tracing and staging the character development of Merida and her mother as well as the personal, societal, and political changes these developments bring about.

At the onset of the film, Merida and her mother are both very set in their ways. At the same time that Elinor tries to impose a certain role onto her daughter, Merida longs for the moments when she does not "have to be a princess," that is, when she can escape the castle and her mother's lessons in proper princess behavior (*Brave*). Time and again, the movie emphasizes the differences between mother and daughter when it delineates that Elinor is all about rules and responsibilities, whereas her daughter tries to eschew both as often as possible. In addition, Merida stresses the fundamental differences she perceives between her and her mother when she yells at Elinor: "I'll never be like you! I'd rather *die* than be like you!" (*Brave*).

The respective roles the two occupy change, however, once Merida accidentally turns her mother into a bear and the two have to hide in the woods and come up with a plan to break the spell and turn Queen Elinor back into a human. Interestingly, during the adventure, the two learn from each other and become more similar to some extent. This is because Merida teaches her mother some of her skills and simultaneously learns to appreciate and make use of the skills which her mother has taught her. While the castle can be regarded as Elinor's terrain, both on the level of the domestic and the political sphere that are connected to it, Merida knows how to survive in the wilderness. Consequently, the princess is the one in charge in the woods as she takes over responsibility and provides food and shelter for her mother and herself. Here, Elinor gets to know a side of her daughter that is new to her: Merida shows herself to be in control, skilled, brave, and level-headed, features that make the queen trust her daughter and take her more seriously.

The movie stages their change in character and how this affects their relationship in a scene during which mother and daughter go fishing. Here, Merida shoots a fish with her bow and arrow and her mother initially applauds her daughter's skills. The princess, however, challenges Elinor and her opinions when she initially denies her the fish and states: "Oh wait, a princess should *not have* weapons, in *your* opinion" (*Brave*). Even though, at first, Elinor vigorously nods assent to this statement, she quickly realizes the fault in her logic, because it is, after all, Merida's weapon that allows her to feed the two. The queen furthermore changes her ideals regarding proper behavior when, instead of using a fork and knife, she devours the fish in a manner that is more bearish than human and therefore breaks her own rule that a princess or queen "does not stuff her gob" (*Brave*). Merida even teaches Elinor how to catch fish herself, thus taking on the role of instructor usually occupied by the latter. The effect of this is that Elinor adopts behaviors of Merida and hence not only becomes more like her daughter, but she also understands her, her dreams and behaviors much better, as she, too, comes to appreciate the freedom the world outside the castle offers. The changes in their characters and relationship are moreover emphasized when the two are shown to increasingly enjoy each other's company, splashing around in the water, and laughing together.

What is more, the changes Elinor in particular undergoes are alluded to when she leaves behind her crown, a marker of her royalty and old self, which she had so far worn even as a bear. Indeed, when she is turned into a bear, the queen initially tries to behave in the same manner as before and attempts to move with the elegance and grace of a queen. To an increasing extent, she is able to let go of her royal habitus and behave in a manner that is more unruly and less restricted by protocol. Ultimately, the fact that Elinor and Merida have grown closer and developed a more equal relationship is also reflected when the queen becomes human again. Whereas her conservatism, strictness, and willingness to abide by traditional rules were mirrored by the fact that she always looked perfectly styled, wearing beautiful gowns, her crown, and an intricate hairstyle that captured her long hair into a single straight braid, instead of returning to her former appearance, in the final scenes of the film, Elinor sports a hairstyle resembling that of her daughter, as she wears her hair loose and lets it flow freely in the wind, an image which clearly symbolizes that the queen has become more lenient with regard to (gender) rules and proper royal behavior.

Merida, on the other hand, realizes that she, too, has to change and that the skills her mother has tried to teach her are actually useful for her. Instead of changing completely, however, Merida's character and actions rather expand to include a larger variety of features. In other words, Merida maintains her old skills at the same time that she develops and becomes a more complex character who embodies aspects that connote both stereotypical femininity and masculinity. In this context, it is important to remark that even though Merida changes and loses some of her more rebellious character traits, she changes in a way that makes her and her family happier and not in order to become a suitable wife and future mother, as is the case with her second wave predecessors. Instead, Merida determines how to maintain her independence and agency without harming or hurting other people. More importantly, she learns to cooperate and work together with others to achieve her aims.

This is articulated in a climactic scene in the second half of the movie, when she asks the clan leaders to change their rules about marriage. The princess explains:

> I've been selfish. I tore a great rift in our kingdom. There's no one to blame but me. And I know now that I need to mend my mistake and mend our bond. And so, there is the matter of my betrothal. I've decided to do what's right. And, and, and break tradition. My mother, the Queen, feels in her heart that I … that *we* be free to write our own story, follow our hearts, and find love in our own time. The Queen and I put the decision to you, my lords. Might our young people decide for themselves who they will love?

In this speech, Merida shows off her skills in public speaking, takes on responsibility for her former behavior, and admits to the importance of traditions and political alliances, all of which are lessons and values that her mother has taught her. Here, the movie works against the narrative tradition found in the majority of Disney princess movies, namely that mature women or mothers do not act as positive or empowering role models. Elinor does act as a role model for her daughter, as it is she who taught Merida some of the central skills she needs to bring about a change in the power system. In fact, she even openly encourages Merida to subvert patriarchal power, when, during the princess' speech, she motions to her that she should ask for a break in tradition. Her mother's lessons and her support enable and encourage the princess to challenge the norms of her society by asking for a change of the rules. Noticeably, she does so not only for herself, but for "our young people," that is all of the heirs of the clans in general. This is an aspect which once again points to the feminist notion of sisterhood and the need of mutual empowerment perpetuated in *Brave*. The fact that Merida is successful in her request stresses that it takes both her old convictions and new insights to change the ancient rules.

In addition to demonstrating how joint action and mutual support can be instrumental in the fight against patriarchal rule, *Brave* also stresses Merida's status as the heroine of the story when, at the end of her heroic journey, she reverses the spell and saves her mother. Once again, the movie defies Disney conventions because it has its princess perform "the final rescue without the involvement of the prince" (England, Descartes, and Collier-Meek 565). Indeed, the act of saving, or rather the manner in which the conflict is solved, is highly unusual, because it rests on the ability to love and forgive rather than on the ability to slay a dragon, kill an evil witch, or share true love's first kiss, as is the case in other Disney princess movies. By contrast, Merida is told that she needs to "mend the bond, torn by pride." In other words, she has to re-establish the relationship with her mother. In the climactic finale of the movie, *Brave* first of all reveals its feminist streaks by showing that an act of true love between a daughter and her mother can be important and valuable, too, as it is Merida's declaration of love and her wish to get her mother back that breaks the spell. Therefore, this princess movie counters the notion that only true love's kiss between a princess and her prince, an act that symbolizes the perpetuation of heteronormative and patriarchal systems, can be regarded as a happy ending to a quest, a fairy tale, or even for girls' lives more generally.

However, the princess mends the bond not only on a metaphorical level, but on a literal one as well. When Merida rides to her mother's rescue after the clan chiefs have discovered Elinor, who is still a bear, in the castle and chased her into the woods in order to kill her, Merida uses needle and thread to repair the slash she cut into her mother's tapestry, thus literally "mending the bond, torn by pride." She hence makes use of skills that connote stereotypical femininity, namely stitching, and masculinity, that is horseback riding, in order to break the spell and save her mother. *Brave* consequently demonstrates that it is the combination of gendered skills that ultimately bring about the happy ending. It also highlights that Merida herself has overcome the internalization of patriarchal gender hierarchies, as she understands that the feminine skill of stitching can potentially be as valuable and important as the masculine skill of riding. *Brave* consequently denounces a patriarchal world view that regards hegemonic masculinity as superior to hegemonic femininity at the same time that it criticizes the Disney princess canon which perpetuates traditional and binary notions of gender and frequently promulgates a concept of femininity that renders women and girls as well as skills and behaviors connected to this gender role as unimportant and ineffectual.

In spite of these innovations, there is also still a fighting scene before the happy ending can be brought about. In this scene, however, it is not men who fight successfully, but the princess and the queen. First of all, Merida stops her father from killing Elinor, who is still a bear, when she shoots a sword out of Fergus' hand when he is just about to bring it down on Elinor's head. The princess then grabs a sword herself, tells her father that she will "not let [him] kill [her] mother," and engages in actual combat with him (*Brave*). In the same moment, another bear starts attacking the clansmen, namely Mor'du, the evil bear who once bit off Fergus' leg. The huge animal easily takes out the clansmen and then tries to kill Merida. When Elinor sees that her daughter is in danger, she comes to her rescue, fighting off Mor'du, who is ultimately killed when a heavy stone collapses onto him. In this scene, *Brave* makes a strong statement about motherly love, as Elinor leaps into action and stands up to an antagonist who is larger and stronger than she is in order to protect her daughter. While this is a trope often found in portrayals of mothers in general, in the context of a Disney princess movie, where mothers are usually absent or unimportant, this staging of Elinor's strength and protectiveness must be read as innovative and subversive. In the end, mother and daughter save each other through their love as well as their ability to physically protect one another. *Brave* once again celebrates traits and behaviors that connote stereotypical femininity and masculinity, respectively, giving a happy ending to a warrior princess who defies gender norms and rules of behavior perpetuated by former Disney princess films.

Conclusion

Even though *Brave* can be regarded as the most radically innovative movie when it comes to the portrayal of its princess and the inclusion of feminist thought and theory, the other Disney princess movies of the third wave, that is *Tangled, The Princess and the Frog, Frozen*, and *Moana*, challenge genre and gender conventions, too. There is, first of all, a general trend in princess movies of the third wave to represent more complete families. Tiana, for instance, is introduced as part of a nuclear family and after the early death of her father, her mother remains an important part of the young woman's life. Rapunzel, too, is able to return to a nuclear family once she has defied her evil stepmother, and although Anna's and Elsa's parents die at the beginning of the movie, family also plays a central role in *Frozen*, as it is the relationship between the two sisters that takes center stage in the film. Moana, too, has a family and even lives in a village whose whole community takes care of the girl. The interest in families, relationships between parents, children, and siblings results in the fact that the movies of the third wave deal with topics and problems with which many young viewers can identify.

Similarly, many third wave princess movies also reduce the importance of romantic love or even completely omit it, so that finding true love becomes "less of a prerogative and more of a secondary storyline" in the princess movies produced after the turn of the century (Stephens 101). Instead of dreaming of finding their prince, these princesses have dreams and ambitions outside of the realm of romance. More importantly, all of the princesses are allowed to achieve these dreams, so that they end up in a more powerful and/or prestigious position at the end of the movies. Noticeably, this change does not come about because they marry a man who elevates them, as was the case with the generations of princesses before them, but because they elevate themselves. Secondly, the representation of romance is also updated, and gender roles and expectations are revised and expanded. To different degrees, all of the third wave princesses are brave, independent, and capable of protecting and rescuing themselves and others, concepts which defy notions of traditional femininity. By contrast, the male love interests often take on roles that connote stereotypical femininity (England, Descartes, and Collier-Meek 563; Law 21; Lester, Sudia, and Sudia 95; Stephens 96, 100). As a result of these innovations, gender roles as well as traditional notions of prince- and princesshood respectively are challenged and negotiated, resulting in a new and more complex portrayal of both female and male characters.

Whereas the innovative features of third wave Disney princess movies reflect that more thorough revisions of princess characters have developed into a staple of the Disney Corporation, the creation and success of *Brave* specifically, not to mention Merida's inclusion into the *official* Disney princess canon, indicates that feminist rewritings and the model of the feminist quest heroine have reached the mainstream, too. After all, through the comparison to the princesses of the second wave in particular, I have shown that, previously, Disney's innovations usually worked on a superficial level only and still perpetuated conservative ideas that maintained traditional gender roles and patriarchal systems. Hence, Disney's creation of a warrior princess such as Merida, who questions notions of female passivity and helplessness and even defies patriarchal power clearly reflects that empowered teenage girls now permeate popular culture on every level. By extension, this also highlights that feminist conceptions of heroism embodied through the feminist quest heroine have successfully entered the mainstream as well since, after all, Merida is the product of a company that arguably represents mainstream American culture and values like no other. Ultimately, the inclusion of feminist discourses into a Disney princess movie demonstrates that feminist thought and theory have not only made it into the mainstream, but are even regarded as worth emulating and valuable.

II

Representations of Girl Warriors in Secondary and Tertiary Texts

◆ ◆ 4 ◆ ◆

Containing Feminist Potential

Girl Warriors in Promotional Paratexts

> Paratexts are not simply add-ons, spinoffs, and also-rans: they create texts, they manage them, and they fill them with many of the meanings that we associate with them.—Gray 6

Paratexts, that is, different types of media which surround, promote, summarize, or expand a given primary text such as a movie, a novel, or a TV show come in manifold forms. Book covers, posters and billboards, newspaper and magazine articles, promotional campaigns, advertisements, trailers, toys, videogames, interviews, or audience discussions belong to it,[1] yet represent merely a fraction of this type of genre (Fiske 118; Gray 4).[1] The sheer number and variety of paratexts already show that the culture industries invest a lot of time, money, and effort into producing these items, whose main function it is, at least at a first glance, to promote and sell products. At a time when immediate success of a movie or TV show is more important than ever, film companies spend at least a third of their budget, and frequently twice as much, on the production of promotional material, while TV networks pass up revenue they could get from selling ad time in order to promote their own shows (Gray 39, 7). With audiences consuming many more paratexts than primary texts, the first make up an important part of contemporary media landscapes, yet, paratexts have long been discarded as mere advertisements and neglected by scholars of media studies or popular culture in favor of analyzing primary texts exclusively (24).

Media scholar Jonathan Gray, however, insists that it would be shortsighted to think of paratexts in economic terms only and regard them as nothing more than money-making entities. He posits that paratexts should

114

be seen as meaning-making entities in their own right and studied as such since they are "often meticulously constructed by their producers in order to offer certain meanings and interpretations" (25). Indeed, paratexts play a central role in establishing a specific style, mood, or genre for the text they represent (49). Consequently, "paratexts often tell us how producers or distributors would prefer for us to interpret a text, which audience demographics they feel they are addressing, and how they want us to make sense of their characters and plots. In short, promos offer 'proper' and 'preferred' interpretations" (72). By establishing a genre, mood, or style, paratexts ultimately set up a frame of appropriate reading strategies and thus also heavily influence the manner in which audiences engage with a primary text (3, 36).

In order for the paratexts to successfully promote and sell a given primary text, they need to give prominence to aspects of said text that are seen as interesting or valuable by the respective audiences. This shows that the two features of paratexts, that is their status as money-making and meaning-making entities, cannot be analyzed separately, as both are inextricably linked and inform and influence each other. Indeed, the selection of genre, characters, mood, or style articulates what is regarded as valuable for, and thus marketable to, a given society. Therefore, paratexts indirectly also comment on and give a voice to a society's contemporary norms and ideals. In the context of this study, it is especially the gender norms and ideals as well as representations of female heroism that are of interest to me. Following the argument just made, just like their primary text counterparts, paratexts articulate and perpetuate the gender norms as well as conceptualizations of heroism of a specific historical moment (cf. Gray; D. Johnson 20).

Before I turn to the paratexts, it is important to briefly note that, in general, the culture industries and the primary texts they produce "[lean] toward genres and markets industrially aimed toward boys and men" (D. Johnson 20). Indeed, there remains a "persistent [...] belief that films featuring women do worse at the box office" (Hickey).[2] Numerous critics have commented on the fact that girls and women are regarded as less important or less valuable when it comes to their representation in primary texts, both on a quantitative and qualitative level (Cart; Geraghty 196; Lauzen; Smith et al.; Wilson). This gender hierarchy found in the primary texts can also be observed with regard to the paratexts. As industry insiders explain, paratexts focus on men and boys specifically because it is widely believed that "women will go to a 'guy's movie' more easily than guys will go to a 'woman's movie'" (Hickey). These gender notions first of all perpetuate the patriarchal myth that, on the one hand, men are put off by anything feminine, but that, on the other hand, women enjoy and value anything masculine, and, as a result, re-establish gendered hierarchies time and again. Secondly, they also reiterate traditional gender roles which suggest that women are willing to sacrifice their own interests to please their male partners. All in all, the assumption that it is men and boys who are the decision makers and are therefore the demographic that needs to be convinced to consume a cultural product ultimately renders them the primary target audience for promotional paratexts and also heavily influences the kinds of genres and gender norms included in such media.

The texts analyzed in this book deviate from said norms of contemporary popular culture in fundamental ways. First of all, they do feature women, or, to be more precise, teenage girls as protagonists. Second, as delineated in the first three chapters, Buffy, Katniss, and Merida are not represented in a stereotypical manner, but challenge traditional gender roles, binary notions of gender, and patriarchal gender hierarchies in a variety of different ways, and can even be called feminist role models. The heroines' feminist potential lies in the very complexity of their characters that defies heroic archetypes along with binary and one-dimensional portrayals of women and girls so often found in other popular culture texts. In addition, the character traits and behaviors connected to stereotypical femininity prove to be as important for the success of their quests as do the ones connected to stereotypical masculinity, so that both genders are presented as equally valuable and potentially heroic. Third, the texts are not produced primarily for male audiences. One could rather describe them as four-quadrant texts, a term that is usually used for movies that "[appeal] to all four of the primary target markets [...]: women under 25, women over 25, men under 25, men over 25," but which can also be applied to TV shows such as *BtVS*, or novels such as the *Hunger Games* trilogy (Kroon 295). The paratexts surrounding these media could thus be unusual as well, since they promote characters and narratives that subvert many of the gender discourses established by the majority of other popular culture texts.

However, the analysis of the paratexts will show that the feminist values promoted by the heroines themselves are not deemed valuable enough to be used in the promotion of the primary texts. In other words, the paratexts show that more complex female characters and feminist ideas are still not deemed interesting and valuable enough the be used to sell the products to a mainstream, that is a male heterosexual, audience. Instead, as I argue in this chapter, much of the promotional material surrounding *BtVS*, *Brave*, and the *Hunger Games* embeds the primary texts and the female heroes into simplified and binary gender discourses and thus reproduces a patriarchal world view that regards masculinity as more valuable than femininity. In the paratexts, masculine and feminine attributes are separated from each other again so that the heroines are turned into one-dimensional characters that resemble the very archetypes and gendered stereotypes they subvert in the primary texts. What is more, a gender hierarchy is established because the features of the heroines that connote masculinity, such as action or physical violence, are used to promote the texts much more frequently than are the ones that connote femininity. The latter, in fact, only comes prominently into play when the heroines are portrayed as sex objects, a gender representation which strips femininity of the empowered potential it is given in the primary text. This return to heroic archetypes and the promotion of themes thought to appeal to a heterosexual male audience demonstrates that the intended audiences for both the paratexts and the primary ones are men, as they are supposedly interested in these issues.[3]

In this chapter, I look at two types of paratexts, namely promotional material such as trailers and posters and licensed merchandise and toys. In each subchapter, I deal with one heroine separately, starting with an analysis of trailers, promos, or posters, and concentrating on the portrayal of gender, heroism, and genre. These paratexts first of all indicate which genres, characters, or other elements of the respective primary text are deemed important or interesting enough to be represented to a mainstream audience. In addition, they also highlight which gender roles and performances are deemed valuable and marketable. I then turn to licensed toys and merchandise, commodities which are usually heavily gendered and frequently reinforce traditional gender roles and performances by enabling certain types of play and rejecting or prohibiting others (D. Johnson 58; Gray 183–84).

Buffy the Vampire Slayer *and Its Paratexts: "A story of blood and sex"*

The tendency to represent the primary text in a manner that appeals to male audiences and to thus marginalize women and girls as target groups can be found in much of the promotional material for *BtVS*. At a first glance, this is quite surprising because the late 1990s and early 2000s are often labeled the high time of Girl Power, a period during which teenage girls became "the most prized segment of the demographic" and many cultural products were produced specifically for them (Murray 44, 45). At the same, however, teenage girls were, and notably still are, also described as consumers that do not need to be convinced to consume a cultural product. Journalist Lynn Hirschberg, for instance, points out that it is believed by those who work in the culture industries that teenage girls "will pretty much see or watch anything" and that they "flock to almost anything that centers on boys and love and high school." The "industry logic [which] assumes that boys are less interested in hour-long dramas such as *Buffy*" and therefore need to be convinced to watch the show through promotional material ultimately led to marketing strategies that frequently deny the show its feminist potential, and instead appropriate aspects thought to appeal to a (heterosexual) male audience (Murray 44).

The network could thus reach a broader spectrum of the demographic and make the show more attractive for advertisers, for instance.

Whereas today, Buffy is hailed as a feminist role model and the show as an example of quality TV, the paratexts which promoted *BtVS* when it first aired worked in the exact opposite direction. In fact, they mainly functioned as "vital mediators for the niche or fan property to a wider audience," as it was their aim to make the show appear more mainstream in order for it to attract a larger audience (Gray 17). This was achieved, for instance, through a simplification and normalization of the show in its paratexts. While it is true, that, in general, paratexts need to simplify the texts they promote to a certain degree, in this case, it was a simplification that worked in the interest of male audiences, as the style of the promos catered to their interests.

Promotional clips which were shown during the series on air in the time slot before *BtVS*, for example, stage the show as almost exclusively concerned with horror, monsters, fighting, and death. In a clip for season two, it is called "the ultimate show for the ultimate scare" (SunnydaleArchives, "Season 2 Promos 1/2"). The promotional clips furthermore feature tropes of the horror genre such as screaming girls and "deadly," "horrible" monsters. They describe the plot as "the ultimate terror" and the setting of the series as "a world of evil where anyone can turn on you," "a world where terror knows no limit," and where "there's evil wherever you turn" ("Season 1"). On the one hand, *BtVS* certainly contains these elements of horror. On the other hand, however, as I briefly delineated in Chapter 1, it mainly uses the familiar tropes in order to undermine the very conventions of the horror genre, especially in the context of gender role portrayals. It is hence noteworthy that the traditional elements that speak to a male audience rather than the subversive elements that establish a feminist subtext are used in the promotional clips, as this choice reflects that the first are deemed more marketable than the latter.

This focus on the genre of horror is also reflected by the fact that the promos mainly present the so-called "monster of the week." While this presentation of the respective antagonist in the weekly installments of the promos makes sense as they tease which monster, demon, or vampire Buffy will have to slay in the next episode, it is still conspicuous that other central aspects, namely those thought to draw a female audience, have almost completely been left out in these short clips (cf. promos seasons 1 to 5). Those are, for example, the romantic elements, the interpersonal relationships, or aspects of high school life, all features of *BtVS* and its unique portrayal of heroism for which the show was also well-known and praised by critics and fans alike. Even though, admittedly, these themes are developed in the series over time and not as easily incorporated into the weekly clips as the newest monster and fighting scenes, it is still striking that, for instance, if the promos show Angel at all, they do so only very briefly and not as the heroine's love interest, let alone as her first great love. In a similar fashion, the clips incorporate Willow or Xander only more prominently when they themselves are directly involved with the respective monster or demon of the week, whereas the friendship between the Scoobies hardly plays a role.

This simplified representation of *BtVS* and its notion of female heroism becomes even more obvious when looking at the promos that aired when the show moved to another network, UPN, in 2001 and the tone of the promos changed fundamentally. Whereas The WB was known as a network for teenagers in general, and teenage girls in particular, UPN's audience comprised an older and largely male audience (Hirschberg; Jensen 64). Thus, the acquisition of *BtVS* was seen as a move to "lure women to its mostly male airwaves," as it stood in stark contrast to the wrestling shows and sci-fi series usually found on this network (Jensen 64). Whereas The WB needed to attract male audiences, and did so by staging *BtVS* as a horror show packed with death and danger, the promotional clips for seasons six and seven are more gender neutral, focusing on the campy elements, witty dialogues, comedic aspects, and personal lives of the different characters (SunnydaleArchives).

This change in tone can also be found in the choice of quotes from critics, which are occasionally fed into the clips. The promos for season one to five quote statements by critics who praise the mainstream appeal of *BtVS* and simplify its genre and plot ("Season 1"). In contrast to this, an early UPN promo chooses a blurb that describes the show as a "kick-ass fantasy action gothic romance pulp horror sex comedy chick-flick existentialist musical coming-of-age drama" ("Season 7 Promos 1/2"). This choice of blurb shows that by the time it moved to a new network, *BtVS* had established itself as a household name that did not need to be simplified and mainstreamed to the same extent as it did in the first seasons. At the same time, the genres that are mentioned in the blurb supposedly appeal to men *and* women, respectively, and can thus be said to be gender neutral or gender inclusive. Still, none of the promos include comments by critics that refer to the feminist aspects of *BtVS*, praise the heroine as an empowering role model for girls and young women, or even simply comment on the protagonist's innovative and subversive role within the contemporary TV landscape, even though those certainly existed at the time of production (cf. Bellafante and McDowell; Moy; Ventura). This omission of the feminist discourse as part of the marketing strategies reflects a general uneasiness with feminism in U.S. culture at large, as it demonstrates that the feminist message of the show was not deemed useful as a marketing tool.

The same tendencies observed in the clips can also be found in promotional photographs published by The WB. There exist some images in which Buffy is dressed in a leather jacket or long pants, but the majority of promotional photographs represent her in a similar manner to the example repro-

Promotional image for *BtVS* Season 2 featuring the main cast including Buffy, the Scoobies, Watcher Rupert Giles, and love interest Angel.

duced here. In this promo image for season two, Buffy is positioned in the middle of the group, framed by Willow and Cordelia who are in turn framed by the male cast (*"Buffy the Vampire Slayer* Poster"). On the one hand, Buffy's central position within the image clearly accentuates her role as the protagonist. On the other hand, however, she is even more skimpily dressed than she usually is on the show, wearing a top with straps that are hardly visible and a mini-skirt with a slit that goes up to the top of her thigh. Similar to

Cordelia, who is wearing a low-cut top and turns to the side so as to display the curves of her breasts, Buffy also positions her leg in a manner that underlines the length of the slit and prominently displays her upper thigh. Whereas on the show, Buffy's strength is, in fact, highlighted through her clothes and she is physically active in every episode, in the promotional images, she is frozen and objectified, posing for people, or, to be more precise, heterosexual boys and men, to gaze at her body on display. This is also emphasized by the lack of any weapon which would symbolize her physical prowess and ability to fight. Since this is a promotional picture supposed to attract audiences that are not regular watchers yet, and therefore not familiar with Buffy's role on the show, downplaying Buffy's physical power in favor of displaying her bodily assets is even more striking and calls attention to the fact that, in a promotional context, her beauty is deemed more instrumental in attracting viewers than are her Slayer powers or her status as a heroine.

Whereas the promotional clips and photographs present *BtVS* as a horror show that features attractive girls in order to draw in a male audience, the merchandise articles target female consumers to a larger extent than male ones. As Josh Stenger describes, merchandised products, especially for teenage girls, could be spun off the show relatively easily because it "repeatedly affirm[ed] consumerism, especially in the realm of fashion" (28). The mentioning of fashion as one important part of merchandised commodities already points out that many of the items perpetuate more traditional gender roles or suggest stereotypical gender performances. Even though there also exist a plethora of merchandise that could be regarded as gender neutral— such as stationary, watches, mugs, or backpacks—clothing items, jewelry, and other accessories still make up a large portion of the products on offer. Necklaces, tank tops, or baby-T's which tightly hug the wearer's body and/or reveal a lot of skin enforce a concept of femininity which aims at presenting the female body as an object for the male gaze or at least as being concerned with one's outer appearance and attractiveness.

In fact, the clothes on offer for the female fans of *BtVS* strongly resemble the very items of fashion which Buffy and Cordelia wear in the promotional photographs, thus inviting girls to present themselves in the same objectified manner as the two actresses. This discourse that emphasizes the importance of outer appearance and female beauty is furthermore affirmed through commodities such as make-up and cosmetics, which became an important part of the show's merchandise not least because Sarah Michelle Gellar was hired as a spokesperson for Maybelline cosmetics (Murray 47). Taken together, the paratexts and merchandise items surrounding *BtVS* follow a binary approach to gender that stands in direct contrast to the gender notions perpetuated in the series itself. The paratexts hence conceal the feminist agenda of the show and deny Buffy's subversive potential.

The Revolution Will Be Merchandised: Paratexts and the Hunger Games

To the same extent that *BtVS* revolutionized the genre of horror, the *Hunger Games* trilogy sets itself apart from previous YA (dystopian) fiction because it features a female protagonist as a heroine. Once again, however, this innovative aspect is not openly addressed by the marketing and promotion campaigns surrounding the novels, demonstrating that such heroines are neither thought to be a selling factor for a wider audience, nor for a niche audience. In fact, whereas the *BtVS* promotion relies on representing its female protagonist, albeit in a sexualized manner, Katniss is hardly anywhere to be found in the promotional material. The marketing campaign for the trilogy addresses a wide variety of possible readers through the focus on a similar variety of topics and themes of the novels; Katniss' role as an innovative heroine, however, is not explicitly mentioned.

In this context, it is important to keep in mind that the marketing of books is fundamentally different from the marketing of other media, because reading a book takes much more time than listening to a song or watching a movie. As Laura Miller explains, it is "essential to grasp the central, maddening paradox that confronts all book marketers [...]: The only thing that reliably sells books is word of mouth, preferably a personal recommendation from a trusted friend" ("Making of"). What is more, it is very hard for books targeting children and young adults to become successful outside of this specific market, because they are separated from other novels on a number of levels. Not only are they sold in different stores or put into separate sections in libraries, but they are also reviewed in publications that specialize in children's and YA fiction ("Making of").

Even though they belong to the genre of YA fiction, from the beginning, the *Hunger Games* aimed at, and ultimately succeeded in, targeting a crossover audience (Dodes and Jurgensen D4). In order to break out of the YA market and attract as many readers as possible, the promotional campaign for the novels addressed a wide variety of potential readers. It did so by publishing promotional material that made use of references to familiar tropes, other successful YA novels, and used blurbs made by well-known and successful authors. The marketers hence drew on the idea that it needs a good friend or person one can trust for people to buy a book only that, in the promotional campaign, actual friends and acquaintances were replaced with popular authors and well-known novels.

The reliance of the marketing campaign on the familiar rather than the innovative first of all results in the fact that one of the most innovative aspects, namely the female protagonist, is relegated to the margins of the campaign. Secondly, this marginalization also reiterates the traditional gender role conceptions that can be found in many other successful YA novels or which are represented by the authors quoted in the campaign. Stephen King, for example, an author who supposedly targets adult audiences and those interested in horror and science-fiction, is quoted on the very top of three of the four pieces of promotional material published by Scholastic, reflecting the value given to the adult men among the potential readership of the trilogy ("Scholastic Publishes *The Hunger Games*"; "Scholastic Publishes *Catching Fire*"; "Critical Praise for *The Hunger Games*"). This is furthermore underlined by the quotes themselves, in which King emphasizes the quality of the writing and the author, whom he describes as a "no-nonsense prose stylist," as well as by his characterization of *The Hunger Games* as a "violent, jarring, speed-rap of a novel that creates nearly constant suspense" ("Critical Praise for *The Hunger Games*"). The quotation by Stephen King is then followed by one from Stephenie Meyer, author of the *Twilight* series, whose praise for the novels is supposed to lure fans of Meyer herself, that is, women and girls interested in romance. As a third major group, the promotional material also quotes professionals from the field of YA fiction, "reminding the wider network that leaders in their field were loving the books" (L. Miller, "Making of").

Through these attempts to simultaneously address and attract a wide variety of potential readers, the promotional material establishes an ambivalent relationship to the female readers and aspects of the novels, such as romantic relationships, that are thought to appeal to women and girls more than to men and boys. On the one hand, quoting Stephenie Meyer and comparing the novels to *Twilight* aims at luring a female readership with the promise of romance and love triangles. Notably, in the quotes that address the love triangle, it appears to be a much larger part of the story than it actually is. On the other hand, and quite paradoxically, in an attempt not to scare off male readers, these aspects of the novels are also played down time and again, and readers of *Twilight* in particular, and romance stories at large, are indirectly devalued through other quotations that question the quality of Meyer's work, such as "who needs vampires?" or "forget Edward and Jacob" ("Critical Praise for *Catching Fire*"). Indeed, the overall impression of the novels that the promotional material communicates is that they do incorporate romantic relationships, but that *in spite* of these, they are still worth reading, as they are of high quality, interesting, and action-packed. Hence, the promos indirectly communicate the idea that traditional femininity and genres that appeal to women and teenage girls are less interesting and valuable and thus re-establish a genre and gender hierarchy that gives value to the masculine aspects of the novels and traditional masculinity in general. Notably, by imposing a binary gender conception through the discourse established in the promotional material, the campaign fails to address one of the central elements of the novels, namely the hybrid gender role conceptions and the importance that is attributed to *both* traditional femininity and masculinity in the context of Katniss' particular type of heroism.

The complicated relationship marketers had to Katniss Everdeen as the protagonist of the trilogy is also reflected in the cover designs. Indeed, the difficulties in finding a suitable image to be printed on the cover of the novels has been described by critics as a "conundrum for Scholastic" (L. Miller, "Making of"), which "considered dozens of cover designs, including portraits of Katniss, before settling on a more 'iconic' image of a bird pendant that plays a role in the story" (Dodes and Jurgensen D4). The decision to use the Mockingjay pin, and hence a *symbol* of the female protagonist instead of an actual image of the teenage girl herself, speaks strongly of the reluctance to represent Katniss, and thus a female protagonist, on the cover of a YA novel. Indeed, the erasure of Katniss goes even further than in other YA novels with a female protagonist. Whereas *Twilight*, for example, in a similar manner to the *Hunger Games*, did initially not feature images of Bella on its covers, opting for symbols such as an apple, a flower, or a chess piece, it did feature the actress and actors of the movies on the covers of the movie tie-in versions. In marked contrast to this, and to the majority of movie tie-ins in general, the tie-in versions of the *Hunger Games* movie series present Jennifer Lawrence as Katniss merely on one cover, namely that of *Catching Fire*, opting again for the Mockingjay symbol for the other two covers. This repeated marginalization of the female protagonist in favor of a more gender neutral icon not only reflects a certain amount of uneasiness with Katniss' image—or the image of a female hero in general—but also speaks strongly of the value that marketers attribute to male readers, who might be turned away by a book which overtly stages its female protagonist on the cover.[4]

When it comes to the promotion of the movie adaptations, a similar concern for male audiences can be found both in statements by journalists and the marketers themselves, as well as in the movie trailers and posters. *Wall Street Journal*'s Rachel Dodes and John Jurgensen, for instance, observe that "Lionsgate has been picking its way through a minefield of gender issues: reeling in male movie-goers without alienating core female fans" (D4). Notably, this minefield was established because many male fans of the trilogy "expressed concern that Lionsgate would try to turn the films into another soapy *Twilight* love triangle" (Graser). As a consequence of this concern for male audiences, instead of "playing up the love triangle," the marketing team consciously avoided tapping into this discourse (Karpel). In fact, and in a similar manner to the erasure of Katniss on the book covers, the promotional team took measures to erase the love triangle on all levels of the marketing campaign, even taking steps "not to show Lawrence, Hutcherson and Hemsworth together in posters, magazine covers or even at events" (Graser).

Here, two discourses surrounding gender and the consumption of media are visible again. First of all, it is the notion that, in contrast to women and girls, men and boys do usually not consume media that are not explicitly promoted to them, which is why they are more explicitly addressed in many paratexts. Secondly, the marketing strategies also reinforce the idea that female fans and genres such as *Twilight* are regarded as less valuable than male-centered films and fandoms, since critics also observed that "guys could be turned off by the perception that female cult fandom has sprung up around the movie, reinforced by the boisterous crowds—predominantly girls—that have gathered at malls where 'Hunger Games' cast members have appeared on a promotional tour" (Dodes and Jurgensen D4). In comparison, no similar concerns were voiced about female fans who could be "turned off" by male ones, a fact that highlights the gender hierarchies at work in the culture industries.

Even though it is still male-centered, the marketing campaign for the movies shows some positive developments when it comes to its portrayal of Katniss. For instance, in comparison to *BtVS*, the promotional material does not disempower, sexualize, and objectify its heroine as did the paratexts surrounding the TV show. Moreover, they do not marginalize Katniss to the same extent as the ones for the novels described above. Still, traces of the promotional strategies of the novel trilogy can be found in the material for the movies, as well. After all, the readers of the trilogy were among the most important addressees of the campaign and consequently, familiar images such as the Mockingjay are heavily used in order to connect the movie adaptations to their literary predecessors. Yet, instead of using the Mockingjay to replace Katniss, it is strategically combined with images of the female protagonist in order to draw attention to her and create a narrative about her empowerment.

In so-called teaser posters, for instance—that is, posters that were published at the beginning of each campaign—the Mockingjay is presented in a manner that creates a story of breaking free from constrains: while it is framed by a circle in the posters for the first three movies, it is depicted with an arrow in the first one, spreading its wings in the third, and ultimately breaking out of its confinement in the fourth and final poster. Since it is the most prominent visual sign in the marketing campaign of the novels, making use of the Mockingjay pin in the context of the movie adaptations makes sense as it allows marketers to draw a strong connection between the novels and the movies and to consequently attract audiences who are already familiar with the imagery of the *Hunger Games*. However, for each of these teaser posters, there also exists a final movie poster that features Katniss Everdeen herself ("*Hunger Games* Poster [#24 of 28]"; "*Catching Fire* Poster [#32 of 33]"; "*Mockingjay—Part 1* Poster [#24 of 25]"; "*Mockingjay—Part 2* Poster [#21 of 29]"):

First of all, that it is the Mockingjay that is used in the *teaser* only, but Katniss herself who is used in the final posters as the "key image" "every successful campaign builds [up] to" points to her overall importance within the campaign (Graser). While she is placed behind the Mockingjay pin in the poster for *The Hunger Games*, which again demonstrates the marketers' attempts to connect the movies to the novels through the visual imagery used in the promotion of the latter, in the rest of the posters, she is put in front of the Mockingjay sign and thus takes on the most central position in the frame. The fact that it is Katniss alone who is represented in the official movie posters reflects Lionsgate's reliance on her as the central character in the promotional material and, by extension, also the willingness to communicate and celebrate that it is a *female* protagonist who takes on the central role in the movies.

Indeed, the posters also underline her defiant character by having her look directly into the camera and project her fighting skills by presenting her in fighting gear—instead of, for example, her elaborate interview dresses— and with her iconic weapon, a bow and arrow ready to fire. This particular visual portrayal of Katniss creates a more complex notion of female power as did, for instance, the promotional posters for *BtVS*. Even though Katniss' body is visibly feminine, the posters also represent her ability to fight and stage her as an active character instead of a passive object for the male gaze. While it still relies on hegemonic notions of feminine beauty, the depiction of her body in the posters complicates binary conceptions of gender to some extent and hence takes up the discourses about gender and heroism already voiced in the novels.

At the same time, Katniss' body is still used to attract male audiences. After all, even though she is not overtly sexualized in these images, each poster still zooms further away from her body, allowing audiences to see more and more of her feminine frame. And even though she is fully clothed in protective gear and sports a weapon, the posture of her body highlights her feminine curves so that (male heterosexual) audiences are assured that this movie will not only be full of action, as symbolized by her weapon, but also sport an attractive female protagonist. Moreover, the posters also suggest that the film adaptations belong to the genre of action movies, thus connecting them to a type of film thought to be interesting for a male viewership. As Gray states, among other functions, movie posters "play a key role in outlining a [film's] genre," and the genre alluded to in these posters is largely that of an action movie (52). After all, representing Katniss as the lone hero "looking

Opposite: Movie posters for *The Hunger Games* adaptations featuring actress Jennifer Lawrence as Katniss Everdeen. Taken together, they tell a story of empowerment and freedom.

steely-eyed and ready for action, with weapons on hand and/or muscles bulging" clearly imitates posters that advertise action films (53).

What is more, the posters also bring to mind traditional quest stories because, taken together, they create a narrative concerned with growing freedom and personal empowerment. The images suggest that, to the same extent that the Mockingjay breaks free from the circle in which it is constrained, Katniss breaks free from the role as a tribute and a victim, empowering herself and, notably, merging with the image of the Mockingjay, which lends her its wings in the final two posters. The posters represent Katniss according to the conventions of the lonely male hero who fights to empower himself so that her character traits and her heroic journey are simplified to exude masculinity. Through the simplification of both the female protagonist's complex character traits and her narrative, a quest story which originally includes a number of aspects that can be read as feminist is re-embedded into a discourse that harks back to archetypes that, even though they present the heroine as powerful, deny her the more complex and innovative aspects of her personality established in the novels.

The majority of the other posters produced in the context of the campaign portray Katniss in a very similarly empowered manner than the one just described. Notably, by leaving out Katniss' struggle for agency and the conflicts that go on behind the scenes, which are central elements that contribute to the feminist message of the novels, the campaign succeeds in establishing Katniss as a character that resembles traditional heroic archetypes rather than a teenage girl struggling with her role within the rebellion. While admittedly, it is hard to imagine how her hesitation or struggle could be incorporated in a poster or poster series, the overwhelming amount of material that presents her as fearless, independent, and confident is still striking and underlines the campaign's aim to establish Katniss as a more archetypical heroic character, representing her as a powerful and determined leader around which the rebels, and by extension the movie audiences, can rally. This demonstrates that heroines who possess features that connote hegemonic masculinity to a larger degree than ones that connote hegemonic femininity are seen as more attractive and marketable than those that present a more equal mixture of gendered character traits and can hence be connected to the model of the feminist quest heroine.

This staging of the movie adaptations as stories filled with action and rebellion is also taken up in the numerous trailers. Generally more complex than posters, trailers are among the most important paratexts from a marketer's point of view, since they are highly influential tools in convincing audiences to see a film in a movie theater (Gray 49). Indeed, they are not only an "important part of the cinema-going experience," but have also found their way into private homes via the Internet (50). Many of the *Hunger Games* movie trailers, for instance, were also published online via YouTube, becoming part of the hype surrounding the release of the films with users posting reaction videos, slow-motion versions, and analyses of the trailers online. In a similar manner to posters, trailers advertise a product, "but they are also a taste test of films to come, offering some of a film's first pleasures, meanings, and ideas," and "may [even] dictate how to read a text" (50, 51). Indeed, they can be seen as part of the film's narrative or a summary thereof, a summary that, again, discloses that film's genre and gives prominence to the most important discourses at work in the movie (51).

Notably, in the case of the *Hunger Games* movies, the trailers are actually not much more complex than the posters analyzed above, because they largely introduce additional characters and themes that contribute further to the conceptualization of the films as action-driven. However, in doing so, the trailers do not distort the central elements of the movie adaptations. On the contrary, following the contemporary Hollywood blockbuster trend, the adaptations have, in fact, turned their source material into films that can be categorized as action movies. This in itself demonstrates the culture industries' reliance on narratives and genres that cater to male audiences. That the trailers focus on and enforce these aspects supports this claim only further. Indeed, the official movie trailers focus on and thus emphasize the elements that connote action, rebellion, and war, underlining that the adaptations are action movies or even war movies, in the case of *Mockingjay* Parts One and Two (Lionsgate Movies trailers; The Hunger Games trailers). The additional themes that are introduced via the trailers are, for instance, the conflict between Katniss and Snow, who are not only portrayed as the main antagonists, but as two power players as well, when, in the novels, it actually takes Katniss a long time to understand the power system at work in Panem. Again, Katniss is depicted as a powerful leader of the revolution and an accomplished archer: there are scenes which show her shooting her bow and arrow in virtually every trailer. Another focus lies on the rebels and their actions, offering audiences a group of people with whom they can identify (The Hunger Games, "*Mockingjay* Part 1"; "*Mockingjay* Part 2—'We March';" "*Mockingjay* Part 2—'Welcome'").

What is more, even though the *movies* do focus on the action sequences and violent themes found in the novels, they also still include elements such as Katniss' struggle for agency, her love for her family, or the love triangle with Peeta and Gale, parts of the narrative thought to appeal to female audiences. However, these "feminine" aspects have found their way into the *trailers* only on a marginal level or not at all. The romantic storyline, for instance, is almost completely left out, with merely one short kissing scene portrayed in the first trailer for *Catching Fire* (Lionsgate Movies, "Official Trailer #1"). Once again, the trailers reflect that, for the movie industries, male audiences are the more valuable ones. Whereas Dodes and Jurgensen describe the discourses at work in the trailers as "gender neutral" (D4), the repeated representations of war, fighting, conflicts, and weapons can rather be said to give prominence to issues connected to hegemonic masculinity and thus made to appeal to male audiences first and foremost.

At the same time, however, the novel adaptations do deviate from the general blockbuster norm, as they feature a female protagonist and not a male one. Indeed, that Katniss would be positioned at the heart of the films' narrative was already established in the very first sneak peek that was shown during the MTV Video Music Awards in 2011, which introduced her, and her alone, to the teenage audience. In this short clip, the focus lies explicitly on Katniss, the audience sees only her while she is hunting in the woods and later in the arena. The clip is accompanied by a voice-over from Gale, who tells Katniss that she is stronger than her competitors and encourages her to "show'em how good" she is (Lionsgate Movies, "VMA"). On the one hand, the teaser addresses male teenagers more specifically, as it introduces the violent themes of the movies by establishing Katniss as an accomplished fighter who stands a good chance at winning the Games. Additionally, the focus on hunting and the weapons also again allude to genre conventions found in action and adventure movies. At the same time, however, the break with conventions when it comes to the gender of the action hero, and the focus on Katniss exclusively, can also be seen as innovative both on the level of the primary text and the paratext. Whereas in the past, movie producers doubted that "any actress [can] carry a film" (Geraghty 196), the focus on Katniss/Jennifer Lawrence once again articulates the marketing team's belief in the female protagonist's ability to attract audiences and carry the movies by herself.

Besides the male teenage audience just mentioned, another demographic that was explicitly targeted by the marketers was that of people over the age of 25. Especially in the trailer for the first movie, the marketing team aimed at introducing not only Katniss, but the Capitol as well (Lionsgate Movies, "*Hunger Games* Official"). This gave them an opportunity to present "the adult cast of the film, who were much more known," thus presenting *The Hunger Games* as a film that features accomplished actors with whom especially older audiences are familiar (Karpel). The stars were thus meant to lure adult audiences, and also indirectly vouched for the overall quality of the film. All in all, it is indeed striking that, in the context of the trailers, basically all possible demographic groups are specifically addressed except for teenage girls, which once again underlines that they are not seen as particularly worthy or important consumers.

When looking at merchandise, licensed toys, or other tie-ins for the *Hunger Games*, there is a relative dearth in products, especially in relation to the hype and success surrounding the franchise at large. However, to limit such products was a conscious effort undertaken by the marketers, as "overt product placement or sponsorship," or an overselling of the movies in general, were considered to be counterproductive and likely to "turn off fans" (Graser). It certainly also has to do with some of the major themes of the *Hunger Games* trilogy itself. After all, being cautious about consumption and the selling of commodities is especially suited for a marketing campaign that promotes movies which are highly critical of these very issues. The heightened awareness of the problems surrounding selling merchandise and tie-in products about films that call out exploitative economic systems, advocate for the poor, and portray hunger as a tool of oppression could, for instance, be seen in the reaction towards the fast food chain Subway, which was harshly judged by fans and the popular press for the insensitivity with which they tried to sell their sandwiches as part of the *Hunger Games* experience (cf. Long).

Since the selling of commodities was seen as counterproductive, and the intended audiences for the movies well beyond the age of playing with toys, the marketers offered fans another opportunity to engage with the *Hunger Games* in a playful manner. They did so by establishing online spaces that blur the line between fiction and reality. In these spaces, fans and audiences can become part of the fictional universe through engagement online. The online magazine *Capitol Couture* and its accompanying blog on Tumblr, for instance, are items that, on the one hand, come across as official publications created by the Capitol for its citizens and, on the other hand, contain photos and articles about the tributes and victors wearing clothes by real-world designers such as Alexander McQueen, Dior, or Jean Paul Gaultier. In addition, the blog on Tumblr or the official Facebook page allow fans to share their own content with that of the marketers, or rather that of the Capitol, so that fiction and reality become blurred even more. Numerous critics and journalists have commented on the online campaign, admiring its ability to communicate with audiences, trigger fan engagement, and create hype (cf. Karpel; Kilinskis; Long; Vary). What has largely been left unnoticed, however, is that, since Katniss plays a central role in the fictional universe into which fans become immersed, they are confronted with her image time and again, which furthermore strengthens her portrayal as the leader of the rebels and the figure around which both the rebels and audiences can rally.

In fact, even though the online campaign was innovative in many respects, one of its primary functions was to spread traditional promotional material and make it more visible. After all, the hype that was created on these online platforms largely surrounded posters such as the ones analyzed above. To name just a few examples, fans were sent on scavenger hunts online to find the newest promotional images which were uploaded on numerous different websites, or they were encouraged to share, like, and comment on said material on their own social media accounts (Kilinskis). In order to ensure a continuous flow of new promotional images, the marketing campaign shot and published a plethora of photo series, such as the *Unite* series, which stars rebels from District 13, the *Throne* series, which depicts Katniss on a throne previously occupied by Snow, one featuring people from the Districts, one that depicts Katniss' star squad, or another one that includes the central characters from *Catching Fire* in their interview outfits (cf. impawards. com). The characters that are represented in these series are the rebels, on the one hand, and Katniss, on the other one. In a similar manner to the paratexts analyzed above, these photographs establish a discourse about the movie adaptations that focuses on the rebellion and its actors as well as on Katniss as a strong and fearless leader of said rebels, and thus further strengthens the message that the movie adaptations belong to the genre of action. Notably, however, by including a lot of propaganda material, they also establish the political discourse as a prominent part of the adaptations, offering fans an opportunity to identify with the people in Panem at large, and the rebels in particular.

The online marketing campaign not only spread traditional promotional material, but it also frequently promoted traditional and binary gender roles. Websites aimed at men, for instance, used themes such as fighting, survival, or training for the Games to make this particular demographic interested in watching the films (Karpel). By contrast, those aimed at women and girls relied on the themes of fashion, style, and make-up to do so. It is striking, for instance, that the online magazine *Capitol Couture*, which pretends to be an official publication created in and for the Capitol, features female models almost exclusively. What is more, when men are included, it is in more traditional contexts and in a more traditional manner, for instance when it comes to styling their beards or wearing a flower in the lapel of their suits. While on *Capitol Couture*, women wear extravagant make-up and hairstyles, as well as colorful and artistic haute-couture fashion, men are shown without make-up and only rarely with extravagant hairstyles or clothes (capitolcouture.pn). The publication thus clearly differs from the world of the novels, where, in the Capitol, gender boundaries are frequently transgressed and it is emphasized time and again that both men and women are interested in fashion, dye their hair, wear extensive make-up and accessories, and even have plastic surgery. Consequently, *Capitol Couture* rather perpetuates the homophobic and transphobic discourses established in the novels, returning to more conventional portrayals of gender roles and gender performances.

The same also holds true for a number of merchandised products. Since fashion and make-up are central elements of the *Hunger Games*, products such as the "Capitol Beauty Collection" make-up line produced by Cover Girl or a series of nail polishes encouraged fans to try out the extravagant looks of the Capitol citizens themselves. However, once again, the target audience for these products is reduced to the female demographic, because in the print advertisements published by both companies, it is female models exclusively who are used to promote the products. Hence, a practice that is portrayed as gender neutral in the novels, as both women and men in the Capitol wear excessive make-up, is reconceptualized as a female practice. What is more, in a similar manner to the Subway sandwiches, these items have also been criticized for "[promoting] further Capitol-like behavior" by glorifying practices that are shown to be part of the exploitative and a-political lifestyle of the Capitol at large (Gagnon 142; see also Asher-Perrin).

When compared to the paratexts of *BtVS*, the *Hunger Games* material follows a more progressive discourse when it comes to the representation of female teenage heroism. In the movie posters and trailers, Katniss is staged as an active and empowered girl warrior and not as a sexualized object, as Buffy was before her. Still, her portrayal largely caters to a male audience interested in action and adventure. In addition, reactionary tendencies can be observed in the context of the marketing campaign for the novels, where Katniss is hardly portrayed at all, as well as in the online campaigns, which hark back to binary notions of gender, selling fashion and make-up to female audiences, and violence and adventure to male ones.

"Every girl can be a princess": Merida and the Disney Princess Canon

As a Disney princess movie, *Brave* belongs to a media franchise which, for decades, has been catering to female audiences first and foremost, with the movies being connected to notions of idealized femininity and heterosexual romance. Since they tend to perpetuate reactionary and narrow gender norms, many of these movies, and the franchise at large, have widely been criticized by scholars from a variety of fields. In light of these stereotypes surrounding Disney princess movies, and in order to be more widely successful, *Brave*, along with the promotional material, needs to appease two critical audiences, namely boys who shy away from anything too feminine or princessy, and (feminist) critics who do the same. Consequently, the promotional material surrounding the movie *Brave* turns out to be yet another example of how stereotypically feminine elements that are a central part of the movie are relegated to the margins of the marketing campaign in order to make it more appealing to male audiences and the mainstream as well as to critics of the franchise's gender role portrayal.

To demonstrate its exceptional status within the princess franchise, the paratexts surrounding and promoting *Brave* focus on the innovative elements of the movie that clearly undermine Disney conventions. It is, however, the innovative elements thought to be of interest for a male audience, such as fighting and danger, rather than the ones with which female audiences can identify, such as the mother-daughter conflict, that are the focus of many paratexts. This is, first of all, visible in the movie title. In contrast to each and every of its predecessors of the first and second wave of Disney princess movies, the title neither contains the princess' name, nor even a description of the female protagonist, as in *The Little Mermaid* or *The Princess and the Frog*. Instead, Merida's name is replaced with the adjective "brave," a word which promises a tale of danger and adventure, concepts thought to appeal to male audiences.[5]

This discourse that puts emphasis on the adventurous and action-filled aspects of the movie is also continued in the movie poster, which bears a striking resemblance to *The Hunger Games* poster ("*Brave* Poster"). It depicts a single heroine poised with bow and arrow who stares defiantly into the camera, thus imitating the action hero pose mentioned in the context of the *Hunger Games* posters, too. In stark contrast to the light and bright color schemes of other Disney princess movies, this poster is held in different hues of dark blue, with Merida's fiery red hair being the only dash of color. The color scheme clearly underlines that *Brave* is not a typical princess movie, a notion which is only furthered through the focus on the weapon, the bow and arrow that are prominently positioned in the foreground. The (movie) genres that the poster establishes or alludes to are thus clearly that of action or adventure and traditional quest stories, with a lonely heroine using violence to fight her opponents. Indeed, when it comes to the opponents, it is notable that in this poster, it is the bear lurking in the background—and not Merida's mother Queen Elinor—who is established as the main antagonist. Admittedly, it is not clear whether the bear is Merida's mother or Mor'du, the evil king-turned-bear encountered in the film. In either case, however, the animal con-notes physical danger rather than the emotional and personal altercations between Merida and her mother that lie at the heart of the film. In fact, those are completely erased in the promotional posters in favor of establishing *Brave* as a dark adventure movie full of action, danger, and fighting.

A similar narrative is also established in the trailers for *Brave*, which focus on the clansmen, shooting and fighting scenes, and the bear Mor'du. It is interesting to note that the latter is featured in the trailers in a much more central position than the one he occupies in the actual movie, thus offering a chance for the trailers to introduce a more traditional type of villain who is a danger to the physical survival of the other characters, thus firmly embed-ding the film in the genre of action. The focus on Mor'du rather than Elinor also reflects the general tendency of the trailers to put the numerous male characters front and center while the female characters, along with the central conflict between them, are relegated to the margins. The trailers also fre-

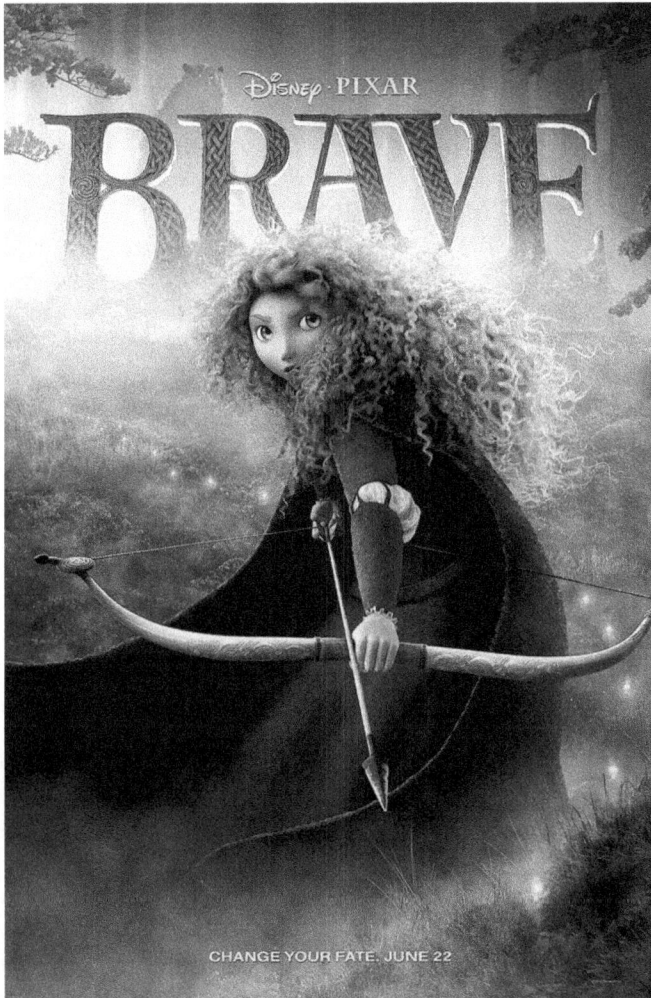

Movie poster for *Brave* depicting protagonist Merida in a manner similar to Katniss in the posters for *The Hunger Games*.

quently portray the rough Scottish landscape, alluding to a plethora of action and adventure movies, such as *Braveheart* (1995), that are set in Scotland and feature masculine heroes and warriors. Indeed, Merida herself describes it as "a land filled with magic and danger," once again contributing to the conceptualization of *Brave* in the promotional material as an action or adventure film (Disney-Pixar, "In Theaters").

In the trailers, male warriors and fighting are, however, not only represented through the numerous clansmen, but the very first trailer actually starts with a voice-over by King Fergus, telling the story of how he fought the evil bear Mor'du and lost his leg, contributing yet another peace to the puzzle of *Brave* paratexts that establish it as a movie about adventure and fighting rather than familial conflicts. The trailers deviate from the movie in this regard, as in the film, it is Merida who narrates her story via voice-over, whereas in the trailers, it is her father, and later her mother, whose voices are heard when they tell stories about their dangerous fights or the traditions of the kingdom (Disney-Pixar, "*Brave* Trailer," "'The Prize'"). Merida herself only gets a voice over in the very last trailer, when she introduces Scotland as the dangerous and mysterious place mentioned above ("In Theaters").

In the instances in which the trailers do give prominence to Merida, she is established in stark contrast to the traditional Disney princess, namely as an adventurous girl with a sense of humor who excels at archery. The difference between Merida and stereotypical princesses is furthermore emphasized because instead of embedding the movie in the context of Disney princess films by referring to her royal predecessors, they rather contextualize *Brave* as part of the Pixar universe, which is well-known for its male protagonists and adventurous plots (Stein). The trailers achieve this by showing audiences that *Brave* was created by the same people who made *Wall-E*, *Toy Story 3*, and *UP*, which are among the most successful Pixar creations (Disney-Pixar, "In Theaters"). On the one hand, this portrayal of Merida mirrors her role in the movie and her innovative status among Disney princesses. The trailers make it clear that this is a princess who is able to stand up for and defend herself. It is also underlined that she is not interested in romance at all. Indeed, all of the trailers contain the scene in which she takes part in the archery contest as a central, or indeed the only element ("'The Prize'"), thus emphasizing her defiant character and superior skills with a bow and arrow. On the other hand, the idea that Merida challenges patriarchal tradition through her use of weapons is not communicated, a negation that erases a central element of the film which adheres to the model of the feminist quest heroine and establishes the feminist message of *Brave*. Besides, even though this particular scene is certainly one of the most important ones of the movie, other scenes which are similarly essential, such as the ones that feature the complicated relationship between Merida and her mother, are largely left out of the trailers. This shows, once again, that the elements of the film which potentially appeal to a male audience are promoted, while the elements that are more reminiscent of genres aimed at female audiences or those that create a feminist subtext are marginalized or omitted.

As part of the Disney princess franchise, a brand whose customers are mostly young girls, *Brave* is also heavily marketed via licensed toys and merchandise. As already briefly mentioned in Chapter 3, Merida belongs to the official Disney princess line, a marketing branch that was established in

2000 and assembles all of the major Disney princesses (Whelan 25). This business move brought in a lot of revenue for the corporation itself and soon became the most successful of its merchandise brands, leading in turn to a hype surrounding the princesses and an ever-increasing amount of merchandised products (cf. Clapp-Itnyre 7). The princess line has since become the number one toy brand for girls in America, offering more than 25,000 products with which young consumers can surround themselves day and night (Stein). In light of the large amount and ensuing omnipresence of these merchandised products, Gray states that, in the case of the Disney Corporation specifically, it "might be foolish to see the film as ipso facto the 'primary text'" (38). Since Disney is a company which "is quite exceptional in the degree to which its paratexts fill stores and lives," critical attention must be paid not only to the movies, but also to paratexts such as toys, merchandise, and costumes, as they are often much more present in a child's life and potentially much more influential (39).

In the context of merchandise and toys, the princess line in particular has come under scrutiny from a number of scholars, not least because its popularity makes it virtually impossible for girls not to encounter these characters at some point. Lyn Mikel Brown, for instance, argues that

> [playing] princess is not the issue, […] the issue is 25,000 Princess products […]. When one thing is so dominant, then it's no longer a choice: it's a mandate, cannibalizing all other forms of play. There's the illusion of more choices out there for girls, but if you look around, you'll see their choices steadily narrowing [qtd. in Orenstein, "What's Wrong"].

However, the problem with the dominance of the princess line lies not only in the increasing limitation of choices for play in general, but also in the increasing limitations of possible gender role performances which girls learn when they play with products from the princess line. According to critics, girls are encouraged to identify with the princesses in order for them to buy more products, but this identification also leads to the learning of particular gender norms and gendered behaviors exemplified by the different princesses (England, Descartes, and Collier-Meek 555). To the same extent that the princess movies have been deemed dis-empowering and reactionary with regard to their gender role portrayal, the princess line, too, has widely been criticized for teaching girls a very limited version of femininity. Indeed, it has even been called "a merchandiser's dream but a feminist nightmare" (DiPaolo 170).

Through the mixing of different princesses from different generations, the brand is said to have unearthed gender norms from the previous century, and is furthermore accused of celebrating these values by promoting them through their toys and merchandise (Rothschild 90). According to Alisa

Clapp-Itnyre, the brand "creates a whole world populated by women whose only desire is to marry a prince" and reinforces traditional gender roles by staging the princesses as "coy, [...] overly appreciative and sweet" (7, 15). What is more, the interactive elements of the toys and website are said to primarily promote activities such as decorating rooms, painting, baking, or dressing up in pretty gowns, in short, activities that are considered to be traditionally feminine, too (15). Cassandra Stover argues that the princess line pushes a post-feminist agenda which turns girls into objects as it "channels female agency not only into purchasing power, but also into the power to make decisions about one's physical appearance" (6). The girls who play with and dress up as princesses "internalize a notion central to post-feminist discourse: the illusion of the power of being looked at," "a process that removes the active heroine from the beautiful body" (6, 7).

Merida, however, presents a disruption to the Disney princess canon with regard to both the movie in which she stars and her role as an official Disney princess marketed through merchandise and licensed toys. When Merida joined the official line-up in 2012, her appearance was initially changed to fit to the rest of the group, whose members had in turn been previously updated themselves. The make-over that the princesses received included changes in physical features, body shape, color and style of dress, make-up, and hair. All in all, they became "more glamorous and more bedazzled" (McKinstry). Their gowns were made to look more colorful and pompous and, in the case of Mulan and Jasmine, the two only princesses who wear pants in their movies, either completely changed or made to look more like a dress. Another fundamental and highly problematic change that occurred with Mulan, Jasmine, and Pocahontas is that their skin was lightened and their facial features changed to look more Caucasian, a move that diminishes the progress that has been accomplished through the inclusion of princesses of color into the princess canon (McKinstry).

What is more, all of the princesses are hyper-feminized and rendered even more conventionally beautiful than they are in the original films. In addition to make-up, pomp, and glitter, the up-dated line-up markets a notion of sexualized femininity to its young customers, as the gowns not only show off the princesses' feminine curves, but their body postures are also reminiscent of pin-up girls as the princesses present their bodies to the camera and gaze submissively at potential onlookers. In many cases, this portrayal of the princesses stands in direct opposition to the role they occupy in their respective films, thus taking away aspects such as their defiance of traditional gender roles, physical fitness and the ability to fight, or any other amount of agency the princesses might have had (Clapp-Itnyre 16; McKinstry).

This reframing of the princesses into more beautiful, sexy, and passive characters is especially obvious in the case of Merida. After all, the appropriation of her character for specific marketing purposes is clearly reflected in the respective paratexts: while the ones surrounding the movie embed the princess and her story into a context of action and adventure in order to make it appealing to a male audience, the princess line merchandise, which targets female audiences, renders Merida a hyper-feminine character in order for her to fit into the gender discourse promoted by the brand: The revised version wears a replica of the exact same gown that Merida was shown to hate in the movie, her hair looks more luscious and less wild, her facial features have been changed completely, and her gown tightly hugs her hips and waist at the same time that it reveals her naked shoulders (cf. image posted by Danckaert). What is more, instead of sporting her bow and arrow, she does not have any weapons at all. This up-dated version has incurred the wrath of critics and audiences alike, with director Brenda Chapman calling it "a blatantly sexist marketing move based on money" that goes into the exact opposite direction of what she envisioned the character to represent (qtd. in Liberatore). Feminist activists even started an online petition entitled 'Keep Merida Brave," explaining that

> by making her skinnier, sexier, and more mature in appearance, you are sending a message to girls that the original, realistic, teenage-appearing version of Merida is inferior; that for girls and women to have value—to be recognized as true princesses—they must conform to a narrow definition of beauty [Danckaert].

Due to the widespread criticism, Disney did change Merida back into a version that adheres more to her look in the movie and also gave her back her weapon.

As a consequence, Merida's page in the Disney online shop stands in stark contrast to the rest of the princess pages not only with regard to the color scheme, but more importantly also when it comes to the activities, clothes, and toys that are sold through this princess character. She thus stands for a disruption to the princess canon established in this online space. Ultimately, the inclusion of a princess who differs so clearly from the standards of princesshood usually represented in the online shop and its merchandised goods results in an expansion of the concept to include traits and activities deemed more stereotypically masculine. For example, the colors used on Merida's page and in the merchandised products are not the stereotypical pinks, violets, or pastels, but rather resemble the ones used in the movie poster, namely dark blues and greens and some red. This also holds true for Merida's gown. Even though the costume dress available still resembles the one Merida disliked in the original film, it does stand out against the rest of the princess gowns as it is dark green-blue. Likewise, the other clothes available also adhere to this color scheme, as the hoodies and shirts are held in blue, grey, and white.

The Disney online shop furthermore expands on the princess canon by including weapons, namely a bow and arrow play set, into the toys available for play. Hence, the concept of playing princess is broadened to include more active and more stereotypically masculine activities. In addition to this, the theme of adventure found in the movie trailer and poster is replicated in the merchandised goods through the inclusion of a variety of books that include such stories, as their titles read *Chasing Magic*, *Fire Falls*, or *Secret Spell*. Thus, the Merida merchandise challenges conceptions of princesshood as well as genre conventions in the context of children's literature. Whereas adventure books for children usually have male protagonists, the ones found on Merida' page feature not only a girl, but a princess.

It is interesting to note, however, that this remasculinization coincides with a marginalization of the character with regard to the official merchandise sold in the Disney online shop. After all, visitors of the online shop can choose between, for example, 146 *The Little Mermaid*, 212 *Beauty and the Beast*, 131 *Cinderella*, 136 *Rapunzel*, and 121 *Snow White* products, whereas fans of Merida can choose from 36 products. The choice is even more limited for fans of Mulan, Pocahontas, Tiana, and Jasmine, whose sites promote 20, 13, 18, and 21 products, respectively (1 Aug. 2017). While some of this imbalance can be explained with recent trends and developments, such as the current popularity of mermaids, or the fact that a live-action *Beauty and the Beast* movie was released at the beginning of 2017, the gap between the different groups is still striking. Moreover, said marginalization not only manifests itself in the number of items that exist for each princess individually, but also in the way they are represented in group settings. In a similar manner to the princesses of color, who appear much less frequently on merchandise products that depict several princesses at the same time, and hardly ever at the center of the group (Clapp-Itnyre 16; DiPaolo 169; McKinstry), Merida, too, is shown less frequently and usually as a character in the background. All in all, the marginalization of the princesses of color first of all reveals an uneasiness with race, which demonstrates that hegemonic femininity in the Disney princess universe is still conceptualized as white. Secondly, the lack of representation of princesses such as Merida, Pocahontas, or Mulan also articulates a refusal to promote characters who more openly subvert the idealization of extreme femininity and the traditional princess narrative.[6]

Whereas the online shop thus largely reiterates traditional discourses about gender and race, a different, or rather more complex narrative can be found on the official princess homepage (princess.Disney.com). First of all, the website does not depict the updated and glamorous versions of the princesses that dominate the online shop, but it uses screenshots from the original movies to represent the female characters. It is also noticeable that, whereas romance plays a major role in many of the movies, the website largely focuses on the princesses as individuals, showing images of them alone both in the majority of banners that head each princess' individual site, as well as in their photo galleries. What is more, even though the general website and the individual ones all contain a section that links to the online shop, princess.Disney.com is more concerned with letting visitors engage with the Disney princess universe and forging connections between the princesses and the audience.

This is achieved, for example, because the princesses are established as role models rather than as commodities ready for consumption. Each individual princess page, for instance, offers life advice for its visitors at the very top of the page. Here, a banner with an image of the respective princess is accompanied by empowering slogans such as "Explore new worlds" (Ariel), "Find your inner warrior" (Mulan), or "Be brave" (Merida). While the previous statements encourage girls to be active, daring, and curious, other pieces of advice, such as Snow White's "Be a friend to all" or Cinderella's "Never give up," also refer back to more traditional notions of femininity. Even though this representation of more traditional princesses along with more traditional feminine characteristics has been criticized for its "blurring [of] gender ideals, which privileges some aspects of femininity and disregards others," the mixture of these ideas can also be said to establish a discourse about femininity that is complex and offers girls who visit the website a variety of role models instead of idealizing and thus perpetuating one concept of femininity only (Stover 7). After all, in contrast to the online shop, all of the princesses are represented in equal measure on the princess website, so that no version of femininity is overtly celebrated or represented as superior to the others.

Indeed, this multilayered concept of femininity and girlhood can also be found in the actual practices made available on the website. On the one hand, Disney has maintained the promotion of many of the more traditional activities derided by other scholars such as dressing up, baking, cooking, or doing arts and crafts (cf. DiPaolo 169; Stover 6). On the other hand, however, Merida's page also includes, for instance, online games in which players can take part in the Highland Games or an archery challenge. The most innovative element of the website, however, is the so-called "Dream Big, Princess" campaign, a series of videos produced by Disney in which sequences of the princess movies are interspersed with clips from girls who engage in a variety of different activities that resemble or imitate the movements or activities of the princesses. To name just a few examples, in these videos, both girls and princesses go horseback riding, practice martial arts, swim and dive, or go on a canoe trip. Notably, princesses such as Merida, Mulan, and Pocahontas are featured much more prominently than others, not least because they are very active in their movies and thus offer a larger number of scenes that can be used for the campaign. In fact, while all of the princesses of the second and third wave of princess movies have a clip dedicated to them individually, this is not the case for Snow White, Aurora, and Cinderella, a fact which reflects and potentially makes audiences aware how limited their roles actually are.

In the Dream Big Campaign, the notion of dreaming, which is a very prominent concept in Disney princess movies in general, is turned from an activity that connotes passivity or dreaming about romance into one that stands for ambition, success, and the development of one's own identity. One clip, for instance, starts out with the slogan "For every girl who dreams big, there's a princess to show her it's possible," in order to then portray scenes in which girls follow their dreams and ambitions in a variety of fields such as sports, academia, or politics (Disney). A scene that presents Rapunzel overcoming her fear and sliding down her hair, for instance, is followed by a girl overcoming her own hesitations and sliding down a rope; Merida and another girl shoot arrows and ride horses; Mulan and her real-life counterpart practice martial arts; and Pocahontas and her counterpart dive off a cliff/platform into the ocean/a pool.

The empowering message of the clip is further emphasized by the choice of music that accompanies the scenes. Instead of using one of the many Disney princess songs, the campaign features The Script's "Hall of Fame," the lyrics of which encourage listeners to strive for greatness and success. The lyrics not only help to establish the general theme of the clip and the campaign as a whole, but are also used to delineate very specific roles girls are encouraged to take on. In addition to the many athletic activities mentioned above, there is a part in the video where even more roles and activities are introduced. The lyrics play a central role to do so, as they specifically describe the girls represented in the clip. While the singer sings, "Be students, be teachers / be politicians, be preachers / be believers, be leaders / be astronauts, be champions," the video shows a girl working on a science project, another helping a younger sibling with his homework, two girls with a megaphone at a demonstration, a girl with a graduation cap, another one campaigning to be elected as class president, and another one in an astronaut costume (Disney). Taken together, this clip, which is only 90 seconds long, offers audiences a wide variety of role models and activities that move away from the stereotype of the passive Disney princesses. Instead, the campaign encourages girl to become active and be ambitious both with regard to physical activities, as well as academic and political ones.

Notably, the campaign strives for inclusiveness not only with regard to the types of activities—after all, more traditional female sports such as dancing or gymnastics are also part of the clips—but also when it comes to the girls themselves. Those that are shown belong to different races and ethnicities, sport different hairdos, and wear different kinds of clothes, for example. The clip also features a young amputee with a prosthetic leg as one of two tap dancers (Disney). Through their increased representation of the more active princesses, many of which are girls of color, and the casting of girl actresses from a variety of backgrounds taking part in a variety of activities, these clips establish a more diverse, active, and empowered notion of both princesshood and girlhood. The campaign thus also stands in stark contrast to the kind of femininity promoted in the online shop, where traditional hyper-feminine ideals are promoted and sold.

All in all, this constant back and forth between innovative and reactionary conceptualizations of femininity and princesshood found on the different platforms that represent and promote the Disney princesses reflects the ongoing struggle over what it means to be a girl in the 21st century. Since these representations are used to market a product, the Disney princesses also reflect which kind(s) of femininity are regarded as valuable and hence marketable to a wider audience. In contrast to Peggy Orenstein, who claims that the meaning of princess "is so broadly constructed that it actually has no meaning" ("What's Wrong"), I suggest that princesses do have meaning: they reflect a notion of ideal girlhood and femininity, albeit one that is constantly under debate and changing. On the one hand, the focus of the stereotypically masculine and adventurous elements of *Brave*, and the various strategies the paratexts undertake to clearly set this film apart from other princess movies, show that in a mainstream context, traditional gender hierarchies are still the norm. With regard to the Disney princess line in particular, however, the inclusion of Merida into the group clearly marks a caesura in the manner Disney princesses are marketed and promoted, as her character and behavior could not as easily be assimilated to the rest of the group, and fans and audiences were able to voice their outrage at the attempts to do so. While aspects of traditional masculinity have hence found their way into the Disney princess canon, notions of traditional femininity have not completely been erased, so that the Disney princess universe establishes a more complex image of femininity and princesshood that accommodates both aspects of traditional femininity and masculinity.

Conclusion

The different paratexts analyzed in this chapter establish and reflect upon a mainstream discourse that can be described as patriarchal, since in it, binary gender notions are frequently reinstated and hegemonic masculinity is attributed more value than hegemonic femininity. The selection of elements used in the paratexts shows that "like Jenkins' poaching fans—[paratexts] take what they can use from the primary text and recontextualize it to serve their own needs and desires" (Vint 17). In the case of the teenage heroines, these needs and desires are to attract mainstream audiences. Notably, the paratexts do so by putting the more conventional elements of the female heroes and their stories, for instance the resemblance to classical action movies, on display. At the same time, more innovative aspects, such as their complex personalities and the manner in which they subvert gender roles, in short, the very features that give the primary texts their feminist flavor, are largely left out of the promotional campaigns. The paratexts thus indirectly make a comment about the culture industries and U.S. society at large, because this elimination demonstrates that reactionary and patriarchal world views are still the norm in both spaces. In spite of the strides feminism has made in the last decades, complex female heroes and feminist ideas are still not considered valuable or a potential device for marketing, at least not for mainstream, that is male heterosexual, audiences.

At the same time however, the patriarchal discourses and gender roles established in the paratexts can, of course, be challenged and negotiated on the level of consumption. As Sherryl Vint claims in her article "'Killing Us Softly'? A Feminist Search for the 'Real' Buffy," the heterogeneous ways in which Buffy is portrayed in the primary text and the paratexts are "concrete representations of the continuing ideological battle over the category of woman" (23). In addition, the very discrepancy between, for example, the active role Buffy takes on in the series, and the manner in which her body is rendered a passive object in promotional images "can introduce fans to a critical consciousness of ideology" and make them aware, as well as critical of, the manner in which she is used to maintain different gender ideologies (23). Indeed, this discrepancy can not only be found between paratexts and primary texts, but also within paratexts themselves, rendering the overarching gender discourses even more complex and complicated, and ultimately showing that often, female characters are used and appropriated to fit specific gender discourses and ideologies. For instance, Merida's make-over, marginalization in the online shop, and prominence in the Dream Big campaign has the potential to make visitors of the websites realize that the specific concept of princesshood represented in *Brave* is accepted and even celebrated in some context, and marginalized in others.

While consumers of paratexts such as online stores, trailers, or posters can become active consumers through their acts of interpretation, an active engagement with the female heroes and their stories is even more directly encouraged through licensed toys and merchandise. When people dress up as their favorite character, play pretend, or visit online spaces that allow them to enter and take part in fictional universes, they have the opportunity to continue, redefine, challenge, or subvert meanings established in both the primary texts and the paratexts (Gray 176, 178). This is especially important in the context of female characters and consumers, because popular culture products themselves, and particularly those that sell merchandised commodities to female consumers, are frequently criticized by (feminist) scholars for catering to a post-feminist agenda which leads women to believe that individual empowerment is possible through consumption (Stover).

The examples analyzed here refute this claim to some extent, as in these particular cases, consuming merchandised products can be a potentially empowering activity. This is because many of the products make it possible for fans to identify with and emulate the characters they encounter in the texts, be it the heroines themselves, or their friends and allies. When female fans buy and wear or use replicas of costumes and weapons, for example, they can not only pretend that they are Buffy, Merida, and Katniss, but they can also aspire to become the kind of female heroes these characters personify. In other words, they can put themselves into the role of a supernaturally strong vampire Slayer, a princess who defies tradition, or a rebel who fights for the freedom of a whole nation. Instead of reinforcing traditional gender roles or turning women and girls into passive and non-political consumers, partaking in the fictional universes of *BtVS*, *Brave*, and the *Hunger Games* offers an opportunity to defy traditional gender roles and performances and potentially even makes aware of the feminist messages found in these texts.

Indeed, a critical analysis of the paratexts is possible because many consumers can be said to occupy an in-between position with regard to the texts, that is, they know both the paratexts and the primary texts. This position enables them to question and complicate the simplified meanings established in many paratexts. To name just two examples of how the reactionary discourses established in the paratexts can be reversed on the level of consumption, I want to look at *BtVS* and the *Hunger Games*. As I claimed above, at a first glance, the tight and revealing clothes Buffy fans could buy as merchandise perpetuate a concept of femininity that encourages women and girls to see themselves as attractive objects. At the same time, however, fans of the series know that Buffy herself wears the exact same kind of clothing items, yet she is never rendered an object and her physical strength is rather underlined through her outfits. Thus, the clothes can be read by fans in two opposing ways, namely as commodities that connote either female passivity or power. In any case, the traditional gender discourse established in the paratexts is rendered more complicated and ambivalent on the level of consumption.

This feat is also achieved by fans of the *Hunger Games* franchise. For instance, *Capitol Couture* magazine and its accompanying Tumblr blog reject the non-binary gender roles encountered in the primary texts by using only female models to represent the fashion items and hair and make-up styles.

On the same sites, however, online users disrupt this discourse as they post pictures of themselves in which both female and male fans dress up in the extravagant fashions of the Capitol described in the novels. They hence not only contribute to the gender discourse established by these paratexts, but render it more complex, inclusive, and innovative and thus rehabilitate the simplified and binary gender notions established in the paratexts.[7] Notably, these fans also comment on the gender discourse established in the novels themselves: whereas in the fictional universe, the gender transgressions in the Capitol are cast in a negative light, the *Hunger Games* fandom celebrates and advocates for less rigid rules when it comes to fashion and gender expression. This demonstrates that paratexts, along with the people who consume and appropriate them, "offer not fixed meanings [...] but a focus in the continuous production and struggle to define and redefine desires, meanings and identities" (Gledhill xvii). The various portrayals of the girl warriors and the manner in which audiences consume and engage with them call attention to the fact that hegemonic femininity, notions of female heroism, and "appropriate" gender roles are constantly fought over, constructed, challenged, and changed.

$\blacklozenge\blacklozenge$ **5** $\blacklozenge\blacklozenge$

Promoting a Queer Agenda
in Femslash Fan Fiction

Have you ever gone to a shitty movie and found yourself [...] won-
dering why you are wasting two hours [...] of your life watching
such a piece of crap? Fem/slashers haven't. Whether it's a fevered
look or a feathery touch [...], fem/slashers will spot the slashiness.
No matter how much the director thought s/he was making a film
about the plight of sea lions, the fem/slasher knows the truth. If
you've never walked out of an awful film saying, "That was totally
worth nine dollars if only for that really gay part ... you know, when
they hugged *like that...*" then you're seriously missing out.
                                                              —Puckity

Fan fiction stories are pieces of "non-commercial writing that [feature]
an original plot using characters and settings from commercially produced
[media]" such as TV shows, movies, computer and video games, comics, or
popular fiction (Cumberland 669). While scholars such as Anne Jamison
point out that the practice of basing one's own work on that of others has a
long literary tradition (Jamison 17–18), critics agree that the literary practice
of fan writing started out during the 1960s and 70s with a relatively small
number of fans who wrote fan fiction based on the TV show *Star Trek* (Cumberland 669). This particular part of fan culture and practice was first analyzed by Camille Bacon-Smith in her seminal study *Enterprising Women:
Television Fandom and the Creation of Popular Myth* (1992) at a time when
fan fiction was still distributed my means of collecting different stories in so-
called "zines," magazines which were copied, bound, and sent around via
mail by fans themselves.[1]
    Many of the fan practices described by early fan scholars such as Bacon-
Smith or Henry Jenkins have changed fundamentally with the advent of the
Internet and the move of fan communities and their practices into online
spaces in the early to mid–1990s (Hellekson and Busse 13). Whereas fan fic-

147

tion had long been regarded as "the ugly, slightly feral stepchild of fandom," "the stigma of writing and reading fanfic has declined massively in recent years" (Adewunmi). Fan fiction as a phenomenon has moved from being "a subculture within a subculture" (Kustritz 372) to becoming a more popular and visible phenomenon increasingly recognized by mainstream culture and studied by academics from a variety of fields (J. Russo 13). Stories produced by fans are no longer regarded as subordinate to the original source, as, for instance, Jenkins proposes in *Textual Poachers* (23), nor are they any longer seen as simply a misinterpretation or misreading of generic codes, as suggested by Bacon-Smith (160–62). Instead, scholars view fan fiction as "related manifestations of equally legitimate forms of desire" (J. Russo 12) and its writers as some of "the savviest of pop culture consumers" (Adewunmi) and "members of an active interpretative community" (Kaplan 135).

Today, online platforms such as fanfiction.net and archiveofourown.com, to name just the two largest ones, provide more than three million registered users a space where they can post, read, comment on, and discuss their stories. The proliferation of the Internet has not only allowed more people from a variety of backgrounds to become involved in the practice of fan writing (Hellekson and Busse 13; Kustritz 372), but the diversification can also be observed with regard to the range of topics, themes, and ideas expressed in stories written by fans (Adewunmi; Jamison 18). Indeed, fan fiction has developed a variety of subgenres, as well as its own terminology and rules.[2] For instance, a distinction is made between canon and fanon. While canon stands for the facts presented in the original work, fanon describes theories or facts which are not explicitly featured in the original, but on which fans widely agree (Hellekson and Busse 9). The stories include headers and disclaimers, which allow readers to decide quickly whether the story is of interest for them. The diversification also shows itself in the range of subgenres, with hurt/comfort, fluff, AU (alternate universe), angst, first time, non-con (non-consensual), PWP (either standing for "porn without plot," or "plot, what plot?"), alpha/omega, kink, or BDSM being just a few of the most common ones into which the fan writings can be categorized.[3]

One of the most popular subgenres of fan fiction is so-called "slash," that is, stories about two characters of the same sex who engage in a romantic and/or sexual relationship. The term itself "actually derives its name from the abbreviations of characters' names linked together by a slash" (Hamming 3). Whereas slash, too, has witnessed a diversification in recent years with more and more male and queer authors taking part in this fan practice, the majority of fan fiction writers are still straight women and girls (Alexander 28). Therefore, works of slash are widely regarded by academics as a form of feminist resistance able to subvert the scripts and conventions not only of mainstream popular culture, but of patriarchal ideologies in general. For example, even though slash deals with same-sex relationships, many theories propose that slash fiction "is not about homosexuality, but about women's desires concerning their own femininity or their relationships with men" (Barker). Notably, many of these desires voiced through the practice of slash writing "are outside the dominant notions of acceptable love relationships" and/or differ from the portrayal of romantic relationships in popular culture texts (Cicioni 175).

In slash, the manner in which relationships are represented is rewritten and negotiated, as the plot tends to delineate the development of said bonds as character-driven, slowly developing, or erotic, aspects that romantic relationships in mainstream popular culture often lack (Cumberland 673; Kustritz 383). Moreover, sexually explicit stories, called "smut" or "PWP," have been viewed as manifestations of female or even feminist pornography (Barker; Hellekson and Busse 17; Penley 316–18), and/or as possibilities for women and girls to imagine sexual relationships between two partners that are equal (Scodari 113). The practice of writing slash can also be regarded as a form of escapism, as the female authors can overcome restrictive gender roles and expectations, and empower themselves, at least on the level of fiction (Cicioni 155; Green, Jenkins, and Jenkins 69). Finally, by reimagining male characters as emotional, loving, sensible, and nurturing, slash writers subvert concepts of hegemonic masculinity, insinuating a "desire for change in the concept of masculinity and in the relations involving men" (Cicioni 174).

There are, however, also scholars who criticize certain aspects of slash, as well as the disproportionate amount of scholarly and public attention it has received (Hellekson and Busse 17). Referring to the idea that writers of slash invariably use two male characters in order to portray equal relationships, Mirna Cicioni proposes that this reflects "a pessimistic unease about the institution of heterosexuality," as the insistence on this particular character constellation implies that an equal relationship between a woman and a man is impossible (169). What is more, the focus on men not only marginalizes women and girls in general, but the fact that even today, when mainstream popular culture does give more prominence to complex female characters, the prioritization of male pairings "validates underlying suspicions of essential female inadequacy" (Scodari 116). The scholarly and public interest in slash and its female writers is furthermore criticized because it is "problematized in a way that male pornography is not" (Barker). Even though lesbian sex scenes can be found in almost any pornographic text aimed at a male audience, male interest in lesbian sex is not questioned, let alone studied to the same extent as slash fics are (Keft-Kennedy 74). Hence, female sexuality is pathologized in a way male sexuality is not. Finally, many texts that deal with and try to explain the lure of reading and writing slash tend to essentialize sexuality and gender, speaking about female emotions, desires, and preferences, when in fact, the wide range of genres, topics, motifs, and ideas that are voiced in the different fics rather stresses the individuality and diversity of their authors.

Since slash focuses on male characters exclusively and is the most popular fan fiction genre, there exists a relative lack of female characters in stories produced by fans. That male pairings are the norm in slash is already insinuated by the usage of the unmarked term "slash" for stories with male pairings, while "femslash" and "het" describe fics that feature two women or two members of the opposite sex, respectively. However, girls and women are not only marginalized in slash fiction but in other genres, too. In fact, the only prominent trope in fan fiction at large that specifically deals with female characters is that of the "Mary Sue," which is "a derogatory name used by fans to refer to an original female character (OFC) who is entirely too extraordinarily perfect to be believable" (Kustritz 380). As a character who is so exceptionally smart, beautiful, and pure that men cannot help but fall in love with her, the Mary Sue represents an idealized and unattainable form of femininity (380). What is more, she

> reproduces the worst aspects of female competition for desirable heterosexual relationship partners. Within this system wherein perfection is a prerequisite for a fulfilling relationship, "average" women are assured that they will never find a community of women who will support them rather than compete with them, and that they can never look upon another woman and feel desire rather than despair or triumph [380].

In short, Mary Sues reinforce heteronormative gender stereotypes regarding women's looks, their behavior, and their relationships to other women. Because of said problematic and unrealistic features, Mary Sue characters are often criticized and derided within fan fiction communities themselves. However, their very existence makes aware of a problem inherent in the source texts, namely that the canon often does not feature female characters, so that these have to be invented and written into the stories by fans (Pugh 93). With its focus on men and male romantic pairings and its reproduction of stereotypical female characters, a lot of fan fiction thus ultimately reproduces the standards of mainstream popular culture, at least when it comes to the portrayal of women and girls: female characters are either represented in a stereotypical fashion or not at all.

The fan fiction genre which most prominently counters these stereotyped and marginalized portrayals of women and girls is femslash. Even though it is still a niche genre, femslash is produced in growing numbers, a development which is partly due to the increasing inclusion of central and complex female characters in mainstream popular culture, as femslash's most popular pairings are taken from texts that not only focus on women and girls, but portray them in diverse and innovative ways.[4] Among the most popular source texts for femslash are not only ones that have been produced in recent years, but notably also *BtVS*, which still has a very active and influential online fandom (cf. Jamison 113; Stenger 27–28). As Meg Barker observes, the series lends itself to fan writers in general, and femslash writers in particular, because it features numerous female characters, some of whom are gay, and often focuses on interpersonal relationships and the feelings and emotions connected to them. Major themes such as sexuality, power, relationships, or gender roles offer numerous points of entry for femslash writers.

This holds, of course, also true for the other two texts with which I engage in this study. *Brave* is about a princess who challenges both genre and gender expectations, whereas the *Hunger Games* trilogy questions established assumptions of genre, gender, and heroism, and is moreover concerned with interpersonal relationships, both platonic and romantic ones. As teenage girls who are hesitant about engaging in heterosexual romantic relationships, Katniss and Merida also open up possibilities for fan writers to queer these girl warriors. These female heroes are hence doubly subversive. Not only do they challenge conventions when it comes to the portrayal of teenage girls on the level of mainstream popular culture, as delineated in the first three chapters, but within the context of fan fiction, their stories have the potential to challenge tropes such as the Mary Sue on the one hand, and the general lack of female characters in fan fiction, on the other one.

In contrast to slash fiction, the amount of academic work conducted on femslash is comparatively small (Isaksson 34; Scodari 114), which makes it all the more important to study this kind of writing, as it can offer interesting insight into the way female writers—just like male slash, femslash is mostly written by women and girls (Alexander 28)—imagine female characters in general, and lesbian ones in particular. As the stories on which I focus furthermore deal with heroic characters, they also allow for an analysis of how female heroism is approached and conceptualized by fan authors. It is my claim that the pieces of femslash portraying the heroines Buffy, Katniss, and Merida follow a decidedly queer agenda that works against hegemonic and heteronormative ideals frequently found in representations of heroic characters in mainstream popular culture by creating heroines that undermine these very ideals. In other words, these stories insist that queer girls, too, can take on the roles of heroines and role models.

Through the portrayal of Buffy, Katniss, and Merida as heroines and as queer characters, the works of femslash fiction also follow a feminist agenda, as the diversification of heroic characters can be seen as a practice that works against the dominance of heteronormative and patriarchal depictions of women and girls in popular culture, strives to include people that are usually not represented in mainstream media, let alone take on the role of heroines, and hence advocates for inclusion and intersectionality.[5] Notably, the feminist discourse is also established because many of the heroic features, behaviors, and traits taken up and celebrated by femslash writers are the ones introduced by the model of the feminist quest heroine. Consequently, notions of gender hybridity, the need for connection, the revaluation of stereotypical femininity, or the subversion of patriarchal systems are taken up and affirmed as potentially heroic in these stories written by fans.

I furthermore argue that these femslash stories follow a didactic approach and that the specific stories in my corpus function as a kind of grassroots sex education for girls and young women. This is because the femslash fics do not merely elaborate on female sexuality in general, but they feature heroines whose ages range from 16 to about 23, so that the focus lies on the sex lives and sexual identity of teenage girls and young adults. This type of sex education is all the more important because it addresses topics that are largely made a taboo both in mainstream U.S. culture and society at large, namely, among others, queer sexualities (Bittner 357) or female sexual desire (Epstein, Kehily, and Renold 249). They also give a voice to children and young adults themselves, which is an aspect that, according to Debbie Epstein, Mary Jane Kehily, and Emma Renold, is regularly neglected in academic works on sex education (252–53). In this context, the writing and discussing of the femslash stories that deal with and instruct about issues of particular importance to (queer) women and girls can also be regarded as a form of the feminist practice of consciousness raising, as it offers the largely female users an opportunity to give a voice to their own experiences and to share them with others.

In order to narrow down the corpus of femslash stories, I decided to only use stories uploaded on archiveofourown.org (AO3), as this platform makes it possible to search for femslash pairings fairly easily due to its tagging system, and because the website has developed into one of the most popular, most diverse, and mostly frequented archives of fan fiction since its launch in 2009. I also limit the number of pairings to one for each primary text, choosing the most popular ones according to the numbers of stories uploaded on AO3.[6] The same-sex couples I investigate are Katniss/Johanna, Buffy/Faith, and Merida/Elsa, respectively.[7] I divided my text into two subchapters, the first of which will focus on innovative conceptualizations of heroism and gender roles in order to show how the changed sexual orientation of Buffy, Katniss, and Merida negotiates and diversifies notions of heroism and the type of role models deemed appropriate for a young adult audience. The second subchapter deals with first-time as well as PWP stories in which the characters engage in lesbian sex. This type of fan fiction is subversive on two levels. First of all, it breaks the taboo of female sexuality as it teaches about sex, female bodies, and pleasure in a very detailed and instructive fashion and, secondly, it deals with lesbian sex, a topic that usually exists only on the margins of popular culture, especially when it comes to texts aimed at young adult audiences. Throughout this chapter, I will also show the extent to which the femslash fics challenge specific ideas about slash established by other scholars.

Negotiating Notions of Heroism in Femslash Stories

The femslash fics in my corpus work against the "heterosexual imperative of heroism" and reject the idea that "heroes must be straight" (Alexander 24). They do so by queering the female protagonists at the same time that they insist that these girls are heroines and role models. They hence call for more diversity when it comes to types of heroic figures represented in popular culture, especially in texts aimed at young adult audiences. In this context, the most crucial aspect is that, in the femslash stories, all of the female protagonists explicitly identify as gay or non-heterosexual. These stories thus clearly differ from both the source texts and conventional slash stories where the attraction between the partners is often based on a special bond only rather than sexual orientation (Cicioni 169). Indeed, several scholars have claimed that the focus on a special and unique bond places many slash stories outside of a homo-erotic or queer context, as it is the special connection, and not sexual orientation, that is responsible for the mutual attraction between the slashed partners (Barker; Isaksson 7; Kustritz 379).

In contrast to this, the texts in my corpus emphasize that their female protagonists are gay and attracted to the same sex in general, and not only to the one particular partner included in the story. There are a number of coming out stories in which the girls openly identify as lesbian or bi (Kennisiou; LauraHollis, "Of Breakfast"; Lilyyuri; RedSneakers; Val_Creative), and, moreover, accepting their sexuality and coming out to others is established as something positive and liberating. This idea is projected, for instance, when the girls maintain that they "wouldn't be able to accept [themselves] or [their] sexuality unless [they] told someone, and made it real" (Kennisiou). In addition, accepting and embracing their sexuality is also described as an act that feels as if a "stupefying burden has been lifted from [their] shoulders" (Flywoman), which makes them "feel a bit more whole" because "who [they] really [are] is finally falling into place" (Bodylikeabattleaxe). In addition to diversifying heroic characters to include girls that openly identify as queer, the femslash fics pertain that accepting and embracing one's sexual orientation is a positive and empowering act for them. They hence establish and celebrate an innovative type of role model rarely found in slash or in texts aimed at a teenage audience.

Still, a number of fics do employ symbols to show why the respective girls fit together. In the case of Merida/Elsa fics, for instance, it is the contrast between Merida's fiery hair and character and Elsa's ice powers that is used to show that the two complement each other (Afterandalasia, "Learn Me"; FlyingFleshEater; Kennisiou). Buffy/Faith fics also hark back to differences in outer appearance such as Buffy's blonde hair and light complexion and Faith's brown hair and dark complexion (Furies). Katniss and Johanna are occasionally shown to belong together on a symbolic level as they share a love for nature and the woods (Theladymore). Whereas these examples show that, occasionally, the femslash writers do employ tropes such as foils or mirrors/doubles when they describe the queer relationships, these symbolic connections are never the only or most important reason for their mutual attraction. Instead, the relationships are more often grounded in their shared status as heroines rather than any lofty symbolic connections. Faith, for instance, says that Buffy is "the only person in the whole goddamn world who bears the same burdens, who can understand her" (LauraHollis, "Of Breakfast"). In a scene resembling this one, Merida admits that she is "still getting the hang of this princess thing," and Elsa remarks: "I know how that feels" (Afterandalasia, "Learn Me"). Johanna also alludes to their similarities both on the level of their experiences and how these have shaped her and Katniss when she states that they share a bond because they are "revolutionaries," "victors," "killers," and "fighters" (Iliveinfantasies).

That their jobs and responsibilities take on a central position in the characters' lives in general as well as in their choice of romantic partners subverts traditional conceptions of both femininity and romantic love stories. In the femslash fics, all of the female characters occupy important and powerful positions within their communities and they find their romantic partners through their jobs or tasks. In the case of Buffy and Katniss, the femslash fics can simply take scenes from the original texts and add the love story. It is especially fighting or training sequences that lead to romantic or sexual interactions between Buffy and Faith. These scenes not only lend themselves to adding erotic context simply because the two girls are alone with each other, but also because in the canon, it is established that "fighting and arousal are intimately linked for Slayers" (Isaksson 8). In the femslash texts, instead of letting out this sexual tension with their boyfriends or other male partners, Buffy and Faith look to each other for personal bonds and sexual satisfaction. For Katniss and Johanna, their shared history as tributes, but, more importantly, the fact that they train together to become rebel soldiers and consequently share a room in District 13, are used to infuse the text with a lesbian love story.

In the case of Merida and Elsa, this works differently, as authors have to find a way to bring together two characters who do not meet in the original movies. Noticeably, instead of harking back to fairy tale conventions and tropes such as the damsel in distress, Merida and Elsa meet on the job when they conduct diplomatic missions or go on state visits, for instance. Their status as rulers and working women is stressed time and again, as their jobs are described in great detail. Elsa is "judge, jury and executioner in this kingdom of hers" (Kennisiou), engages in "diplomatic royal work" (PTlikesTea), and has "much work to do" (MoonGirll155). Both she and Merida speak several languages (PTlikesTea; Afterandalasia, "Learn Me"), preside over meetings in which they find "themselves as much mediating as discussing the matter themselves," and bond by discussing "what it means to be Queen, or to know that you were to become one" (Afterandalasia, "Learn Me"). While the source texts concentrate on what happens before Merida and Elsa take over these responsibilities and the tensions and conflicts that emerge because of their unwillingness to be princess or queen, the femslash texts show what happens to them after they have overcome these conflicts and embraced their responsibilities. These fics hence not only celebrate and reinforce the innovative ideas voiced in the source texts, namely that women and girls can be competent leaders and rulers, but they also work against stereotypical depictions of Disney princesses as passive and powerless wives.

This focus on jobs and responsibilities furthermore allows the femslash writers to conceptualize the female protagonists as heroines. Even though they are deeply concerned with characterization and feelings and emotions, the stories neglect neither the actions nor the heroic deeds of the female protagonists. Indeed, they maintain that being (future) queens, revolutionaries, and Slayers takes up such a central status in the teenage girls' lives that they are profoundly influenced by these roles. While at a first glance, it is the exploration of character rather than action that lies at the heart of these fics, at a closer look, both aspects are essential parts of these stories. After all, in the majority of texts, even in those that do not specifically feature action sequences or fighting scenes, the young women's thoughts, feelings, and emotions revolve around such actions, their roles as warriors or leaders, and their successes as well as the emotional fallout of having to bear these responsibilities. Some stories even feature in-depth discussions about the nature of heroism along with the questions who can be a heroine and which actions and characteristics can be considered to be heroic. In "All Cracked Up," for example, Faith explains: "Agency, Buffy. It's what makes a hero a hero. [...] You choose, B. We all choose. That's what makes us heroes" (Furies).

What is more, the femslash fics celebrate female power and heroism as they emphasize that the heroic deeds of Buffy, Katniss, and Merida have a positive effect not only on the young women's lives, but on their societies as a whole. This holds especially true for fics that take place after the original stories have ended. These stories show that Katniss has turned Panem into a free, peaceful, and safe nation (Bodylikeabattleaxe; TiggerFace, "Little Things"), or that Merida ended patriarchal traditions, overcame the conflict with her parents as well as her aversion against taking over the responsibilities of being a princess, and is turning into a competent ruler (Lilyyuri). In this context, the stories also regularly take up a notion of heroism established by the model of the feminist quest heroine in the primary texts, namely the importance of heterarchical power systems as well as sisterhood and the necessity to empower not only oneself, but others, too. After all, the heroic deeds of Katniss, Buffy, and Merida subvert patriarchal gender hierarchies and systems of power and result in societies in which people in general and not only the heroines themselves have a higher amount of freedom and agency, which is a feature that is regularly emphasized and celebrated in the works written by fans.

Many of the femslash stories are also decidedly political and tackle issues such as homophobia, equal rights, and gay marriage (Folie_a_yeux; Fresh-Brains; Kennisiou; Nikmood; Phoebe1901, "Anything"; PTlikesTea; Shamrock; The_Eclectic_Bookworm; TiggerFace). They hence make aware of many of the personal challenges queer people encounter in their everyday lives, such as coming to terms with one's sexual orientation, coming out, or finding a partner (Folie_a_yeux; Kennisiou; LauraHollis; Lilyyuri; MonaLover07; Musicaltaco; Orphan_account; Pinebundles; Pop_Punk_Jolras; Radioclubjp; Theladymore; TiggerFace, "And Then"; Val_Creative). In fact, the femslash stories establish a type of quest particular to the experience of queer teenagers as the proverbial dragons which the heroines slay, that is the obstacles and discrimination they face, are specific challenges queer teenagers and young adults might face as well. Hence, readers can find encouraging role models in the heroines who tackle or overcome discrimination in addition to their other obligations. Taken together, these stories establish a political online space where, through the use of fiction, queer users and straight allies can engage in political discussions. This is an observation that clearly counters the notion expressed by many (feminist) scholars, which is that teenage girls are not interested in politics or unaware of heteronormative patriarchal oppression (cf. Genz and Brabon 36–37).

Femslash fics also critically respond to mass culture simply because they focus on and give a voice to female characters. They expand on the already well-established characterizations of the respective girl warriors by offering detailed insight into their thoughts, relationships, motivations, desires, and actions and therefore produce characters that are even more multidimensional than they are in the canon. In addition, the femslash fics also give prominence to the secondary female characters that are not as prominently featured in the source texts. They create backstories for them and give an account of their actions, feelings, and emotions in great, and frequently innovative, detail. Readers of Katniss/Johanna fics, for instance, learn how Johanna lost her family (Bodylikeabattleaxe; Pinebundles), what life in her home district was like (Amsay), or how her upbringing in District 7 influenced her (Amsay; Bodylikeabattleaxe). The same holds true for Faith, as fans fill in the gaps left in *BtVS* and come up with stories of Faith's life before she became a Slayer and what happened to her during the time she was not part of the series (Electra126; Furies; M_phoenix). In this context, Faith and Johanna are not represented as the tough and strong young women they are made out to be in the canon, but the fan stories articulate that they have a soft and gentle side. Johanna, for instance, is described as a "hard-ass" who carries "an ax on each hip" but who also takes care of her daughter by "doing adorably cute and soft-hearted things" with her (TiggerFace, "Everyday"; see also Theladymore for Johanna and Folie_a_yeux and Theconcomingwolf for Faith). By expanding on these female characters in a manner that establishes them as young women who are both strong and gentle, tough and caring, these fics work against stereotypical and binary notions of gender. While both Faith and Johanna are rather masculinized in the canon, especially with regard to their behavior and character traits, they evade categorization in the fanon.

In addition, the portrayals of Faith and Johanna insist that they are not sidekicks but fully developed and equally important characters and heroines in their own right. Time and again, the stories point out how similar Faith and Johanna are to Buffy and Katniss. In one fic, for instance, Katniss observes that "Johanna always reminded [her of herself]" (District_7_Profanity, "Help"), whereas Faith points to the similarities between her and Buffy when she states: "I'm the Slayer; you're the Slayer. [...] [S]o I figure we're the same person, right?" (JaneDavitt). Notably, their personalities and actions are also characterized as heroic. For instance, many fics underline that Johanna played a central role in the rebellion against President Snow, too, because she did not give away any information about the rebels, even though she was tortured, and she is also shown to protect Katniss and to support her in becoming a soldier (cf. District_7_Profanity, "She Doesn't"; Pinebundles). In "And Then Comes," for instance, Johanna maintains: "I got you out of the room with your family and into an environment that let you become an actual force in the war effort" (TiggerFace). In the case of Buffy/Faith femslash, many stories feature fighting or training scenes which underline that Faith employs a different technique, but is ultimately as strong and successful as Buffy. By featuring not one, but two queer women as heroines and role models, these femslash stories make their demand for more diversity clear and, at the same time, offer their readers a variety of empowering characters with whom they can identify.

By depicting Faith and Johanna as multi-dimensional and heroic characters who are equal to and equally important for the stories as Buffy and Katniss, the femslash fics also work against generic representations of women and girls in popular culture texts that include more than one female character. To be more precise, they subvert the convention that secondary female characters are usually employed either as evil antagonists or as foil characters whose mere function it is to highlight certain characteristics of the protagonist. Indeed, this is a tendency that can be observed to varying degrees in all of the source texts: Queen Elinor, the only other central female character in *Brave*, is Merida's main antagonist, at least in the beginning of the movie; Faith acts as a dark foil to Buffy's characterization as the good Slayer; and Johanna can be said to function as a dark foil, too, as she is the only young female tribute/victor besides Katniss. Consequently, her portrayal in the novels as someone who is unhinged and has lost her whole family can be seen as a warning about what might have happened to Katniss after the Hunger Games if the rebellion had not taken place.

In the femslash texts, Johanna and Faith are shown to be more than merely dark foils whose main function it is to emphasize the goodness of the female protagonist. Instead, they take on the roles of lovers, supporters, and heroines. What is more, the dark or deviant aspects of their characters are also explained or justified. In stories that feature Faith, this tendency has been observed by Amanda L. Hodges and Laurel P. Richmond, who state that fans "seek to justify or excuse her 'bad girl' persona" by depicting it as "a product of her class and background" (6.6, 6.4). The fanon imagines Faith as an insecure, lonely, and distrustful person unable to give and receive love because she had a terrible childhood, no father figure, and an alcoholic mother who did not take care of her. Frequently, she is also portrayed as a victim of violence, rape, and assault (Australooithecushomo; Bruteaous; Electral26; M_phoenix; Stormwreath). Similarly, Johanna is traumatized due to her experiences during and after her participation in the Hunger Games, when she lost not only friends and mentees, but also her family, who were killed because she did not abide by the Capitol's rules (Bodylikeabattleaxe; District_7_Profanity, "She Doesn't"; Pinebundles).

Along with these characterizations, in the fan texts, the tensions and conflicts that exist between the female heroes and the secondary characters in the canon are shown to be based on love and/or desire rather than hate or animosity. In a fic entitled "Choices," for instance, Faith admits: "'I never wanted to be you, B,' [...] 'I just wanted to be worthy of you'" (Folie_a_yeux). Consequently, the story arc found in the original series, namely that Buffy feels threatened by Faith when she first arrives in Sunnydale ("Faith, Hope & Trick"), is put into a different context in which Faith tries to impress Buffy and win her friendship rather than sidelining her or diminish her achievements and skills. Johanna's cold and dismissive attitude towards Katniss is shown in a different light as well, namely as a protection mechanism used by Johanna, who is in love with Katniss but convinced that her feelings are not reciprocated (MonaLover07; TiggerFace, "And Then").

This apparent need of fans to find reasons for and hence justify the bad behavior of characters such as Faith and Johanna can be seen as problematic, as it reiterates the idea that girls should not be violent, evil, moody, or vengeful without having a reason for it, such as traumatic experiences in their past. I suggest, however, that this particular portrayal of these specific characters can also be regarded as innovative. After all, the creation of individual background stories and more complex characterizations serves as a strategy to establish more nuanced female characters. In addition, as Hodges and Richmond have already observed when it comes to Faith, the stories about beating the odds and dealing with trauma also celebrate the strength of these female characters and show that they are heroines and survivors who were able to overcome or at least deal with the traumatic events of their past (6.6). This is another instance in which the femslash stories echo the concept of heroism brought forth by the feminist quest heroine, as they, too, attribute heroic status to secondary characters and thus expand on the notion of who can be a hero.

The responsibilities, obstacles, and traumas they face, and how they deal with and/or overcome these issues, also challenge assumptions regarding heroism and gender roles. In this context, I focus on stories that belong to the genre of hurt/comfort, as these specifically deal with such issues. Hurt/comfort fics, "as the name implies, revolve around a character being injured and another character comforting him" (Hellekson and Busse 10–11). The use of the pronoun "him" already alludes to certain genre conventions: usually, hurt/comfort stories are about a masculine male hero who goes on an adventure and is hurt, and a feminized male sidekick who takes care of the injuries and nurtures the hero back to health. Hurt/comfort is regarded by many fan fiction scholars as a subversive genre as it breaks with patriarchal and hegemonic gender notions on a number of levels. It challenges both hegemonic masculinity and heroism as it portrays the hero as someone who can get hurt and is in need of help. At the same time, hurt/comfort also celebrates the ability to nurture and comfort others, skills which are traditionally connected to stereotypical femininity and thus regarded as less valuable than, for instance, the heroic deeds conducted by the male hero (Derecho 72; Kustritz 347).

On the one hand, the hurt/comfort stories that feature female characters are rather similar to those that focus on male characters as they, too, challenge patriarchal gender hierarchies. They do so by maintaining that the ability to nurture and comfort is as important for the survival of the heroines themselves and those they protect as the ability to fight. Katniss, for instance, suffers from severe PTSD including recurrent flashbacks and nightmares; Buffy is not only severely injured and dies on several occasions throughout the series, but she also struggles with her role as the Chosen One and the responsibility and isolation it brings. Even though these issues are already dealt with in the canon to some extent, as the model of the feminist quest heroine includes the notion that feminine skills such as nurturing are valuable and potentially heroic, the heroines do not receive the same amount of comfort and support they get from their female partners in the femslash fics. Katniss observes, for instance, that "Johanna offers [her] a security that [she] can't seem to understand. It's not like the comfort Peeta afforded in his arms, or even the gentle familial comfort of sleeping in bed with [her] sister. It's something else entirely" (District_7_ Profanity, "Help"). Unlike Peeta, Johanna makes Katniss "feel like her old self" (Pinebundles) and allows her to share and come to terms with the "feelings [she] kept behind stone walls" (Bodylikeabattleaxe). Faith also offers Buffy physical as well as emotional comfort which she cannot get from any other character in the story, including her boyfriends (Elizabeth_Scripturient; Furies; Newrromantics). These fics thus not only give value to the feminine practice of nurturing, but by having their protagonists compare their female partners to male ones, they also further promote a queer agenda by celebrating gay relationships. After all, these are shown to be more effective in overcoming the traumatizing effects that being warriors has on Buffy and Katniss.

On the other hand, femslash stories are even more subversive than their male slash counterparts, because the latter frequently perpetuate heteronormative conceptions of romantic relationships. This is mostly because more often than not, the respective roles of hero and nurturer are taken on by the same character across different stories. In *Star Trek* slash, for instance, Kirk is usually given the role of the hero and Spock that of the feminized nurturer. Hurt/comfort featuring male characters therefore not only reflects the binary patterns of heteronormative relationships, but ultimately also constructs gender as a fixed and stable entity. By contrast, the femslash hurt/comfort stories challenge patriarchal gender hierarchies *as well as* heteronormative romance patterns, the perpetuation of binary gender roles, and conceptions of gendered identities as fixed and stable. This is possible because the femslash fics deviate from genre conventions when it comes to the question who takes on which role. Instead of invariably assigning the role of the injured masculinized hero to the protagonists of the source texts, and the nurturing and feminized part to the secondary characters, the femslash stories envision the young women in changing roles.

While they do take care of Buffy, Katniss, and Merida, Faith, Johanna, and Elsa also receive comfort from their female partners. In addition to Faith's physical injuries which are taken care of by Buffy, their relationship offers Faith a sense of home and belonging and makes it possible for her to overcome her traumatic childhood (Folie_a_yeux). Similarly, Elsa is able to deal with her anxieties and insecurities with the help of Merida (Lilyyuri; Thelinksthat-connectus). In the context of the *Hunger Games*, one of the most central motifs besides PTSD and nightmares that is taken up time and again is Johanna's fear of water, which she developed after being tortured in the Capitol. Numerous stories revolve around scenes in which Katniss enables Johanna to overcome her trauma by helping her to shower, take a bath, or go swimming (Fembuck; Pinebundles; Thesewordselope). By emphasizing their ability to move between roles that are usually ascribed to stereotypical femininity and masculinity, the femslash texts hence depict gender roles as performative and subject to change. The different roles which the female characters take on emphasize that romantic relationships do not have to involve one masculinized and one feminized partner. These femslash stories thus model for their teenage readers relationships that offer an alternative to the binary patterns still encountered in the majority of portrayals of romantic relationships, even in ones that include same-sex couples.

Through their detailed accounts of bodily injuries and psychological trauma, the femslash fics work against stereotypical depictions of romantic relationships on an additional level. As Anne Kustritz states:

> Slash characters are far from perfect, but they don't have to be. They receive the love of their desired partner not because of their physical and psychological resemblance to the airbrushed *Playboy* (or *Playgirl*) centerfold, but because they trust their partners enough to show them all the hidden things and broken places [379–80].

While portrayals of women and girls in mainstream culture frequently project the idea that both outer and inner perfection are needed for them to be deserving of romantic partners, in femslash, it is exactly the other way around: the characters are loved because of their imperfections, not in spite of them. This particular depiction of the girl warriors not only breaks with conventional representations of female characters to be found in mainstream popular culture, but also with the ones permeating fan fiction. To be more precise, it is the trope of the Mary Sue character that these stories criticize, as they maintain that even though they are not perfect, the young women are worthy of love and affection.

This can most clearly be seen in the fact that, frequently, the fics "make explicit references to each partner acknowledging and accepting the other's physical and emotional shortcomings" (Cicioni 161). For example, in "An Evergreen Forest," Katniss states that she "still got remnants of the battle" on her body and that she feels "a bit embarrassed" about them. Johanna, however, "lightly kisses each scarred piece of skin [and] whispers, 'you're beautiful, Katniss'" (Bodylikeabattleaxe). Similar notions are also expressed in *BtVS* femslash, as Buffy describes:

It [her body] is littered with the same bruises [as] Faith's body; mirroring the same war you've been through. It's the first time you've seen the damage of what you do reflected on somebody else. [...] It feels more real to see it up close. It feels less lonely to know that Faith goes through it, too: the push and pull, the kick and punch, the bruises and the pain [Newrromantics].

In this scene, Buffy characterizes Faith's body as a mirror image of hers, bearing the same marks as her body. This scene hence not only underlines the equal status of the two Slayers, but it also projects the idea that their shared experiences and the resulting bodily and mental injuries bring them together, make them understand each other, and allow them to "feel less lonely." In short, it is blemishes and bruises and not idealized bodies that make the respective partners appear attractive to each other. All in all, this particular portrayal of girls' bodies as attractive not in spite, but because of particular imperfections establishes an alternative and empowering conception of female bodies in general because it celebrates their strength and their resilience. It also includes notions of female beauty not usually found in mainstream popular culture or fan fiction.

The portrayal of queer characters as heroines follows a queer agenda as it expands on notions of heroism to include girls who do not identify as straight. These stories hence insist that conceptualizations of heroism should be opened up to include queer girls and young women. At the same time, these stories also follow a feminist agenda, because many of the features that are established as heroic in the femslash stories can already be found in the primary texts, or the model of the feminist quest heroine, to be more precise. The femslash fics insist that heroines do not need to be invariably masculine but that stereotypically feminine features also contribute to their heroism; they celebrate the overcoming of patriarchal power structures and the establishment of more equal societies; they elevate secondary characters and additional traits and behaviors into the realm of the heroic; and show that connections to others and mutual empowerment depicted through the same-sex relationships are important for the success of the warrior girls.

(Queer) Desire, Sex and Female Bodies

In this subchapter, I turn to genres of fan fiction that feature explicit sex scenes between two female characters. These stories subvert norms and conventions with regard to portrayals of girl warriors and role models because they feature queer teenage heroines who actively engage in sex and clearly enjoy it. In this context, PWP is especially well suited for an analysis, because it often focuses on sex scenes exclusively. Aside from hurt/comfort, it is probably also the most studied genre of fan fiction with different scholars commenting on its relation to pornography and romance (cf. Alexander; Driscoll, "One True"; Woledge), as well as its potential to subvert "cultural assumptions about what women want from sexually explicit material designed to produce sexual arousal" (Isaksson 33). In addition, I will also look at first time stories that not only narrate the story up until the point where the characters have sex for the first time and then fade out, but which also include actual sex scenes. These fics are interesting, as, very often, first time refers not only to sexual encounters with the particular partner, but to the fact that those are the heroines' first sexual encounters in general. Hence, these femslash fics once again address a teenage audience in particular by including topics that are relevant for a younger readership. Again, I will deviate from the patterns established by other scholars to some extent, as my focus lies on the manner in which lesbian sex and teenage girls' or young women's bodies are portrayed in these fics, rather than on the relationship to other types of texts that feature sex scenes or on the possible responses and desires of readers.[8]

Instead of romanticizing and idealizing first sexual encounters, many first time stories address the inexperience and uncertainties of the female characters as well as the awkwardness that these encounters potentially entail. For instance, the girls experience feelings of "dread [...] instead of pleasure" and find the prospect of having sex "nerve-wracking" (District_7_Profanity, "Help"; Phoebe1901, "Anticipation"). Often, they simply "don't know what to do" (District_7_Profanity, "Help"), or they are timid and blush (Bodylike-abattleaxe; Kennisiou). Their inexperience is furthermore pointed out when the fics state that they are not "exactly an expert on what naked women [feel] like" (Lysippe; see also Lilyyuri). However, it is not just the fearful emotions and feelings of being inadequate that are articulated in these fics, but they also give an account of intimate acts themselves that do not go exactly as planned. The femslash stories describe "teeth [that are] getting in the way more often than not" (Kennisiou), and young women who are "clumsy" or "freeze up" during sex (Bodylikeabattleaxe; Lilyyuri). Notably, the problems and anxieties the heroines encounter are always openly addressed and eventually solved, because they are met by the respective partners with openness and understanding. Often, the inexperienced partner is also offered guidance (Bodylikeabattleaxe; Folie_a_yeux). All in all, it is shown that sex does not have to be perfect in order to be pleasurable, because in spite of their clumsiness, the partners are shown to have a positive experience, or even "the best time of [their lives]" (Kennisiou).

Another important element addressed in these femslash fics is the issue of consent. The willingness of the respective partners to engage in sexual activity is not merely alluded to through the use of focalization, as delineated by Isaksson,[9] but the partners communicate and explicitly ask for permission to proceed in their actions, be it touching, undressing, or kissing the other girl. Time and again, the fics stop in their descriptions of the action in order to have their characters "[ask] for permission" (Jonisstrash), "lift an eyebrow in search for permission" (Johannas_Motivational_Insults), or "look up into [their partner's] eyes, a question on [their] face" (Electra126). More importantly, the girls only proceed after they have actually received permission to do so, either by nods (Iliveinfantasies; Johannas_Motivational_Insults; MonaLover07) or verbal requests (Electra126). Moreover, the girls also make sure that what they do feels good for their respective partners, as there are a number of scenes in which they ask whether what they are doing is okay (Kennisiou; Pop_Punk_Jolras).

Another important characteristic of the stories is that even though in the majority of fics, permission is willingly given, there are also some stories in which one partner is not ready for sex. These stories are not only important when it comes to the topic of consent as they emphasize that it is okay for someone to not engage in sexual activity if they do not want to, but they also model appropriate behavior by describing the feelings and reactions of the respective partners. Faith, for instance, accepts her girlfriend's hesitation to become intimate in spite of her own feelings: "She wanted Buffy badly, but she respected her above all else and didn't want to pressure her" (Radioclubjp). Likewise, Johanna accepts Katniss' nervousness regarding sex and does not do anything that might hurt or scare her (Phoebe1901, "Anticipation").

By including these short sequences that address different aspects of consent, namely how to ask for it, give it, and how to react if it is denied, these femslash fics make aware of a topic that is not only important in the context of queer sexuality, but of sex in general. In recent years, the issue of consent has been given increased importance and visibility in the mainstream media and U.S. society, especially because of the covering of rape and sexual assault in colleges, and is an important part of sex education in general.[10] These works of fan fiction take part in this discourse and teach their readership about consent by showing that it should be an integral part of sexual encounters. The inclusion of consent can thus be regarded as an additional aspect of the metanarrative of femslash that teaches its young readership about queer sexuality in particular, and sexual activity more generally.

The femslash stories that feature sex scenes, regardless of whether they belong to the genre of first time or PWP, also work against traditional notions and gendered stereotypes about sexual capacities. In mainstream media and culture, women and girls are still widely portrayed as passive and restrained, especially in comparison to boys' and men's sexual needs and desires (Isaksson 22, 32; Kapurch 449; Kustritz 382; Stone 47).[11] This is also visible in *Brave*, the *Hunger Games* and *Buffy the Vampire Slayer*. Out of the three female characters analyzed in this book, Buffy is the only one who has sex, who is allowed to be active both in bed and in the pursuit of her male partners, and who is shown to have a sex drive. In contrast to this, Merida, as a Disney princess, does not have any kind of sexuality at all, and Katniss experiences only one instant that can be described as sexual arousal, namely when she kisses Peeta on the beach during the Quarter Quell. However, the novel abstains from offering any details, let alone mentioning intimate body parts, when Katniss observes that "the sensation inside [her] grows warmer and spreads out from [her] *chest*, down through [her] body, out along [her] *arms and legs*. [...] Instead of satisfying [her], the kisses have the opposite effect, of making [her] need greater" (Collins, *CF* 352–53; emphasis added).

These rather chaste portrayals are, of course, influenced and regulated by the genre of the respective text and by the age of target audiences. Nevertheless, they demonstrate a reluctance to engage with or address teenage girls' sexuality, especially for characters who are established as heroines and role models. In contrast to the mainstream texts, fan fiction as a grassroots phenomenon can engage with teenage girls' sexuality and arousal more openly and thus addresses a topic that is of interest for a teenage audience. These pieces of fan fiction thus ultimately also affirm that female characters who actively engage in sex can still act as heroines and role models.

Whereas in the original texts and mainstream popular culture at large, "sexual pleasure and desire for girls continue to operate as both a societal threat and taboo," the femslash fics clearly articulate women's and girls' rights to their own pleasure and to control how that pleasure is depicted (Epstein, Kehily, and Renold 252–53). The femslash texts speak freely of the heroine's sex drive and their feelings of pleasure and arousal and they do mention more intimate body parts or areas. Instead of talking about legs and arms, for instance, the Katniss/Johanna stories locate the place of arousal "between [Katniss'] legs" (Bodylikeabattleaxe), or in "the groin" (District_7_Profanity, "Help"). In a Merida/Elsa fic, it is "in the cradle of [the] hips [...] where the heat [is] flaring hottest" (FlyingFleshEater). What is more, the stories also underline that their sex drive is very strong. Katniss, for instance, observes that her desire for sex is "strong enough to override common sense" (District_7_Profanity, "Help"), whereas Buffy "never [...] knew it was possible to be this turned on, to want something this bad" (Beersforqueers). Other fics characterize the desire for sex as something uncontrollable or a desperate need (FlyingFleshEater; Kennisiou).

Notably, the femslash fics portray sexual arousal not only as something natural that all of the girls experience, but also as something that has a right to be fulfilled. In my corpus, there is not one story in which the female characters are left unsatisfied. Indeed, their sexual needs are regarded as something positive, as the respective partners enjoy seeing the other's arousal and giving them pleasure (Bodylikeabattleaxe; District_7_Profanity, "Help";

DJMeep; Kennisiou; MonaLover07). For example, in the fic entitled "What I Want," the idea that the fulfillment of one's own wishes and desires, sexual and non-sexual ones, is something important, is made very explicit. As the title suggests, the story engages with Katniss' needs and wishes, both personal ones as well as sexual ones. The fic projects Katniss as someone who has lost any sense of her own needs and thus also a sense of self, because, as the Mockingjay, she is forced to fulfill the demands of the people around her. Johanna tries to convince her that she has a right to her own wants and needs. While Katniss observes that "it's a strange feeling, to be concentrating solely on making myself feel good. I try to think of the last time I've used my body for my own pleasure, and can't," her fellow victor states that "wanting something for yourself, even something idiotic like getting yourself off in the middle of the night, when no one can stop you from taking all the pleasure your beat-up body can still feel? [...] Sometimes that does matter" (Doctornerdington).

The motif of wanting something for yourself is significant on two levels. In the context of sexual desire and pleasure, it is an important statement to affirm the right of girls to receive or feel sexual pleasure. On a larger scale, the notion of wanting something for oneself, of focusing on personal wishes instead of those of others, also undermines the traditional gender conception of women as selfless nurturers who take care of others. Focusing on herself and her needs is cast as an act of rebellion against the role that Katniss is supposed to take on as the Mockingjay and the icon of the rebellion. This femslash fic hence insists that girls have a right to receive sexual pleasure and a right to take care of themselves and their own well-being. Since it is her role as the Mockingjay which causes Katniss to negate her own needs in the first place, this story also negotiates conceptualizations of heroism to include the notions that heroines should be allowed to take care of themselves both in general and when it comes to their sex lives.

Ultimately, "What I Want" also promotes masturbation as a form of self-care and stress-relief and as an important part of female sexuality. This is a progressive thought, especially when uttered in the context of teenage girls' sexuality. Whereas female masturbation and orgasms are still a taboo in mainstream popular culture—only very few movies include scenes where women, let alone teenage girls, have sexual agency and such scenes are often censored[12]—many femslash fics break with said taboo by not only including scenes in which the young women pleasure themselves, but also by describing this in detail (District_7_Profanity; Escritoireazul; Phoebe1901, "Anticipation"; Pseudo_sweetheart). The attention to detail is what makes these fics didactic, as the descriptions potentially teach readers how to masturbate. Lengthy masturbation scenes outline exactly what the girls do and how they feel:

I start with just my fingertips, swirling them over my cheeks, my throat, my collarbones [...]. When I touch both nipples at the same time, everything intensifies even further, and I gasp aloud. [...] I press my hand between my legs, thrusting my hips experimentally once or twice against my own strength. It isn't enough. [...] It almost tickles, almost itches, but in the sensation I feel the promise of something more. [...] I slide my finger in, slightly, parting my lower lips to feel the place where I'm slippery and wet. Everything is slick, and I can't stop myself from moving there, pressing, teasing, flicking. [...] It's not enough, what I'm feeling, and I speed my hand. [...] And then. My mind is blessedly blank, filled with an expanding pleasure that seems limitless [Doctornerdington].

With their attention to detail and their chronological accounts of actions, scenes such as this one can be seen as a kind of step-by-step tutorial on how to masturbate. In other fics, the didactic approach is included in an even more literal manner, as there are stories that explicitly feature a character who gives tips and offers instructions. In "Finding Solace," for instance, Johanna tells Katniss:

All you have to do is stick your hand in your underclothes [...]. Then you keep at it until you feel a sort of pressure, but a good kind. Eventually you'll reach the point where you'll ... what's a good way to say it? It'll feel like a tingly drug rushing through your veins, and afterwards you'll feel relaxed, like you've flushed your system of toxins in an instant. [...] Also, most people's nipples will respond, so playing with them with your other hand can be pleasant [Pseudo_sweetheart].

Taken together, the femslash fics that present masturbation scenes and instructions on how to pleasure oneself work against the lack of representations of female sexuality and pleasure found in both the mainstream media and U.S. society at large. More importantly, through this particular portrayal of masturbation scenes, these fics communicate a number of positive ideas regarding this issue. For instance, they insist that women and girls are sexual beings who have desires and needs. In addition, they advocate for the right to have and to satisfy said needs and desires, both when it comes to sex, but also on a more general level. Finally, they propose that taking care of those needs can be an empowering and subversive act, as it defies the gendered notions that girls are less sexual than boys or that they should be more concerned with the well-being or the satisfaction of the needs of others than with their own.

The attention to detail when it comes to the naming and description of body parts and the sequence of actions themselves cannot only be found in the masturbation scenes just analyzed, but they are also included in the portrayals of sexual intercourse between the female characters. Again, these fics offer guidance and information about female bodies as well as the actual act of having sex, and they speak freely of the sensations, both physical and emotional ones, experienced by the female protagonists during intercourse and climax. The sexual acts in these particular femslash fics are also decidedly queer and focused on women: they are non-phallic, do not focus on penetration, and put female pleasure and the female orgasm at their center. Indeed, there is only one fic in which a phallic object is included in the sex scene, and in none of the fics in my corpus is it penetration alone that brings the young women to orgasm.

The didactic nature of these fics manifests itself in the fact that the authors use anatomically correct terms to talk about the specific body parts of the girls. They distinguish between the vulva and the vagina, name labia and clitoris, and talk about the g-spot. More importantly, they also explain where these body parts are, how to find them, and what to do with them in explicit detail. Sex scenes recount Elsa "running her tongue across the same spots over and over [...]. Letting her mouth grow soft as she kisses lower, making her lips firmer as she rubbed them against Merida's clit" (Salmon_Pink). In other scenes, characters get actual verbal advice on what to do. When Buffy, for instance, tells Faith that she "[needs] some guidance," Faith gives her rather specific instructions (Folie_a_yeux). Again, fics such as this one underline the importance of communication and show that sexual inexperience is not negative or shameful, but that asking what to do and trying out different things can be a pleasurable experience for both partners. The importance of practice and taking time is also articulated in stories that talk about finding and stimulating the g-spot. After all, one fic describes that Johanna "had spent months searching for" it (Amsay), whereas several other ones offer specific instructions on how to stimulate it: "Faith rotated her hand so her palm was facing upward. She moved her index finger in a 'Come hither' motion and knew that she had found Buffy's g-spot when the blonde moaned out in pleasure and stuttered out her name" (DJMeep; see Amsay; Garnigal; Johannas_Motivational_Insults for similar scenes).

What is more, girls' orgasms are described in detail, both when it comes to bodily reactions and emotions. One fic, for instance, delineates that Buffy's "body shivered visibly, but that was no comparison to the maelstrom she could feel within. Every nerve ending had just fired. Lights danced behind her eyes, her lungs gasped for air and wave upon wave of pleasure rushed through her body" (Garnigal). Indeed, the focus on the female orgasm, how to achieve it, and what it feels like is subversive in itself as it goes against portrayals of female sexuality in mainstream culture and society. It is also subversive when it comes to the genre of fan fiction and slash. While in traditional slash stories, "heterosexual female desire [is] inscribed as long, detailed descriptions of male bodies as objects of desire and male arousal and orgasm as sources of joy and gratification for both partners," in femslash, it is exactly the other way around (Cicioni 167). It is queer female desire that is inscribed in these stories and the focus is on girls' bodies, their arousal, and their orgasms.

In addition to breaking with gender role portrayals of girls having a weaker sex drive, these fics also go against the assumption that they are, or should be, passive when it comes to sexual encounters. In the femslash fics collected in my corpus, girls receive pleasure from their female lovers, but they are also active both when it comes to pursuing their potential partners and to sexual acts themselves. Through these portrayals, the femslash stories challenge a claim voiced by Elizabeth Woledge, who posits that "perhaps the heteronormative patterns typically associated with sexual intimacy in our culture are almost impossible to transcend" (109). The femslash fics demonstrate that heteronormative patterns can actually be transcended, because the sex scenes subvert binary and heteronormative notions of romantic and sexual relationships as they show that each partner is able to take on and move between different subject positions as both active giver and passive receiver of pleasure, roles which are traditionally connected to stereotypical masculinity and femininity, respectively.

The explicit lesbian sex scenes between the female characters can furthermore be regarded as innovative and subversive because they differ from lesbian sex scenes found in both mainstream popular culture and pornography. Unlike its mainstream and pornographic counterparts, femslash is produced mainly by female writers for a female audience. As a consequence, these stories do not only *not* cater to a male gaze, but they also put lesbian sex scenes front and center instead of treating them "as one of the compulsory 'numbers' that constitute traditional heterosexual porn" (William qtd. in Isaksson 3). In these stories, it is not only a male gaze that is negated, but the gaze is also queered as it is a girl—often explicitly identified as queer—who looks at another girl and receives pleasure from this act of looking, as described in the following scenes: Merida "realised that Elsa was wearing only a bra underneath. Not just that, but a bra made of her own ice, glittering blue-white and more delicate than any lace. Merida's throat went dry" (Afterandalasia, "Looking"). Likewise, Katniss finds Johanna "on [her] bed, stark naked. She [is] stretched out like a cat, exposing every inch of her body to [her]. [...] [She] couldn't help but stare at her slender form" (MonaLover07).

Conventional conceptions of the gaze are challenged on an additional level as the act of looking does not implicate any kind of hierarchy or power relation. This is because the young woman who is looked at in these stories is either portrayed as active and strong, such as in a scene in which Johanna receives pleasure from looking at Katniss chopping fire wood (Amsay), or as consciously using her looks for seductive purposes, as in a story where a naked Johanna looks at Katniss "like a hunter stalking its prey" (MonaLover07), or Faith strips for Buffy (Shelley). Stable allocations are also subverted through the fact that the roles of the one who gazes and the one who is gazed at either constantly shift between the two characters or that both become onlookers as delineated in the following scene: "I look down to watch, and our foreheads press together; *we share our enjoyment of the spectacle we're making*" (Doctornerdington; emphasis added). Here, the gaze is not only a decidedly queer one, as it is two girls who watch their own lovemaking in a story that is aimed at a female readership, but they are both in the same position, receiving pleasure from looking at the sexual act in which they are both actively partaking. Ultimately, these femslash fics hence also undermine the idea that women and girls "can never look upon another woman and feel desire rather than despair or triumph," which, in many works of fan fiction, is projected through female characters such as the Mary Sue (Kustritz 380).

While the act of looking and the pleasure received from both gazing and being gazed at certainly plays an important role in the femslash fics, the sex scenes also put emphasis on all of the other senses. In addition to learning what the characters look like, readers also get to know how they feel, smell, sound, and taste. Consequently, the femslash fics draw a very complex and detailed picture of sex that goes beyond the mere description of what is done. As mentioned above, the questions of what is done, how it is done, and to what effect are a central and important part of these specific femslash fics, but through their inclusion of taste, sound, touch, and smell, sex is portrayed as more than just a sequence of specific actions, namely as a sensual experience in the truest sense of the word. Whereas accounts of the sounds that the girls emit during intercourse can be found in basically each of the explicit fics, taste and smell also feature prominently. In fact, it is insinuated that both are major factors that contribute to the mutual attraction between the partners and are also shown to be potentially arousing. Johanna, for instance, states that Katniss' "neck smelled forever of forest in the spring, leather from the jacket and mint from her pores [...]. It was absolutely intoxicating, Johanna thought as she pressed her face into the crook of Katniss' neck, inhaling deeply before she sunk her lips into the flesh, to taste" (Amsay). Other fics are rather more explicit when it comes to the connection between taste, smell, and arousal. They recount, for instance, that during or before cunnilingus, Elsa "[inhales] the scent of sex there, the scent of *want*" (Salmon_Pink), or that Buffy "[gives] up a sharp spicy smell. Faith can taste her, sweet and thick at the corners of her mouth" (Folie_a_yeux).

With their focus on and detailed descriptions of not only girls' smell, but the smell of intimate body parts and the fluids they secrete, the femslash fics also rework established conventions regarding misogynist portrayals of female bodies in literature and art. To be more precise, they simultaneously call upon and challenge the model of the female grotesque established by Mary J. Russo, who argues that female bodies have traditionally been portrayed as fluid, cavernous, and open; depictions which used to maintain a misogynist discourse that represents the female body as unaesthetic, inferior, repulsive, and even monstrous (2, 8). In the femslash stories, the heroines' bodies adhere to this model, as they are shown to be penetrable, open, cavernous, rough, and secreting fluids. What is more, they are not smooth and delicate, either, because they have body and pubic hair or are marked by scars which symbolize their physical strength and heroism (Amsay; Bodylikeabattleaxe; Electra126; Jonisstrash; Kennisiou; M_phoenix; Newrromantics; Salmon_Pink; Thesewordselope; TiggerFace, "Little Things";). In addition to the bodily fluids mentioned before, they also sweat or bleed (Doctornerdington; Folie_a_yeux; Iliveinfantasies; Johannas_Motivational_Insults; LauraHollis, "Baby"; Lilyyuri; M_phoenix; Newrromantics; Stormwreath).

At the same time that they bring to mind the female grotesque, the femslash fics undermine the notion of inferiority and repulsiveness connected to it by stressing that these bodies are erotic, desirable, and beautiful. Indeed, frequently, they are even shown to be attractive because of these features and not in spite of them. The femslash fics hence undermine the idea that bodies that do not adhere to impossible standards of feminine beauty are unattractive or a potential source of shame. This is all the more important because Russo also mentions that such notions are frequently internalized by girls and women themselves, who try to erase or hide the signs that would mark their bodies as abject, grotesque, and unattractive (2). By portraying the heroines' bodies in such an unconventional way, the femslash fics establish a discourse that is empowering and body positive, which is all the more important for a young readership whose own bodies are still developing.

Gay sex is, in a sense, also portrayed as a crucial part of the girls' heroism, as it is instrumental for the female warriors' ability to keep fighting or overcome challenges in general. This is because in many stories, it is specifically gay sex that is shown to have special powers: it is healing and/or magical. Being queer is thus conceptualized in a radical manner, namely as a potentially heroic feature. Having sex with Merida, for instance, helps Elsa to let go of her anxieties and insecurities, and she allows herself to feel instead of think (Lilyyuri). Similarly, after having sex with Johanna, Katniss feels "happier than [she has] been in a long time" (District_7_Profanity, "Help"), and she is able to live in the moment instead of being "constantly overcome with fear" (Pseudo_sweetheart). Indeed, bodily affections are literally described as healing on numerous occasions, for instance when Katniss states "I let her hold me […]. I let her heal me. With her touch, with her hold, with her lips. She touches her lips to mine, warms them with her warmth, breathes air into my chest" (Flipflop_diva).

This trope of lesbian sex as magical and/or healing figures most prominently in Buffy/Faith femslash. In "Magnetic," for instance, bodily contact in general, and having sex in particular, further improves the Slayers' already supernatural healing powers. Faith explains that "every caress is a bruise being healed, every kiss a scar erased. [...]. Her orgasm washes over her and she's reborn, no longer the girl who hurt everyone but the girl who came back to help" [...]. "She feels strong, she feels whole, she feels unstoppable" (Electra126). Lesbian sex and female orgasms are also given an empowered meaning when in a story that slightly deviates from the canon, it is Buffy's and Faith's orgasm, and not Willow's magic, that activates the magic of the scythe and the potential Slayers (Folie_a_yeux).

By staging the teenage heroines as girls who have a sex drive and engage in sexual activities with their partners, the femslash texts expand on the notion of heroism to include not only queer girls, but sexually active ones, too. Some of them even depict gay sex as an important part of the girls' ability to fight, or rather heal after fighting. These stories break with conventional and fetishized portrayals of lesbian sex found in both mainstream popular culture and pornography. Instead, they normalize lesbian sex at the same time that they promote it as erotic and pleasurable. In addition, by making queer sex accessible to a (young) readership, these fics allow queer readers to explore their own sexual orientation and find pleasurable reading material. They also offer valuable information for young female readers regardless of their sexual orientation. After all, they work against the taboo surrounding (young) women's sexuality and instead engage with and instruct about important issues such as consent, pleasure, or masturbation, and model for their teenage readership a notion of female beauty that includes and even celebrates imperfections.

Conclusion

The femslash fics analyzed in this chapter use their respective source texts as stepping stones to affirm and expand on the innovative conceptualizations of heroism, female characters, and gender roles already established in the latter ones. The fics promote and establish as heroic many features already put forth by the model of the feminist quest heroine. To be more precise, they celebrate the female heroes' defiance of traditional and binary gender roles, revalue traits and behaviors connected to traditional femininity, emphasize the empowering potential of connections, or focus on secondary characters and attribute them heroic potential, too. However, by queering the heroines, the fan texts broaden their approach to heroism to include the issues of sexual orientation and sexual identity, so that their subversive potential is informed by both the protagonists' gender as well as their sexuality. In other words, the femslash fics call for more diverse conceptions of heroism and question the heteronormative standard found in representations of both male and female heroes. By staging the teenage heroines as girls who have a sex drive and engage in sexual activities with their partners, the femslash texts expand on the notion of heroism to include not only queer girls, but sexually active ones, too.

Even though the femslash fics that deal with the different heroines have a lot in common and cater to the same discourses about gender roles, heroism, queerness, or female sexuality, different issues appear in the respective texts in different proportions and to different extents. At the same time that the femslash fics openly defy and criticize certain elements of the canon, they are also always embedded in and influenced by the respective source text, so that major themes and motifs of the canon are taken up in the slash fics.

Although there exists explicit Merida/Elsa slash, for instance, many texts are rather restrained, going no further than having the two royals share a kiss, a touch, or even just a look. Slash writers are apparently influenced by the more traditional norms and values inscribed in the Disney canon and the company's status as wholesome family entertainment. User Lilyyuri, for instance, notes: "You have no idea how hard it is to try and write a sex scene with Disney's characters! I'm feeling like I'm ruining their innocence." As this comment insinuates, slash writers who write sex scenes in general, and lesbian ones in particular, have to work against the canon to a large degree. What is more, they also have to work against societal assumptions and norms about young women's sexuality, many of which are perpetuated by the conception of Disney princesses as innocent and pure. This results in the fact that there are fewer PWP stories in the context of Disney princess movies than there are in the cases of the *Hunger Games* and *BtVS*. Major themes, on the other hand, are Merida's and Elsa's roles as (future) rulers of their kingdoms. Almost all of the fics in my corpus celebrate the empowered status of the two Disney princesses, promote female leadership, and consequently endorse these innovative aspects of *Brave* and *Frozen*.

In the case of the *Hunger Games*, the fact that the franchise is darker and geared towards an older audience than the Disney movies is clearly reflected in the slash stories. After all, PTSD, war, and even suicide are the most prominent topics, as is the process of healing and overcoming traumatic events. Notably, the femslash fics promote the same-sex relationship between Katniss and Johanna, and not the heterosexual one between Katniss and Peeta, as the best means to do so, thus defying the heteronormative agenda established in the canon. The stories are also very explicit when it comes to the description of sexual acts, defying the notion of Katniss as a teenage girl without any sexual desires or needs in particular, and, on a larger scale, the portrayal of YA heroines as non-sexual.

Both the age difference of target audiences and the topics that the source text deals with are reflected in the stories written by *BtVS* fans. In a similar manner to the *Hunger Games* femslash, these fics, too, deal with issues such as violence, trauma, and death. What is more, the Buffy/Faith fics are the ones to include the most, and the most explicit, sex scenes, which is mostly due to the prevalence of said issue in the source text itself.

All in all, the femslash fics analyzed in this chapter reflect and celebrate the cultural and societal changes regarding the status of women and girls that have occurred in recent years at the same time that they call for even more progress. The prevalence of male slash that has existed ever since the genre first emerged in the late 1960s and is still observable today mirrors the dominance of male characters in, as well as the patriarchal ideals perpetuated through, the mainstream media.[13] After all, scholars find the reasons why female fans mainly write about men in the stereotypical and often misogynist ways women and girls are portrayed in the media themselves, as well as in the patriarchal discourses of U.S. society at large. Even though girl warriors and female heroes enter popular culture in increasing amounts, in many TV shows, movies, comics, or computer games, men continue to take on the role of the protagonist who is not only complex and interesting, but also at the center of the action. As a consequence, fans are more likely to identify with male characters than with female ones, who are, if not non-existent, often one-dimensional, unimportant for the development of the plot, or possess traits with which the average girl or woman might not be able to identify (Busse 211; Green, Jenkins, and Jenkins 67).

Still, the growing number of femslash mirrors the fact that there are more and more media that feature female characters who are interesting, complex, and central to the action. In other words, the mainstream media increasingly produce female characters which fans deem worthy to engage and identify with. Whereas for a long time, the argument ran that "because of the limitations in media and cultural representations of women, women cannot imagine themselves as heroes unless they imagine themselves as male" (Barker), the femslash fics featuring Buffy, Merida, and Katniss demonstrate that these limitations are slowly breaking down. The female characters serve as heroines both in the source texts as well as in the fan texts and thus mirror the progress in both culture and society that has been made in recent years. What is more, by portraying the heroines as queer, the femslash fics ask for even more progress when it comes to the level of inclusiveness of mainstream media and culture.

◆ ◆ 6 ◆ ◆

Affirming Feminism,
Challenging Whiteness
Girl Warriors in Fan Art

The power of a visual piece is automatic, visceral, and deeply impact-
ful, often instantaneously. Users can connect to the visual for its aesthetic pleasure, but also for the strong emotional response that it
garners.—Gilliland 5.1

Fan art is very similar to fan fiction insofar as both genres can be
described as creative outlets for fans' reactions to and interpretations of popular stories and characters. While authors of fan fiction use the written word
exclusively in order to react to said stories and characters, fan artists create
images to do so.[1] These images can take on a number of different forms, so
that "broadly defined, [fan art] would include fan drawing and painting, as
well as digital image manipulations, mash-ups, and even potentially animated
GIFs" (Scott 150). When it comes to content, fan art is even more diverse
than it is on the level of form. Some fan artists copy scenes or characters but
change the style of the respective piece by making it more realistic, or turn
realistic original texts into comics or anime, for instance. They also draw and
paint in order to give a face to characters from popular novels, or rework
well-known characters' outer appearance. Others produce cross-overs in
which characters from different fictional universes come together, or imagine
romantic scenes featuring either already established couples or, in a similar
manner to writers of fan fiction, slash characters by portraying them as same-
sex partners. Even though fan art occasionally ties into the same discourses
as fan fiction, as a medium that relies heavily on the visual, it is less concerned
with the representation of character traits or inner thoughts and feelings,
and more with outer appearance and the representation of bodies. In recent
years, fan artists have, for instance, commented on the homogenous manner

in which popular mainstream media portray especially central characters by changing the shape, gender role, race, or ethnicity of these characters.

One other central aspect that sets fan art apart from fan fiction is its larger potential to become viral. Although fan fiction has shed its status as a marginal phenomenon of fan culture and is written, read, and studied by an increasing number of people, its visibility pales in comparison to that of many pieces of fan art, which are shared, liked, reblogged, and discussed on sites such as Tumblr, DeviantArt, or Pinterest in the thousands and ten thousands, occasionally reaching up to more than a million likes and shares. This is possible because the platforms are regularly used and visited by millions of people: DeviantArt has "over 38 million registered members and [...] over 65 million unique visitors per month" ("About DeviantArt"); Pinterest is visited by more than 150 million users per month (Chaykowski); and Tumblr attracts about 550 million visitors a month ("Tumblr") and contains 342.3 million blogs and 147.4 billion posts ("About").

Notably, images are the central element of these sites: whereas Pinterest and DeviantArt feature images exclusively, Tumblr users have the opportunity to choose between eight different types of posts—photos, texts, quotes, audio, video, chat, answer, and link—but with almost 80 percent of overall posts, images represent the vast majority (Y. Chang et al. 22). Admittedly, with the exception of DeviantArt, not all of the pictures uploaded on these platforms are fan art, but one can still find a plethora of items that belong to this genre. Users and fan artists also frequently upload and reblog fan art across these different platforms. This shows that fan art is not only more likely to become viral because of the sheer number of users who engage with it, but also because in contrast to fan fiction, it is quicker to consume and share. In fact, the posting, reblogging, and discussing of the images not only happens on the specific platforms themselves, but popular images are also frequently taken up by journalists, bloggers, and users of other social media such as Facebook.

Not least due to their popularity, in recent years, online platforms such as Pinterest and Tumblr have aroused the interest of academics to an increasing degree, with scholars studying demographics, levels of social interaction, quality and type of content, or the representation of gender roles and interactions (Y. Chang et al.; S. Chang et al.). Other scholars have investigated their potential as political spaces in general, and feminist spaces in particular (Connelly; Milner; Retallack, Ringrose, and Lawrence), observing that "it is increasingly clear that the internet has facilitated the creation of a global community of feminists who use the internet both for discussion and activism" (Munro 23). One of the most important effects of this move into online spaces it the possibility to include and represent more marginalized groups and to establish networks and discussions more easily. In other words, "because the internet allows people to vocalize their experiences of oppression in a globalized world, active and present forms of intersectionality is a real possibility in internet feminism" (Connelly 37).

Nevertheless, even though it offers new possibilities and opportunities for feminist activism and engagement, scholars posit that, instead of seeing the Internet as either a utopian or dystopian environment, it should rather be regarded as a highly contested space "of tough struggles for gender and sexuality," where feminist voices, anti-feminist voices, and opinions from everyone in between the two poles are spread and discussed (Carstensen 117).[2] In this context, social media platforms are one prevalent space in which said struggles take place.

While research has been conducted on a number of features as well as the kinds of discourses that take place in these online spaces, one aspect that is largely missing from the corpus of academic work on online spaces and their potential impact is an engagement with image content itself (Y. Chang 29). Whereas statistics, user demographics, photo captions, discussions, and written content have been analyzed by a number of scholars (Connelly; Y. Chang et al.; S. Chang et al.), the images themselves have largely been neglected. Similar tendencies can be observed with regard to fan art specifically, which, as Suzanne Scott explains, is studied to a far lesser extent than other types of fan practices and creations (150).

In this chapter, I want to bring together the two different strands of analysis—image content of fan art and feminist online spaces—with my own research on female heroes and the representation of female characters in popular culture by analyzing works of fan art that engage with Buffy, Katniss, and Merida. I am primarily interested in the different ways fan artists represent and adapt the girl warriors and the claims these images make about the characters, their outer appearance, their stories, and the concepts of heroism their narratives establish. I am using the term "claims" here because, after all, just like fan fiction, fan art should be seen as an interpretation of the source texts and fan artists as members of an "active interpretative community" (Kaplan 135). I argue that fan artists engage in the affirmation of feminist theory and activism as crucial features of (female) heroism at the same time that they imagine and establish new and more diverse heroic characters. I also show that users create and share pieces of fan art about the female heroes in order to engage in a variety of intersectional feminist online discourses that are concerned with the representation of women and girls (of color) in the mainstream media.

Since I am primarily interested in feminist discourses, I will neglect pieces of fan art that embed the young women into heteronormative, sexist, or racist discourses.[3] In order to further narrow down my objects of analysis, I take a look at two online platforms and two specific genres of fan art. With regard to platforms, I focus on Tumblr and Pinterest, two sites which, at a first glance, are very different in nature. Tumblr, for example, is mainly used by people between the ages of 13 and 24 (Connelly 3; Y. Chang et al. 21), whereas most Pinterest users are between 24 and 44 years old (Y. Chang et al. 22). Eighty percent of registered users on Pinterest are women (S. Chang et al. 674), whereas no such information exists for Tumblr because users do not have to indicate their sex when they register. That it is not necessary to define or articulate one's sex on Tumblr underlines the site's progressive nature. In fact, both among users and scholars, Tumblr is widely regarded as "a platform for highly involved feminist dialogue" and "one of the most significant locations of political commentary, activism, and community on the internet because of user's dedication to social justice and political correctness" (Connelly 2, 1). This is an important aspect that counters the notion described in the introduction, namely that (teenage) girls or young women are nonpolitical or do not take part in feminist discourses, as many of the young female Tumblr users do exactly that. In contrast to this, Pinterest is primarily used for saving and sharing images connected to lifestyle or consumption (S. Chang et al. 674). Nevertheless, during my research, I have found that boards with feminist content and fan art do exist on Pinterest as well, albeit as a niche category. Still, the very existence of feminist fan art on two platforms that are so fundamentally different speaks for the pervasiveness of feminist thought and theory in online spaces at large.

The two fan art genres on which I focus are image macro memes and racebent fan art. Image macro memes are digitally manipulated images which combine a picture or screenshot from a TV show, movie, commercial, etc., with a written comment or punchline set in a simple white font (cf. Milner 2365). They are a subcategory of memes, a term that, in general, describes an item of digital culture—a picture, a video, a tweet, a hashtag, etc.—that is rapidly spread online ("Meme"). Research has shown that, while in the past, memes have often been neglected due to their seemingly shallow, trivial, and ephemeral nature, they do, in fact, have a central and influential social function within and outside of digital culture because they "are tied directly to ways of interacting with others, to meaning making, and to ways of being, knowing, learning and doing" (Knobel and Lankshear 221). Communication studies scholar Limor Shifman even draws a connection between memes and myths, as she describes the first as a kind of "(post)modern folklore, in which shared norms and values are constructed through cultural artifacts" (15). In this chapter, I look at the image macro memes that portray Buffy, Katniss, and Merida in order to find out more about the norms and values regarding gender roles, female heroes, and feminism that are spread through these items of digital culture.

The second genre of fan art I analyze are racebent images. Originally, the term "racebending" referred to the changing of a character's racial or ethnic background in general. As delineated by Lori Kido Lopez in "Fan Activists and the Politics of Race in *The Last Airbender*," the racebending movement emerged in December 2008 as a reaction to the casting of white actors for the live-action adaptation of the animated series *The Last Airbender*. The casting choices left many fans outraged because the series was set in a space many of them perceived to be Asian, as it used "cultural practices, architecture, religious iconography, costumes, calligraphy, and other elements from East Asian and Inuit cultures" (431). Therefore, fans argued, the actors who took on these roles should have been Asian as well. Today, however, the terms "racebent" and "racebending" have come to describe a fan practice in which a fictional character who is white or Caucasian is transformed into a person of color (POC). Visual representations of said transformations, or, in other words, fan art, is used to envision these fundamental changes with fans altering outer appearances either digitally through photoshopping or manually through sketching and drawing.[4] Racebent fan art that portrays the heroines Buffy, Katniss, and Merida contributes to an intersectional feminist discourse that advocates for the representation of girls of color in the mainstream media. The pieces of fan art included in my analysis furthermore maintain that they should be portrayed in non-stereotypical and heroic roles.

Even though both genres of fan art analyzed in this chapter draw from the same primary texts, they engage with, interpret, and comment on *BtVS*, the *Hunger Games*, and *Brave* in ways that differ from each other to a large extent and shed light on different aspects of these items of popular culture. Indeed, they perfectly illustrate Jenkins' claim that "fandom [...] is born of a balance between fascination and frustration: if media content didn't fascinate us, there would be no desire to engage with it; but if it didn't frustrate us on some level, there would be no drive to rewrite or remake it" (*Convergence* 258). On the one hand, the fascination with the innovative and empowered heroic roles Buffy, Merida, and Katniss take on is reflected in the image macro memes that celebrate these particular aspects of the texts. These memes do not make any fundamental changes regarding the heroines' outer appearance or their stories. Rather, they focus on and increase the feminist potential of the texts and promote the heroines themselves along with their stories as progressive and feminist. Notably, the do so by emphasizing central traits and plot elements that are characteristic of the model of the feminist quest heroine, such a girls' physical prowess, agency, notions of sisterhood and the importance of friends and allies, or the reworking of hegemonic and binary gender scripts. On the other hand, the simultaneous frustration with said pieces of popular culture is captured in racebent fan art. The act of racebending Buffy, Merida, and Katniss not only changes their outer appearance, but makes it possible for fan artists and online users to criticize the primary texts for their lack of diversity, to denounce different aspects regarding the representation of women and girls of color in the mainstream media at large, and to create new heroines who broaden conceptualization of the heroic to include non-white characters and non–Western stories.

Notably, it is particularly because of the different aspects with which they engage that, taken together, these pieces of fan art contribute to a larger intersectional feminist online discourse which strives to include and represent women and girls with diverse backgrounds. At the same time that they celebrate the empowered status of characters such as Buffy, Merida, and Katniss, they also reflect on the need for people of color to be seen in popular culture not only more frequently but also in central and non-stereotypical roles that present them as heroines and role models. These works of fan art attest to the idea that representation matters, because whether and how marginalized groups and minorities are represented by the media at large and by popular culture in particular can have a profound influence on the way members of these groups see themselves and others (cf. Bruce 2; Hines and Ayres 4; Wanzo 1.5; Whelan 26–27). On a basic level, the plethora of images created and shared by the online community calls for an increase in numbers of powerful female characters and role models. This is because both the original and the racebent versions simply multiply the female heroes and thus increase their visibility. The pieces of fan art hence first of all work against the general lack of female characters (of color) in popular culture simply by producing more of them. Secondly, the images also suggest that it is important how these characters are represented. Instead of reproducing and promoting gendered and racial stereotypes, as many popular media do, the fan art I analyze here calls for an innovative and complex portrayal of female characters by celebrating their heroic and empowered status at the same time that they challenge the white hegemony at work in these texts.

In this chapter, I first take a look at the image macro memes in order to show how their combination of pictures and punchlines makes it possible to engage with a variety of feminist issues and discourses. Since these ideas and discourses are present in all three primary texts, this subchapter will follow a thematic approach that explains how different types of memes contribute to or advocate for different aspects of the overarching feminist discourse. I suggest categorizing image macro memes into three different types. The first and least complex type of meme works on an intra-textual level as it draws from one primary text exclusively and combines screenshots and quotes from or about the female protagonist of this text. The second type of meme uses intertextual references in order to highlight a specific heroine's strength or to communicate more general messages about female empowerment. Finally, the third type of meme does not directly engage with the primary texts themselves, but works on a meta-level as it uses comments from the people involved in the creative process, that is, writers, directors, or actresses and actors, to underline the feminist aspects of the respective texts. For many of the memes analyzed here, users have posted a number of similar examples that share the same scenes, images, characters, and/or quotations, albeit with slight variations. The repeated representation of specific scenes, quotes, and screenshots demonstrates that these scenes and statements are "important, meaningful, or in some way striking enough to have formed an accessible memory" (M. Butler 226). Consequently, the simple fact that many Internet users create memes that represent female heroes in an empowered manner is in itself an important finding because it shows that the online community is eager to engage with and spread feminist ideas and concepts.

After analyzing the image macro memes, I turn to the pieces of racebent fan art and look at different strategies that are used by fans in order to make aware of and tackle the problem of the lack of representation of women and girls of color, the hegemony of Western beauty ideals, or acts of whitewashing conducted by the culture industries. Similar to the image macro memes, the viral nature of the racebent images reflects that intersectionality, and the inclusion of girls of color in particular and people of color in general, are issues close to the heart of online fandoms and the online community at large. However, since the different primary texts represent and engage with issues of race and ethnicity in very different ways, this subchapter is structured in a manner that analyzes *BtVS*, *Brave*, and the *Hunger Games* individually one after the other. While I concentrate on the image content, I will also include analyses of the written words surrounding these images, such as comments, descriptions, user names, or titles of blogs, as these are instrumental in understanding the meaning of the different works of fan art.

Visualizing Feminist Heroines in Image Macro Memes

The first type of meme discussed in this chapter is what I call intratextual image macro memes. These focus exclusively on one heroine and her story. Text and image work together in order to draw attention to what the creators of these images deem the most important ideas and statements propagated in a particular narrative. Interestingly, these memes often represent exactly those features of the heroines and their stories that have been revised by replacing the archetype of the warrior or damsel with the feminist quest heroine.

In the case of Princess Merida, the female protagonist of the animated movie *Brave*, creators of memes identify those scenes as essential in which the young woman defies notions of female passivity or breaks with patriarchal traditions. A plethora of memes show her shooting her bow and arrow or riding her horse. Another scene that is frequently used is when Merida rejects her parents' wish to get married. She resists parental control by beating all of her male suitors in an archery contest held for the purpose of finding her a prospective husband. This act of defiance can be regarded as a feminist moment because Merida not only shows that she is a more capable archer than the male contestants, but she also subverts the ancient patriarchal tradition of arranged marriage of her society by winning her own hand and thus self-ownership. Through these plot points, the movie, and by extension also the memes that deploy scenes like the ones described above, deconstruct the stereotypical image of the (Disney) princess, who can be regarded as "a variation of the damsel in distress stereotype" (Rothschild 9). Instead of perpetuating the trope of female weakness and dependence, the memes emphasize Merida's resistance and infuse the role of the princess with new connotations, namely of agency, mobility, and defiance of patriarchal systems.

In addition to representing her strength visually, the majority of intratextual image macro memes combine images of Merida with captions that draw from the voice-over narration of the movie where Merida herself acts as the narrator. She states: "There are those who say fate is something beyond our command, that destiny is not our own. But I know better. Our fate lives within us, you only have to be brave enough to see it" (*Brave*). As the plethora of memes that makes use of this statement suggests, many users see this as the central statement of the movie because it articulates the alternative concept of bravery propagated in the film. Whereas traditional bravery is depicted through the characters of Merida's father King Fergus and Merida herself as skilled warriors who do not shy away from physical altercations, the movie also presents standing up to structures that would otherwise shape your life as a demanding and brave task. Merida possesses the courage to defy her own family in order to change the patriarchal system and to choose her own path in life. Singling out and drawing attention to Merida's strength, agency, and defiant character, the memes emphasize the new role of Merida as an active and self-reliant teenage girl who does not need to be saved by a prince in shining armor.

Many of the intra-textual memes portraying Katniss Everdeen stage her development from a non-political and oppressed tribute to an empowered rebel. A typical example which originally appeared on Tumblr and was then reposted by user Ericka Smith on Pinterest, for instance, features a close-up of Katniss with the words sister, daughter, archer, rebel, hero, girl on fire, Mockingjay written next to it. The meme constructs a narrative about her development from a sister and archer to a rebel and to her becoming the Mockingjay, the symbol of the rebellion against President Snow. Through its focus on her development and empowerment, this meme dramatizes one of the central features of the feminist quest heroine, namely coming into political consciousness, which is an indispensable tool to fight and overcome patriarchal oppression. Notably, the meme also maintains that Katniss, her behavior, and her development are heroic, as the description includes the term "hero." Indeed, taken together, the captions draw attention to the complexity of her character, as they demonstrate that she takes on numerous roles throughout her story and thus subverts stereotypical portrayals or stock characters such as the strong female character. The captions point out that Katniss is not one-dimensional and/or decorative, but complex and influential. The meme thus not only celebrates Katniss' development and complexity, but by calling her a hero, it also offers a clear and unambiguous interpretation of her role within the trilogy. Finally, even though, through the use of lighter colors, it suggests that her roles as sister and daughter are not as important as her role as girl on fire and the Mockingjay, it still also makes aware of another feature typical of the feminist quest heroine, and that is her connection to others: this meme insinuates that Katniss is not an unattached and lonely warrior, as suggested in the movie posters analyzed in Chapter 4, for example, but part of a family.

The memes of the second category, intertextual memes, do not focus on one heroine exclusively but employ intertextual references. Shifman considers this intertextual practice to be "a central attribute" of Internet memes in general (2). By referring to multiple texts, putting them into opposition to each other, or highlighting parallels between them, these memes achieve two effects: they draw attention to the female heroes' potential to function as (feminist) role models and they make general claims about the role of female heroes in contemporary popular culture. Two examples are the portrayals of Buffy (Macey) and Katniss ("We Will Rebel") in the role of the iconic Rosie the Riveter in the "We Can Do It" poster. While the background story of the original image is rather complex,[5] the "depiction of Rosie has become an empowering symbol for women" and she is often regarded as a "feminist icon" in the popular imagination (Kimble and Olson 537, 533). This is because Rosie the Riveter represents the idea that women can successfully take on jobs and roles traditionally reserved for men. Indeed, the comparison between Rosie the Riveter, Katniss, and Buffy is convincing because both girls occupy roles that have been reserved for men within Western culture for centuries. This holds true for their status as heroines in general, but also for their roles as warrior, political icon, and rebel in the case of Katniss, and warrior and superhero in the case of Buffy. Through the allusion to the well-known image of Rosie the Riveter, the memes establish Buffy and Katniss as feminist icons in their own right.

In addition, the feminist concept of sisterhood, which is a central element of the feminist quest heroine, is evoked by the use of the pronoun "we" in the respective captions of the images, as the memes call for unity and group effort and represent Buffy and Katniss as representatives of a larger group of people. While the meme-makers slightly changed the captions from the original "We Can Do It" into "We Can Slay It" and "We Will Rebel" to fit the contexts of the different primary texts, the personal pronoun "we" was left unchanged. This is important as it suggests that the two young women want to include and encourage others to follow their lead and to rebel against, and metaphorically slay, patriarchal and other oppressive forces in their respective societies. Indeed, the pronoun draws attention to the notion of sisterhood represented in the primary texts through the specific manner in which both Buffy and Katniss bring down the oppressive forces in their respective fictional universes delineated in Chapters 1 and 2: instead of accumulating individual power, they empower themselves *and* others.

In addition, these memes also partake in an intersectional feminist discourse that advocates for diversity. Even though these memes represent white, heterosexual, able-bodied, and conventionally beautiful young women, they are merely two examples of a large corpus of similar memes that replace Rosie the Riveter with a variety of girls and women. In these memes, the role of Rosie is taken over, for example, by little girls, pregnant women, women of different races, ethnicities, and religions, but also by celebrities who have become feminist icons or role models in their own right, such as Beyoncé, Michelle Obama, or Malala Yousafzai. Taken together, these memes advocate for the notion of sisterhood propagated by third wave feminism by including "more diverse voices, including those of men and those of non-white heritage" (Payne-Mulliken and Renagar 58).

Intertextual memes do not only suggest similarities and parallels between feminist characters such as Rosie the Riveter, Buffy, and Katniss, but intertextual references can also be used to emphasize how differently gender roles are portrayed in popular culture. One set of prominent examples for this strategy are memes depicting Bella Swan, the protagonist of the popular *Twilight* series, who is widely regarded as the exact opposite of characters such as Buffy and Katniss because she is clumsy, helpless, and passive.[6] The sheer number of memes that make use of intertextual references to *Twilight* "suggests a broad-based community of interest" with regard to the characters themselves, but especially to the gender roles they project and the type of role model they represent (M. Butler 224).

In this case, intertextuality is used to draw a clear distinction between Bella, on the one hand, and Katniss or Buffy, on the other one. The creators of these specific memes underline the extraordinary position of strong girls like Buffy or Katniss by comparing them to a female character that they do not deem empowered or worth emulating. While the memes that compare Bella Swan with Katniss Everdeen mainly focus on the differences in behavior, mobility, and strength—Katniss wins a televised fight to the death while Bella is the stereotypical damsel in distress who needs to be rescued by her male friends and love interests time and again—the comparisons to Buffy often use the two young women's romantic relationships with vampires to comment explicitly on the issues of gender and sexuality. Here, the critique hinges on *Twilight*'s compliance with traditional gender roles, conventions of romance, and the reiteration of the damsel in distress archetype, whereas Buffy is celebrated as the protagonist of an innovative, exciting, and entertaining TV show that breaks with these very conventions.

The meme "Lessons from Twilight vs. Lessons from Buffy" (Nichols) is a typical example of how differently the two characters are perceived. The meme criticizes the *Twilight* characters and celebrates the romantic relationship represented in *BtVS*. Under the caption, the meme shows images of the two couples, Edward and Bella on the left and Angel and Buffy on the right, in a comic strip style, each couple having a conversation that implicitly characterizes their respective relationship. The meme has Edward proclaim that in addition to stalking, manipulating, and physically abusing his girlfriend, he will treat her like a child and contemplate killing her. Bella's reaction in the meme is to accept his behavior; she responds: "That's okay, I will just internalize your abuse as my fault. After all, you're a man so you must be right" (Nichols). Bella's body language—she is sitting on a bed staring into space—underlines her passivity. Drawing attention to the often-voiced complaint that *Twilight* portrays a controlling and abusive relationship as the epitome of romantic love (cf. Ames 39, 41; Platt 71–72), the meme criticizes that the novels and film adaptations teach feminine obedience and masculine superiority: Edward is the one in charge and Bella accepts his masculine authority. The meme exhibits the dynamics in which women hold themselves responsible for being mistreated and interpret their partners' abusive behavior as expressions of their love and care. It openly addresses a tabooed pattern of behavior and provides an alternative on the right-hand side of the meme.

Here, Angel offers Buffy his help in killing an enemy and saving her at the last minute, which Buffy refuses because she is clearly capable of handling the opponent herself. Buffy's agency and power are not only portrayed through her snappy remark when she tells Angel, "Let me just slice this misogynist bastard in half [...]. Then we can snuggle," but also through the image which shows her with weapon in hand, ready to attack. In contrast to Bella, Buffy remains in charge in her role as the Slayer and, noticeably, also in her love life. It is Buffy who proposes that she and Angel can snuggle after she is done fighting. Even though Buffy's and Angel's relationship might resemble that of Edward and Bella insofar as both couples engage in more or less conventional heterosexual relationships, what sets them apart is the fact that *BtVS* undermines heteronormative standards to a large degree. This is because, in the series, Buffy and Angel do very often not act according to their designated gender roles: Buffy, for example, frequently takes on the role of the hero because she rescues her male love interest on several occasions. Through the representation of Angel as passive and helpless—he is, for instance, poisoned ("Graduation Day [Part 1]"), or kidnapped and tortured ("What's My Line [Part 2]") and thus in need of saving—the stereotypical image of the damsel in distress is replaced by a "dude in distress" in these episodes (Coulombe 212). This innovative portrayal of gender roles and romantic relationships is emphasized and celebrated in this meme.

Intertextual memes work in a similar fashion to the intra-textual memes analyzed above in calling attention to the empowered status of one individual heroine within her respective story. In addition, intertextuality is used in feminist memes to provide more general commentary on the status of female heroes as role models, their growing visibility and popularity, and their influence on users' perceptions of gender roles. These memes usually bring together a larger number of heroines in order to support the claims made in the captions (cf. Emerson).

For instance, stereotypes about (teenage) girls in particular are undermined in memes that reinterpret and give new meaning to the saying "You fight like a girl." In these memes, images of different teenaged heroines are brought together and overlaid with the caption "You fight like a girl," sometimes followed by the punchline "Thanks," as in the meme represented below (E. Schultz). Traditionally, the allegation that someone does something "like a girl," i.e., running, throwing, or fighting, has been used as an insult that not only targeted women and girls, but also boys and men as it insinuates that their skills are inferior and not properly developed.[7] The memes that take up the phrase "You fight like a girl" work against this stereotype because they depict physically strong and trained young women instead of weak and clumsy ones. All of the teenage girls depicted in this meme are characters from some of the most popular young adult novels and movie adaptations of recent years: Hermione Granger (top left, *Harry Potter*) and Clarissa Fairchild (bottom left, *The Mortal Instruments*) have magical abilities that allow them to fight their enemies, Katniss Everdeen is portrayed as a skilled archer, and Annabeth Chase (top right, *Percy Jackson*) and Beatrice Prior (middle right, *Divergent*) are shown in a fighting stance, ready to attack.

In this meme, the very discrepancy between the stereotypes expressed by the saying "You fight like a girl" and the characters depicted in the images calls attention to the fact that, in this context, 'fighting like a girl' means fighting like a skilled and brave warrior. Indeed, the punchline "Thanks" unmistakably demonstrates that fighting like a girl should be seen as a compliment. Memes such as this one show that even though the sexist stereotype still exists, the discourse is slowly changing, not least because of the innovative

Meme entitled "You Fight Like a Girl" featuring teenage heroines from popular YA novels and movie adaptations. Creator unknown.

portrayal of teenage heroines in popular culture. The large number of memes such as the one depicted above reflects that there are now a large number of role models for (teenage) girls and women that challenge the notions that they are inferior to men when it comes to physical strength or abilities such as running, throwing, or even fighting. In fact, these memes not only represent, but celebrate these fictional female characters and insists that instead of regarding (teenage) girls as silly, weak, or inferior, they should be seen as skilled, strong, brave, and powerful.

The last category of image macro memes to be discussed in this chapter features quotations from interviews or official statements on characters given by directors, creators, or actresses and actors who have been known to directly comment on the topics of gender roles, heroism, or feminism in their films.

These memes draw attention to the fact that female heroes and gender roles are part of feminist discourses outside of the fictional and the digital world. Instead of referencing the fictional texts only, these memes broaden the discourse to include meta-comments that deal with feminist aspects surrounding the movies and shows, but also the processes of creating and marketing these items of popular culture. Notably, through the transformation into memes, discourses that are established offline are incorporated into digital spaces and hence contribute to feminist discussions on the Internet, be it as part of feminist blogs, in Twitter feeds, or on social media sites such as Facebook, Pinterest, or Tumblr. In addition to drawing attention to the circumstances surrounding the creation of popular culture, the memes also emphasize the potentially feminist aspects of the movies and shows. They shed light, for instance, on the innovative gender politics of these particular productions that set themselves apart from the majority of movies and TV shows by centering on a female protagonist and working against traditional gender roles. They also represent the thoughts and aims of the people involved in processes of cultural production to call attention to the fact that this is a potentially political activity.

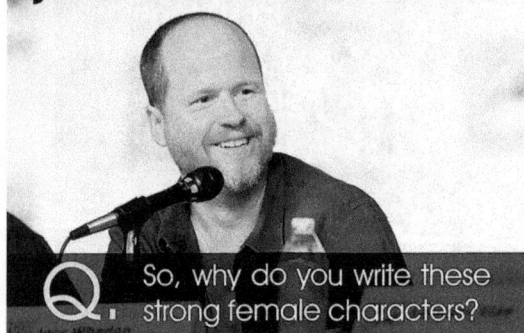

Meme featuring Joss Whedon's reaction to an interview question about strong female characters tweeted by AMightyGirl. Photographs by Gage Skidmore.

The memes about *BtVS* mostly feature writer and director Joss Whedon, rather than Sarah Michelle Gellar, the actress who plays Buffy Summers, as the latter has, in contrast to the first, only rarely spoken out about feminist issues on the TV show. The variety of statements contained in the different memes makes it clear that Whedon has often discussed feminism in general and Buffy as a feminist character in particular. One of his statements, however, is more often featured in memes than others: his answer to the question why he writes strong female characters. This question, along with Whedon's simple and snappy retort that he does so because people still ask him that question, is featured, for instance, in this meme tweeted by amightygirl.

Through the combination of the caption and the images, this meme pokes fun at and consequently criticizes the interviewer in particular as well as mainstream culture in general. Not only is the question itself ridiculed through Whedon's dismissal of it and by the reaction shots which show him in a state of bemused exasperation, but his answer furthermore insinuates that these kinds of questions prove the need for more female characters that resemble the ones he creates. Noticeably, at the same time that the meme criticizes mainstream culture and media, it celebrates Whedon by depicting him as subversive and defiant of media conventions because he keeps writing empowered and complex female characters in spite of these questions and in spite of the persistent refusal of the media industries to do the same.[8] In addition, the repetition of the question also insinuates that it is even more noteworthy when men create innovative female characters. The meme heroizes Whedon as it projects him as somebody with a feminist agenda, as a trailblazer and innovator and also underlines that feminism is an important project for both women and men. It thus calls attention to the fact that men can be feminists, too, echoing an important issue propagated by third wave feminism and the feminist quest heroine.

In the case of the *Hunger Games*, there exists a large number of memes that feature an image of Jennifer Lawrence, who plays Katniss Everdeen, together with quotations from interviews in which she talks about the sense of responsibility she felt when taking on this role (cf. Colom; Hodgens). In these memes, the shape and look of the heroine's body is often a central issue. There is a vast number of memes that include different statements by Lawrence about what she wanted the character she portrays to look like. One meme, for example, quotes her saying:

> In the first movie, when it was obviously being talked about, like 'It's *The Hunger Games*, you have to lose 10 pounds.' I said 'We have control over this role model. Why would we make her something unobtainable and thin?' This is a person that young girls will be looking up to, so why not make her strong? Why not make her beautiful and healthy and fit? I was very adamant about that, because I think that [the film] industry doesn't take enough responsibility for what it does to our society [...] [Colom].

This statement features a number of different ideas close to the heart of (online) feminism and fandoms. First, the media are criticized for their idealized and unrealistic portrayal of female bodies. Second, Katniss is praised as a strong and exceptional role model for young women and girls. Moreover, the meme also indirectly praises Jennifer Lawrence as an advocate for breaking with conventions, for challenging beauty ideals, and for being aware of and taking responsibility for the influence she has not only on audiences in general, but as a role model for girls in particular.

Although people have criticized Lawrence for speaking out against beauty ideals while she herself can be regarded as the embodiment of these very standards (cf. Trout), her criticism should not be neglected only because it comes from someone who fits these standards more than others do. If anything, the way in which Lawrence herself has been treated draws even more attention to the unobtainability of the beauty ideals propagated by Hollywood and the media industries since the actress was chastised by producers, agents, film critics, and even fans for being too heavy to play Katniss (cf. Garriott 169). Her statement hence not only shows that no matter how women look, their bodies will very likely be criticized, but by speaking out about these issues, Lawrence also inscribes herself into a larger (online) discourse that can be subsumed under the title of "body positivity."[9] After all, in the quotation shown above, she redefines notions of beauty to include physical strength, health, and fitness. These are aspects that do not only refer to what a body might look like, but also to what it can do: a woman who is fit and healthy does not necessarily have to be thin, but she is able to take care of herself and her body. Thus, Lawrence's notion of beauty is also one of self-love and independence. By converting Lawrence's remark into a meme, users can easily and quickly share, discuss, and spread the ideas contained in the actress' statement. They hence contribute to the feminist online discourse surrounding female heroes in a very effective and far-reaching manner.

As these memes are concerned with the portrayal of female bodies and body positivity, it is also notable that the images used in combination with Lawrence's statements largely portray her in close-ups or medium shots, focusing on her face rather than her whole body. In the cases where her body is visible, she is often clothed professionally, wearing a blazer (Fangirl) or a formal dress. While a quick online search will show that there exists a large number not only of full body shots of the actress, but also of sexualized images in particular, hardly any of these have been used in this specific type of meme. The memes featuring Lawrence, then, do not only work against the objectification and stereotypical depiction of female bodies in the mainstream media through their use of quotations, but also through their deliberate choice of pictures that avoid portraying the actress as a sexual object and instead depict her as a professional, engaged, and responsible young woman.

The focus on Lawrence's professionalism or the exasperation expressed through Whedon's sarcasm exemplify an important aspect in which the memes contained in my corpus differ from established genre conventions. Unlike the vast majority of memes on the Internet (cf. Shifman 67), many of the memes in my corpus do not primarily aim at making people laugh. Whereas sardonic humor can be found in some examples, such as "Lessons from Twilight vs. Lessons from Buffy," for instance, the feminist memes often comment on social and cultural issues without using sarcasm, thus setting themselves apart from many other political memes (cf. Knobel and Lankshear 211). Instead of only engaging with, commenting on, and representing oppressive systems or misogynist characters, these memes take a more positive and empowering stance by focusing on, portraying, and celebrating characters they deem heroic and feminist. The effect is that these memes are not only critical, but at the same time empowering for their audiences. Even though these memes still criticize oppressive forces through their depiction of girls who fight against them, they simultaneously offer positive role models with which audiences can identify and heroines which they can emulate. Celebrating female heroes as positive role models fits the overall purpose of these feminist memes, as they not only want to teach audiences about feminist issues, but potentially also encourage them to become politically active themselves. Hence, portraying these role models—both fictional and real ones—in addition to criticizing the status quo enlarges the political potential of these memes.

In summary, the innovative portrayal of teenage girls as feminist quest heroines is celebrated by fans who spread the ideas of female strength and equality online by producing and sharing pieces of fan art such as the image macro memes analyzed in this chapter. In doing so, they single out and confirm the feminist potential and impact of the primary texts by spreading discourses about innovative conceptions of gender roles and female heroism. What is more, they expand on these discourses by creating intertextual and meta-textual memes that look at female heroism as a contemporary phenomenon that reaches across texts and characters. They also demonstrate that popular culture, its creators, producers, and actresses can have a feminist agenda. Still, the heroines discussed in this book represent a very specific group of young women: white, heterosexual teenage girls who possess bodily features that follow the Western beauty ideal to a large degree. Indeed, it is highly problematic that there are no girls of color, queer young women, or ones that do not look conventionally beautiful in the most successful installments that feature a female teenage protagonist. This is a perceived wrong that fan artists posting under the hashtag #racebent are trying to right.

Racebent Fan Art: Challenging White Western Hegemony One Artwork at a Time

Whereas the image macro memes employ screenshots or images without changing them in order to emphasize and celebrate elements of the original texts which users deem empowering, heroic, and progressive, the racebent drawings and digital items challenge elements of the texts by transforming the visual appearance of the female characters. By doing so, fans and the online community at large not only participate in the creation of new heroines, but they also engage in an intersectional feminist discourse by criticizing the lack of diversity with regard to heroic female characters in particular, and mainstream popular culture in general. This is because visual items such as original drawings or photoshopped images are especially suited to address outer appearances, to transform them, and to thus challenge and resist the idealized and uniform representations of women and girls in the mainstream media. As there is a (relative) lack of diversity in *Brave*, *BtVS*, and the *Hunger Games*, it comes as no surprise that all of the texts have been included in the racebent online discourse. While racebent fan art in general is concerned with questions of race, ethnicity, and representation, the individual pieces I analyze in this chapter deal with the particular primary texts and the individual manners in which they address or neglect issues of race and ethnicity more specifically.

Before I turn to the analysis of the works of fan art, it is important to clearly define the different terms, as some of them are frequently used interchangeably or to describe different phenomena. As delineated above, the term "racebending" started out as a play on words of the title and content of the animated series *The Last Airbender* to describe the casting of white actors for roles that were originally occupied by people of color (Lopez 433). However, it is now more often used for practices that do the exact opposite. To be more precise, racebending is now widely used to describe the replacement of white characters with people of color (cf. Gilliland 1.6), whereas the term whitewashing is used when white actors are cast in roles that are originally occupied by people of color. Indeed, it is crucial to clearly distinguish between the two practices, as the former one promotes the representation of people of color while the latter one erases it. With regard to *BtVS*, *Brave*, and the *Hunger Games* franchise, both racebending and whitewashing play a role in the way fan artists engage with and transform the primary texts.

It is equally important to note that, at the same time that racebending is celebrated by online communities for its efforts to promote diversity, the danger that certain pieces of such fan art potentially essentialize or stereotype people of color and use them as token characters is also frequently addressed both among academics and within online communities themselves. The criticism that racebending faces in this context is twofold. On the one hand, only changing the skin color and nothing else is seen as problematic as it "[rids] a character of the important cultural facets that have shaped her [and hence] essentially erases the importance of her individual story" (3.8). According to this direction of criticism, proper representation does not stop at the color of the skin, but includes alternative narratives, cultures, histories, and the identities that have been shaped by them. On the other hand, critics also warn against the marking of certain tropes as belonging to one specific culture only. As Lopez observes in the context of *The Last Airbender* fandom, the idea that the practices, architecture, and outer appearance of the characters within the fictional universe are distinctly Asian "contributes to an essentialized or fixed notion of Asia" and has even led to "accusations of Orientalism" (435). All in all, the most basic problem racebent fan art faces is the idea "that identity and representation can be collapsed within an actor's [or actress'] body" (435).

However, the majority of fan artists and the online community in general are not only highly aware of the various problems that might arise in the context of their work, but they also take steps to avoid said accusations. They do so by commenting on their pieces and offering background information about the characters they portray, by engaging in discussions with other users, and by offering constructive feedback. In short, they hold "each other accountable" for the types of representation they spread (Gilliland 4.10). This is also one of the reasons why it is essential to analyze the written comments that accompany the racebent images.

When it comes to *BtVS*, fan art is used to make aware of and criticize the general lack of people of color in the series' main cast. As mentioned in Chapter 1, the question whether racial and ethnic diversity is included in the TV show to an adequate amount and in an adequate manner is a highly debated topic. On the one hand, some scholars suggest that racial diversity is symbolized through the monsters and vampires (Fuchs 105–6) or that the show addresses diversity in the final episode of the series when Buffy shares her powers with a "heterogeneous group" of potential Slayers from all over the world (Pender, "Kicking Ass" 8). On the other hand, fans and scholars alike reprimand the show both for its lack of diversity and for its stereotypical and, at times, derogatory depiction of people of color (validcriticism; Ono). Not only did the original cast of *BtVS* almost exclusively consist of white actresses and actors, but the show featured people of color predominantly as background actors, sidekicks, or villains.

The most prominent type of fan art to right this perceived wrong are so-called fan casts, images in which the original characters are replaced with actresses and actors that, according to the specific artist's opinion, are a better fit for the respective role. Fan casts are a popular genre among fans in general and not only used to give visibility to people of color, but also, for example, to imagine casts that are completely female. They are a very prevalent genre in the larger context of racebent fan art, and the most popular one when it comes to racebending practices engaging with *BtVS* specifically. The fan casts establish an innovative and inclusive representation by transforming Buffy and the Scoobies, that is, her friends and allies, into a racially and ethnically diverse group of people.

To be more precise, there are two types of fan cast images that achieve two different effects. One criticizes the show for its lack of diversity and calls for more representation of people of color in general, while the other one communicates the same ideas but additionally insinuates that people of color can be heroines and heroes, too. The first type of fan cast combines the pictures of new actresses and actors, all of whom are people of color, and the names of the original characters. There is no further visual reference to the original text, such as screenshots, for instance, so that the text, or rather the names, are needed for audiences to understand that it is this specific show that is being recast. Often, a large number of characters or the complete main cast are featured in one image, as it allows to show many people at the same time and to reimagine the cast as a whole. This type of fan art engages in a discourse concerned with questions of representation and the importance of the inclusion of people of color into mainstream popular culture products. These fan casts can be seen as pieces of art that tie into this discourse by representing people of color in large numbers and in central roles. They also underline a demand for people of color to be cast if not as protagonist then at least in central roles.

The idea that people of color can and should be represented not only in leading roles but as heroines and heroes is more strongly insinuated in the second type of fan cast. This type works differently as it combines photographs from new actresses and actors with screenshots or images from central scenes of the show or iconic objects connected to a specific character. The meme posted by user Visennyatargaryen on a Tumblr blog entitled "Fuck yeah, racebending," for instance, contains screenshots—the book Giles presents to Buffy when she first visits the library at Sunnydale High, her iconic cross-shaped necklace, as well as the scythe that allows her to kill the First Evil in the final episode—along with photos of English-Jamaican actress Antonia Thomas instead of Sarah Michelle Gellar ("Antonia Thomas"). The connection between the new actress and the original series is made even stronger by the fact that the scenes contained in the fan cast are filmed from Buffy's point of view. In contrast to the first type of fan cast, the act of reimagining and transforming the original piece of popular culture works more thoroughly, as the actress is quite literally inserted into the original piece.

What is more, these fan casts insinuate that this young woman of color has the potential to be as heroic as the white actress who originally occupied this role. After all, the meme imagines Antonia Thomas in scenes which trace Buffy's development and growing power as the Slayer from the very beginning to the end of the series and emphasize her physical and mental strength. These images thus suggest that the woman of color featured in the image is as capable of successfully fulfilling the role and overcoming the obstacles of being the Slayer as her white counterpart. Notably, all of this is achieved through the combination of three portraits and three screenshots, and hence reveals the complexity and expressiveness of these visual items.

The piece of fan art just analyzed is part of a larger series of *BtVS* fan casts including Willow and Xander, as well as Dawn, Angel, and Darla. This series combines the promotion of people of color as heroines and heroes with the demand also articulated in the first type of fan cast, namely to have more diverse casts in mainstream popular culture in general. As delineated in Chapter 1, Buffy's friends and allies are established as heroines and heroes in their own right during the course of the series. The fan casts take up this idea, because in a similar manner to the recast of Buffy, they combine screenshots that characterize Willow as a powerful witch (Visennyatargaryen, "Ellen Wong") or Xander as a loyal friend ("Suraj Sharma"). At the same time, they replace the white actress and actor with people of color and can hence expand on the claim that those should be featured in heroic roles, too.

Besides that, the memes also name specific actresses and actors of color who are currently pursuing acting careers, which promotes these people on a meta-level: through these works of fan art, they are literally made visible and it is underlined that there exist people of color who could play these roles. This inclusion of names can be found in virtually every fan cast, speaking strongly of the genre's aim to promote diversity on the level of texts themselves, but also on a meta-level with regard to the cultural industries and their choice of actresses and actors. What is more, the specification of who exactly is recast into the iconic roles of Buffy and the Scoobies further emphasizes the attempt to achieve a high level of diversity in these fan casts. After all, a quick online research reveals that the new cast featured in this series is truly diverse when it comes to their racial and/or ethnic background: Antonia Thomas is of English-Jamaican descent, Ellen Wong is a Canadian actress whose parents are of Cambodian descent, and Suraj Sharma is an Indian actor. Amandla Stenberg, who is given the role of Dawn, is African-American and Danish, Seychelle Gabriel as Darla is Mexican and French-Italian, and Michael Obiora as Angel is of Nigerian descent. This focus on diversity and the inclusion of non–Western characters and cultures can also be found in the context of racebent Disney fan art to which I now turn.

As delineated in Chapter 3, Disney princesses have reached new heights of popularity in recent years. This has not only led to an increase in debates and criticism among academics, journalists, and the public at large, but also inspired fan artists to engage with, change, and subvert a variety of attributes of these well-known female characters. As a consequence, today, Merida and her fellow Disney princesses are probably among the most popular characters represented in fan art at large. Fan artists portray the princesses with, what they call, "realistic" hair, waistlines, or eyes. They are drawn as bruised and scarred victims of domestic abuse, punks and pin-up girls, superheroes, hipsters, feminists, high school and college students, or burlesque dancers. The list could be continued, but should suffice to underline the prominence of Disney princesses among fan artists. More importantly, this list also reflects that it is very specific elements of the (Disney) princess archetype that are reworked in these images. Even though the princesses and their roles have constantly evolved, to varying degrees, the majority of them still represents an idealized version of femininity, that is white, slim, and innocent young women whose behavior frequently perpetuates traditional gender roles. In contrast to this, fan artists imagine the princesses as educated, strong, hard-working, or sexual human beings, thus creating not only additional types of role models, but notably more diverse and progressive ones.[10]

Disney princesses are also frequently racebent by fan artists who, through their pieces of art, participate in a variety of discourses about femininity, race, popular culture, and how they intertwine. On the most general level, the portrayals of the princesses as girls and women of color question the type of female beauty ideal perpetuated by the Disney Corporation. For decades, Disney movies at large, and Disney princesses in particular, represented and thus perpetuated white, Western beauty ideals and gave prominence to stories situated in European or Northern American spaces. Although some princesses of color, such as Pocahontas, Mulan, or Tiana were added during the installments of the second and third waves, Disney princesses remained predominantly white and Western. If any, girls of color have usually only one princess that represents their own racial or ethnic background. In contrast to this, with brunette Belle, red-headed Ariel and Anna, black-haired Snow White, and blonde Aurora, Cinderella, and Rapunzel, there are seven Caucasian princesses. As Marc DiPaolo elaborates, "the grouping encourages Caucasian girls of every major hair color to pick their favorite princess to identify with, thereby imagining themselves in the tiara and regal gown" and, ultimately, as princesses, too (168–69). Fan artists who racebend these iconic characters counter this dominance along with the ideas and ideals communicated and maintained through the Disney movies.

Images which transform Disney princesses into characters with darker skin and hair are liked, shared, and reblogged in the thousands and ten thousands, reflecting both the demand for and popularity of princesses of color. What is more, these pieces of fan art also trigger comments by and discussions among users. On a Tumblr entitled "Disney for Princesses," which features a variety of racebent fan art, user swedishheroine remarks:

> I am Hispanic. I have never seen a Princess who looks like me. I have [an] 8 year old sister. She's dark skinned and her favorite princess is usually Ariel or Tiana [the first African-American Disney princess]. Ariel because of the fact she's a mermaid, Tiana

because she loves her dress and she identifies with her, she sees Tiana as closely resembling her. I want her to keep having more Tianas, *in a sense more princesses she identifies with*. More princesses all my siblings and cousins can identify with ["Why It's Problematic"].

This statement takes up an idea contained in basically any piece of racebent fan art, namely that representation matters. Not only does user swedishheroine point to and criticize the lack of diversity in Disney princess movies, but she also speaks of the importance for girls of color to find positive role models in the mainstream media. Indeed, statements such as this one hark back to and exemplify academic studies which claim that Disney, as one of the most popular providers of entertainment for children, has the potential to strongly influence the way they perceive and understand themselves and the world around them (Bruce 2; Hines and Ayres 4; Whelan 26–27). It has been argued, for example, that a lack of representation in general, as well as stereotypical and derogatory portrayals of people of color, can potentially have negative effects on children of color (Hurley). In other words, "the impact of conveying primary narratives through the bodies of white actors while engaging with only extraneous people of color and their culture cannot be underestimated" (Lopez 435). Since Disney princesses are arguably the most popular female role models for girls all over the world, the issue of representation in these specific movies gains even more significance than it does for many other popular culture texts.

Notably, while they do change the color of the skin and hair, many of the racebent images that feature Disney princesses do not change any other features of the characters, such as the roles they take on in the narrative. They could thus be criticized for perpetuating more traditional gender roles and ideals. I suggest, however, that they rather open up roles and subject positions for girls of color which these are usually not allowed to occupy. In other words, in the same manner that the image macro memes show that white teenage girls can be warriors instead of damsels in distress, the racebent pieces of fan art insist that women and girls of color can be princesses, too; that they can take on the role of the beautiful, elegant, and privileged protagonist. Hence, both image macro memes and racebent Disney princess fan art follow a feminist agenda by advocating for inclusion and diversity through their portrayal of women and girls in roles they have traditionally been denied.

In addition to negotiating beauty ideals and opening up the iconic role of the (Disney) princess for girls of color, there is a second discourse that is established with these works of fan art. To be more precise, works that merely change the outer appearance of these female characters also frequently engage with and challenge canonical portrayals of European history. The drawing by Juliajm15 shown below, for example, depicts Princess Merida as a biracial character without changing much about her look other than the color of her skin and hair. On Tumblr, this drawing and the comments and discussions it has triggered are used to answer to a point of criticism fan artist who racebent Disney princesses face time and again. The argument runs that the outer appearance of the original characters is more realistic since the majority of fairy tales are set in Europe in or before the Middle Ages, so the princesses must be white because the population was also white. According to this argument, a biracial Merida could not exist simply because biracial interactions in any form did not take place during the time the story is set.

First of all, it is rather striking that audiences find a biracial Disney princess to be unrealistic, but do not comment on the plausibility of one of the major plot points of the film, in which a magic potion turns the queen into a bear, for example. Indeed, the fact that suspension of disbelief frequently applies to magical or supernatural elements of movies, but is questioned when it comes to outer appearance or skin color is repeatedly commented on and debated by users. Secondly, there are a number of posts that undermine the assumptions of historical inaccuracy and show that the societies portrayed in *Brave* and other Disney movies have potentially been more diverse than these films account for. They do so by posting racebent fan art, citing historical and other academic sources,[11] or posting original works of art in which white people and people of color interact, thus enlarging the visual counter narrative to include not only fan art but actual historical paintings (Swedishheroine, "POC in Europe"; A-Crow-Girl). The racebending fan art and the various posts that accompany it thus paint a different picture of European history

Fan drawing entitled "Princess Merida Racebend" presents the Disney princess as a girl of color. © Julia Jacob Mori (Juliajm15).

and show that the population was more diverse than many people believe. These discourses make aware that it is not only popular culture that constructs and represents a certain view of the world, but they emphasize that history, too, is constructed to serve a white Western hegemony. The fan art and discussions surrounding it challenge the whitewashing that takes place when it comes to accounts of European history in general, but also the manner in which mainstream media such as Disney portray these time periods.

In spite of the important statements that these pieces of racebent fan art make about beauty ideals, role models for girls of color, or the whitewashing of European history, fan artists are still frequently criticized for using the characters they portray as token characters by merely changing their skin color and nothing else. In the context of Princess Merida and the other Disney princesses, many fan artists escape this trap by specifying the cultural background the new rendition of the princess belongs to as well as changing her appearance according to this cultural background. These fan-made images not only comment on the general lack of diversity in Disney princess movies by changing white princesses into young women of color, but they also engage with the criticism regarding a lack of authenticity by attempting to create images that more deeply engage with the cultures and societies they represent.

The racebent series entitled "A Whole New World," which includes all of the major Disney princesses as well as a number of central female characters from other Disney movies (TT), is an excellent example to illustrate this. In this series, the princesses are transformed in order to reflect a very specific cultural background. In addition to the visual changes, the artist also included specific information concerning the new cultural background of the reimagined female character in the description of her work. To name just a few, Merida is portrayed as Brazilian, Snow White is Spanish, Cinderella is Japanese, Belle is Arab and portrayed with a headscarf, and Jamaican Aurora sports dread locks (TT, "Compilation"). Along with the color of their skin, the princesses' hair styles and textures, as well as clothes, make-up, and accessories were adapted in order to adequately represent the respective culture. This attempt at authenticity is celebrated in the Tumblr community not only through a large number of notes—taken together, the four parts of the series and the compilation have been liked, reblogged, and shared more than a million times—but also through comments that compliment the artist's work and her willingness to more consciously engage with the princesses, their cultural identity, and their outer appearance. User bandersnatchedsouls, for example, writes: "I love how you put time and effort into making them look like they could actually be a different race. Some race-bending artists just change the skin color and go 'DUHVERSITY!'"

Interestingly, these pieces of fan art not only give a face to a group of people that is underrepresented in mainstream popular culture and the Disney princess universe in particular, namely women and girls of color, but they also give a voice to alternative narratives, thus replacing the Western fairy tale tradition and Eurocentrism contained in the majority of Disney princess movies. This is because the images featuring the Disney princesses are not only accompanied by descriptions of the artists' themselves, but they frequently trigger comments that provide background information with regard to the cultures and narratives portrayed, or they inspire fan fiction authors to write alternative stories for the princesses. All in all, "these online spaces often become a place for people of color to use technology to discuss issues of their cultures" or those of others (Gilliland 5.2).

User gooseweasel, for instance, drew inspiration from the racebent Disney series just mentioned and conducted extensive research on non–Western myths, fairy tales, and historical figures in order to "give [these reimagined princesses] stories and fairy tales of their own" "rather than just seeing them as different versions of the original characters." The pieces of fan fiction are, indeed, quite diverse, telling the stories of historical figures such as Muslim queen and pirate leader Sayyida al Hurra or Jamaican national hero Queen Nanny.[12] In addition, they are inspired, among others, by Japanese, Turkish, Native American, and Hawaiian legends and folk tales, or are retellings of European fairy tales with a twist, incorporating, for instance, elements from Chinese culture or Pakistani flora and fauna. On her Tumblr account, user gooseweasel not only opens up a space for marginalized women, cultures, and their stories, but she also opens up a space for discussion and learning by telling other users: "I'll try my best to do right by these characters and cultures, and if there is something horribly offensive, please let me know *how I can fix it.*"

The fan fiction and the accompanying descriptions, comments, and narratives engage with and challenge a variety of issues, both when it comes to the primary texts they rework, as well as the practice of fan art itself. They first of all avoid the criticism of tokenism and superficial engagements with other peoples and cultures as they portray diversity on different levels, that is, with regard to a person's look, her experiences, and her historical and cultural background. Secondly, these fan-made images and the conversations they trigger question and actively work against the Eurocentric worldview perpetuated by Disney through the choice of princesses and narratives the corporation chooses to represent in its movies (cf. Ginneken 27–32). In contrast to this, the fan artists and online users give a voice to non–European versions and predecessors of many of the well-known fairy tales collected by Charles Perrault or the Brothers Grimm.

In a sense, these pieces of fan art and fan fiction can also be seen as attempts to revise history by turning history into herstory, a feminist neologism that describes the retelling of history from a female perspective or that focuses on the historical roles of women (cf. Mills 118). After all, they do not remain on the fictional level exclusively, but instead, many of them merge the fictional princesses with real-life historical figures. These historical figures are not only mostly unknown in both Western cultures and the ones from which they originate (cf. Gottlieb; Lebbady), but, more importantly, they were also powerful and exceptional women. These items of fan art and fan fiction hence give a face and a voice to these female leaders whose stories have largely been neglected by official accounts, and consequently challenge the official narratives of white Western patriarchal hegemony. By including these female leaders into their works of fan art and fan fiction, users also diversify the type of role models available for women and girls to include real-life, non–Western women whose political careers and lives defy traditional gender roles.

Whereas racebent Disney princess fan art criticizes the whitewashing of European history along with the erasure of women in official historical accounts, fans of the *Hunger Games* criticize the whitewashing of characters. To be more precise, they use their racebent art to offer a visual counternarrative that criticizes the casting of Caucasian actress Jennifer Lawrence to play the role of Katniss Everdeen in the movie adaptations of the popular novel trilogy. Along with this, the casting choices regarding a number of secondary characters, such as Gale Hawthorne, Johanna Mason, or Haymitch Abernathy, are criticized as well. In these cases, fans bend the filmic representations of these characters from white to non-white in order to return to and affirm Katniss' look as it is described in the novels. In contrast to blonde and blue-eyed Lawrence, Katniss is described as having "straight black hair," "olive skin," and "grey eyes" (Collins, *HG* 8). Whereas these are "physical traits that could be possessed by someone of any ethnicity—including people of mixed ethnicity," the casting call itself asked for white actresses exclusively to audition, stating that they "should be Caucasian, between ages 15 and 20, who could portray someone 'underfed but strong,' and 'naturally pretty underneath her tomboyishness'" (Lee). While the demand for a female actress who is "underfed" and "pretty" to play a role in a movie primarily aimed at teenage audiences can be seen as problematic in itself, the clearly stated preference for white actresses has caused even more outrage among fans and was widely criticized in the media at large (Lee).

The casting call and the selection of white actresses and actors for the main roles were seen as prime examples that exposed Hollywood as "an industry that perpetuates the systematic erasure of minorities from the media" (Lopez 443). Indeed, whitewashing is a prevalent practice in Hollywood and is seen as problematic because it diminishes the visibility of people of color and takes away roles which are already few and far between in mainstream popular culture anyway.[13] Thus, casting Lawrence was perceived as a missed opportunity for this highly popular franchise in particular and Hollywood in general to promote diversity and practice inclusion (katnissisoliveskinned-dealwithit; Lee; monsterjumper). In addition, whitewashing is not only criticized for its erasure of people of color from the mainstream media, but also for the way it deals with whiteness itself. As Lopez observes, "whitewashing is particularly dangerous because of the way that these representations reify whiteness as both invisible and dominant" (435).

In reaction to the controversy regarding the movie adaptations, numerous fan artists came up with creative responses that work against the whitewashing of the *Hunger Games*. One of the most prominent platforms on which various pieces of art are collected, shared, and commented on is a Tumblr entitled katnissisoliveskinneddealwithit. Under the headline "We do not condone. All of this is wrong," the bloggers explain their reasons for establishing the blog along with their aims:

> This is a blog about the white-washing of Katniss Everdeen, Gale Hawthorne, Haymitch Abernathy, and the rest of the Seam in the *Hunger Games* movie adaptations. The books presented an interesting view of racism and colorism, with the darker olive-skinned Seam class being confined to the lower-paying mining jobs within District 12. This was negated with the casting of Jennifer Lawrence and Liam Hemsworth. [...] Feel free to submit any information or art.

This description of the blog not only offers a condensed yet fitting analysis of how some aspects of racial difference and hierarchy are dealt with in the trilogy, but the request to send both fan art and information is also central in order to understand how this blog works. While the majority of postings on this site are indeed fan art, the written word in the form of descriptions and comments is also very important. After all, both are used together to achieve a certain effect and communicate specific ideas. To be more precise, the combination of images and comments effectively criticizes the movie industry as a whole, offers detailed and insightful discussions about race and ethnicity in both fictional worlds and reality (cf. Pauldierden), and ultimately establishes a counter-narrative that presents diverse visual alternatives to the whitewashed images found in the movie series along with important background information regarding the practice of whitewashing and the subversive role fan art can play in this context.

As can be seen in the example, fan artists use a range of art forms, the most prominent of which are portraits, fan casts, and drawings that reimagine central scenes, in order to visualize Katniss as she is described in the novels and to work against her canonization as a white girl. As this image exemplifies, many fan artists draw portraits of Katniss that closely adhere to her description in the novels, that is with olive skin, black hair, and grey eyes (MJ Erickson, cf. also Sophie C. or Marsha). Sometimes, these portraits are paired with images of Jennifer Lawrence in order to underline the difference in outer appearance, but more often, they stand on their own, thus erasing the Caucasian presence and dominance and establishing a more diverse representation of the beloved character. In addition to these basic traits, the hand-drawn portraits feature the heroine's iconic hairstyle, the Mockingjay pin, or her bow and arrow. They present Katniss with a rather somber or fierce facial expression, or portray her as someone who is bloody or visibly scarred by her experience in the Hunger Games and the ensuing rebellion. All of these features refer back to Katniss' central and powerful role in the story itself. The Mockingjay pin not only provides context and makes it possible to recognize the girl in the picture as Katniss

Fan drawing of Katniss Everdeen which more closely adheres to the description in the novel. Artist MJ Erickson, site kreugan.com.

Everdeen without any further descriptions, but it also marks her as the icon of the rebellion against President Snow. Her facial expression reflects her defiant and rebellious character, and the weapon, along with the blood and scars, shows that she is able to physically fight her opponents and that she takes on an active and dangerous part in the rebellion. By portraying Katniss together with these symbolic elements, the drawings establish the idea that the young woman portrayed in these images is a heroine, and, more importantly, a heroine of color.

While the portraits focus more on the girl warrior's outer appearance alone, drawings that represent Katniss in some of the most central scenes of the *Hunger Games* connect the new character, and thus a girl of color, more directly to the action of the story. The drawing below, which was originally posted by user Ari on her Tumblr account and later reblogged on katnissisoliveskinneddealwithit, recreates one of the most iconic scenes of the *Hunger Games* trilogy: it captures the moment in *Catching Fire* in which Katniss shoots an arrow into the force field surrounding the Quarter Quell arena. This scene is iconic as it contains a number of important aspects with regard to the rebellion against the Capitol as well as Katniss' personal development and her role in said rebellion. On a basic level, it marks the climax of the novel and the end of the Quarter Quell, which, notably, it brought about by yet another defiant action carried out by the female heroine. The destruction of the force field underlines Katniss' growing political awareness when she decides to attack the Capitol and Gamemakers instead of her fellow tributes. It also marks Katniss' transition from a tribute and victor into the Mockingjay, the symbol of the rebellion, as she is rescued by the rebels from District 13 who actively engage her in the cause of the rebellion. Moreover, when she is transported to District 13, Katniss also becomes aware that there is an official political movement that strives to bring down the Capitol and President Snow.

Notably, the fan drawing not only recreates this scene to present a girl of color in this role, but the composition strongly emphasizes the darker hue of Katniss' skin. This is achieved, first of all, because the color of her skin stands in stark contrast to both the background and the foreground of the image as well as the heroine's clothes and her hair. All of the latter four elements are depicted in dark blues, dark grey, or black, a basis against which the brown, beige, and light yellow elements clearly stand out. Said features of the drawing which are portrayed in lighter colors are Katniss's face and her arms and hands on the one hand, and

Fan drawing portraying Katniss Everdeen shooting a bow and arrow at a force field to end the Quarter Quell. Artist Ari (Walkingnorth).

fire, on the other one. Notably, these lighter elements, most of all the flaming arrow Katniss aims above her head, form a frame around and illuminate her face and arms, giving prominence to the color of her skin. Last but not least, her head and her arms are situated in the very center of the image, giving them prominence and depicting them as the most important part of this drawing. Through this specific composition, which centers around and frames Katniss' face, hands, and arms, this image does not merely contain the darker color of her skin as one element of many, but celebrates it as the most important one. What is more, by portraying Katniss as a person of color in one of the most iconic scenes of the trilogy, the fan drawing inserts this female character directly into the action of the story, stages her as a skilled archer as well as a defiant girl, and thus maintains that girls of color can be heroines and icons in their own right, too.

A problem that remains with regard to the fan practice of racebending is that, at a first glance, it reaffirms and essentializes racial categories and differences and potentially stereotypes ethnic groups. After all, not every woman who is Spanish has black hair and wears a flower in it, and neither do all Arab women wear a headscarf, as the Disney princess compilation analyzed above suggests. By looking at the larger discourses surrounding these images, however, it becomes clear that fan artists portray difference not to establish boundaries but to overcome them and achieve equality. The particular ethnic groups included in the compilation, for example, are largely marginalized and hardly ever portrayed in mainstream popular culture, let alone in the Disney fictional universe, so that the fan-made images advocate for equality in representation on a quantitative level. The same holds true for basically all of the other fan-made images, as they, too, portray and promote women and girls of color. Of course, while they strive for authenticity, fan artists have to simplify these characters to some extent, as one image or one individual representation can never capture the diversity of a whole ethnic group.

What is more, racebending fan art does not merely advocate for equality on a quantitative level, but on a qualitative one, as well. The images of racebent princesses, for instance, maintain that girls of color can have the same abilities and characters traits as the Disney princesses and thus make available a category of role models for little girl of color previously unavailable to them. In addition, the pieces of fan art that engage with *BtVS*, the *Hunger Games*, or *Brave* maintain that girls of color can be heroines, too, and should be represented as such, thus communicating the idea that when it comes to (heroic) character traits, there is no difference between white girls and girls of color. As the numerous examples that replace white heroines with heroines of color analyzed in this chapter have shown, racebent fan art visualizes racial and ethnic differences in order to emphasize that women and girls of color are not different from white women and girls, and that they should be represented in mainstream popular culture to an equal amount and in equally important and central roles. Finally, it is also important to keep in mind that neither of the racebent images stands on its own but is a part of a larger online discourse that includes innumerable amounts of racebent images that portray a variety of, and variety within, racial and ethnic groups, so that taken together, the overarching discourse that is established through these pieces of fan art works against stereotyping and essentialism even more than the individual pieces of fan art can.

Conclusion

At a first glance, the two different manners in which fan art engages with *BtVS*, *Brave*, and the *Hunger Games* seem rather contradictory and mutually exclusive, as one celebrates the source text while the other criticizes it. Nevertheless, even though they are borne out of very different emotions or evaluations, both types of fan art ultimately follow a feminist agenda, as they portray the feminist features of the primary texts as heroic and valuable and furthermore expand on notions of heroism to be more diverse and inclusive. Fan artists also contribute to feminist online discourses more generally, as they use their works to illustrate, support, or incite discussions about topics propagated by third wave feminism such as the representation of girls and women in the media, intersectionality, feminist movies and TV shows, feminist actresses, writers, and producers, gender roles, or critical readings of the primary texts to which they refer. Consequently, these pieces of fan art demonstrate that active audiences can affirm and perpetuate certain ideas about heroism made in the primary texts or even create new and innovative heroic figures that counter the conventions of casting white, privileged men in heroic roles. Fans create art to voice their opinions about the movies and TV shows themselves, but also about larger issues, such as feminism and gender roles, race and ethnicity, or casting practices and the culture industries.

One other important aspect that the image macro memes and the racebent fan art have in common is that they are fairly accessible and easy to understand, even without the comments, blog titles, or discussions surrounding them. This is because in both cases, the choice of images and punchlines, or the representation of names, symbols, screenshots, or iconic scenes makes it possible for audiences to understand the images even if they have only some basic knowledge about the source texts. This high level of accessibility reflects the central role these fan-made images play as part of an intersectional feminist online discourse that puts emphasis on creating a sense of community and of learning about intersectional feminist ideas through creating, discussing, and analyzing fan art as well as the primary texts with which it engages (cf. Gilliland 1.6). After all, if it is the aim to increase the number of female and feminist voices online and to spread feminist ideas such as female agency, self-determination, or gender equality, and the inclusion of marginalized groups, to make these issues entertaining, interesting, and accessible, the images that communicate these ideas must be accessible as well.

In fact, this focus on inclusion rather than exclusion is an aspect of feminist fan art that holds importance across genre boundaries. After all, in this respect, the image macro memes in particular move away from established genre conventions. First of all, users usually need a certain set of skills and knowledge, or so-called "meme literacy," to understand the meaning of a specific meme (Shifman 100). Secondly, memes are frequently used to create and maintain group boundaries and to keep people out of these groups rather than to include them (Nissenbaum and Shifman 3). In contrast to this, there are no "symbolic barriers" or "communal walls" that have to be overcome in order to be able to take part in the discourse surrounding the memes or the works of racebent fan art (Miltner). Since it is a feature of both types of fan art analyzed in this chapter, accessibility seems to be a central attribute of political or feminist fan art in general.

At the same time, even though the images themselves do take on a central role on the various online platforms, both image macro memes and racebent fan art also rely heavily on the written word. While image macro memes use a punchline, the racebending fan art uses hashtags, the titles of works of art, blog titles, user names, and comments in order to make its intended meaning explicit and to embed it into a specific context. As mentioned before, this is especially important for the racebent fan art, as artists want to avoid allegations of tokenism or stereotyping, which are more likely to occur in images that stand on their own. After all, as Elizabeth Gilliland explains, the meaning of a fan-made image depicting a black Ariel from *The Little Mermaid*, for instance, "changes dramatically if that poster is [made or consumed by] a woman of color who grew up longing to see someone like herself in the Disney princesses she grew up watching, rather than a white man who likes to photoshop pictures of 'exotic' women into seashell bikini tops" (4.4). This meaning, however, can only be fully determined through a written explanation that clearly states the intent of a respective image. In other words, the punchlines, hashtags, and written commentary can be seen as forms of disambiguation and clarification with regard to the meaning of the fan art itself as well as the primary texts with which they engage.

Fans and users who produce, post, and share pieces of fan art such as the ones included in this analysis inscribe themselves into specific intersectional feminist discourses. They are able to spread and discuss the ideas contained in said discourses through the viral nature of the fan art they employ, thus "bringing feminist analysis and voices into the mainstream" (Martin and Valenti 14). People who know the movies and shows can share and discuss these images and are consequently exposed to the ideas contained in them. Therefore, in a similar manner to fan fiction, fan art can also be said to have a didactic function, as it visualizes feminist role models that challenge conceived notions of heroism, gender roles, as well as racial stereotypes.

Conclusion
Girl Power Politics

> New politics increasingly works at the level of culture, representation, and narrative, as well as dramatic direct action and public performance. Alternative media are central to these politics.
> —Harris 158

Anita Harris' definition of contemporary politics makes it possible to conceptualize the retellings of heroic quest stories as well as fan engagement and the production of fan texts as political activism. From this vantage point, then, Girl Power media and its consumers are not, as often assumed, non-political and complicit, but rather subversive and resistant. While I do not want to suggest that this holds true for all of Girl Power culture and all young women, an engagement with the subversive and resistant girl warriors analyzed in this book frequently inspires fans and audiences to criticize and work against oppression and marginalization in the context of both (popular) culture and Western societies at large.

On the level of the primary texts themselves, quest stories that cast teenage girls as warriors who fight patriarchal oppression reflect on and potentially also drive changes in culture, narrative conventions, and patterns of representation, especially when it comes to the conceptualization of heroism and gender. The importance of the fact that there exist girl warriors who counter notions of young women as passive, helpless, and vulnerable cannot be overestimated. After all, numerous studies have shown that adolescents consume a large variety of media every day, which greatly impacts their identity and how they view the world and their place in it (cf. Arnett; Giles and Maltby; Larson; Lem and Hassel; Turner). In this context, a number of scholars have pointed out that the reiteration of norms of traditional femininity combined with a lack of innovative role models has a potentially negative influence on girls and young women. Hayley Dohnt and Marika Tiggemann, for instance, found dissatisfaction with body image in girls as young as six years (142) and Mary Polce-Lynch and her co-authors report that adolescent girls have lower self-esteem than boys (226). Notably, both studies regard the media and their portrayal of women and girls as one of the most important factors leading to these problems (Dohnt and Tiggemann 142; Polce-Lynch et al. 227, 239). By contrast, the stories of Buffy, Katniss, and Merida challenge the notion that heroes must be male, visibly strong, and powerful and instead offer role models that show girls that they, too, can be active, resistant, and drivers of change. As feminist quest stories, these narratives also suggest that young women have the right or even the obligation to fight against patriarchal oppression and marginalization.

Indeed, that more and more female heroes and warriors populate popular culture texts indicates a change in culture and patterns of representation. While they are, admittedly, still fewer in number, female warriors can be found in popular culture in increasing amounts. In movies and TV shows such as *Wonder Woman* (2017), *Agent Carter* (2015–16), *Supergirl* (2015–), or *Jessica Jones* (2015–), they have not only taken over the role of protagonist, but also successfully acted as soldiers, agents, or superheroines. Girl warriors in particular can be found across a variety of genres. Novel trilogies and series such as *The Hunger Games* (2008–10), *Divergent* (2011–13), or *The Mortal Instruments* (2007–14) feature teenage girls as protagonists who know how to fight. On TV's *Game of Thrones* (2011–19), Arya Stark's sword plays such an important role in her live that she even gives it a name, and in the Netflix hit show *Stranger Things* (2016–), a young girl named Eleven regularly saves her friends from dangerous monsters with the help of her superpowers. On the big screen, warrior princesses such as Merida or Snow White from *Snow White and the Huntsman* (2012) have exchanged their tiaras for weapons which they skillfully wield. What is more, in Marvel comics, the role of Iron Man, which has so far been occupied by Tony Stark, a white rich man, will soon be taken over by Riri Williams, a fifteen-year old black girl. Indeed, even the modern-day quest hero par excellence, that is, Luke Skywalker, has been replaced as protagonist of the *Star Wars* movies by 19-year-old Rey, a young woman who is an accomplished fighter, pilot, and technophile.

Yet, the culture industries have not developed into a feminist utopia. While there exist girl warriors such as Buffy, Katniss, and Merida, whose stories contain and celebrate feminist ideas and ideals, many of the characters mentioned above are certainly empowered, but their stories do not necessarily further or include feminist thought and theory. For instance, Tris Prior, protagonist of the *Divergent* trilogy, dies towards the end of the story, which reiterates the idea that "the death of a woman is necessary for the establishment or the restoration of civil order" (Krimmer and Raval 156). What is more, while Arya Stark is an accomplished fighter and has survived the game of thrones longer than many male characters, she did so because she completely rejects femininity. Consequently, her character and accomplishments rather reinforce and celebrate notions of traditional male heroism. Similarly, as a girl warrior who leads an army, the Snow White in *Snow White and the Huntsman* stands in stark contrast to her princess predecessor, yet the fact that she fights the only other female character present in the film, that is, her stepmother the Evil Queen, simultaneously perpetuates traditional notions of female enmity and the fear of power-craving women so often found in princess stories.

Female superheroes are not immune to this reactionary treatment, either: whereas Wonder Woman is canonically bi-sexual in the Marvel comics, in the recent movie adaptation, she engages in a heterosexual relationship only, and it is the love to a man that enables her to defeat her enemy in the final battle of the film. Likewise, in *Thor: Ragnarok* (2017), a scene that highlights the lesbianism of female superhero Valkyrie was cut from the final version of the movie. Last but not least, it also remains to be seen on what kind of heroic quest *Star Wars'* Rey will go, and whether the newest trilogy will enforce more innovative concepts of gender and heroism, or whether she will share a similar fate to Padmé Amidala, who initially took on a more empowered role in the *Star Wars* prequel trilogy, but then died from a broken heart, thus returning to a more stereotypically feminine gender position. Taken together, these examples ultimately show that female heroes are highly complex and ambiguous figures and more critical attention needs to be paid to their representation in contemporary popular culture as they can be both, drivers of change and preservers of traditional gender roles. What all of the female heroes do have in common, however, is that their stories can be described as politically charged, as they engage with issues of gender ideals.

However, it is not only the texts themselves, but fans and audiences, too, that can be described as political or politically active. Critics increasingly regard fan engagement and the struggle over meanings and representations as forms of political activism and have accordingly labeled them "participatory politics" (Jenkins et al. 2). In this context, scholars point to two crucial similarities between fan engagement in participatory cultures and engagement in political activism that allows them to conceptualize the activities of fans as political work. They argue that, first of all, both groups are able to imagine alternative societies or cultures, since "fandom provides a space to explore fabricated worlds that operate according to different norms, laws, and structures than those we experience in our 'real' lives" (Dahlgreen qtd. in Jenkins et al. 34). The second skill that fans and activist share is their ability to create communities of interest and advocate for common demands (34). In fact, studies have shown that people who engage in participatory politics online are more likely to vote, so that "online communities may be as much a predictor of civic participation as traditional afterschool clubs such as newspaper, debates, or student government or service learning and community volunteering" (44, 54).

In spite of the positive potential they detect in fan activity, scholars have also increasingly pointed out that fandoms are not invariably empowering, resistant, or progressive and might even affirm racist, xenophobic, or misogynist attitudes (Jenkins, *Textual* 34; Wanzo 1.4). In addition, people might also be excluded from participating in fandoms based on their race, class, language abilities, or access to the Internet (Jenkins, *Convergence* 269; Keller 7). In other words, just like popular culture, online spaces are no utopias either, but are rather characterized by a constant struggle over meaning and power, too. Regardless of the direction or content of these political discourses, however, their very existence shows that "youth may be pursuing politics through different means than have historically been acknowledged within research on institutional politics and social movements" (Jenkins et al. 8).

In this context, girls in particular have come under increased scrutiny, as they populate fandoms, social media, and other online spaces in larger amounts than their male peers or adults (Harris 161; Keller 2, 3, 7). Anita Harris, for instance, identifies online spaces as "ideal locales for the creation of narratives that disrupt hegemonic discourses about young womanhood" and maintains that they "have a particular role in undermining, questioning, and playing with the dominant paradigms by which young women's lives are so commonly represented and shaped in current times" (163, 165).[1] Jessalynn Keller also calls attention to the various texts female users produce and remarks that instead of regarding girls as passive consumers only, as has so often been done in previous academic works about girls and girl culture, scholars should "recognize the potential for resistance and agency within girls' media production practices" (6).

Indeed, it could be argued that girls in particular are still frequently considered to be non-political because online activism at large is not yet widely recognized as activism in its own right. One of the reasons that might hinder scholars, critics, and the public in general to recognize girls' online engagement as political activism is the fact that both the actors and their actions stand in direct opposition to more traditional models. Political activists are still usually cast as "white, middle-class, heterosexual, Western adult men" whose activism involves "mobilization, voting, petitioning, protest, and labor organizing" (Keller 50; Jenkins et al. 39). By contrast, more contemporary concepts of activism acknowledge that politics can also involve advocating for changes in cultural narratives or representation, which is exactly what happens in many online communities (Harris 158). Lori Kido Lopez even warns that "we must be careful about suggesting that their lack of face-to-face mobilizing represents a failure to become truly politicized, or that a group cannot be considered to be engaged in 'real activism'" because theirs takes place online (441).

In fact, to the same amount that the girl warriors analyzed in this book fight against authorities, rigid hierarchical structures, traditions, and norms, so do fans and audiences struggle, affirm, protest, and resist when it comes to the representation of (heroic) girls and women in and outside of popular culture texts. When young women write fan fiction that represents a canonically heterosexual heroine as gay or when fan artists draw images that racebend a white heroine, they advocate for a variety of changes in the representation of female characters and heroines.[2] Indeed, in addition to the fan texts already discussed in Chapter 5 and 6, fan activism can take on many forms. Petitions, online blogs and articles, tweets, podcasts, or online videos are just some of the media through which concepts of heroism and femininity are negotiated and change is called for.

To focus on one more example of fan activism online, it is interesting to look at petitions. For instance, the treatment of Rey outside of the fictional universe has been cause for criticism because the female protagonist was initially not included in the *Star Wars* action figure set, which only featured the male characters of the film. Notably, this was not a mere oversight, but a conscious decision on the marketers' part, as they believed that boys, the target group of the merchandise, were not interested in playing with a female doll or might even be put off by it, thus not buying the set at all (Davis). However, in a similar manner to the petition that demanded that Merida be turned back from her sexy and glamorous makeover when she joined the official princess line, people also successfully called for a Rey action figure to be added to the play set (O'Connor). Indeed, change.org is currently hosting yet another petition focused on the representation of female heroes, namely one that is asking Warner Brothers to depict Wonder Woman as a bisexual character in the upcoming film sequel.

In this context, it is important to note that, frequently, this kind of activism is successful and leads to a change in representations, narratives, and norms. After all, that female action figures are added to merchandised products, that princess makeovers are repealed, that a white male hero (Tony Stark) is replaced by a girl of color, or that rewritings of quest stories are made by companies such as Disney suggests that there exists a "feedback effect" between audiences and industries (Hamming 17). This shows that fan activism is taken seriously by the culture industries and that the political work done by the different groups not simply comments on, but actually influences the creative processes of those involved in the production of popular culture items.

What is more, in addition to their engagement online, girls and young women also take part in more traditional forms of political activism. Sonya

Sawyer Fritz, for instance, cites a number of studies that suggest that girls are indeed very likely to engage in movements for social change or socially conscious rebellion (26). In this context, it is important to note that the means and discourses employed in online and offline spaces overlap and resemble each other. While Keller claims that scholars frequently establish a "false boundary between online and offline spaces" (9), I want to take this argument one step further and suggest that there is, indeed, a false boundary between online spaces, offline spaces, and the fictional universes of popular culture in general, and Girl Power culture in particular, as all of them inform, influence, and inspire each other.

The Women's March on Washington, which took place one day after Donald Trump's inauguration on January 21, 2017, can serve as an example to support this claim, as it started out online, took to the streets of Washington, D.C., and employed popular culture heroines to illustrate demands, articulate feminist issues, or criticize the political system at large. In this context, the girl warriors and the political and resistant discourses established in the primary texts were appropriated in protest signs as a source to make complex statements and voice political dissent, bearing slogans such as "Down with the Capitol," or "Buffy wouldn't stand for this shit." Others stage Merida as a feminist or proclaim the importance of Girl Power, or rather insinuate that marching in a protest is an example of girl power and thus celebrate girls' political activism. During the Women's March, protesters used the "popular narratives" about Buffy, Katniss, and Merida as "shared resources that facilitate […] conversation," and as "entry [points] for political conversations" (Jenkins et al. 18, 31). Indeed, in a similar manner to the memes discussed in Chapter 6, drawing from these popular culture texts with which many people are familiar allowed the protesters to effectively spread their ideas and messages.

In fact, the protest signs bear a striking resemblance to online memes, both when it comes to form and content. Just like their digital counterparts, on the one hand, the signs use the girl heroines and their stories to make statements about political oppression ("Down with the Capitol") or the need for girls and women in particular to fight patriarchal power systems through feminist activism ("Buffy wouldn't stand"). At the same time, they also once again work as a means of disambiguation and interpretation by focusing on the feminist and/or political aspects of the primary sources and amplifying them through the usage in a protest march for women's and girls' rights. In this context, using the words "Girl Power" on a protest sign also fills the term with political and resistant meaning, thus claiming it as a feminist notion rather than an anti-feminist one. These examples only further call attention to the non-existent or at least highly permeable boundaries between online and offline spaces, as memes were turned into protest signs and, after the march, many protest signs found their way into online spaces. The signs also signify the overlap between online spaces, offline spaces, and popular culture, as many protesters use the popular culture heroines to underscore their political demands in both online and offline spaces.

Ultimately, the usage of the girl warriors in these protest signs counters two central claims about Girl Power media and their young audiences. Critics first of all claim that "prevailing representations" of girls and girl heroes in popular culture "do not open girlhood to the kind of critical analysis that could harness girl power to movements for social justice" (Currie, Kelly, and Pomerantz 49). However, the exact opposite can be observed in the examples above, where representations of Buffy, Katniss, and Merida are used in a social justice movement. The second idea that the protest signs, along with the people who carry them, most of which are girls and women, refute, is the notion that "girl power feminism does not encourage girls to consider the structural forces that contribute to the need for change, the ongoing oppression of girls and women, or the collective nature of social change movements" (Zaslow 159–60). During the Women's March, girls and women came together as a collective to protest structural oppression, voice their resistance, and advocate for change, and they did so by using girl power heroines.

All of these examples show that Girl Power media that engage with girl warriors can be highly political if they change or subvert traditional representations of gender and heroism. What is more, fan activities online have the potential to establish and push political and feminist agendas, too, either by creating more diverse role models on the one hand, or by openly criticizing and discussing problematic or regressive representations in both the primary texts and paratexts. Finally, Girl Power discourse and representatives such as Buffy, Katniss, and Merida are also used in more traditional forms of political activism such as protest signs, where they enable easy and effective communication of subversive and/or feminist ideas and ideals. It remains to be seen whether the different types of (fan) activisms will succeed in fostering change in the political sphere and/or keep on influencing the production of popular culture texts. The future will show, for instance, whether the diversification of heroic characters found in fan art and fan fiction will also move into mainstream popular culture, rendering representations of girl warriors and female heroes even more inclusive. So far, the feedback effects and developments observable in this context do suggest that fans and audiences can advocate for change and that their opinions, ideas, and demands will not be left unanswered.

Chapter Notes

Introduction

1. Pearson and Pope cite a number of similar studies, or, as they call them, "classical works on the hero," such as Lord Raglan's *The Hero: A Study in Tradition, Myth and Drama* (1937), Jessie Weston's *From Ritual to Romance* (1957), and Dorothy Norman's *The Hero: Myth/Image/Symbol* (1969). Campbell's study, however, even though it was written seventy years ago, is the most influential one, both among those who tell heroic stories and those who study them. Not only do heroes such as Harry Potter, *Star Wars'* Luke Skywalker, the protagonists of the *Lord of the Rings* trilogy, or modern superheroes such as Spiderman adhere to the model established by Campbell, but it is also regularly called upon by scholars who work on conceptions of the heroic (cf. J. Campbell, *Hero's Journey* 175; L. Campbell; Drucker and Gumpert; Early and Kennedy; Pearson and Pope; Strate; Stuller). I am not interested, however, in simply applying the model to the narratives that I analyze, but I focus on the moments of deviance from said model to see how and to what effect it is reworked and subverted rather than perpetuated.

2. I use the terms "warrior" and "hero" interchangeably, as all of the characters I analyze are warriors who are able to use weapons and do not shy away from physical altercations.

3. Indeed, there exists a certain uneasiness among scholars both with regard to definitions of girlhood and womanhood and terminology in general. First of all, within feminist discourse, the term "girl" still carries negative connotations, as it has traditionally been used to belittle and trivialize adult women (Currie, Kelly, and Pomerantz 5). In *Future Girls*, Anita Harris includes an appendix entitled "Who Is a Girl?," in which she delineates the issues that surround the usage of the term "girl" in academic analyses. She points out that the concept of girlhood has frequently been used to naturalize something that rather is in constant flux and "subject to historical and social specificities" (191). At the same time that Harris makes aware of the problems of working with the concepts of girl and girlhood, she still offers guidance by naming "some parameters to our shared understandings of the period of contemporary Western young womanhood," suggesting that while, for many girls, the transition into womanhood starts already in their late pre-teens, their girlhood "is not perceived to be entirely completed until the mid- to late twenties" (191). I use the terms "(teenage) girl," and "young woman" interchangeably, emphasizing the youth of these characters not to belittle them, but in order to underline that their liminal status between girlhood and womanhood is an important analytical frame as it influences the portrayal of both gender and heroism in these stories. A similar uneasiness with the terms "heroine" and "female hero" can be observed as well. Pearson and Pope, for instance, use the term "hero" to talk about female characters throughout their book and remark that the female form "heroine" has traditionally been used to describe secondary or supporting characters and thus connotes inferiority (18). By contrast, Lori Campbell uses "female hero," and insists that it is "a *positive* term in its ability to highlight and celebrate [a character's] fe-

maleness in tandem with her heroism" (7). For similar reasons, I use both "heroine" and "female hero" not only to reclaim the first one as a positive term, but also to highlight the heroines' femininity, which represents an important aspect of their ability to transgress binary gender roles.

4. Fans have been studied in detail since the early 1990s when Henry Jenkins first published his seminal study *Textual Poachers: Television Fans and Participatory Culture* (1992). Similar works such as Camille Bacon-Smith's *Enterprising Women* (1992) and Lisa Lewis' *The Adoring Audience* (1992) focus on fans and gender more specifically. Other works which Jenkins wrote or coauthored, such as *Convergence Culture* (2008), *Spreadable Media* (2013), or *By Any Media Necessary* (2016) have shed new light on the study of fandoms, especially with regard to the usage of new media and fans' involvement in political activism.

5. For more detailed descriptions and criticism of the trope, refer to McDougall or Valibeigi.

Chapter 1

1. The format of the TV series serves as a medium that is especially well-suited to portray Buffy's long and complex journey towards maturation, selfhood, and agency (Kearney, "Changing Face" 33). As different critics have noted, since they usually run over several seasons and contain numerous episodes, TV series are able to explore and portray a character's personal development in much greater detail than movies, for instance. This is a feature that allows this particular genre to create protagonists that are interesting, complex, and authentic, which in turn encourages audiences to view actively instead of consuming passively (cf. Kearney "Changing Face"; Allrath, Gymnich, and Surkamp). Therefore, the genre has developed into the "principal storyteller in contemporary American society" (Kozloff qtd. in Allrath, Gymnich, and Surkamp 1). With its seven seasons that ran over the course of seven years, *BtVS*, for instance, comes up to more than a hundred hours of running time, which is equivalent to about seventy movies.

2. Even though Buffy is strong and able to defeat her opponents in every fight, she and the Scoobies often refrain from using violence or killing their enemies (Early 18). In "Once More, with Feeling," for instance, the Scoobies negotiate with the demon about the contract that summoned him and once the situation is solved, they let him leave unharmed. In doing so, *BtVS* counters yet another feature of male warriorhood, namely the glorification of violence (Early 20). For a detailed analysis of violence in the context of *BtVS*, refer to Parks.

3. Buffy's relationship with Riley Finn will not be dealt with in detail here, since Riley can be regarded as a representative of traditional masculinity. Refer to Simkin or Durand for more detailed analyses.

4. This is not to say that the desire for connectedness is a natural given tendency. Indeed, Gilligan herself has remarked that it is rather caused by differences in education and upbringing, as well as by the roles men and women traditionally take on in everyday life (7). Still, it can be observed in women and girls more often and hence serves as an additional feature that connotes stereotypical femininity.

5. Even though she sacrifices herself, Buffy does not actually die but is reanimated by Xander, a plot point which further stresses the importance of the Slayer's group of friends. Besides that, it has been claimed that *BtVS* "sends the message that passive self-sacrifice, however noble, is not only a waste of a good person, but also unhealthy for society as a whole. The show subverts the Western tradition that 'the death of a woman is necessary for the establishment or the restoration of civil order'" (Chandler 26). In fact, it is Buffy's survival, and not her death, which is necessary for the restoration of order, because once she is reanimated, she kills the Master and saves the world from an apocalypse. This trope is actually so important in the series that it is featured in a second instance at the end of season five when Buffy once again sacrifices herself, but is later resurrected by the Scoobies.

Chapter 2

1. In this chapter, I focus on the novels exclusively, because in comparison to the movie adaptations, they more extensively portray Katniss' character, her thoughts and feelings, and her development, which makes

it possible to analyze the portrayal of both gender and heroism in a more detailed manner.

2. Henceforth, I abbreviate the titles of the novels, referring to *The Hunger Games* as *HG*, *Catching Fire* as *CF*, and *Mockingjay* as *MJ*.

3. Several scholars have engaged with the gender role portrayals in the *Hunger Games* trilogy. See, for example, W. Jones, Lem and Hassel, Jaques, Mitchell, Firestone, Lethbridge, J. Miller.

4. In this context, her gender identity is aptly symbolized by her weapon of choice, a bow and arrow. On the one hand, it is fatal and dangerous, which signifies Katniss' violent and masculine side, since she uses it without hesitation on animals and also on humans if the circumstances call for it (Collins, *HG* 233; *MJ* 314, 372). Still, it also triggers feminine connotations, as bow and arrow have been weapons of female fighters throughout history, for instance in Greek and Roman myths and legends where the Amazons, as well as the goddesses Artemis and Diana, were portrayed as bow wielding warriors and hunters (Hansen 161–62; Jaques).

5. Refer to W. Jones for a more detailed analysis of this device.

6. Through the portrayal of Gale, the novels also criticize hegemonic masculinity by showing that patterns of thought and behavior attributed to violent masculinity must be seen as harmful and destructive. This is because Gale's inclination for violence and unforgiving and vengeful nature ultimately result in the loss of innocent people, above all Katniss' sister Prim (Collins, *MJ* 367).

7. Christina Van Dyke also regards the inhabitants of District 13 as docile bodies. For a more detailed elaboration on this issue, see pages 260–62.

8. Peeta's involvement in the rebellion, as well as that of other male characters such as Haymitch, Gale, or Cinna also draws attention to the need for men to become involved in feminist projects such as that symbolized by the rebellion. Notably, it is not only Peeta who represents a more innovative notion of male heroism, but so do Cinna and Haymitch. Neither of them is physically strong, but they still support Katniss and the rebels in the fight against the Capitol and become part of the revolution. Cinna even does so by making use of a skill usually connected to stereotypical femininity, namely fashion design.

9. At the same time that they are innovative because they criticize hierarchical power systems, the novels promote some of the most traditional American values and beliefs with regard to politics at large and political systems more specifically. To be more precise, they celebrate democracy at the same time that they condemn fascism and communism. The political system to be established in Panem after the rebellion is described as a democratic one, namely "a republic where the people of each district and the Capitol can elect their own representatives to be their voice in a centralized government" (Collins, *MJ* 84). The Capitol, by contrast, represents fascism, as it is led by one powerful person, uses false propaganda, mass surveillance, and brute force in order to restrict its citizens with regard to freedom of speech and movement ("Fascism"), and District 13 is reminiscent of communism, as it can be described as a socialist society where "the means of production and subsistence belong to the community" ("Communism" 96). Since they present fascism and communism in a similar manner, namely as two sides of the same coin, the *Hunger Games* clearly perpetuate traditional American values and world views which celebrate democracy. To some extent, the story also expresses the idea that it is necessary or just to use warfare to overthrow such systems. Even though the novels do not celebrate violence and depict the traumatic consequences war has on those who fight in it, they still present fighting as the only viable solution to overcome the oppressive forces at work in Panem.

10. Even though Katniss later alters her view of her prep-team to some extent, as she comes to understand that Octavia, Flavius, and Venia are not inherently evil, she still regards them as "Other," and ultimately inferior, as according to her, they are still childlike, naïve, less human, and thus irrevocably different from the people in the districts.

Chapter 3

1. For a detailed historical overview and analysis of the genre of the fairy tale, turn to Jack Zipes' *Fairy Tale as Myth, Myth as Fairy Tale*.

2. It is, of course, also important to mention that this kind of gender role portrayal is not beneficial for a male audience either, as boys are not only indirectly taught to see women as submissive and helpless objects, but are also confronted with an outdated image of masculinity which contains aspects that they should not emulate.

3. The outdated portrayal of gender roles is not the only source of criticism Disney faces on a regular basis. Issues such as race, ethnicity, class, and sexuality are also often used to draw attention to the company's conservative world view (cf. Bean 53; Lester 294; Wilson).

4. This even happens in *Brave*. Even though the marginalization of female characters is not as pronounced as in many other princess movies, Princess Merida and Queen Elinor are still the only women to take on a central role in this film. Other female characters—except for some female servants and the witch—are completely missing from the plot. Male characters, on the other hand, especially due to the large number of male clansmen, are represented in the hundreds. Although *Brave* has taken first steps into the direction of portraying men and women in a more balanced and equal manner, there is still work to be done when it comes to the representation of secondary and tertiary female characters in Disney's princess movies, as for now, they are quasi non-existent.

5. For a detailed description and analysis of the princesses' bodies in the context of dance, see Bell.

6. In recent princess movies, the relationship between princesses and animals has often been mocked and parodied, pointing out the exaggerated depiction of the young women as sweet, domestic, and in tune with nature. In Disney's *Enchanted* (2007), for instance, Princess Giselle cleans a New York apartment with the help of cockroaches, rats, and scruffy pigeons, while in *Once upon a Time*, Snow White only sings to a bird in an attempt to lure it into the house and then kill it with a broom ("Heart of Darkness"). Another animal is harmed in *Shrek* (2001), when Princess Fiona wants to sing a duet with a bird and it explodes when she hits a high note.

7. Sarah Rothschild observes that "no more than half the screen time is allotted to the princesses" (78). The relegation of the princesses from the screen goes so far that Princess Aurora is only given 18 minutes of screen time in a movie that is 75 minutes long ("Sleeping Beauty"). In fact, the first time the audience actually sees her face is after about 20 minutes into the film, at which point the prince has already been introduced.

8. The topic of romance is introduced even earlier on, namely in the opening sequences during which a love song plays. This stylistic device sets the tone, or rather the romantic mood, before the movies have even properly begun (cf. Bordwell, Staiger, and Thompson 25–26).

9. Pocahontas and Mulan are not only more innovative when it comes to the diversification of beauty ideals and body types, but also with regard to their behavior as they "take part in stereotypically masculine activities, such as conducting diplomacy and war" (England, Descartes, and Collier-Meek 563). However, both eventually step away from these responsibilities and choose a domestic life instead of a public one. In this light, the adventures of Mulan and Pocahontas must simply be seen as detours on the way to the life that they were supposed to lead all along, as their allegedly rebellious acts in the end merely set the young women on the path to finding true love (cf. England, Descartes, and Collier-Meek 563; Henke, Zimmermann Umble, and Smith 246; Rothschild 152).

Chapter 4

1. The term "paratext" was first coined by Gerard Genette to describe aspects of books that are not part of the narrative itself. He divided paratexts into "peritexts": paratexts within the book such as the title, the name of the author, illustrations or prefaces, and "epitexts": paratexts outside the book such as interviews or reviews (1, 3). The media described as paratexts by Genette are also frequently called "peripherals" or "secondary texts" by other scholars (Fiske 118; Gray 5). I use paratexts in a similar manner to Jonathan Gray, namely as an umbrella term for all types of texts that surround and promote what could be called a primary text.

2. This myth has not only been debunked in a study conducted by Hickey himself, but there are also various examples, such as the

Hunger Games, *Frozen*, or *Wonder Woman* (2017), that demonstrate that female-led movies can be highly successful. In fact, Hickey found out that films that feature female characters in central and complex roles show a higher return on investment than movies that do not.

3. I do not want to perpetuate the stereotype that men and boys are, in fact, interested in action while women and girls are interested in romance. Nevertheless, these are the gender categories with which the producers of the paratexts work and it is hence important to name them as such (cf. Aubrey, Walus, and Click; Brown 7; Dodes and Jurgensen; Graser; Hickey; D. Johnson; Karpel; Meehan; Wilson). On the level of consumption or actual interest, these gender binaries are, of course, frequently broken and questioned.

4. The *Harry Potter* series also clearly exemplifies this gender hierarchy: while drawings of Harry can be seen on virtually every cover of the series, J. K. Rowling was reportedly advised to only use the initials of her name as a "marketing ploy designed to make her work acceptable to boys, who actively choose not to read books by women" (Savill). *The Hunger Games*, on the other hand, give prominence to Suzanne Collins' name. Again, however, this is in order to attract male audiences, as she was already well-known for writing a popular book series featuring a male protagonist, namely *The Underland Chronicles*. Her name, then, was more openly advertised because it carried notions of previous success and because it held strong connotations to stories that appealed to boys. Moreover, the erasure of the female protagonist on the cover can not only be observed with regard to the cover image, but also when it comes to the title of the novel. In the case of the *Hunger Games* trilogy, only the last installment—*Mockingjay*—alludes to Katniss herself, albeit in a very indirect manner. Other YA novels that feature female protagonists such as *Twilight*, *Divergent*, or *The Mortal Instruments* follow the same strategy. Once again, the *Harry Potter* series can be used as a telling comparison, as every single title of the series starts with the male protagonist's name followed by a short description or allusion to the main plot of the respective novel.

5. This replacement of the princess' name with one single adjective is a trend found in many installments of the third wave of Disney princess movies, namely *Tangled*, *Brave*, and *Frozen*. In order to appear attractive to a wider audience, and boys in particular, these films use the same strategy found in YA novels, namely to replace the name of the female protagonist with a gender neutral title that promises some kind of adventure or conflict.

6. At the same time, Disney apparently also strives to be more inclusive. While at the beginning of June 2017, princess costumes were only available for Belle, Rapunzel, Cinderella, and Aurora, the shop has since added at least one costume for each of the other princesses, too.

7. Fans of the *Hunger Games* franchise also became politically active in other contexts, as a number of them engaged in actual political campaigns by using the signs and symbols from the novels, movies, and marketing campaigns. The three finger salute, for example, was used by people in Thailand to protest the taking over of power by the military government in 2014 (Ehrlich), while in Ferguson in the same year, people sprayed the rebel slogan "If we burn, you burn with us" on a landmark during the protests against police brutality (Bates).

Chapter 5

1. For a more detailed account of the *Star Trek* fandom specifically, see Bacon-Smith. For more general overviews of the history of media fandoms and fan fiction, see, for instance, Black 10–12, S. Jones 80, or Coppa.

2. Several scholars point out that, within fan fiction communities, there exist rules, power relations, and hierarchies that govern discourses and influence what can be written and discussed (Hodges and Richmond 3.1; Jenkins, *Textual* 34; J. Russo 29; Scodari 111). Therefore, even though it tends to undermine and resist certain mainstream ideologies and conventions, "the world of fan-fiction is not all happy anarchy" (Jamison 20).

3. For a more detailed list of subgenres, terms, and definitions, see Hellekson and Busse 9–12 and Keft-Kennedy 52–53. Fanlore.org also provides an extensive wiki entitled "List of Tropes in Fanworks."

4. According to user toastystats, who conducted research on archiveofourown.org,

femslash accounted for about 10 percent of all the works published on the platform in 2015. Male slash made up about 50 percent of all the published works that same year. Still, femslash is on the rise. Not only did its percentage increase from about 4 percent in 2010, but the absolute number of works has also significantly grown from about 4,000 stories in 2010 to more than 60,000 in 2015. The most popular pairings are, for example, the women of the TV series *Once upon a Time* (2011–), *The 100* (2014–), *Glee* (2009–15), or *Marvel's Agent Carter* (2015–16). Other frequently femslashed texts are *Harry Potter*, *The Avengers*, or the *Pitch Perfect* movies.

5. Different studies have shown that in U.S. mainstream media, heterosexuality is still the norm. A study entitled "Inequality in 700 Popular Films," for instance, revealed that the most popular movies of 2014 did not represent any lesbian or bisexual female characters in leading roles (Smith et al. 1). In the same year, out of 4,610 speaking characters in the 100 most successful films, "only 19 were lesbian, gay or bisexual. *Not one transgender* character was portrayed. Only 14 movies sample wide featured an LGB depiction and *none of those films were animated*. Of the LGB characters coded, nearly two-thirds were male (63.2 percent) and only 36.8 percent were female" (2; emphasis added). See also "Status of Women" for accounts of LGBTQ characters in additional media.

6. At the time of research, there were 2,139 Buffy/Faith, 1,131 Katniss/Johanna, and 184 Merida/Elsa stories on AO3. In order to further narrow down my corpus, I decided to only include stories from AO3 that were a) categorized as femslash, b) between 250 and 5,000 words long (still, some exceptions reach up to 28,000 words) and, c), feature relationships between two girls that can be described as non-platonic. This is why I chose to focus on Buffy/Faith rather than Buffy/Willow. Although there exists a considerable amount of Buffy/Willow fics (3,826) on AO3, a scan of them showed that many of these stories are about the platonic friendship and not about a romantic/sexual relationship.

7. Elsa is, of course, not a secondary character but a protagonist in her own movie *Frozen*. That fans need to write so-called "cross-over" fics, which bring together characters from different movies

once again demonstrates that even in the newest Disney princess movies, there still remains a general lack of female characters. In both *Brave* and *Frozen*, a second central female character exists, but they are a mother and a sister, respectively. If fans want to write fiction that is not incestuous, and there exists Anna/Elsa slash, they have to look to other (Disney) movies to find a same-sex partner.

8. I also decided not to include BDSM or kink fics. Even though these more deviant practices are an integral part of femslash, they are certainly not the only sexual practices represented. Yet, they have received attention by a relatively large number of scholars such as Jenny Alexander, Kristina Busse, Malin Isaksson, and Virginia Keft-Kennedy. While this attention to deviant and stigmatized sexual practices is relevant as it offers readings and analyses that make such practices visible and understandable, and potentially challenge the taboos connected to them, it also creates a distorted image of the types of sexual practices portrayed in (fem)slash fiction at large.

9. Consent is addressed in a rather ambiguous manner in the Buffy/Faith BDSM and kink stories analyzed by Isaksson, where frequently, "only a small detail distinguishes the seduction from rape, namely the insertion of the seduced heroine's perspective, signaling that she actually enjoys what is happening" (14). Other stories even feature actual non-con (for non-consensual) or rape scenes (Alexander 5).

10. Incidents such as the Steubenville rape case or the documentary *The Hunting Ground* (2015) brought the topic into the public consciousness. Additionally, in 2014, then vice-president Joe Biden, as a representative of the White House Task Force to Prevent Sexual Assault, helped launch "It's on Us," a campaign that aims to "end sexual assault" by informing people and inciting conversations about sexual assault and consent ("Our Story").

11. A number of scholars have commented on the bifurcated way in which girls and young women are portrayed in popular culture and the mainstream media. On the one hand, they are sexualized and represented in a manner that caters to a male gaze by appearing in sexy clothes and make-up (cf. Epstein, Kehily, and Renold 252; Smith et al. 2; "Status of Women" 51, 57). On the

other hand, female sexuality is frequently regulated and tamed by the mainstream media (Stover 2) and it is also presented as a threat from which girls need to be protected (Epstein, Kehily, and Renold 249; Stone 47).

12. Numerous articles published in the popular press, for instance, demonstrate that movies get higher MPAA ratings if they include scenes that show women and girls enjoying sex or having orgasms (Chemaly; Kang; Kim; Zutter).

13. Indeed, the enduring dominance of male slash can also be observed in the case of the texts with which I engaged. After all, the numbers of stories written about male pairings matches, and at times exceeds, that of stories featuring female pairings even in these texts that do have female leads and several female characters (*BtVS*: Buffy/Faith 2,139, Spike/Angel 2,197, Spike/Xander 2,664, Angel/Xander 1,302; *Hunger Games*: Katniss/Johanna 1,131, Peeta/Gale 1,320) (AO3, Dec. 2016).

Chapter 6

1. Fans frequently collaborate and communicate across different platforms, expanding on and enriching their fan works to include a variety of forms and practices. So-called "prompts" on Tumblr, for instance, contain requests to create fan art or write fan fiction. These items will then be uploaded on archiveofourown.org. In other cases, fan fiction may also inspire fan artists to draw pictures that illustrate the characters or scenes of a story. These are sometimes included in the story itself, but also uploaded on Tumblr or DeviantArt.

2. In spite of these positive developments, in general, the Internet is still a male-dominated space where hardcore pornography, online (sexual) harassment, and sexism are the norm rather than the exception (Carstensen 107, 119; Arvidsson and Foka).

3. Indeed, there is a plethora of images that depicts women and girls, both fictional and real ones, in overly sexualized or even pornographic poses. This does not only happen, however, with drawings, but photoshopped images or actual nude pictures are also frequently used to blackmail women into paying money to or having sex with men who threaten to post said pictures if

the women do not obey the demands. This practice has become so common that it has even received its own term, namely "sextortion" (Chawki and Shazly 76).

4. In this analysis, I will solely concentrate on the issue of race and racebent fan art. Nevertheless, sexuality, sexual orientation, or beauty ideals other than those connected to race and ethnicity are also central elements of feminist fan art shared online. See, for instance, #genderbent, #gaydisney, or #curvy. For academic articles analyzing these phenomena, refer to Scott or Kapurch.

5. According to Kimble and Olson the "poster has come to represent a past that never was" (562). When it was first created, the Rosie-poster was "not nearly as empowering of home-front women as it might seem" (533). Women who went to work in factories were confronted with prejudices (534), they often took on these jobs to earn money and not for patriotic reasons, and they did not have a lasting impact on women's roles in society (535). Contrary to popular belief, the poster was not created by the government to be publicly shown, but by an advertising agency for the Westinghouse factories, "where wartime security ensured that its audience was limited to workers and management" (536). In fact, it was "virtually unknown before the mid-1980s" (537). Today, the poster has not only become one of the best-known images representing the 1940s in the U.S. (536), but it has also taken on a mythic status for U.S. society as the depictions of Rosie "function as a charactertype [sic], narrative, and enactment of U.S. culture's key values" (537).

6. For more detailed comparisons, see Berlatsky, Firestone, or L. Miller "*Hunger Games.*"

7. For a detailed analysis of gender differences in bodily motions see Young.

8. Studies show that out of 700 popular movies that were released between 2007 and 2014, only 30.2 percent featured women in speaking roles, and only roughly 20 percent featured women or girls as protagonists (Smith et al. 1). On TV, women are outnumbered almost 2 to 1 in comparison to men when it comes to leading roles, both in reality TV, cable, and network shows ("Status of Women" 31).

9. The body positivity movement advocates the idea that "all bodies are good bodies," and "strives for the representation of

marginalized bodies. [...] Fat bodies, queer bodies, and bodies of color" (Bustle). When taken alone, Lawrence's statements can be seen as one voice defending a certain body type, viewed in an online context however, they become part of a larger discourse on body positivity in which many different body types—both ones that are closer to the Western beauty standards and ones that are not—are represented, defended, and celebrated.

10. Other highly popular fan art discourses are concerned with the princess' sexuality and the gender role performances of both princesses and princes. Practices such as slash, genderbending (in which the characters are portrayed in a more ambiguous and fluid manner regarding their gender role performance, i.e., changes in clothes, hairstyle, stance, body shape) or genderswap (in which the roles of the female and male characters are reversed), challenge the heteronormative and binary notions of gender and sexuality promoted by Disney.

11. For academic sources on POC in Europe and Scotland before and during the Middle Ages, refer to Fryer, Hsy, or R. Jones.

12. Sayyida al Hurra "was a personage of considerable historical and political significance" who "was involved in ruling Tetouan [a city in Northern Morocco] for some thirty years in the beginning of the sixteenth century" (Lebbady 134). Queen Nanny, too, is an "extremely important" historical figure (Gottlieb xiiv). Born in the late 17th century, she became "the military, religious, and cultural leader of the Windward Jamaican Maroons [a community of escaped slaves that lived on the Eastern Side of the island] during the height of their resistance against the British" (xv–xvi).

13. Racebent fan art not only criticizes the culture industries, but also frequently addresses fans, fandoms, and the fact that they, too, tend to neglect and marginalize people of color. As Elizabeth Gilliland states, "these pieces of fan art can inform discussions that may cause users to identify their own beliefs about the current whitewashing [...] in their own practices, which traditionally tend to favor white characters in fan-generated blogs, fiction, and art. As such, these users can begin to challenge not only the norm of media, but also their complacency toward it and efforts in perpetuating it" (5.2).

Conclusion

1. In this context, a number of scholars and feminists such as Jennifer Baumgardner, Courtney Martin, or Vanessa Valenti have proclaimed that a new wave, a fourth wave of feminism, has emerged. They regard contemporary feminisms as fundamentally different from the third wave not only when it comes to the ideas and concepts for which they advocate, but with regard to the means by which they try to foster change. To be more precise, they draw attention to the increased visibility and pervasiveness of feminisms today through their usage of online spaces and celebrate the new possibilities these spaces hold for feminist discussions, consciousness raising, and political mobilization. For an in-depth discussion of fourth wave feminism, see Baumgardner, Martin and Valenti, or Munro.

2. Notably, it is not only fans and audiences who engage in this struggle over the manner in which female characters are represented within and outside of popular culture texts. In a similar manner to Jennifer Lawrence, who resisted the demands that she lose weight when she played Katniss in the *Hunger Games* movie adaptations, actress Emma Watson insisted that specific features of Belle, the Disney princess she plays in the live-action adaptation of *Beauty and the Beast*, be changed as well. Watson refused to wear a corset that would make her appear thinner, and she also convinced the writers to portray Belle as an inventor, a role previously occupied by her father (Giannini). Last but not least, even though it does not pertain to the character she plays in particular, but to the movie industries more generally, actress Gal Gadot successfully threatened not to reprise her role in the *Wonder Woman* sequel if producer Brett Ratner, who is accused of sexual misconduct, remained involved with the film project (Golgowski).

Bibliography

"About." Tumblr.com. Tumblr, n. d. Web. 5 Apr. 2017.

"About DeviantArt." DeviantArt.com. DeviantArt, n. d. Web. 5 Apr. 2017.

A-Crow-Girl. "I Apologize." Tumblr.com. Tumblr, 2014. Web. 2 May 2017.

Adewunmi, Bim. "Why *The Walking Dead* Has Become Fanfiction's Muse." BuzzFeed.com. BuzzFeed, 14 Nov. 2016. Web. 11 Jan. 2017.

Afterandalasia. "Learn Me Right." Archiveofourown.org. Organization for Transformative Works, 2 Feb. 2014. Web. 20 Jan. 2017.

_____. "Looking a Gift (Bear) in the (Crossed) Eyes." Archiveofourown.org. Organization for Transformative Works, 6 Dec. 2014. Web. 20 Jan. 2017.

"After Life." *Buffy the Vampire Slayer: Season 1–7*. Season 6, episode 3. Writ. Jane Espenson. Dir. David Solomon. Fox, 2010. DVD.

Alexander, Jenny. "A Vampire Is Being Beaten: DeSade through the Looking Glass in *Buffy* and *Angel*." *Slayage: The Online International Journal of Buffy Studies* 4.3 (2004): 29 pars. Web. 25 Nov. 2017.

Allrath, Gaby, Marion Gymnich, and Carola Surkamp. "Towards a Narratology of TV Series." Introduction. *Narrative Strategies in Television Series*. Ed. Gaby Allrath and Marion Gymnich. New York: Palgrave Macmillan, 2005. 1–43. Print.

Ames, Melissa. "*Twilight* Follows Tradition: Analyzing 'Biting' Critiques of Vampire Narratives for Their Portrayals of Gender and Sexuality." *Bitten by* Twilight: *Youth Culture, Media, and the Vampire Franchise*. Ed. Melissa A. Click, Jennifer Stevens Aubrey, and Elizabeth Behm-Morawitz. New York: Lang, 2010. 37–53. Print. Mediated Youth 14.

AMightyGirl (amightygirl). "Joss Whedon on Writing Strong Women and Mighty Girl Characters!" 13 Nov. 2014, 12:39 p.m. Tweet.

Amsay. "The Way You Grab Me (Must Wanna Get Nasty)." Archiveofourown.org. Organization for Transformative Works, 28 Dec. 2013. Web. 20 Jan. 2017.

Ari (Walkingnorth). "This is a WIP." Tumblr.com. Tumblr, 18 Aug. 2013. Web. 16 June 2017.

Arnett, Jeffrey Jensen. "Adolescents' Uses of Media for Self-Socialization." *Journal of Youth and Adolescence* 24.5 (1995): 519–33. *Springer Link*. Web. 25 Nov. 2017.

Arvidsson, Viktor, and Anna Foka. "Digital Gender: Perspective, Phenomena, Practice." *First Monday* 20.4 (2015): n. p. Web. 16 Nov. 2015.

Asher-Perrin, Emily. "Is the Capitol Couture Clothing Line Sending the Wrong Message to *Hunger Games* Fans?" TOR.com. Macmillan, 18 Sep. 2013. Web. 27 May 2017.

Aubrey, Jennifer Stevens, Scott Walus, and Melissa A. Click. "*Twilight* and the Production of the 21st Century Teen Idol." *Bitten by* Twilight: *Youth Culture, Media, and the Vampire Franchise*. Ed. Melissa A. Click, Jennifer Stevens Aubrey, and Elizabeth Behm-Morawitz. New York: Lang, 2010. 225–41. Print. Mediated Youth 14.

Auden, Wystan Hugh. "The Quest Hero." *Tolkien and the Critics: Essays on J. R. R. Tolkien's*

The Lord of the Rings. Ed. Neil David Isaacs and Rose A. Zimbardo. Notre Dame: University of Notre Dame P, 1968. 40–61. Print.

Australooithecushomo. "I Don't Deserve This." Archiveofourown.org. Organization for Transformative Works, 3 June 2015. Web. 20 Jan. 2017.

Averill, Nancy Issow. "Sometimes the World is Hungry for People Who Care: Katniss and the Feminist Care Ethic." The Hunger Games and Philosophy: A Critique of Pure Treason. Ed. George A. Dunn and Nicolas Michaud. Hoboken: Wiley, 2012. 162–76. Print. Blackwell Philosophy and Pop Culture Ser.

Ayres, Brenda, ed. "The Poisonous Apple in Snow White: Disney's Kingdom of Gender." The Emperor's Old Groove: Decolonizing Disney's Magic Kingdom. New York: Lang, 2003. 39–50. Print.

Bacon-Smith, Camille. Enterprising Women: Television Fandom and the Creation of Popular Myth. Philadelphia: University of Pennsylvania Press, 1992. Print.

Baker-Sperry, Lori, and Liz Grauerholz. "The Pervasiveness and Persistence of the Feminine Beauty Ideal in Children's Fairy Tales." Gender and Society 17.5 (2003): 711–26. JStor. Web. 22 Nov. 2017.

Bandersnatchedsouls. "Racebent Disney Princesses." Tumblr.com. Tumblr, n.d. Web. 1 May 2017.

Barker, Meg. "Slashing the Slayer: A Thematic Analysis of Homo-Erotic Buffy Fan Fiction." Paper presented at Blood, Text and Fears: Reading around Buffy the Vampire Slayer, University of East Anglia, 19–20 Oct. 2002. The Open University. Web. 25 Nov. 2017. PDF file.

Bates, Daniel. "Ferguson Protesters Scrawl Hunger Games Slogan on Landmark as Tense Town Waits for Grand Jury Decision on Indicting Officer Darren Wilson over Killing of Michael Brown." DailyMail.co.uk. Associated Newspapers, 24 Nov. 2014. Web. 22 July 2017.

Baumgardner, Jennifer. F'em!: Goo Goo, Gaga, and Some Thoughts on Balls. Berkeley: Seal, 2011. Print.

Baumgardner, Jennifer, and Amy Richards. "Feminism and Femininity: Or How We Learned to Stop Worrying and Love the Thong." All About the Girl: Culture, Power, and Identity. Ed. Anita Harris. New York: Routledge, 2004. 59–67. Print.

_____. Manifesta: Young Women, Feminism, and the Future. New York: Farrar, Straus and Giroux, 2000. Print.

"Becoming (Part 2)." Buffy the Vampire Slayer: Season 1–7. Season 2, episode 22. Writ. and dir. Joss Whedon. Fox, 2010. DVD.

Bean, Kelly. "Stripping Beauty: Disney's 'Feminist' Seduction." The Emperor's Old Groove: Decolonizing Disney's Magic Kingdom. Ed. Brenda Ayres. New York: Lang, 2003. 53–64. Print.

Beauty and the Beast. Dir. Gary Trousdale and Kirk Wise. Walt Disney Pictures, 1991. Film.

Beersforqueers. "No Sugar." Archiveofourown.org. Organization for Transformative Works, 7 June 2016. Web. 20 Jan. 2017.

Bell, Elizabeth. "Somatexts at the Disney Shop: Constructing the Pentimentos of Women's Animated Bodies." From Mouse to Mermaid: The Politics of Film, Gender, and Culture. Ed. Elizabeth Bell, Lynda Haas, and Laura Sells. Bloomington: Indiana UP, 1995. 107–24. Print.

Bellafante, Ginia, and Jeanne McDowell. "Bewitching Teen Heroines." Time.com. Time, 5 May 1997. Web. 25 Nov. 2017.

Bergman, David, ed. Introduction. Camp Grounds: Style and Homosexuality. Amherst: University of Massachusetts Press, 1993. 3–16. Print.

Berlatsky, Noah. "Twilight vs. The Hunger Games: Why Do So Many Grown-Ups Hate Bella?" TheAtlantic.com. The Atlantic Monthly Group, 15 Nov. 2011. Web. 19 Nov. 2017.

Bittner, Robert. "Queering Sex Education: Young Adult Literature with LGBT Content as Complementary Sources of Sex and Sexuality Education." Journal of LGBT Youth 9.4 (2012): 357–72. Taylor and Francis Online. Web. 25 Nov. 2017.

Black, Rebecca W. *Adolescents and Online Fan Fiction*. New York: Lang, 2008. Print. New Literacies and Digital Epistemologies 23.

Blasingame, James. "An Interview with Suzanne Collins." *Journal of Adolescent & Adult Literacy* 52.8 (2009): 726–27. *MLA International Bibliography*. Web. 19 Nov. 2017.

Bluestone, George. *Novels into Film: The Metamorphosis of Fiction into Cinema*. Berkeley: University of California Press, 1957. Print.

Bodylikeabattleaxe. "An Evergreen Forest." Archiveofourown.org. Organization for Transformative Works, 29 Aug. 2014, updated 27 Dec. 2015. Web. 20 Jan. 2017.

Bordwell, David, Janet Staiger, and Kristin Thompson. *The Classical Hollywood Cinema: Film Style and Mode of Production to 1960*. New York: Columbia University Press, 1985. Print.

Bowman, Laurel. "*Buffy the Vampire Slayer*: The Greek Hero Revisited." Department of Greek and Roman Studies, University of Victoria, 2002. Web. 24 Nov. 2017.

Braithwaite, Elizabeth. "Post-Disaster Fiction for Young Adults: Some Trends and Variations." *Papers: Explorations in Children's Literature* 20.1 (2010): 5–19. Web. 19 Nov. 2017. PDF file.

Brannon, Julie Sloan. "'It's About Power': Buffy, Foucault, and the Quest for Self." *Slayage: The Online International Journal of Buffy Studies* 6.4 (2007): 14 pars. Web. 22 Aug. 2017.

Brave. Dir. Mark Andrews and Brenda Chapman. Walt Disney Pictures and Pixar Animation Studios, 2012. Film.

"*Brave* Poster (#3 of 17)." Impawards.com. Internet Movie Poster Awards, 22 Feb. 2012. Web. 29 July 2017.

Brown, Jeffrey A. *Dangerous Curves: Action Heroines, Gender, Fetishism, and Popular Culture*. Jackson: University Press of Mississippi, 2011. Print.

Bruce, Alexander M. "The Role of the 'Princess' in Walt Disney's Animated Films: Reactions of College Students." *Studies in Popular Culture* 30.1 (2007): 1–25. *JStor*. Web. 22 Nov. 2017.

Bruteaous. "Don't Die." Archiveofourown.org. Organization for Transformative Works, 5 Aug. 2014. Web. 20 Jan. 2017.

"*Buffy the Vampire Slayer* Poster (#11 of 15)." Impawards.com. Internet Movie Poster Awards, 10 July 2003. Web. 20 July 2017.

Busse, Kristina. "Crossing the Final Taboo: Family, Sexuality, and Incest in Buffyverse Fan Fiction." *Fighting the Forces: What's at Stake in* Buffy the Vampire Slayer. Ed. Rhonda V. Wilcox and David Lavery. Lanham: Rowman and Littlefield, 2002. 207–17. Print.

Bustle. "What Is the Body Positive Movement." Online video clip. *YouTube*. YouTube, 18 Nov. 2015. Web. 29 Feb. 2016.

Butler, Judith. *Gender Trouble: Feminism and the Subversion of Identity*. 1990. New York: Routledge, 2007. Print.

_____. "Imitation and Gender Insubordination." *Cultural Theory and Popular Culture: A Reader*. Ed. John Storey. Harlow: Pearson, 2006. 255–70. Rpt. of "Imitation and Gender Insubordination." *Inside Out: Lesbian Theories, Gay Theories*. Ed. Diana Fuss. London: Taylor & Francis, 1992. 13–31. Print.

Butler, Michelle Markey. "The Wisdom of the Crowd: Internet Memes and *The Hobbit: An Unexpected Journey*." The Hobbit *and Tolkien's Mythology: Essays on Revisions and Influences*. Ed. Bradford Lee Eden. Jefferson: McFarland, 2014. Print.

Buttsworth, Sara. "'Bite Me': *Buffy* and the Penetration of the Gendered Warrior-Hero." *Continuum: Journal of Media and Cultural Studies* 16.2 (2002): 185–99. Print.

Byers, Michele. "*Buffy the Vampire Slayer*: The Next Generation of Television." *Catching a Wave: Reclaiming Feminism for the 21st Century*. Ed. Rory Dicker and Alison Piepmeier. Boston: Northeastern University Press, 2003. 171–87. Print.

Campbell, Joseph. *The Hero's Journey: The World of Joseph Campbell*. Ed. Phil Cousineau. San Francisco: Harper and Row, 1990. Print.

_____. *The Hero with a Thousand Faces*. 1949. Princeton: Princeton UP, 1971. Print. Bollinger Ser. XVII.

Campbell, Lori M., ed. Introduction. *A Quest of Her Own: Essays on the Female Hero in Modern Fantasy*. Jefferson: McFarland, 2014. 4–14. Print.

Camron, Marc. "The Importance of Being the Zeppo: Xander, Gender Identity and Hybridity in *Buffy the Vampire Slayer*." *Slayage: The Online International Journal of Buffy Studies* 6.3 (2007): 18 pars. Web. 24 Nov. 2017.

Carstensen, Tanja. "Gender Trouble in Web 2.0: Gender Relations in Social Network Sites, Wikis and Weblogs." *International Journal of Gender, Science and Technology* 1.1 (2009): 105–27. Web. 16 Nov. 2015.

Cart, Michael. *Young Adult Literature: From Romance to Realism*. Chicago: American Library Association, 2010. Print.

Chandler, Holly. "Slaying the Patriarchy: Transfusions of the Vampire Metaphor in *Buffy the Vampire Slayer*." *Slayage: The Online International Journal of Buffy Studies* 3.1 (2003): 62 pars. Web. 24 Nov. 2017.

Chang, Shuo, et al. "Specialization, Homophily, and Gender in a Social Curation Site: Findings from Pinterest." *CSCW '14: Proceedings of the 17th ACM Conference on Computer Supported Cooperative Work & Social Computing*: 674–86. *ACM Digital Library*. Web. 23 Nov. 2017.

Chang, Yi, et al. "What is Tumblr: A Statistical Overview and Comparison." *ACM SIGKDD Explorations Newsletter* 16.1 (2014): 21–29. *ACM Digital Library*. Web. 23 Nov. 2017.

Chawki, Mohamed, and Yassin el Shazly. "Online Sexual Harassment: Issues and Solutions." *Journal of Intellectual Property, Information Technology and Electronic Commerce Law* 4.2 (2013): 71–86. Web. 15 June 2017.

Chaykowski, Kathleen. "Pinterest Reaches 150 Million Monthly Users, Boosts Engagement Among Men." Forbes.com. Forbes Media, 13 Oct. 2016. Web. 1 June 2017.

"Checkpoint." *Buffy the Vampire Slayer: Season 1–7*. Season 5, episode 12. Writ. Douglas Petrie and Jane Espenson. Dir. Nick Marck. Fox, 2010. DVD.

Chemaly, Soraya. "The MPAA's Backwards Logic: Sex Is Dangerous, Sexism Is Fine." Salon.com. Salon Media Group, 6 Nov. 2013. Web. 16 Mar. 2017.

"Chosen." *Buffy the Vampire Slayer: Season 1–7*. Season 7, episode 22. Writ. and dir. Joss Whedon. Fox, 2010. DVD.

Cicioni, Mirna. "Male Pair-Bonds and Female Desire in Fan Slash Writing." *Theorizing Fandom: Fans, Subculture and Identity*. Ed. Cheryl Harris and Alison Alexander. Cresskill: Hampton, 1998. 153–77. Print. Hampton Press Communication Ser.

Cinderella. Dir. Clyde Geronimi, Hamilton Luske, and Wilfred Jackson. Walt Disney Productions, 1950. Film.

Clapp-Itnyre, Alisa. "Help! I'm a Feminist But My Daughter is a 'Princess Fanatic'!: Disney's Transformation of Twenty-First-Century Girls." *Children's Folklore Review* 32 (2010): 7–22. Web. 22 Nov. 2017. PDF file.

Clemente, Bill. "Panem in America: Crisis Economics and a Call for Political Engagement." *Of Bread, Blood and* The Hunger Games: *Critical Essays on the Suzanne Collins Trilogy*. Ed. Mary F. Pharr and Leisa A. Clark. Jefferson: McFarland, 2012. 20–29. Print.

Clover, Carol J. *Men, Women, and Chainsaws: Gender in the Modern Horror Film*. Princeton: Princeton UNiversity Press, 1992. Print.

Collins, Suzanne. *Catching Fire*. New York: Scholastic, 2009. Print.

_____. *The Hunger Games*. New York: Scholastic, 2008. Print.

_____. *Mockingjay*. New York: Scholastic, 2010. Print.

Colom, Adriana. "14 Celebrity Quotes on Women and Equality." HerCampus.com. Her Campus Media, 11 Mar. 2015. Web. 11 Jan. 2016.

"Communism." *The Concise Oxford Dictionary of Politics*. 3rd ed. Ed. Iain McLean and Alistair McMillan. Oxford: Oxford University Press, 2009. 96–99. Print.

Connelly, Sarah M. "'Welcome to the Feminist Cult': Building a Feminist Community of Practice on Tumblr." *Student Publications* Paper 328 (2015). The Cupola: Scholarship of Gettysburg College, n.d. Web. 29 May 2017.

Coppa, Francesca. "A Brief History of Media Fandom." *Fan Fiction and Fan Communities in the Age of the Internet: New Essays*. Ed. Karen Hellekson and Kristina Busse. Jefferson: McFarland, 2006. 41–59. Print.

Corliss, Richard. "Katniss, Meet Merida." *Time Magazine* 25 May 2012: 68. *Academic Search Premier.* Web. 22 Nov. 2017.

Coulombe, Renee T. "'I Had It All Wrong': New Vampires, Grrrl Heroes and the Third Wave Body in *Buffy the Vampire Slayer.*" *Nostalgia or Perversion?: Gothic Rewriting from the Eighteenth Century until the Present Day.* Ed. Isabella van Elferen. Newcastle: Cambridge Scholars, 2007. 206–22. Print.

"Critical Praise for *Catching Fire.*" Mediaroom.Scholastic.com. Scholastic, n.d. Web. 12 June 2017. PDF file.

"Critical Praise for *The Hunger Games.*" Mediaroom.Scholastic.com. Scholastic, n.d. Web. 14 July 2017. PDF file.

Culver, Jennifer. "'So Here I Am in His Debt Again': Katniss, Gifts, and Invisible Strings." *The Hunger Games and Philosophy: A Critique of Pure Treason.* Ed. George A. Dunn and Nicolas Michaud. Hoboken: Wiley, 2012. 90–101. Print. Blackwell Philosophy and Pop Culture Ser.

Cumberland, Sharon. "Private Uses of Cyberspace: Women, Desire, and Fan Culture." *The Gender and Media Reader.* Ed. Mary Celeste Kearney. New York: Routledge, 2012. 669–79. Print.

Currie, Dawn H., Deirdre M. Kelly, and Shauna Pomerantz. *Girl Power: Girls Reinventing Girlhood.* New York: Lang, 2009. Print. Mediated Youth 4.

Danckaert, Carolyn. "Say No to the Merida Makeover and Keep Our Hero Brave!" AMighty Girl.com. A Mighty Girl, 10 May 2013. Web. 22 Nov. 2017.

Davis, Cindy. "Here's the Ugly Truth about Why Rey Was Missing from *Star Wars* Merchandise." Pajiba.com. Disqus, 21 Jan. 2016. Web. 17 Nov. 2017.

Day, Helen. "Simulacra, Sacrifice and Survival in *The Hunger Games*, *Battle Royale*, and *The Running Man.*" *Of Bread, Blood and* The Hunger Games: *Critical Essays on the Suzanne Collins Trilogy.* Ed. Mary F. Pharr and Leisa A. Clark. Jefferson: McFarland, 2012. 167–77. Print.

Day, Sara K., Miranda A. Green-Barteet, and Amy L. Montz, eds. "From 'New Woman' to 'Future Girl': The Roots and the Rise of the Female Protagonist in Contemporary Young Adult Dystopias." Introduction. *Female Rebellion in Young Adult Dystopian Fiction.* Farnham: Ashgate, 2014. 1–14. Print. Ashgate Studies in Childhood, 1700 to the Present.

Dean, Marissa, and Karen Laidler. "A New Girl in Town: Exploring Girlhood Identities through Facebook." *First Monday* 18.2 (2013): n.p. Web. 16 Nov. 2015.

Derecho, Abigail. "1. Archontic Literature: A Definition, a History, and Several Theories of Fan Fiction." *Fan Fiction and Fan Communities in the Age of the Internet: New Essays.* Ed. Karen Hellekson and Kristina Busse. Jefferson: McFarland, 2006. 61–78. Print.

Dicker, Rory, and Alison Piepmeier, eds. Introduction. *Catching a Wave: Reclaiming Feminism for the 21st Century.* Boston: Northeastern UP, 2003. 3–28. Print.

DiPaolo, Marc. "Mass-Marketing 'Beauty': How a Feminist Heroine Became an Insipid Disney Princess." *Beyond Adaptation: Essays on Radical Transformations of Original Works.* Ed. Phyllis Frus and Christy Williams. Jefferson: McFarland, 2010. 168–80. Print.

Disney. "Dream Big, Princess—Be A Champion | Disney." Online video clip. *YouTube.* YouTube, 11 Feb. 2016. Web. 2 Aug. 2017.

Disney-Pixar. "*Brave* Trailer." Online video clip. *YouTube.* YouTube, 16 Nov. 2011. Web. 29 July 2017.

Disney-Pixar. "*Brave* 'The Prize' Trailer." Online video clip. *YouTube.* YouTube, 22 Feb. 2012. Web. 29 July 2017.

Disney-Pixar. "*Brave* Trailer—In Theaters June 22." Online video clip. *YouTube.* YouTube, 6 June 2012. Web. 29 July 2017.

District_7_Profanity. "Help." Archiveofourown.org. Organization for Transformative Works, 26 Jan. 2015. Web. 20 Jan. 2017.

_____. "She Doesn't Say I Love You." Archiveofourown.org. Organization for Transformative Works, 12 Oct. 2014, compl. 15 Nov. 2014. Web. 20 Jan. 2017.

DJMeep. "It's Only Love." Archiveofourown.org. Organization for Transformative Works, 21 Feb. 2014. Web. 20 Jan. 2017.

Doctornerdington. "What I Want." Archiveofourown.org. Organization for Transformative Works, 29 Oct. 2014. Web. 20 Jan. 2017.

Dodes, Rachel, and John Jurgensen. "Gender Games: *The Hunger Games* Must Clear Tricky Marketing Hurdles." *The Wall Street Journal* (Eastern Edition) 56.259 (2012): D4. Print.

Dohnt, Hayley K., and Marika Tiggemann. "Body Image Concerns in Young Girls: The Role of Peers and Media Prior to Adolescence." *Journal of Youth and Adolescence* 35.2 (2006): 141–51. *Academic Search Premier*. Web. 6 July 2017.

Dominus, Susan. "Suzanne Collins's War Stories for Kids." Nytimes.com. The New York Times Company, 8 April 2011. Web. 27 Nov. 2017.

Do Rozario, Rebecca-Anne C. "The Princess and the Magic Kingdom: Beyond Nostalgia, the Function of the Disney Princess." *Women's Studies in Communication* 27.1 (2004): 34–59. *Communication and Mass Media Complete*. Web. 22 Nov. 2017.

Driscoll, Catherine. "2. One True Pairing: The Romance of Pornography and the Pornography of Romance." *Fan Fiction and Fan Communities in the Age of the Internet: New Essays.* Ed. Karen Hellekson and Kristina Busse. Jefferson: McFarland, 2006. 79–96. Print.

_____. *Girls: Feminine Adolescence in Popular Culture and Cultural Theory.* New York: Columbia University Press, 2002. Print.

Driver, Susan. *Queer Girls and Popular Culture: Reading, Resisting, and Creating Media.* New York: Lang, 2007. Print.

Drucker, Susan J., and Gary Gumpert, eds. *Heroes in a Global World.* Cresskill: Hampton, 2008. Print. Hampton Press Communication Ser.

Durand, Kevin K., ed. "It's All about Power." Buffy *Meets the Academy: Essays on the Episodes and Scripts as Text.* Jefferson: McFarland, 2009. 45–56. Print.

Early, Frances H. "Staking Her Claim: *Buffy the Vampire Slayer* as Transgressive Woman Warrior." *Journal of Popular Culture* 35.3 (2001): 11–27. *Wiley Online Library.* Web. 24 Nov. 2017.

Early, Frances, and Kathleen Kennedy, eds. "Athena's Daughters." Introduction. *Athena's Daughters: Television's New Women Warriors.* Syracuse: Syracuse University Press, 2003. 1–10. Print.

Ehrlich, Richard S. "Thailand Protests Meet *Hunger Games* as Demonstrators Arrested for Three-Finger Salute." WashingtonTimes.com. The Washington Times, 20 Nov. 2014. Web. 22 July 2017.

Electra126. "Magnetic." Archiveofourown.org. Organization for Transformative Works, 11 Jan. 2015. Web. 20 Jan. 2017.

Elizabeth_Scripturient. "Bring on the Night." Archiveofourown.org. Organization for Transformative Works, 26 Dec. 2002. Web. 20 Jan. 2017.

Emerson, Rebecca. "A Woman Can…" Pinterest.com. Pinterest, n.d. Web. 10 Apr. 2016.

Enchanted. Dir. Kevin Lima. Walt Disney Studios Motion Pictures, 2007. Film.

"End of Days." *Buffy the Vampire Slayer: Season 1–7.* Season 7, episode 21. Writ. Jane Espenson and Doug Petrie. Dir. Marita Grabiak. Fox, 2010. DVD.

England, Dawn Elizabeth, Lara Descartes, and Melissa A. Collier-Meek. "Gender Role Portrayal and the Disney Princess." *Sex Roles* 64 (2011): 555–67. *Education Source.* Web. 22 Nov. 2017.

Epstein, Debbie, Mary Jane Kehily, and Emma Renold. Editorial. *Gender and Education* 24.3 (2012): 249–54. *Education Source Publications.* Web. 25 Nov. 2017.

Escritoireazul. "Mutual Masturbation." Archiveofourown.org. Organization for Transformative Works, 20 Dec. 2008. Web. 20 Jan. 2017.

"Faith, Hope & Trick." *Buffy the Vampire Slayer: Season 1–7.* Season 3, episode 3. Writ. David Greenwalt. Dir. James A. Contner. Fox, 2010. DVD.

Faludi, Susan. *Backlash: The Undeclared War Against American Women.* 1991. New York: Three Rivers, 2006. Print.

_____. *The Terror Dream: Fear and Fantasy in Post-9/11 America*. New York: Metropolitan Books, 2007. Print.

Fangirl. "What Are You Going To Do." Pinterest.com. Pinterest, n.d. Web. 5 June 2017.

"Fascism." *The Concise Oxford Dictionary of Politics*. 3rd ed. Ed. Iain McLean and Alistair McMillan. Oxford: Oxford University Press, 2009. 193–94. Print.

Fembuck. "Marginally Okay." Archiveofourown.org. Organization for Transformative Works, 31 May 2011. Web. 20 Jan. 2017.

Firestone, Amanda. "Apples to Oranges: The Heroines in *Twilight* and *The Hunger Games*." *Of Bread, Blood and* The Hunger Games: *Critical Essays on the Suzanne Collins Trilogy*. Ed. Mary F. Pharr and Leisa A. Clark. Jefferson: McFarland, 2012. 209–18. Print.

Fisher, Jerilyn, and Ellen S. Silber. "Good and Bad beyond Belief: Teaching Gender Lessons through Fairy Tales and Feminist Theory." *Women's Studies Quarterly* 28.3/4 (2000): 121–36. Print.

Fisher, Mark. "Precarious Dystopias: *The Hunger Games, In Time,* and *Never Let Me Go*." *Film Quarterly* 65.4 (2012): 27–33. JStor. Web. 19 Nov. 2017.

Fiske, John. *Television Culture: Popular Pleasures and Politics*. London: Methuen, 1987. Print.

Flipflop_diva. "Lost but for Her Touch." Archiveofourown.org. Organization for Transformative Works, 10 Nov. 2013. Web. 20 Jan. 2017.

FlyingFleshEater. "Trade Negotiations." Archiveofourown.org. Organization for Transformative Works, 6 Jan. 2014. Web. 20 Jan. 2017.

Flywoman. "Hungry." Archiveofourown.org. Organization for Transformative Works, 22 Aug. 2001. Web. 20 Jan. 2017.

Folie_a_yeux. "Choices We Never Made." Archiveofourown.org. Organization for Transformative Works, 3 Jan. 2015. Web. 20 Jan. 2017.

"Fool for Love." *Buffy the Vampire Slayer: Season 1–7*. Season 5, episode 7. Writ. Douglas Petrie. Dir. Nick Marck. Fox, 2010. DVD.

Foucault, Michel. *Discipline and Punish: The Birth of the Prison*. New York: Vintage, 1995. Print.

FreshBrains. "Mama Bears." Archiveofourown.org. Organization for Transformative Works, 24 June 2015. Web. 20 Jan. 2017.

Fritz, Sonya Sawyer. "Girl Power and Girl Activism in the Fiction of Suzanne Collins, Scott Westerfeld, and Moira Young." *Female Rebellion in Young Adult Dystopian Fiction*. Ed. Sara K. Day, Miranda A. Green-Barteet, and Amy L. Montz. Farnham: Ashgate, 2014. 17–31. Print. Ashgate Studies in Childhood, 1700 to the Present.

Frozen. Dir. Chris Buck and Jennifer Lee. Walt Disney Pictures, 2013. Film.

Fryer, Peter. *Staying Power: The History of Black People in Britain*. London: Pluto, 2010. Print.

Fuchs, Cynthia. "'Did Anyone Ever Explain to You What 'Secret Identity' Means?': Race and Displacement in *Buffy* and *Dark Angel*." *Undead TV: Essays on* Buffy the Vampire Slayer. Ed. Elana Levine and Lisa Parks. Durham: Duke University Press, 2007. 96–115. Print.

Furies. "All Cracked Up." Archiveofourown.org. Organization for Transformative Works, 5 Sep. 2010. Web. 20 Jan. 2017.

Gagnon, Mollie. "Media and Hyperreality in the Film Adaptations of Suzanne Collins' *Hunger Games* Trilogy." *The Fantastic Made Visible: Essays on the Adaptation of Science Fiction and Fantasy from Page to Screen*. Ed. Matthew Wilhelm Kapell and Ace G. Pilkington. McFarland, 2015. 133–44. Print.

Garnigal. "Friends." Archiveofourown.org. Organization for Transformative Works, 6 Mar. 2008. Web. 20 Jan. 2017.

Garriott, Deidre Anne Evans. "Performing the Capitol in Digital Spaces: The Punitive Gaze of the Panopticon among Fans and Critics." *Space and Place in* The Hunger Games: *New Readings of the Novels*. Ed. Deidre Anne Evans Garriott, Whitney Elaine Jones, and Julie Elizabeth Tyler. Jefferson: McFarland, 2014. 160–83. Print.

Genette, Gérard. *Paratexts: Thresholds of Interpretation*. Cambridge: Cambridge University Press, 1997.

Genz, Stéphanie, and Benjamin A. Brabon. *Postfeminism: Cultural Texts and Theories*. Edinburgh: Edinburgh University Press, 2009. Print.

Geraghty, Christine. "Re-Examining Stardom: Questions of Texts, Bodies and Performance." *Reinventing Film Studies*. Ed. Christine Gledhill and Linda Williams. London: Arnold, 2000. 183–201. Print.

"Get It Done." *Buffy the Vampire Slayer: Season 1-7*. Season 7, episode 15. Writ. and dir. Douglas Petrie. Fox, 2010. DVD.

Giannini, Ally. "How Emma Watson's Belle Differs from the Character in the Original *Beauty and the Beast*." BusinessInsider.com. Business Insider, 6 Mar. 2017. Web. 17 Nov. 2017.

"The Gift." *Buffy the Vampire Slayer: Season 1-7*. Season 5, episode 22. Writ. and dir. Joss Whedon. Fox, 2010. DVD.

Giles, David C., and John Maltby. "The Role of Media Figures in Adolescent Development: Relations between Autonomy, Attachment, and Interest in Celebrities." *Personality and Individual Differences* 36 (2004): 813–22. *Science Direct*. Web. 25 Nov. 2017.

Gilligan, Carol. *In a Different Voice: Psychological Theory and Women's Development*. Cambridge: Harvard University Press, 1982. Print.

Gilligan, Carol, Nona P. Lyons, and Trudy J. Hanmer. *Making Connections: The Relational Worlds of Adolescent Girls at Emma Willard School*. Cambridge: Harvard University Press, 1990. Print.

Gilliland, Elizabeth. "Racebending Fandoms and Digital Futurism." *Transformative Works and Cultures* 22 (2016): 7 pars. Web. 13 Mar. 2017.

Ginneken, Jaap van. *Screening Difference: How Hollywood's Blockbuster Films Imagine Race, Ethnicity, and Culture*. Lanham: Rowman and Littlefield, 2007. Print.

Gledhill, Christine, ed. Introduction. *Stardom: Industry of Desire*. London: Routledge, 1991. Print.

Golgowski, Nina. "Gal Gadot Confirms Brett Ratner Is Out of *Wonder Woman* Sequel." HuffingtonPost.com. Oath, 16 Nov. 2017. Web. 17 Nov. 2017.

Gooseweasel. "With Permission from Lettherebedoodles." Tumblr.com. Tumblr, 27 Dec. 2015. Web. 1 May 2017.

Gottlieb, Karla. *"The Mother of Us All": A History of Queen Nanny, Leader of the Windward Jamaican Maroons*. Trenton: Africa World Press, 2000. Print.

"Graduation Day (Part 1)." *Buffy the Vampire Slayer: Season 1-7*. Season 3, episode 21. Writ. and dir. Joss Whedon. Fox, 2010. DVD.

Graser, Marc. "Lionsgate's Tim Palen Crafts Stylish Universe for *Hunger Games: Catching Fire*." Variety.com. Variety Media, 29 Oct. 2013. Web. 27 May 2017.

"Grave." *Buffy the Vampire Slayer: Season 1-7*. Season 6, episode 22. Writ. David Fury. Dir. James A. Contner. Fox, 2010. DVD.

Gray, Jonathan. *Show Sold Separately: Promos, Spoilers, and Other Media Texts*. New York: New York University Press, 2010. Print.

Green, Shoshanna, Henry Jenkins, and Cynthia Jenkins. "'Normal Female Interest in Men Bonking': Selections from the Terra Nostra Undergrounds and Strange Bedfellows." *Fans, Bloggers, and Gamers: Exploring Participatory Culture*. Ed. Henry Jenkins. New York: New York University Press, 2006. 61–88. Print.

Haas, Lynda. "'Eighty-Six the Mother': Murder, Matricide, and Good Mothers." *From Mouse to Mermaid: The Politics of Film, Gender, and Culture*. Ed. Elizabeth Bell, Lynda Haas, and Laura Sells. Bloomington: Indiana University Press, 1995. 193–211. Print.

Hagelin, Sarah. *Reel Vulnerability: Power, Pain, and Gender in Contemporary American Film and Television*. New Brunswick: Rutgers University Press, 2013. Print.

Hains, Rebecca C. "Power Feminism, Mediated: Girl Power and the Commercial Politics of Change." *Women's Studies in Communication* 32.1 (2009): 89–113. Web. 21 Nov. 2017.

Hamming, Jeanne E. "Whatever Turns You On: Becoming-Lesbian and the Production of Desire in the Xenaverse." *Genders* 34 (2001): 29 par. Web. 10 Aug. 2016.

Hansen, Kathryn Strong. "The Metamorphosis of Katniss Everdeen: *The Hunger Games*, Myth, and Femininity." *Children's Literature Association Quarterly* 40.2 (2015): 161–78. *Project Muse*. Web. 7 Mar. 2016.

Harris, Anita. *Future Girl: Young Women in the Twenty-First Century*. New York: Routledge, 2004. Print.

"Heart of Darkness." *Once upon a Time*. Season 1, episode 16. Writ. Andrew Chambliss and Ian Goldberg. Dir. Dean White. ABC, 2012. DVD.

Heldman, Caroline. "*The Hunger Games*, Hollywood and Fighting Fuck Toys." Web blog post. *Ms. Magazine Blog*. News Theme, 6 Apr. 2012. Web. 9 Oct. 2017.

Helford, Elyce Rae. "'My Emotions Give Me Power': The Containment of Girls' Anger in *Buffy*." *Fighting the Forces: What's at Stake in* Buffy the Vampire Slayer. Ed. Rhonda V. Wilcox and David Lavery. Lanham: Rowman & Littlefield, 2002. 18–34. Print.

Hellekson, Karen, and Kristina Busse, eds. "Work in Progress." Introduction. *Fan Fiction and Fan Communities in the Age of the Internet: New Essays*. Jefferson: McFarland, 2006. 5–32. Print.

"Helpless." *Buffy the Vampire Slayer: Season 1–7*. Season 3, episode 12. Writ. David Fury. Dir. James A. Contner. Fox, 2010. DVD.

Henke, Jill Birnie, Diane Zimmermann Umble, and Nancy J. Smith. "Construction of the Female Self: Feminist Readings of the Disney Heroine." *Women's Studies in Communication* 19.2 (1996): 229–49. Print.

Hickey, Walt. "The Dollar-and-Cents Case Against Hollywood's Exclusion of Women." FiveThirtyEight.com. FiveThirtyEight, 1 Apr. 2014. Web. 30 June 2017.

Hills, Elizabeth. "From 'Figurative Males' to Action Heroines: Further Thoughts on Active Women in the Cinema." *Screen* 40.1 (1999): 38–50. *MLA International Bibliography*. Web. 21 Nov. 2017.

Hines, Susan, and Brenda Ayres. "(He)gemony Cricket! Why in the World Are We Still Watching Disney?" Introduction. *The Emperor's Old Groove: Decolonizing Disney's Magic Kingdom*. Ed. Brenda Ayres. New York: Lang, 2003. 1–12. Print.

Hirschberg, Lynn. "Desperate to Seem 16." Nytimes.com. The New York Times Company, 5 Sep. 1999. Web. 8 July 2017.

Hodgens, Chrissy. "Jennifer Lawrence." Pinterest.com. Pinterest, n.d. Web. 6 June 2017.

Hodges, Amanda L., and Laurel P. Richmond. "Taking a Bite out of Buffy: Carnivalesque Play and Resistance in Fan Fiction." *Transformative Works and Cultures* 7 (2011): 8 pars. Web. 10 Aug. 2016.

Hopkins, Susan. *Girl Heroes: The New Force in Popular Culture*. Annandale: Pluto, 2002. Print.

Hsy, Jonathan. *Trading Tongues: Merchants, Multilingualism, and Medieval Literature*. Columbus: Ohio State University Press, 2013. Print. Inventions: New Studies in Medieval Culture.

"*The Hunger Games* Poster (#24 of 28)." Impawards.com. Internet Movie Poster Awards, 19 Jan. 2012. Web. 20 July 2017.

"*The Hunger Games: Catching Fire* Poster (#32 of 33)." Impawards.com. Internet Movie Poster Awards, 30 Sep. 2013. Web. 20 July 2017.

"*The Hunger Games: Mockingjay—Part 1* Poster (#24 of 25)." Impawards.com. Internet Movie Poster Awards, 10 Sep. 2014. Web. 20 July 2017.

"*The Hunger Games: Mockingjay—Part 2* Poster (#21 of 29)." Impawards.com. Internet Movie Poster Awards, 30 Sep. 2015. Web. 20 July 2017.

Hurley, Dorothy L. "Seeing White: Children of Color and the Disney Fairy Tale Princess." *The Journal of Negro Education* 74.3 (2005): 221–32. JStor. Web. 23 May 2017.

Iliveinfantasies. "Just Enough." Archiveofourown.org. Organization for Transformative Works, 5 Dec. 2015. Web. 10 Jan. 2017.

Imondi, Bethany. "Pixar's Princess Takes on a New Role." TheHoya.com. The Hoya, 21 June 2012. Web. 22 Nov. 2017.

"Inka Mummy Girl." *Buffy the Vampire Slayer: Season 1–7*. Season 2, episode 4. Writ. Matt Kiene and Joe Reinkemeyer. Dir. Ellen S. Pressman. Fox, 2010. DVD.

"Innocence." *Buffy the Vampire Slayer: Season 1–7*. Season 2, episode 14. Writ. and dir. Joss Whedon. Fox, 2010. DVD.

Isaksson, Malin. "Buffy/Faith Adult Femslash: Queer Porn with a Plot." *Slayage: The Online International Journal of Buffy Studies* 7.4 (2009): 34 pars. Web. 11 Aug. 2016.

"I Was Made to Love You." *Buffy the Vampire Slayer: Season 1–7*. Season 5, episode 15. Writ. Jane Espenson. Dir. James A. Contner. Fox, 2010. DVD.

Jakubowski, Kaylee. "No, the Existence of Trans People Doesn't Validate Gender Essentialism." EverydayFeminism.com. Everyday Feminism, 9 Mar. 2015. Web. 17 June 2016.

Jamison, Anne. *Fic: Why Fanfiction Is Taking over the World*. Dallas: Smart Pop, 2013. Print.

JaneDavitt. "All Work and No Play." Archiveofourown.org. Organization for Transformative Works, 27 Apr. 2011. Web. 20 Jan. 2017.

Jaques, Zoe. "'This Huntress Who Delights in Arrows': The Female Archer in Children's Fiction." *A Quest of Her Own: Essays on the Female Hero in Modern Fantasy*. Ed. Lori M. Campbell. Jefferson: McFarland, 2014. 150–71. Print.

Jenkins, Henry. *Convergence Culture: Where Old and New Media Collide*. New York: New York University Press, 2008. Print.

_____. *Textual Poachers: Television Fans and Participatory Culture*. New York: Routledge, 1992. Print. Studies in Culture and Communication.

Jenkins, Henry, et al. *By Any Media Necessary: The New Youth Activism*. New York: New York University Press, 2016. Print. Connected Youth and Digital Futures.

Jenkins, Henry, Sam Ford, and Joshua Green. *Spreadable Media: Creating Value and Meaning in a Networked Culture*. New York University Press, 2013. Print.

Jensen, Jeff. "*Buffy the Vampire Slayer*: To Hell and Back." *Entertainment Weekly* 7 Sep. 2001: 60–65. Print.

Johannas_Motivational_Insults. "Fireside." Archiveofourown.org. Organization for Transformative Works, 26 Dec. 2014, compl. 26 Dec. 2015. Web. 20 Jan. 2017.

Johnson, Derek. *Media Franchising: Creative License and Collaboration in the Culture Industries*. New York: New York University Press, 2013. Print.

Johnson, Melissa. "Appetite and Destruction: Issues of Consumption and Containment in Season 2 and 3 of *Buffy the Vampire Slayer*." Paper given at The *Slayage* Conference on the Whedonverses. Gordon College, Barnesville, GA, May 26–28, 2006. Web. 24 Nov. 2017.

Jones, Rebecca. *Roman Camps in Scotland*. Edinburgh: Society of Antiquaries of Scotland, 2011. Print.

Jones, Sara Gwenllian. "The Sex Lives of Cult Television Characters." *Screen* 43 (2002): 79–90. *Oxford Academic*. Web. 25 Nov. 2017.

Jones, Whitney Elaine. "Katniss and Her Boys: Male Readers, the Love Triangle and Identity Formation." *Space and Place in* The Hunger Games: *New Readings of the Novels*. Ed. Deidre Anne Evans Garriott, Whitney Elaine Jones, and Julie Elizabeth Tyler. Jefferson: McFarland, 2014. 60–82. Print.

Jonisstrash (roxysk8rgrrl). "After Pride." Archiveofourown.org. Organization for Transformative Works, 10 Aug. 2015. Web. 20 Jan. 2017.

Juliajm15. "Another Attempt to Redesign […]." Tumblr.com. Tumblr, 3 Feb. 2015. Web. 28 Apr. 2017.

Kang, Inkoo. "Feminist Filmmaking Means NC-17 Rating from MPAA." Indiewire.com. Penske Business Media, 20 Dec. 2013. Web. 16 Mar. 2017.

Kaplan, Deborah. "5. Construction of Fan Fiction Character Through Narrative." *Fan Fiction and Fan Communities in the Age of the Internet: New Essays*. Ed. Karen Hellekson and Kristina Busse. Jefferson: McFarland, 2006. 134–52. Print.

Kapurch, Katie. "Rapunzel Loves Merida: Melodramatic Expressions of Lesbian Girlhood and Teen Romance in *Tangled*, *Brave*, and Femslash." *Journal of Lesbian Studies* 19 (2015): 436–53. *Taylor and Francis Online*. Web. 25 Nov. 2017.

Karpel, Ari. "Inside *The Hunger Games* Social Media Machine." fastcompany.com. Fast Company, 4 Sep. 2012. Web. 15 July 2017.

Karras, Irene. "The Third Wave's Final Girl: *Buffy the Vampire Slayer*." *Thirdspace: A Journal of Feminist Theory & Culture* 1.2 (2002): n.p. Web. 24 Nov. 2017.

Katnissisoliveskinneddealwithit. "We Do Not Condone. All of This Is Wrong." Tumblr.com. Tumblr, n.d. Web. 8 May 2017.

Kearney, Mary Celeste. "The Changing Face of Teen Television, Or Why We All Love Buffy." *Undead TV: Essays on* Buffy the Vampire Slayer. Ed. Elana Levine and Lisa Parks. Durham: Duke University Press, 2007. 17–41. Print.

_____. *Girls Make Media.* New York: Routledge, 2006. Print.

Keft-Kennedy, Virginia. "Fantasising Masculinity in *Buffyverse* Slash Fiction: Sexuality, Violence, and the Vampire." *Nordic Journal of English Studies* 7.1 (2008): 49–80. Web. 25 Nov. 2017.

Keller, Jessalynn. *Girls' Feminist Blogging in a Postfeminist Age.* New York: Routledge, 2016. Print.

Kennisiou. "Anna the Matchmaker." Archiveofourown.org. Organization for Transformative Works, 2 Sep. 2015, compl. 16 Nov. 2015. Web. 20 Jan. 2017.

Kilinskis, Mandy. "Masters of Word of Mouth: *The Hunger Games* Marketing Team." Web blog post. *Branding Beat.* Quality Logo Products, n. d. Web. 22 July 2017.

Kim, Sylvia. "The Subtle Sexism in Movie Ratings." Attn.com. ATTN:, 10 Jan. 2016. Web. 16 Mar. 2017.

Kimble, James J., and Lester C. Olson. "Visual Rhetoric Representing Rosie the Riveter: Myth and Misconception in J. Howard Miller's 'We Can Do It!' Poster." *Rhetoric and Public Affairs* 9.4 (2006): 533–69. *Project Muse.* Web. 23. Nov. 2017.

Kimmel, Michael. *Manhood in America: A Cultural History.* 4th ed. Oxford: Oxford University Press, 2017. Print.

Knobel, Michele, and Colin Lankshear, eds. "Online Memes, Affinities, and Cultural Production." *A New Literacies Sampler.* New York: Lang, 2007. 199–227. Print. New Literacies and Digital Epistemologies 29.

Kord, Susanne, and Elisabeth Krimmer. *Hollywood Divas, Indie Queens, and TV Heroines: Contemporary Screen Images of Women.* Lanham: Rowman & Littlefield, 2005. Print.

Krimmer, Elisabeth, and Shilpa Raval. "'Digging the Undead': Death and Desire in Buffy." *Fighting the Forces: What's at Stake in* Buffy the Vampire Slayer. Ed. Rhonda V. Wilcox and David Lavery. Rowman and Littlefield, 2002. 153–64. Print.

Kroon, Richard W. *A/V A to Z: An Encyclopedic Dictionary of Media, Entertainment and Other Audiovisual Terms.* Jefferson: McFarland, 2010. Print.

Kustritz, Anne. "Slashing the Romance Narrative." *Journal of American Culture* 26 (2003): 371–84. *Wiley Online Library.* Web. 25 Nov. 2015.

LaRossa, Ralph. *The Modernization of Fatherhood: A Social and Political History.* Chicago: University of Chicago Press, 1997. Print.

Larson, Reed. "Secrets in the Bedroom: Adolescents' Private Use of Media." *Journal of Youth and Adolescence* 24.5 (1995): 535–50. *Springer Link.* Web. 25 Nov. 2017.

Latham, Don, and Jonathan M. Hollister. "The Games People Play: Information and Media Literacies in the *Hunger Games* Trilogy." *Children's Literature in Education* 45 (2014): 33–46. *Springer Science and Business Media.* Web. 19 Nov. 2017. PDF file.

LauraHollis. "Baby Girl You Know We're Gonna Be Legends." Archiveofourown.org. Organization for Transformative Works, 15 Sep. 2016. Web. 20 Jan. 2017.

_____. "Of Breakfast Clubs and Bobby Pins." Archiveofourown.org. Organization for Transformative Works, 31 July 2016. Web. 20 Jan. 2017.

Lauzen, Martha M. "Boxed in Women in 2015–16: Women on Screen and Behind the Scenes in Television." Womenintvfilm.sdsu.edu. Center for the Study of Women in Television and Film, Sep. 2016. Web. PDF file.

Law, Michelle. "Sisters Doin' It for Themselves: *Frozen* and the Revolution of the Disney Heroine." *Screen Education* 74 (2014): 16–25. *Communication and Mass Media Complete.* Web. 18 May 2015.

Lebbady, Hasna. "Women in Northern Morocco: Between the Documentary and the Imaginary." *Alif: Journal of Comparative Poetics* 32 (2012): 127–50. *JStor.* Web. 23 May 2017.

Lee, Marissa. "Media Takes Note of *The Hunger Games* Casting." Racebending.com. Racebending.com, 4 Mar. 2011. Web. 6 May 2017.

Leitch, Thomas. *Film Adaptations and Its Discontents: From* Gone with the Wind *to* The Passion of the Christ. Baltimore: Johns Hopkins UP, 2007. Print.

Lem, Ellyn, and Holly Hassel. "'Killer' Katniss and 'Lover Boy' Peeta: Suzanne Collins's Defiance of Gender-Genred Reading." *Of Bread, Blood and* The Hunger Games: *Critical Essays on the Suzanne Collins Trilogy.* Ed. Mary F. Pharr and Leisa A. Clark. Jefferson: McFarland, 2012. 118–27. Print.

Lester, Neal A. "Disney's *The Princess and the Frog*: The Pride, the Pressure, and the Politics of Being a First." *Journal of American Culture* 33.4 (2010): 294–308. *Wiley Online Library.* Web. 22 Nov. 2017.

Lester, Neal A., Dave Sudia, and Natalie Sudia. "Race, Gender and the Politics of Hair: Disney's *Tangled* Feminist Messages." *Valley Voices: A Literary Review* 13.2 (2013): 83–101. *Academic Search Premier.* Web. 29 Oct. 2017.

Lethbridge, Stefanie. "Girl on Fire: Antihero, Hero, Hunger Games." *Helden. Heroes. Héros: E-Journal zu Kulturen des Heroischen* 3.1 (2015): 93–104. Web. 22 July 2017.

Levine, Elana. "Buffy and the 'New Girl Order': Defining Feminism and Femininity." *Undead TV: Essays on* Buffy the Vampire Slayer. Eds. Elana Levine and Lisa Parks. Durham: Duke University Press, 2007. 168–89. Print.

Lewis, Lisa. *The Adoring Audience: Fan Culture and Popular Media.* London: Routledge, 1992. Print.

Lewit, Meghan. "Casting *The Hunger Games*: In Praise of Katniss Everdeen." TheAtlantic.com. The Atlantic Monthly Group, 9 Mar. 2011. Web. 19 Nov. 2017.

Liberatore, Paul. "*Brave* Creator Blasts Disney for 'Blatant Sexism' in Princess Makeover." Marinij.com. Marin Independent Journal, 11 May 2013. Web. 14 May 2014.

Lilyyuri. "Unlimited." Archiveofourown.org. Organization for Transformative Works, 5 Aug. 2014. Web. 20 Jan. 2017.

Lionsgate Movies. "*The Hunger Games* (2012 Movie)—Official Theatrical Trailer—Jennifer Lawrence & Liam Hemsworth." Online video clip. *YouTube.* YouTube, 14 Nov. 2011. Web. 17 July 2017.

_____. "*The Hunger Games* (2012)—VMA Sneak Peek!" Online video clip. *YouTube.* YouTube, 29 Aug. 2011. Web. 17 July 2017.

_____. "*The Hunger Games: Catching Fire* (2013)—Exclusive Teaser Trailer." Online video clip. *YouTube.* YouTube, 11 July 2013. Web. 17 July 2017.

_____. "*The Hunger Games: Catching Fire* (2013)—Official Trailer #1." Online video clip. *YouTube.* YouTube, 15 Nov. 2013. Web. 17 July 2017.

_____. "*The Hunger Games: Catching Fire* (2013)—Official Trailer #2." Online video clip. *YouTube.* YouTube, 15 Nov. 2013. Web. 17 July 2017.

"List of Tropes in Fanworks." *Fanlore.org.* Fanlore, 8 Oct. 2016. Web. 4 Mar. 2017.

The Little Mermaid. Dir. Ron Clements and John Musker. Walt Disney Pictures, 1989. Film.

"Living Conditions." *Buffy the Vampire Slayer: Season 1–7.* Season 4, episode 2. Writ. Marti Noxon. Dir. David Grossman. Fox, 2010. DVD.

Long, Heather. "Total Misfire: Brands like CoverGirl and Subway Miss Point of *Hunger Games*." TheGuardian.com. Guardian News and Media, 22 Nov. 2013. Web. 29 May 2017.

Lopez, Lori Kido. "Fan Activists and the Politics of Race in *The Last Airbender*." *International Journal of Cultural Studies* 15.5 (2011): 432–45. Web. 13 Mar. 2017.

Lorditch, Emilie. "*Brave* Features Hair-Rising Animations." InsideScience.org. Inside Science News Service, 20 June 2012. Web. 22 Nov. 2017.

Lysippe. "No Apologies in Bed." Archiveofourown.org. Organization for Transformative Works, 22 Nov. 2015. Web. 20 Jan. 2017.

Macey, Gracey. "We Can Slay It." Pinterest.com. Pinterest, n.d. Web. 7 Dec. 2015.

Magee, Sara. "High School is Hell: The TV Legacy of *Beverly Hills, 90210,* and *Buffy the Vampire Slayer*." *Journal of Popular Culture* 47.4 (2014): 877–94. *Wiley Online Library.* Web. 5 Oct. 2015.

Magoulick, Mary. "Frustrating Female Heroism: Mixed Messages in *Xena, Nikita,* and *Buffy*." *Journal of Popular Culture* 39.5 (2006): 729–55. *Wiley Online Library.* Web. 21 Oct. 2016.

Manley, Kathleen E. B. "Disney, the Beast, and Woman as Civilizing Force." *The Emperor's*

Old Groove: Decolonizing Disney's Magic Kingdom. Ed. Brenda Ayres. New York: Lang, 2003. 79–89. Print.

Marsha. "Lil Doodle to Go with a Lil Psa." Tumblr.com. Tumblr, 21 Nov. 2014. Web. 8 May 2017.

Martin, Courtney E., and Vanessa Valenti. "#FemFuture: Online Revolution." *New Feminist Solutions* 8 (2012): 1–34. Barnard Center for Research on Women. Web. 18 Nov. 2015.

McCaughey, Martha. *Real Knockouts: The Physical Feminism of Women's Self-Defense*. New York: New York University Press, 1997. Print.

McCracken, Allison. "At Stake: Angel's Body, Fantasy Masculinity, and Queer Desire in Teen Television." *Undead TV: Essays on* Buffy the Vampire Slayer. Ed. Elana Levine and Lisa Parks. Durham: Duke University Press, 2007. 116–44. Print.

McDougall, Sophia. "I Hate Strong Female Characters." NewStatesman.com. NS Media Group, 15 Aug. 2013. Web. 9 Oct. 2017.

McKinstry, Shavon. "Bright Like a Diamond, White Like a Princess." SparkMovement.org. Spark Movement, 17 Apr. 2013. Web. 29 May 2017.

McRobbie, Angela. "Young Women and Consumer Culture: An Intervention." *Cultural Studies* 22.5 (2008): 532–50. *MLA International Bibliography*. Web. 21 Nov. 2017.

Meehan, Eileen R. "Gendering the Commodity Audience: Critical Media Research, Feminism, and Political Economy." *Sex and Money: Feminism and Political Economy in the Media*. Ed. Eileen R. Meehan and Ellen Riordan. Minneapolis: University of Minnesota Press, 2002. 209–22. Print. Commerce and Mass Culture Ser.

"Meme." Def. 2. Oxforddictionaries.com. Oxford University Press, n.d. Web. 7 Dec. 2015.

Miller, Jessica. "'She Has No Idea. The Effect She Can Have': Katniss and the Politics of Gender." The Hunger Games *and Philosophy: A Critique of Pure Treason*. Ed. George A. Dunn and Nicolas Michaud. Hoboken: Wiley. 145–61. Print. Blackwell Philosophy and Pop Culture Ser.

Miller, Laura. "The Making of a Blockbuster." Salon.com. Salon Media Group, 18 Mar. 2012. Web. 8 June 2017.

_____. "*The Hunger Games* vs. *Twilight*." Salon.com. Salon Media Group, 6 Sep. 2010. Web. 8 June 2017.

Mills, Jane. "Herstory." *Womanwords: A Vocabulary of Culture and Patriarchal Society*. London: Virago, 1991. Print.

Milner, Ryan M. "Pop Polyvocality: Internet Memes, Public Participation, and the Occupy Wall Street Movement." *International Journal of Communication* 7 (2013): 2357–90. Web. 17 Nov. 2015.

Miltner, Kate M. "'There's No Place for Lulz on LOLCats': The Role of Genre, Gender, and Group Identity in the Interpretation and Enjoyment of an Internet Meme." *First Monday* 19.8 (2014): n.p. Web. 16 Nov. 2015.

Mitchell, Jennifer. "Of Queer Necessity: Panem's Hunger Games as Gender Games." *Of Bread, Blood and* The Hunger Games: *Critical Essays on the Suzanne Collins Trilogy*. Ed. Mary F. Pharr and Leisa A. Clark. Jefferson: McFarland, 2012. 128–37. Print.

MJ Erickson (Kreugan). "Finished *The Hunger Games*." Tumblr.com. Tumblr, 1 Apr. 2012. Web. 8 May 2017.

Moana. Dir. Ron Clements and John Musker. Walt Disney Pictures, 2016. Film.

MonaLover07. "The After Party." Archiveofourown.org. Organization for Transformative Works, 3 Feb. 2016. Web. 20 Jan. 2017.

Monsterjumper. "Okay People Real Talk." livejournal.com. Live Journal, 13 Mar. 2013. Web. 8 May 2017.

MoonGirl1155. "Frosted Flowers." Archiveofourown.org. Organization for Transformative Works, 13 July 2015. Web. 20 Jan. 2017.

Moy, Suelain. "Girls Who Fight Back." *Good Housekeeping* 228.4 (1999): 86. *Academic Search Premier*. Web. 13 July 2017.

M_phoenix (liminalsmith). "Coming Home." Archiveofourown.org. Organization for Transformative Works, 26 Feb. 2014. Web. 20 Jan. 2017.

Mulan. Dir. Tony Bancroft and Barry Cook. Walt Disney Pictures, 1998. Film.

Mulvey, Laura. "Visual Pleasure and Narrative Cinema." *Film Theory and Criticism: Intro-ductory Readings*. Ed. Leo Braudy and Marshall Cohen. New York: Oxford University Press, 1999. 833–44. Print.

Munro, Ealasaid. "Feminism: A Fourth Wave?" *Political Insight* 4.2 (2013): 22–25. Web. 16 Nov. 2015.

Murray, Susan. "I Know What You Did Last Summer: Sarah Michelle Gellar and Crossover Teen Stardom." *Undead TV: Essays on* Buffy the Vampire Slayer. Ed. Elana Levine and Lisa Parks. Durham: Duke University Press, 2007. 42–55. Print.

Musicaltaco. "Kisses in the Cold." Archiveofourown.org. Organization for Transformative Works, 16 Mar. 2015. Web. 20 Jan. 2017.

Myers, Abigail E. "Why Katniss Chooses Peeta: Looking at Love Through a Stoic Lens." The Hunger Games *and Philosophy: A Critique of Pure Treason*. Ed. George A. Dunn and Nicolas Michaud. Hoboken: Wiley, 2012. 134–44. Print. Blackwell Philosophy and Pop Culture Ser.

"A New Man." *Buffy the Vampire Slayer: Season 1–7*. Season 4, episode 12. Writ. Jane Espenson. Dir. Michael Gershman. Fox, 2010. DVD.

"New Moon Rising." *Buffy the Vampire Slayer: Season 1–7*. Season 4, episode 19. Writ. Marti Noxon. Dir. James A. Contner. Fox, 2010. DVD.

Newrromantics. "Hands to Myself." Archiveofourown.org. Organization for Transformative Works, 30 Mar. 2016. Web. 20 Jan. 2017.

Ng, Vincent. "How Disney Princesses Became a Multi Billion Dollar Brand." mcngmarketing. com. MCNG Marketing, 18 Mar. 2013. Web. 30 Jan. 2015.

Nichols, Amy. "Lessons from *Twilight* vs. Lessons from *Buffy*." Pinterest.com. Pinterest, n.d. Web. 7 Dec. 2015.

Nikmood. "Bedtime Stories." Archiveofourown.org. Organization for Transformative Works, 22 Feb. 2012. Web. 20 Jan. 2017.

Nissenbaum, Asaf, and Limor Shifman. "Internet Memes as Contested Cultural Capital: The Case of 4chan's /b/ Board." *New Media and Society*: 1–19. Web. 23 Nov. 2017.

Norman, Dorothy. *The Hero: Myth/Image/Symbol*. New York: New American Library, 1969. Print.

O'Connor, Clare. "After Outcry, Disney Launches New Rey Toys For *Star Wars* Fans." Forbes.com. Forbes Media, 12 Jan. 2016. Web. 17 Nov. 2017.

Olthouse, Jill. ""I Will Be Your Mockingjay': The Power and Paradox of Metaphor in the *Hunger Games* Trilogy." The Hunger Games *and Philosophy: A Critique of Pure Treason*. Ed. George A. Dunn and Nicolas Michaud. Hoboken: Wiley, 2012. 41–54. Print. Black-well Philosophy and Pop Culture Ser.

"Once More, with Feeling." *Buffy the Vampire Slayer: Season 1–7*. Season 6, episode 7. Writ. and dir. Joss Whedon. Fox, 2010. DVD.

Ono, Kent A. "To Be a Vampire on *Buffy the Vampire Slayer*: Race and ('Other') Socially Marginalizing Positions on Horror TV." *Fantasy Girls: Gender in the New Universe of Science Fiction and Fantasy Television*. Ed. Elyce Rae Helford. Boston: Rowman and Lit-tlefield, 2000. 163–86. Print.

Orenstein, Peggy. *Schoolgirls: Young Women, Self-Esteem, and the Confidence Gap*. New York: Doubleday, 1994. Print.

_____. "What's Wrong with Cinderella?" nytimes.com. The New York Times Company, 24 Dec. 2006. Web. 22 Nov. 2017.

Orphan_account. "Showtime." Archiveofourown.org. Organization for Transformative Works, 19 Nov. 2012. Web. 20 Jan. 2017.

"Our Story." *Itsonus.org*. It's on Us, n.d. Web. 19 May 2017.

"Out of My Mind." *Buffy the Vampire Slayer: Season 1–7*. Season 5, episode 4. Writ. Rebecca Rand Kirshner. Dir. David Grossman. Fox, 2010. DVD.

Owen, Susan A. "Vampires, Postmodernity, and Postfeminism: *Buffy the Vampire Slayer*." *Journal of Popular Film and Television* 27.2 (1999): 24–31. *MLA International Bibliogra-phy*. Web. 24 Nov. 2017.

Parks, Lisa. "Brave New Buffy: Rethinking 'TV Violence.'" *Quality Popular Television: Cult TV, the Industry and Fans.* Ed. Mark Jancovich and James Lyons. London: British Film Institute, 2003. 118–33. Print.

"Passion." *Buffy the Vampire Slayer: Season 1-7.* Season 2, episode 17. Writ. Ty King. Dir. Michael Gershman. Fox, 2010. DVD.

Pauldierden (Gabi). "Katniss." Tumblr.com. Tumblr, 27 Jan. 2016. Web. 9 May 2017.

Payne-Mulliken, Susan, and Valerie Renagar. "Buffy Never Goes It Alone: The Rhetorical Construction of Sisterhood in the Final Season." *Buffy Meets the Academy: Essays on the Episodes and Scripts as Text.* Ed. Kevin K. Durand. Jefferson: McFarland, 2009. 57–77. Print.

Pearson, Carol. *The Hero Within: Six Archetypes We Live By.* 1986. San Francisco: Harper & Row, 1989. Print.

Pearson, Carol, and Katherine Pope. *The Female Hero in American and British Literature.* New York: Bowker, 1981. Print.

Pender, Patricia. "'I'm Buffy and You're ... History': The Postmodern Politics of *Buffy.*" *Fighting the Forces: What's at Stake in* Buffy the Vampire Slayer. Ed. Rhonda V. Wilcox and David Lavery. Lanham: Rowman & Littlefield, 2002. 35–44. Print.

_____. "'Kicking Ass is Comfort Food': Buffy as Third Wave Feminist Icon." Paper given at Staking a Claim: Exploring the Global Reach of Buffy. University of South Australia, Adelaide. 22 July 2003. 1–14. Web. 2 July 2012.

Penley, Constance. "Feminism, Psychoanalysis, and the Study of Popular Culture." *Visual Culture: Images and Interpretations.* Ed. Norman Bryson, Michael Ann Holly, and Keith Moxey. Middletown: Wesleyan University Press, 1994. 302–24. Print.

Phoebe1901. "Anticipation." Archiveofourown.org. Organization for Transformative Works, 20 Apr. 2014, updated 21 Apr. 2014. Web. 20 Jan. 2017.

_____. "Anything for You." Archiveofourown.org. Organization for Transformative Works, 20 Apr. 2014. Web. 20 Jan. 2017.

Pinebundles. "If You're a Fire then I Wanna Burn." Archiveofourown.org. Organization for Transformative Works, 31 July 2015. Web. 20 Jan. 2017.

Pipher, Mary. *Reviving Ophelia: Saving the Selves of Adolescent Girls.* New York: Putnam, 1994. Print.

Platt, Carrie Anne. "Cullen Family Values: Gender and Sexual Politics in the *Twilight* Series." *Bitten by* Twilight: *Youth Culture, Media, and the Vampire Franchise.* Ed. Melissa A. Click, Jennifer Stevens Aubrey, and Elizabeth Behm-Morawitz. New York: Lang, 2010. 71–102. Print. Mediated Youth 14.

Pocahontas. Dir. Mike Gabriel and Eric Goldberg. Walt Disney Pictures, 1995. Film.

Polce-Lynch, Mary, et al. "Adolescent Self-Esteem and Gender: Exploring Relations to Sexual Harassment, Body Image, Media Influence, and Emotional Expression." *Journal of Youth and Adolescence* 30.2 (2001): 225–44. *Academic Search Premier.* Web. 29 June 2017.

Pop_Punk_Jolras. "Ace of Hearts." Archiveofourown.org. Organization for Transformative Works, 25 Apr. 2015. Web. 20 Jan. 2017.

The Princess and the Frog. Dir. Ron Clements and John Musker. Walt Disney Pictures, 2009. Film.

Projansky, Sarah. *Spectacular Girls: Media Fascination and Celebrity Culture.* New York: New York University Press, 2014. Print.

"Prophecy Girl." *Buffy the Vampire Slayer: Season 1-7.* Season 1, episode 12. Writ. and Dir. Joss Whedon. Fox, 2010. DVD.

Pseudo_sweetheart. "Finding Solace." Archiveofourown.org. Organization for Transformative Works, 19 May 2014. Web. 20 Jan. 2017.

PTlikesTea. "Four Times Arendelle Was More Progressive than Dunbroch (and One Time Dunbroch Was More Progressive than Arendelle)." Archiveofourown.org. Organization for Transformative Works, 12 Aug. 2015. Web. 20 Jan. 2017.

Puckity. "In Honor of ISD/IDF: 'How Slash and Femslash Make You a Better Person.'" Archiveofourown.org. Organization for Transformative Works, 2 July 2007. Web. 11 Mar. 2017.

Pugh, Sheenagh. *The Democratic Genre: Fan Fiction in a Literary Context*. Bridgend: Seren, 2005. Print.

Quraishi, Tarina. "The Gender-Neutral Games." Thecrimson.com. Disqus, 26 Mar. 2012. Web. 19 Nov. 2017.

Radioclubjp (morspraematura). "Joyride." Archiveofourown.org. Organization for Transformative Works, 3 Apr. 2015. Web. 20 Jan. 2017.

Raglan, Lord. *The Hero: A Study in Tradition, Myth and Drama*. New York: Oxford University Press, 1937. Print.

RedSneakers. "Little Worlds." Archiveofourown.org. Organization for Transformative Works, 12 Feb. 2014, updated 14 Apr. 2014. Web. 20 Jan. 2017.

Retallack, Hanna, Jessica Ringrose, and Emilie Lawrence. "'Fuck Your Body Image': Teen Girls' Twitter and Instagram Feminism in and around School." *Learning Bodies: The Body in Youth and Childhood Studies*. Ed. Julia Coffey, Shelley Budgeon, and Helen Cahill. Singapore: Springer, 2016. 85–103. Print. Perspectives on Children and Young People.

Riordan, Ellen. "Commodified Agents and Empowered Girls: Consuming and Producing Feminism." *Journal of Communication Inquiry* 25.3 (2001): 279–97. Web. 10 Aug. 2017.

Robertson, Barbara. "The Royal Treatment." *Computer Graphics World* 35.4 (2012): 11–19. *Academic Search Premier*. Web. 22 Nov. 2017.

Rohy, Valeria. "On Homosexual Reproduction." *Differences: A Journal of Feminist Cultural Studies* 23.1 (2012): 101–30. Web. 18 June 2016. PDF file.

Ross, Deborah. "Escape from Wonderland: Disney and the Female Imagination." *Marvels and Tales* 18.1 (2004): 53–66. *Academic Search Premier*. Web. 14 Apr. 2014.

Rothschild, Sarah. *The Princess Story: Modeling the Feminine in Twentieth-Century American Fiction and Film*. New York: Lang, 2013. Print.

Russo, Julie Levin. "New Voy 'Cyborg Sex' J/7 [NC-17] 1/1: New Methodologies, New Fantasies." J-l-r.org. Web. 25 Nov. 2017. PDF file.

Russo, Mary J. *The Female Grotesque: Risk, Excess and Modernity*. New York: Routledge, 1994. Print.

Sainato, Susan Butvin. "Not Your Typical Knight: The Emerging On-Screen Defender." *The Medieval Hero on Screen: Representations from Beowulf to Buffy*. Ed. Martha W. Driver and Sid Ray. Jefferson: McFarland, 2004. 133–46. Print.

Salmon_Pink. "Flurry." Archiveofourown.org. Organization for Transformative Works, 3 Feb. 2014. Web. 20 Jan. 2017.

Savill, Richard. "Harry Potter and the Mystery of J K's Lost Initial." Telegraph.co.uk. Telegraph Media Group, 19 July 2000. Web. 15 July 2017.

Schippers, Mimi. "Recovering the Feminine Other: Masculinity, Femininity, and Gender Hegemony." *Theory and Society* 36. 1 (2007): 85–102. *Academic Search Premier*. Web. 10 Nov. 2017.

"Scholastic Publishes *Catching Fire*." Mediaroom.Scholastic.com. Scholastic, n.d. Web. 12 June 2017. PDF file.

"Scholastic Publishes *The Hunger Games*." Mediaroom.Scholastic.com. Scholastic, n.d. Web. 14 July 2017. PDF file.

Schultz, Elyssa. "You Fight Like a Girl. Thanks." Pinterest.com. Pinterest, n.d. Web. 19 Sep. 2017.

Schultz, Lauren. "Concepts of Identity When *Nancy Drew* Meets *Buffy*." Buffy *Meets the Academy: Essays on the Episodes and Scripts as Text*. Ed. Kevin K. Durand. Jefferson: McFarland, 2009. 187–202. Print.

Scodari, Christine. "Resistance Re-Examined: Gender, Fan Practices, and Science Fiction Television." *Popular Communication* 1.2 (2003): 111–30. *Taylor and Francis Online*. Web. 25 Nov. 2017.

Scott, Suzanne. "The Hawkeye Initiative: Pinning Down Transformative Feminism in Comic-Book Culture through Superhero Crossplay Fan Art." *Cinema Journal* 55.1 (2015): 150–60. *Project Muse*. Web. 28 Mar. 2017.

Shamrock. "A Simple Kind of Life." Archiveofourown.org. Organization for Transformative Works, 16 Nov. 2012. Web. 20 Jan. 2017.

Shelley (jedi_penguin). "Busted." Archiveofourown.org. Organization for Transformative Works, 16 Nov. 2010. Web. 20 Jan. 2017.

Shifman, Limor. *Memes in Digital Culture*. Cambridge: MIT Press, 2014. Print.

"Showtime." *Buffy the Vampire Slayer: Season 1–7*. Season 7, episode 11. Writ. David Fury. Dir. Michael Grossman. Fox, 2010. DVD.

Shrek. Dir. Andrew Adamson and Vicky Jenson. DreamWorks Pictures, 2001. Film.

Simkin, Stevie. "'Who Died and Made You John Wayne?': Anxious Masculinity in *Buffy the Vampire Slayer*." *Slayage: The Online International Journal of Buffy Studies* 3.3–4 (2004): 36 pars. Web. 24 Nov. 2017.

Sleeping Beauty. Dir. Clyde Geronimi et al. Walt Disney Productions, 1959. Film.

"Sleeping Beauty Trivia." imdb.com. IMDb.com, n.d. Web. 22 Nov. 2017.

Smith, Anna. "Frozen in Time: When Will Disney's Heroines Reflect Real Body Shapes?" Theguardian.com. Guardian News and Media, 17 July 2014. Web. 22 Nov. 2017.

Smith, Ericka. "Sister. Daughter. Archer. Rebel. Hero. Girl on Fire. Mockingjay." Pinterest.com. Pinterest, n.d. Web. 4 Dec. 2017.

Smith, Stacy L., et al. "Inequality in 700 Popular Films: Examining Portrayals of Gender, Race, and LGBT Status from 2007–2014." annenberg.usc.edu. Media, Diversity, and Social Change Initiative, USC Annenberg. Web. 29 Feb. 2016. PDF file.

"Snow Falls." *Once Upon a Time*. Season 1, episode 3. Writ. Liz Tigelaar. Dir. Dean White. ABC, 2012. DVD.

Snow White and the Seven Dwarfs. Dir. David Hand et al. Walt Disney Productions, 1937. Film.

Sontag, Susan. *Against Interpretation and Other Essays*. New York: Farrar, Straus and Giroux, 1967. Print.

Sophie C. "Katniss from *The Hunger Games*." Tumblr.com. Tumblr, 2012. Web. 8 May 2017.

Spicer, Arwen. "'Love's Bitch but Man Enough to Admit It': Spikes Hybridized Gender." *Slayage: The Online International Journal of Buffy Studies* 2.3 (2002): 24 pars. Web. 24 Nov. 2017.

"The Status of Women in the U.S. Media 2015." Womensmediacenter.com. The Women's Media Center, n.d. Web. 29 Feb. 2016. PDF file.

Stein, Joel. "Pixar's Girl Story." *Time International* 5 March 2012: 36–41. *Business Source Premier*. Web. 22 Nov. 2017.

Stenger, Josh. "The Clothes Make the Fan: Fashion and Online Fandom When *Buffy the Vampire Slayer* Goes to eBay." *Cinema Journal* 45.4 (2006): 26–44. *MLA International Bibliography*. Web. 25 Nov. 2017.

Stephens, Jena. "Disney's Darlings: An Analysis of *The Princess and the Frog, Tangled, Brave* and the Changing Characterization of the Princess Archetype." *Interdisciplinary Humanities* 31.3 (2014): 95–107. *Academic Search Premier*. Web. 18 May 2015.

Stone, Kay. "Things Walt Disney Never Told Us." *The Journal of American Folklore* 88.347 (1975): 42–50. *JStor*. Web. 25 July 2018.

Storey, John. *Cultural Theory and Popular Culture: An Introduction*. 4th ed. Athens: University of Georgia Press, 2006. Print.

Stormwreath. "(Dis)Connect." Archiveofourown.org. Organization for Transformative Works, 9 Sep. 2009. Web. 20 Jan. 2017.

Stover, Cassandra. "Damsels and Heroines: The Conundrum of the Post-Feminist Disney Princess." *LUX: A Journal of Transdisciplinary Writing and Research from Claremont Graduate University* 2.1 (2013): Article 29. *Academic Search Premier*. Web. 16 Apr. 2014.

Strate, Lance. "Heroes and/as Communication." *Heroes in a Global World*. Ed. Susan J. Drucker and Gary Gumpert. Cresskill: Hampton, 2008. Print. Hampton Press Communication Ser.

Stuller, Jennifer K. *Ink-Stained Amazons and Cinematic Warriors: Superwomen in Modern Mythology*. London: Tauris, 2010. Print.

Sullivan, Nikki. "Transmogrification: (Un)becoming Other(s)." *The Transgender Studies Reader.* Ed. Susan Stryker and Stephen Whittle. New York: Routledge, 2006. 552–64. Print.

SunnydaleArchives. "*Buffy*—Season 1 Promos." Online video clip. *YouTube.* YouTube, 21 July 2010. Web. 8 July 2017.

_____. "*Buffy*—Season 2 Promos 1/2." Online video clip. *YouTube.* YouTube, 13 May 2010. Web. 8 July 2017.

_____. "*Buffy*—Season 2 Promos 2/2." Online video clip. *YouTube.* YouTube, 13 May 2010. Web. 8 July 2017.

_____. "*Buffy*—Season 3 Promos 1/2." Online video clip. *YouTube.* YouTube, 14 May 2010. Web. 8 July 2017.

_____. "*Buffy*—Season 3 Promos 2/2." Online video clip. *YouTube.* YouTube, 14 May 2010. Web. 8 July 2017.

_____. "*Buffy*—Season 4 Promos 2/2." Online video clip. *YouTube.* YouTube, 19 June 2010. Web. 8 July 2017.

_____. "*Buffy*—Season 5 Promos 1/2." Online video clip. *YouTube.* YouTube, 7 July 2010. Web. 8 July 2017.

_____. "*Buffy*—Season 5 Promos 2/2." Online video clip. *YouTube.* YouTube, 8 July 2010. Web. 8 July 2017.

_____. "*Buffy*—Season 6 Promos 1/2." Online video clip. *YouTube.* YouTube, 4 Aug. 2010. Web. 8 July 2017.

_____. "*Buffy*—Season 6 Promos 2/2." Online video clip. *YouTube.* YouTube, 5 Aug. 2010. Web. 8 July 2017.

_____. "*Buffy*—Season 7 Promos 1/2." Online video clip. *YouTube.* YouTube, 14 Aug. 2010. Web. 8 July 2017.

Swedishheroine. "POC in Europe Masterpost." Tumblr.com. Tumblr, 2013. Web. 2 May 2017.

_____. "Why It's Problematic." Tumblr.com. Tumblr, 2013. Web. 2 May 2017.

Tangled. Dir. Nathan Greno and Byron Howard. Walt Disney Pictures, 2010. Film.

The_Eclectic_Bookworm. "Loose Lips Sink Ships." Archiveofourown.org. Organization for Transformative Works, 29 Mar. 2016. Web. 20 Jan. 2017.

Theconcomingwolf. "Playtime." Archiveofourown.org. Organization for Transformative Works, 23 June 2015. Web. 20 Jan. 2017.

The Hunger Games. "*The Hunger Games: Mockingjay Part 1*—'The Mockingjay Lives' Official Trailer." Online video clip. *YouTube.* YouTube, 15 Sep. 2014. Web. 17 July 2017.

_____. "*The Hunger Games: Mockingjay Part 2* Official Trailer—'We March Together.'" Online video clip. *YouTube.* YouTube, 23 July 2015. Web. 17 July 2017.

_____. "*The Hunger Games: Mockingjay Part 2* Official Trailer—'Welcome to the 76th Hunger Games.'" Online video clip. *YouTube.* YouTube, 6 Oct. 2015. Web. 17 July 2017.

Theladymore. "Something That I Never Could Erase." Archiveofourown.org. Organization for Transformative Works, 9 Dec. 2013. Web. 20 Jan. 2017.

Thelinksthatconnectus (orphan_account). "Magic in Its Own Right." Archiveofourown.org. Organization for Transformative Works, 17 Apr. 2014. Web. 20 Jan. 2017.

Thesewordselope (jadebloods). "Husking." Archiveofourown.org. Organization for Transformative Works, 21 Apr. 2012. Web. 20 Jan. 2017.

TiggerFace. "All the Little Things." Archiveofourown.org. Organization for Transformative Works, 31 Dec. 2013. Web. 20 Jan. 2017.

_____. "And Then Comes." Archiveofourown.org. Organization for Transformative Works, 16 Dec. 2013. Web. 20 Jan. 2017.

_____. "Everyday." Archiveofourown.org. Organization for Transformative Works, 4 Jan. 2014. Web. 20 Jan. 2017.

Toastystats (destinytoast). "[Fandom Stats] F/F Stats (Femslash February 2016)." Archiveofourown.org. Organization for Transformative Works, 17 Feb. 2016. Web. 11 Mar. 2017.

Towbin, Mia Adessa, et al. "Images of Gender, Race, Age, and Sexual Orientation in Disney Feature-Length Animated Films." *Journal of Feminist Family Therapy* 15.4 (2004): 19–44. *Taylor and Francis Online.* Web. 22 Nov. 2017.

Trout, Jenny. "Jennifer Lawrence Body-Shames You More than You Might Realize." TheHuffingtonPost.com. Oath, 1 Mar. 2014. Web. 1 Mar. 2016.

TT. "A Whole New World Part III." Tumblr.com. Tumblr, n.d. Web. 1 May 2017.

_____. "Here's a Compilation of My Racebent Series […]." Tumblr.com. Tumblr, n.d. Web. 1 May 2017.

"Tumblr." Wikipedia.org. Wikimedia Foundation, 1 Apr. 2017. Web. 5 Apr. 2017.

Turner, Graeme. *Understanding Celebrity*. London: Sage, 2004. Print.

Val_Creative. "Unstoppable Forces." Archiveofourown.org. Organization for Transformative Works, 26 Feb. 2016. Web. 20 Jan. 2017.

Valibeigi, Bijhan. "Strong Female Characters are Rarely Strong and Barely Characters." The marysue.com. The Mary Sue, 21 Sep. 2015. Web. 27 Nov. 2017.

Validcriticism. "Can We Talk About the Racism in *Buffy the Vampire Slayer*? Part 1." Tumblr.com. Tumblr, 2014. Web. 22 May 2017.

Van Dyke, Christina. "Discipline and the Docile Body: Regulating Hungers in the Capitol." *The Hunger Games and Philosophy: A Critique of Pure Treason*. Ed. George A. Dunn and Nicolas Michaud. Hoboken: Wiley, 2012. 250–64. Print. Blackwell Philosophy and Pop Culture Ser.

Vary, Adam B. "5 Things You Should Know About the Curious New Marketing Campaign for *The Hunger Games: Catching Fire*." BuzzFeed.com. BuzzFeed, 23 Aug. 2013. Web. 29 May 2017.

Ventura, Michael. "Warrior Women." *Psychology Today* 31.6 (1998): 58–61. *Academic OneFile*. Web. 13 July 2017.

Vint, Sherryl. "'Killing us Softly?' A Feminist Search for the 'Real' Buffy." *Slayage: The Online International Journal of Buffy Studies* 2.1 (2002): 26 pars. Web. 24 Nov. 2017.

Visennyatargaryen. "Racebent *Buffy the Vampire Slayer*: Antonia Thomas as Buffy Summers." Tumblr.com. Tumblr, 25 June 2013. Web. 25 Apr. 2017.

_____. "Racebent *Buffy the Vampire Slayer*: Ellen Wong as Willow Rosenberg." Tumblr.com. Tumblr, 26 June 2013. Web. 25 Apr. 2017.

_____. "Racebent *Buffy the Vampire Slayer*: Suraj Sharma as Xander Harris." Tumblr.com. Tumblr, 26 June 2013. Web. 28 Apr. 2017.

Wanzo, Rebecca. "African American Acafandom and Other Strangers: New Genealogies of Fan Studies." *Transformative Works and Cultures* 20 (2015): 6 pars. Web. 22 Aug. 2016.

"Welcome to the Hellmouth." *Buffy the Vampire Slayer: Season 1–7*. Season 1, episode 1. Writ. Joss Whedon. Dir. Charles Martin Smith. Fox, 2010. DVD.

Weston, Jessie. *From Ritual to Romance*. Garden City: Doubleday, 1957. Print.

"The Weight of the World." *Buffy the Vampire Slayer: Season 1–7*. Season 5, episode 21. Writ. Doug Petrie. Dir. David Solomon. Fox, 2010. DVD.

"We Will Rebel." Tumblr.com. Tumblr, 20 Jan. 2012. Web. 7 Dec. 2015.

"What's My Line (Part 1)." *Buffy the Vampire Slayer: Season 1–7*. Season 2, episode 9. Writ. Howard Gordon and Marti Noxon. Dir. David Solomon. Fox, 2010. DVD.

"What's My Line (Part 2)." *Buffy the Vampire Slayer: Season 1–7*. Season 2, episode 10. Writ. Howard Gordon and Marti Noxon. Dir. David Solomon. Fox, 2010. DVD.

Whelan, Bridget. "Power to the Princess: Disney and the Creation of the 20th Century Princess Narrative." *Interdisciplinary Humanities* 29.1 (2012): 21–34. *Academic Search Premier*. Web. 22 Nov. 2017.

"When She Was Bad." *Buffy the Vampire Slayer: Season 1–7*. Season 2, episode 1. Writ. and dir. Joss Whedon. Fox, 2010. DVD.

Wilcox, Ronda V. "'Who Died and Made Her the Boss?': Patterns of Mortality in *Buffy*." *Fighting the Forces: What's at Stake in* Buffy the Vampire Slayer. Ed. Rhonda V. Wilcox and David Lavery. Lanham: Rowman & Littlefield, 2002. 3–17. Print.

Wilcox, Rhonda V., and David Lavery, eds. Introduction. *Fighting the Forces: What's at Stake in* Buffy the Vampire Slayer. Lanham: Rowman & Littlefield, 2002. Xvii–xxix. Print.

Willmore, Alison. "Roman Polanski's New Movie Explores the Real Meaning of 'Strong Female Character.'" BuzzFeed.com. BuzzFeed, 19 June 2014. Web. 9 Oct. 2017.

Wilson, Natalie. "Pop Goes Feminism: *Tangled* Shows No Sign of Cutting Disney's White, Male Roots." Web blog post. *Girl w/ Pen*. The Society Pages, 28 Nov. 2010. Web. 11 May 2015.

Woledge, Elizabeth. "3. Intimatopia: Genre Intersections between Slash and the Mainstream." *Fan Fiction and Fan Communities in the Age of the Internet: New Essays*. Ed. Karen Hellekson and Kristina Busse. Jefferson: McFarland, 2006. 97–114. Print.

"The Yoko Factor." *Buffy the Vampire Slayer: Season 1–7*. Season 4, episode 20. Writ. Douglas Petrie. Dir. David Grossman. Fox, 2010. DVD.

Young, Iris Marion. "Throwing Like a Girl: A Phenomenology of Feminine Body Comportment, Motility, and Spatiality." *On Female Body Experience: "Throwing Like a Girl" and Other Essays*. Ed. Iris Marion Young. Oxford: Oxford University Press, 2005. 27–45. Print.

Zaslow, Emilie. *Feminism, Inc.: Coming of Age in Girl Power Media Culture*. New York: Palgrave Macmillan, 2009. Print.

Zipes, Jack. *Breaking the Magic Spell: Radical Theories of Folk and Fairy Tales*. Austin: University of Texas Press, 1979. Print.

_____. *Fairy Tale as Myth, Myth as Fairy Tale*. Lexington: University of Kentucky Press, 1994. Print.

_____. *Happily Ever After: Fairy Tales, Children, and the Culture Industry*. New York: Routledge, 1997. Print.

Zutter, Natalie. "The MPAA Rates Movies More Harshly If Women Seem to Be Enjoying Sex." Alloy.com. Defy Media, 6 Apr. 2011. Web. 16 Mar. 2017.

Index

www.ingramcontent.com/pod-product-compliance
Lightning Source LLC
Chambersburg PA
CBHW031126270326
41929CB00011B/1513